ZOMBIE CSU

BOOKS BY JONATHAN MABERRY

NOVELS

Assassin's Code * Bad Moon Rising * Bits & Pieces * Broken Lands: A Rot & Ruin novel * Code Zero * Dark of Night (with Rachael Lavin) * Dead Man's Song * Dead of Night * Deep Silence * Dogs of War * Dust & Decay * Extinction Machine * Fall of Night * Fire & Ash * Flesh & Bone * Ghost Road Blues * Ghostwalkers: A Deadlands novel * Glimpse * Ink * Kill Switch * King of Plagues * Lost Roads: A Rot & Ruin novel * Mars One * Patient Zero * Predator One * Rage * Rot & Ruin * Still of Night (with Rachael Lavin) * The Dragon Factory * The Orphan Army—The Nightsiders, Book 1 * The Unlearnable Truths * The Wolfman * V-Wars * Vault of Shadows—The Nightsiders, Book 2 * Watch Over Me * World of Eli * X-Files Origins: Devil's Advocate

SHORT STORY COLLECTIONS

A Little Bronze Book of Cautionary Tales * Beneath the Skin * Darkness on the Edge of Town * Hungry Tales * Joe Ledger: Special Ops * Strange Worlds * The Sam Hunter Case Files * Whistling Past the Graveyard * Wind Through the Fence

GRAPHIC NOVELS

Age of Heroes: Black Panther * Black Panther: DoomWar * Black Panther: Klaws of the Black Panther * Black Panther: Power * Captain America: Hail Hydra * Marvel Universe vs. The Avengers * Marvel Universe vs the Punisher * Marvel Universe vs Wolverine * Marvel Zombies Return * Pandemica * Punisher: Naked Kills * Road of the Dead: Highway to Hell * Rot & Ruin: Warrior Smart * V-Wars: All of Us Monsters * V-Wars: Crimson Queen * V-Wars: God of Death * V-Wars: The Collection * Wolverine: Flies to the Spider

ANTHOLOGIES (as editor)

Aliens: Bug Hunt * Don't Turn Out the Lights: A Tribute to Scary Stories to Tell in the Dark * Hardboiled Horror * Joe Ledger: Unstoppable (co-edited with Bryan Thomas Schmidt) * New Scary Stories to Tell in the Dark * Nights of the Living Dead (co-edited with George A. Romero) * Out of Tune, Volume I * Out of Tune, Volume II * Scary Out There: Baker Street Irregulars (co-edited with Michael Ventrella) * The Game's Afoot (co-edited with Michael Ventrella) * The X-Files: Secret Agendas * The X-Files: The Truth Is Out There * The X-Files: Trust No One * V-Wars * V-Wars: Blood and Fire * V-Wars: Night Terrors * V-Wars: Shockwaves

NONFICTION BOOKS

Vampire Universe * The Cryptopedia (with David Kramer) * Zombie CSU: The Forensic Science of the Living Dead * They Bite (with David Kramer) * Wanted Undead or Alive (with Janice Gable Bashman) * Ultimate Jujutsu: Principles and Practices * Ultimate Sparring: Principles and Practices * The Martial Arts Student Handbook * Judo and You

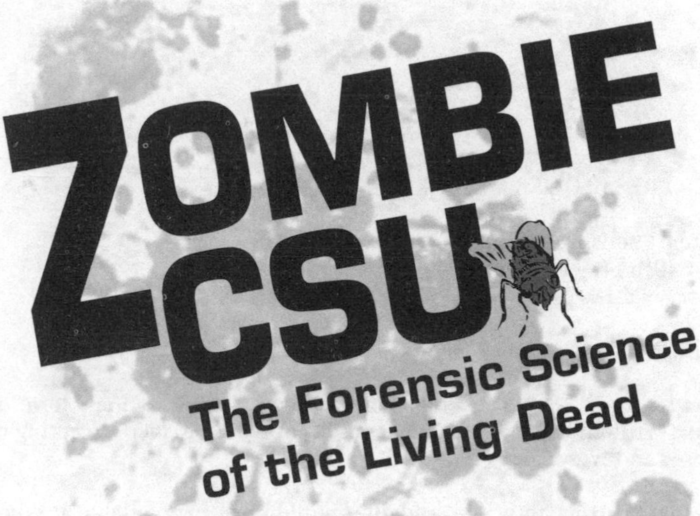

ZOMBIE CSU
The Forensic Science of the Living Dead

Jonathan Maberry

CITADEL PRESS
Kensington Publishing Corporation
www.kensingtonbooks.com

CITADEL PRESS BOOKS are published by

Kensington Publishing Corp.
119 West 40th Street
New York, NY 10018

All Kensington titles, imprints, and distributed lines are available at special quantity discounts for bulk purchases for sales promotions, premiums, fund-raising, educational, or institutional use. Special book excerpts or customized printings can also be created to fit specific needs. For details, write or phone the office of the Kensington sales manager: Kensington Publishing Corp., 119 West 40th Street, New York, NY 10018, attn: Sales Department; phone 1-800-221-2647.

First printing: September 2008

10 9 8 7 6 5 4

Printed in the United States of America

ISBN-13: 978-0-8065-4140-2
ISBN-10: 0-8065-4140-7

Electronic edition:

ISBN-13: 978-0-8065-3461-9 (e-book)
ISBN-10: 0-8065-3461-3 (e-book)

To Richard Matheson, for taking time long, long ago to sit me down to explain how science and logic can make everything just a little bit scarier. I still have the copy of *I Am Legend* you gave me. I've read it at least twenty times and expect to read it twenty more.

And, as always, to my beloved Sara Jo.

Contents

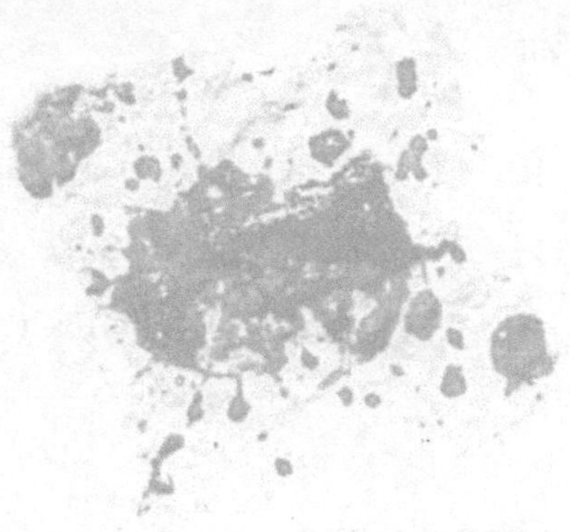

Acknowledgments

Thanks to my agent, Sara Crowe of Harvey Klinger, Inc., and my editor at Kensington, Michaela Hamilton. This has sure been a wild ride.

Thanks to the many experts who provided their insight and knowledge to this rather strange project. Since we're talking about zombies here, I think we can all agree that their comments do not necessarily reflect the opinions of any organization to which they belong. Any technical errors to be found in the book are purely the author's doing. The following people have contributed their advice, opinions, and insights:

Allen Steingold, Esq.; Andrea Campbell; Andy Bark; Geoff Brough, editor of *Revenant* magazine; B. Burt Gerstman, M.D., San Jose State University; Bernardo Gutierrez; Bob Fingerman; Bowie Ibarra; Brady Howard; Brian Keene; Brinke Stevens; Bruce Bohne; Bryan Chrz, past president of the American Board of Forensic Odontology; Dr. Bruno Vincent of the L'Institut de Pharmacologie Moléculaire et Cellulaire; Bryon Morrigan; C. J. Henderson; Calvin Watson; Captain Daniel Castro, commanding officer, Philadelphia Forensic Science Bureau; Cass Brennan; Catherine McBride, department lab director, Philadelphia Forensic Science Bureau; Cathy Buburuz, editor of *Champagne Shivers;* Chandra Singh, M.D.; Charles Amuzzie, M.D., African Society for Toxicological Sciences; Christopher Welch; Collin Burton; Combat-Handguns Yahoo! Group; Constance Link; D. L. Snell; Dale Blum, RPh; Damian Gonzalez; Damien Rogers; Dan O'Bannon; Dan McConnell; Daniel Conklin; Danielle Ackley-McPhail; David A. Prior; David Chalmers, Ph.D.; David Chiang; David Christman; David Jack Bell; David F. Kramer; David Moody; David Pantano, CounterStrike Kenpo Karate; Lieutenant David Smith, LAPD Coroner's Investigations Division; David Wellington; Dena Procaccini; Dennis Miller, LAPD (retired);

Derrick Sampson; Detective Michael Buben, Tullytown Police Department; Detective Joseph Sciscio, Bensalem Police Department; Captain Dick Taylor, U.S. Army (retired); Donna Burgess; Donna Sims; Doug Clegg; Drue Russell; Dwane S. Hilderbrand; Edward Dugan, forensic lab manager, Philadelphia Forensic Science Bureau; Elaine Viets; Elizabeth Becka; Ellen Datlow; Eric Gressen, M.D., assistant professor of radiation oncology, Jefferson Medical College; Eric S. Brown; FEMA; Frank Dietz; Fredericka Lawrence, Bucks County 911; G. Harris Grantham; Garden State Horror Writers (GSHW); Gary A. Braunbeck; Dr. Robert Hall, associate vice chancellor for research, University of Missouri; Gayle Brown-Harris; Geff Bertrand; George A. Romero; George Martzoukos; George Schiro, MS, consulting forensic scientist; Greg Dagnan, CSI/Police/Investigations Faculty, Criminal Justice Department, Missouri Southern State University; Georgia Stanley; Greg Lamberson; Greg Schauer, Between Books; Gerald and Kathleen Hill, MJF Books; Gregg Winkler; Harry Matsushita; Horror Writers Association (HWA); Herschel Goldman, M.D.; International Thriller Writers (ITW); J. N. Rowan; J. A. Konrath; J. Curtis Daily, American Board of Forensic Odontology; J. L. Comeau; Jack Spangler; Jacob Parmentier; James Gunn; Jamie Russell; Jane Dalkieth; Jason Broadbent; Jeremy Simmons; Jerome Wilson, NYPD (retired); Jerry Waxler, MS; Jill Hunt and the Baltimore Zombie Crawl; Jim Dolan; Jim O'Rear; Jim Winterbottom; Joe Augustyn; Joe Bob Briggs; Joe DiDomenico, Teddy Scares; Joe Lansdale; Joe McKinney; Joe Student; John Lutz; John Passarella; Jonathan Coulton; Jonathan Santlofer; Josh "the Viper" Gallagher; Joyce Kato, Coroner's Investigations Division, LAPD; Joyce Kearney, Ph.D.; Judee Tallman; Kanchana Patel, Ph.D.; Karl Gretz, Ph.D.; Karl Rehn, KR Training; Katherine Ramsland, Ph.D., DeSales University; Chief Inspector Keith R. Sadler, Philadelphia Forensic Science Bureau; Ken Bruen; Keith Harrop, ZombieWorld News; Chief Ken Coluzzi, Lower Makefield Police Department; Ken Foree; Kenneth Storey, Ph.D., Carleton University; Kevin Breaux; Kim Paffenroth, Ph.D.; Kyle Ladd, Zombie Squad; L. A. Banks; Lisa Gressen; Lisa Morton; Louis Michael Sanders; Lynn and Bill Koehle; Mark McLaughlin; Mark Rainey; Martin Leadbetter, chairman, The Fingerprint Society; Martin Schöenfeld; Max Brooks; Michael Arnzen; Michael Augenbraun, M.D., Brooklyn University; Michael E. Witzgall; Michael Kelly; Michael Pederson, M.D.; Michael R. Burrows; Michael Sicilia, Homeland Security; Michael Tresca; Mike Segretto; Monica O'Rourke; Mort Castle; Mystery Writers of America (MWA); Nancy Barr; Nancy Kilpatrick; Natalie Mtumbo, M.D.; Nate Kenyon; National Center for Reanimation Prevention and Control (NCRPC); Nicholas Grabowsky; Nick Comeaux; Nick Ladany, Ph.D., Lehigh University; Nick Mamatas; Nicole Blessing; Nicole M. Brooks (a.k.a. The Zombie Cheerleader); Office of Homeland Security; Helen Poland, NP; Chief Pat Priore, the Tullytown Police Department; Patricia Tallman; Paul Tremblay; Pawel P. Liberski, M.D., Department of Molecular Pathology and Neuropathology, Medical University of Lodz, Poland; Pete Hynes; Peter Lukacs, M.D.; Peter Mihaichuk; PhillyGeek Yahoo! Group; Rabbi Michael Shevack; Ramsey Campbell; Raymond Hook; Raymond Singer, Ph.D.; Rene Sampier; Richard F. Kuntz, RN, first deputy coroner, Bucks County; Richard Matheson; Richard V. Greene, Ph.D.; Rick Hautala; Rick A. Shay; Rick Robinson; Robert Kirkman; Robin Dobson, M.D.; Rocky Wood; Russ Hassert, MS; Sam Anderson; Sarah Langan; Science Fiction and Fantasy Writers of America (SFWA); Scott A. Johnson; Scott Cramton; Scott Johnson; Scott Nicholson; Sean Gallagher; Shelley Handen; Stephen Susco; Steve Alten; Steve Swickard; Steven Feldman; Steve Vernon; Stephen Jones; Susanna Reilly; Tactical-Rifle Yahoo! Group; Tapaswi Dhamma; Rick Smith, CEO, Taser, Inc.; Tom Smith, chairman, Taser, Inc.; Ted Krimmel, SERT; Thomas Jefferson Johnson III; Tim Waggoner; Tony Finan; Tony Timpone, editor, *FANGORIA*; Tony Todd; Trevor Strunk; United States Department of Justice; Van Nguyen, Ph.D.; Vincent L. DeNiro; Wade Davis, Ph.D.; Walt Stenning Ph.D., former head of psychology at Texas A&M University; Warren Harvey; Weston Ochse; Zach Martini; Yvonne Navarro; and the Zombie Squad. Thanks to the many wonderful bookstore managers and community relations managers who made the tours for my previous books such a joy!

Please visit the official website for the Pine Deep series: www.zombiecsu.com and the website for my official author site, www.jonathanmaberry.com. Visit the MySpace page for the book at www.myspace.com/zombiecsu.

JONATHAN MABERRY

Introduction

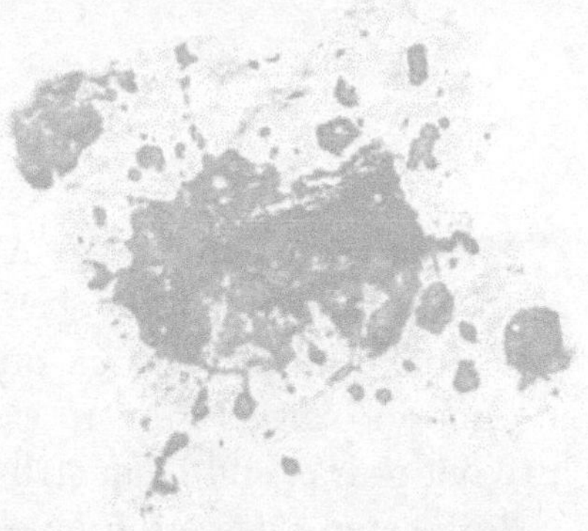

They're Coming by Peter Mihaichuk.

"My works are photo-based illustrations, so I'm often inspired by the models I work with. They usually have certain features that call to be exaggerated and pulled upon. In the case of visualizing zombies, it can get quite disturbing when you look at people and automatically picture them as the walking dead—especially when you start to see grandma in a whole new light!"—Artist Peter Mihaichuk

I was ten when George A. Romero's *Night of the Living Dead* was released in October 1968. That movie did more than just make an impression on a very impressionable kid. In fact, it's not an exaggeration to say that movie *marked* me. It took a bite out of me, and I can still feel the scar.

By age ten I'd seen double my share of vampire and werewolf flicks. I'd seen every giant bug flick they'd show during the Saturday double features at the Midway Theater in my hometown of Philadelphia. Two monster flicks, two cartoons, and at least a half dozen movie trailers for thirty-five cents. I'd always sneak in to the front row of the balcony and hunker down with my Hires Root Beer and my big box of Day 'n' Nights and watch revivals of old Karloff and Lugosi films, or dig into a tub of popcorn while Christopher Lee put the bite on bosomy rural gals (and I was still young enough to be more entranced by the monsters than the maidens). Or I'd stay up past my bedtime to watch both parts of *Double Chiller Theater*—grooving along with the *Brain That Wouldn't Die, Monster of Piedras Blancas*, and *The Tingler*. I went a little *Psycho*, hunted with the *Witchfinder General*, learned *Whatever Happened to Baby Jane*, tucked into the *Blood Feast*, visited the *Haunted Palace*, and settled down to patiently *Wait Until Dark*.

But you see, I was kind of a weird little kid, and none of these films actually scared me. In a weird sort of way I was safe with them. The monsters and the monster hunters were friends of mine; we'd play together in the dark.

All that changed when I saw *The Night of the Living Dead*. That was the first movie that truly and thoroughly scared the bejesus out of me.

Vampires I could deal with (or thought I could). Lugosi was cool, but to a kid in mid–Vietnam era 1968 he wasn't really all that scary. Frankenstein's Monster was more sad than frightening. The Wolf Man was tragic, and, besides, Claude Raines beat the piss out of him with a walking stick. And don't get me started on the Mummy. I was an inner city kid—if my buddies and I had seen Imhotep (or Kharis) limping along, wrapped in dusty old bandages and acting all grabby, we've have either stomped him to powder or flicked matches at him.

So, when I sat down to watch one of those films you knew—I mean really *knew*—that it was just a matter of time before Dracula tripped over his own opera cloak and fell onto a piece of pointy wood; and come dawn the Wolf Man would go back to being Larry-fricking-Talbot. No matter how bad these monsters were, they had built-in vulnerabilities. And besides, there was just *one* of them. In rare cases (as with Dracula's brides) there were a few others. We were too jaded to be afraid of that sort of thing.

George Romero changed the game on us, and it knocked the smug smiles off of our faces.

In *Night of the Living Dead*[1] all recently deceased people were rising from the grave or mortuary slab to attack the living. All of them. Not to drink blood, not to tear out the occasional throat. Oh no . . . these things were eating the living . . . and rather graphically, too.

I remember very clearly sitting in my balcony seat watching that movie and becoming suddenly very aware of how big and dark that balcony was. How far from the lights of the lobby it was. How remote it was.

It was like a hand reached into my brain and turned the dial on my imagination up. All the way up.

It made me think about what I would do if something like that really happened. I'd always worked out scenarios for handling monsters. I'd started taking martial arts lessons when I was six, so by age ten I was pretty sure I was one tough monkey. If a vampire came after me, I knew that all I had to do was grab a couple of sticks and make a cross. If it was a werewolf, I could lock myself in a room (the projection booth had a steel door) until morning. I knew for sure I could outrun the Mummy; and all I had to do to scare off the Tingler was to scream. I was ten, my voice hadn't broken yet, and I could scream high enough to crack a wineglass.

But if all the dead rose, then what could I do? What could anyone do? How do you outrun hundreds of thousands of walking

1. John Russo cowrote the screenplay and has been active in zombie pop culture ever since.

"Zombies scare me. No seriously, they break every rule of horror. You have to go find most other monsters, but Zombies come to you . . . and not in ones or twos."

—Max Brooks, author of *Zombie Survival Guide* and *World War Z*

corpses? Where can you flee where death has never been? How can you outlast something that doesn't need to go back to its grave at sunrise or won't change back into a normal guy at dawn?

I sat in the dark and thought about how overwhelming a rising of the dead would be, and I got really, really *scared*.

I left the theater and stepped into the chilly darkness of an early October evening. I was only ten years old and my older sisters were supposed to be minding me, but they hated horror flicks and always just dumped me at the box office, knowing that I could walk the four blocks home on my own. Until now this had been a perfect arrangement: I never wanted my sisters around when I had some monster movie watching to do.

On that October evening, however, I would have welcomed all four of my sisters and would probably have wanted to hold their hands. I was *that* scared.

As I raced home, trying to beat full darkness, watching every shadow, I tried to work out how I would survive an attack of the living dead. I worked out a hundred scenarios, a thousand. The numbers were against me, though. If the dead rose, if they were present in such overwhelming numbers, then we'd all be . . . well . . . *overwhelmed*.

A thought like that doesn't fit comfortably into a kid's head. I've since learned that it doesn't fit comfortably into the heads of a lot of adults, too. There was always a part of me that either *believed* in the possibility of zombies, or wanted to believe. That I grew up to write horror novels and books like this is a surprise to no one.

Not that I wanted humanity to fall down and become sushi for the postmortem set, but it was so darn fascinating. Especially the problem of how to survive the zombie apocalypse.

Then at around age eleven I started reading crime novels, particularly the 87th Precinct police procedurals by Ed McBain. If you haven't read those books, especially the early ones like *Lady, Lady I Did It, Give the Boys a Great Big Hand, Ax*, and *He Who Hesitates*, do yourself a favor and raid your local bookstore. I devoured these books, and what really enchanted me was the humanity of the main characters. They were cops. Not supercops like on TV, but ordinary guys. A bunch of working schlubs who happen to be detectives chasing down killers in the big, bad city. These books did more than present a crime and offer a solution—the McBain books took you through every step, showed every detail of the process, even to the point of including mock police reports, fingerprint cards, and other "official" forms in the book. What I learned is that no matter how smart the villain, no matter how impossible the case, ordinary step-by-step police work usually paid off in the end. It wasn't the devil that was in the details, but rather a little fluff from angel wings. This was good guys winning in the end by hard work, doggedness, and most crucial of all, *routine*.

Routine—the use of established procedures, method, and techniques—could give even a Detective Three working stiff a real shot at bagging a clever crook.

That got me to thinking. It kicked off the "what if" process in me.

What if the zombie uprising had started in the fictional city of Ed McBain's 87th Precinct? Would Steve Carella and Meyer Meyer become zombie lunchmeat, or would they investigate the first zombie killings and work the clues and process the evidence to take them to the source? If they could do that, would they be able to stop the plague before it spread?

At eleven I wondered. I had a lot of faith in cops. At first it was proxy faith given to cops because of the McBain books; but in the decades since, I've come to know and work with a large number of police officers and detectives. In the movies they're sometimes played as buffoons, but that's more propaganda than fair assessment. No matter what the raw intelligence may be of any given person when he or she joins the department, they are surrounded and reinforced by routine, process, hard science and cutting-edge technologies. Cops are a hell of a lot smarter and more resourceful than most people give them credit for. Our prisons are packed with crooks who thought that they were smarter.

Partnered with investigatory routine is the vast and ever-expanding world of forensic science. DNA testing, gas chromatography, touch evidence, 3-D computer modeling, chemical reagents, electron microscopes—the mind boggles at the technology developed for and available to modern law enforcement.

When I decided to write this book, it gave me a chance to take these two powerful childhood influences—the living dead and their awful potential and the relentless and inventive police investigators—and merge them into a whopping big "what if" project.

As I launched into my research, contacting cops, scientists, medical doctors, and forensics experts, I was delighted but not entirely surprised to find out that many of them had been thinking along the same lines. When I floated the question of how forensics would cope with the zombie threat, instead of getting doors slammed in my face, I got a wide welcome from men and women who, just like me, had sat in the dark as kids and watched zombie flicks and wondered . . . what if? Folks who, as professionals now in their fields, actually have some answers to those questions.

What if there were zombies? Could the routine and infrastructure of law enforcement and the combined strength of modern science be able to recognize and adequately respond to the threat?

You know . . . it just might.

Let's go find out.

Reading This Book

So what if zombies existed? What if the very first zombie who rose from the dead killed someone? How would the police react? Would they be able to understand the nature of the crime . . . and the nature of the assailant? Would forensic evidence collection and medical science be able to discover the cause of the zombie plague? And, most important of all, would we be able to stop the wave of killing before a zombie apocalypse occurred?

In order to give us a framework on which we can build our case, we need to decide which kind of zombie attack is in question. The flesh-eating ghouls as shown in the majority of zombie films, and particularly in those of George A. Romero, will be our target. These are creatures that have been reanimated by some process currently unknown. In the Romero films there is an early theory that radiation from a returning space probe caused the rising. We'll be discussing the likelihood of that, and also explore other theories that have been floated in zombie stories, particularly the idea of a virus. There are more zombie films and books with that as a basis than any other, and we'll delve deep into the sciences of infectious disease and epidemiology. Since we're in the realm of hard science here, we're not only going to look at how collected evidence may help police track down the zombie and the source of the infection; we'll also explore whether medical science can support the concept of a corpse that rises from the dead and attacks the living.

To explore the forensics of the living dead, we'll construct a mock crime scene, taking it from the 911 call all the way to the attempt to apprehend the perpetrator. When you take a big picture view of a ghoul attacking and killing a person, you are really looking at a standard murder scene. There will be an incident, possibly witnesses to the event; police will respond in a certain way, following specific established and effective procedures; the scene will be secured and observed; evidence will be collected and processed; investigatory leads will be followed. Whether the perpetrator is Joe Ordinary, Jack the Ripper, or Bub the Zombie, a murder scene is a murder scene.

So let's take it step by step.

But First a Word About Zombies

Images of the Living Dead by Jacob Parmentier.

"The first Zombie movie I ever saw was *Night of the Living Dead* and it was the original as well. I remember having dreams night after night of fighting off brain-sucking zombies for days afterward; but I think my true favorite of all the zombie movies would have to be *The Evil Dead*. I had a friend that had a VHS copy of this movie and I remember how taboo it was to have watched it."

There's an old adage popular among big-game hunters that goes: "Before you can hunt anything you have to understand it."

That logic is so fundamental that it applies equally to wild animals, human enemies, or monsters from the grave.

Another variation on that thought is this one, roughly translated[1] from the Hmong language of the Laotian mountain people, which observes: "If I know it then I can hunt it; if I do not know it then it can hunt me."

So what are we talking about when we use the word *zombie*? What kind of monster are we hunting?

A Ghoul by Any Other Name . . .

Zombie. The very word conjures disturbing images. Close your eyes and picture the living dead. You can see their pale, decaying faces; their vacant eyes sunk into dark pits; their slack and expressionless mouths. If you listen real hard, you can just about hear the slow, scuffling steps of a zombie as it shambles out of the shadows, tottering unsteadily as it approaches. You can hear the low moan that tells of a hunger so deep that it can never be satisfied. Take a whiff—that's the smell of rotting flesh, the sickly sweet perfume of the open tomb.

But what are they? Historically *zombie* has meant different things to different people. To just about anyone born in the mid-to-early twentieth century (and yes, a lot of you are reading this, too), a zombie is a shambling living-dead person associated somehow—and you may not know *exactly* how—with the Haitian religion of voodoo. Those zombies are actually a real-world phenomenon . . . but are they the creatures we see in horror movies?

For an answer to that question, I asked one of the world's great experts on the subject, Dr. Wade Davis, an ethnobotanist and

1. Translation courtesy of Dr. Van Nguyen, formerly of Temple University.

author of a dozen books, including *The Serpent and the Rainbow*[2] and *Passage of Darkness*. "Hollywood, and indeed much of the popular and political culture, has maintained a racist view of Haitian culture, vodoun,[3] and zombies. American culture was demonstrably uncomfortable with the existence of Haiti—a nation whose slaves revolted and overthrew the white slave masters. The views of Haitian culture, whether written, spoken or filmed painted a picture totally at odds with the people and their beliefs. This propagandized view denigrates an entire religion."

So then, what is a zombie?

"The zombie, by Haitian belief," Dr. Davis explains, "is an individual who has lost their soul and been cast into purgatory. By that view the act of making a zombie is a magical act. The victims have lost their animus—their true personality—and their conscious control. In my books, *Serpent and the Rainbow*, and, more specifically, *Passage of Darkness*, I discuss how this is accomplished partly through what's called 'zombie powder,' a concoction made from toad skin and the chemical tetrodotoxin,[4] which is harvested from a species of puffer fish, which is the same order of fish as the Japanese *fugu* fish. The tetrodotoxin blocks sodium channels and lowers metabolic rates. A zombie of the vodoun kind is created in part by zombie powder and partly by the structure of the culture. Believing that becoming a zombie is possible helps to make it possible. It has a clear chemical base, but the creation of a zombie is a social event with spiritual, political, sociological basis."

Are these zombies the same thing as the creatures that appear in modern horror films and in best-selling books like *World War Z*[5] by Max Brooks?

2. *The Serpent and the Rainbow*, 1985, Simon & Schuster; *Passage of Darkness: The Ethnobiology of the Haltian Zombie*, 1988, The University of North Carolina Press

3. Vodoun is the correct name for the religion known popularly as voodoo. Also known as vudu, Vodon, Voudou, Vodu. The word *Voodoo* is considered offensive to the practitioners of that faith, largely due to the way it has been portrayed by Western culture in film, literature, etc.

4. Tetrodotoxin (unhydrotetrodotaxin 4-epitetrodotaxin, tetrodonic acid or TTX) is a potent neurotoxin.

5. *World War Z* by Max Brooks, published by Crown Books in 2006.

Art of the Dead – Brian Orlowski

Drawn of the Dead

"Zombies have always scared me, much more than monsters or psychos or ghosts. Mainly because they start out as us. I think we are actually looking at our own reflection when faced with the undead. Your neighbors, family, spouse, they can all turn on you when you let your guard down and bad things happen. They are also so terrifying because they easily outnumber us. Whether it is the classic slow-moving corpse or the running, crazed ghoul, as quickly as you dispatch of one or two, ten more fall in to replace it. It's the fear of a losing struggle, like fighting against quicksand. And the disease spreads from corpse to corpse, multiplying exponentially, until the Earth is rampant with the undead and we, as humans, have lost the fight. That is scary.

"However my art is predominantly humorous cartoons. So I use gore and violence for laughs. Whether it be *queasy* gross-outs or shock value gags, the reactions I get most are; 'funny,' 'cool,' 'gross,' and 'you're sick.' And, yes, there's social commentary built in as well."

Dr. Davis is emphatic on this point. "No! The zombies in movies like *Night of the Living Dead* have no connection at all to the zombies of Haiti. It is not a correct or fair use of that word. Haitian zombies are not ghouls."

Fair enough, but the word *zombie* is associated with another cultural phenomenon—and one that has had a massive global impact. Unlike the creatures of Haiti, the zombies known to the general population are, in point of fact, flesh-eating ghouls. They are the recent dead, returned to a semblance of life, and their only apparent point for existing is to attack humans for food. They hunt and kill, hunt and kill, without rest, without sleep, without thought. And though it's hard to admire savage cannibalism, one has to respect the degree of focus involved—it makes a person with OCD look fickle by comparison.

Technically our monster is a kind of ghoul . . . but even then we're not being totally PC because *ghoul* also has an older and far different cultural connection related to desert demons variously known as the *ghul* and *algul* from pre-and-post Islam Arabic legend. Even here, though, the folkloric monsters had a number of different qualities that included intelligence (at times), cunning, and the ability to shape-shift.[6]

However, the Anglicized word *ghoul* has taken on a somewhat different and very specific meaning in Western culture: that of a dead creature that has risen from the grave to feast on human flesh. The movie version of this monster archetype—at least as defined in the earliest films of the genre—has no intelligence, no cunning at all, no ability to change shape, no qualities of any kind except an insatiable hunger and zero detectable brain function.[7] The zombies in our pop-culture sensibility are actually mindless flesh-eating ghouls.

Zombie culture, as we know it today, really began in 1968 when George A. Romero, a young Pittsburgh industrial filmmaker, decided

6. Shape-shifting, or theriomorphy, is a common trait of many folkloric monsters including vampires and werewolves.

7. There are a few exceptions to this, notably the creatures from the Dan O'Bannon *Return of the Living Dead* series of films who not only possess the power of speech but are also gourmets rather than gourmands—they only eat brains, eschewing the rest of the body.

he was tired of doing the corporate stuff and wanted to try his hand at making a new kind of horror movie. His inspiration came neither from Haitian culture or Arab folklore, but drew instead on the neo-folklore of modern pop culture.

Mind you, these creatures weren't actually *called* zombies until ten years after the whole "zombie craze" got started. That name became associated with it only after the sequel, *Dawn of the Dead* (1978), was released in the United States, and was then recut for European release by producer Dario Argento. He called it *Zombi*. Even then, the word is used very briefly in *Dawn of the Dead* (by the character Peter, played by an imposing Ken Foree), but it clearly wasn't intended as a defining label at that point. With the European release the name stuck and here we are talking about *zombies* in the twenty-first century. And though this is on a par with calling all tissues Kleenex or all copiers Xerox it is the name that's now hardwired into the consciousness of the mass popular culture. Zombie it became, and zombie, for good or ill, it will probably always be, I say this with genuine apologies to the people of Haiti and with respect to their cultural beliefs.

Besides, zombie is a handy, short, easily spelled, easy-to-remember label. After all, calling them *reanimated flesh-eating corpses* is a bit unwieldy.

Zombie Roots

There are several classic movie genres and subgenres that have clearly influenced Romero's work, but for the fabric of it, the material substance on which created what would become his own genre, he looked away from film and into fiction. He looked at Richard Matheson's groundbreaking novel, *I Am Legend*, in which the author blended the vampire and science fiction genres into a single story that used science to ratchet up the fright.

Matheson's story tells of a plague (*bacillus vampiri*) that sweeps the earth and turns everyone into vampires except one man. The book then explores the protagonist's struggle to survive against an overwhelming army of the walking dead. *I Am Legend*, though a short novel by today's standards, is dense with implied social and political commentary as well as insightful psychological subtext.

Art of the Dead – Mark McLaughlin

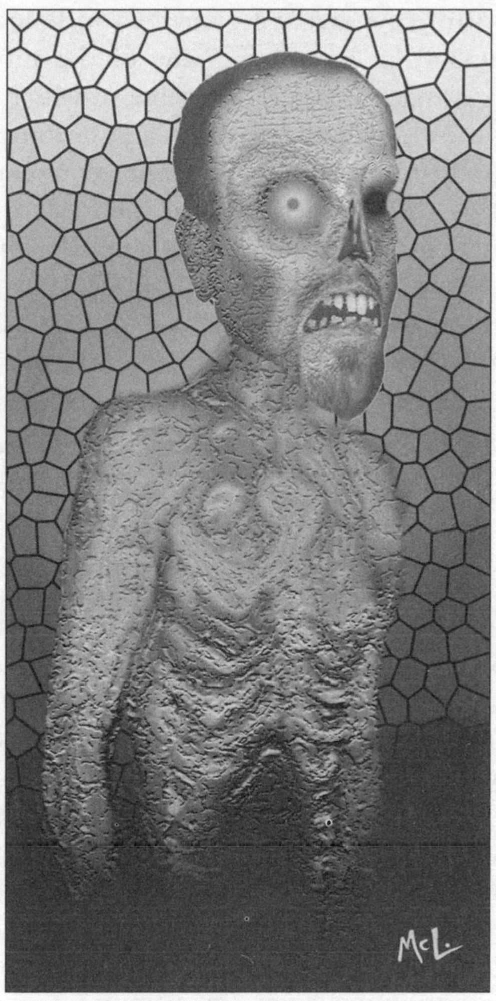

Advanced Decay

"Why did they come back to life? Who knows! A person can come up with any number of reasons—horrific, fantastical or science-fictional. Their flexible nature appeals to me, and so I use them in my artwork, and my fiction, too."

This is a thinking person's horror story, and arguably one of the most important books in the twentieth-century cannon of both science fiction and horror.

In terms of film, the strongest obvious influence was Alfred Hitchcock's 1963 film *The Birds*,[8] one of the most significant entries in the "revenge of nature" subgenre in which a normal part of the natural world suddenly changes and becomes deliberately threatening. Hitchcock used birds, but the genre explored a lot of variations of this theme with decidedly mixed results. We had some exceptional entries beginning with an onslaught of giant ants in *Them!* (1954) and one really pissed-off shark in *Jaws* (1974); a few decent chillers like the rat-infested *Willard* (1971) and *Ben* (1972); a mixed bag of so-so flicks like the killer-whale gonna get you *Orca* (1977) and the weirdly wormy *Squirm* (1976); and some truly appalling pieces o' crap like *Night of the Lepus* (1972), in which a southwestern town is attacked by flesh-eating killer bunnies (I'm not making this up!). In each of these films nature decides to stop being passive and takes a bite out of mankind. All great inspiration for George Romero.

The revenge of nature subgenre overlaps with "disaster films," which typically pit a dwindling group of people against a natural (or in some cases man-made) catastrophe. Typical of the later zombie genre, it's often the infighting among the struggling survivors that leads to their high mortality rate. Disaster films have been a staple of cinema since the industry's earliest days, with early outstanding examples like *Fire* (1901), *San Francisco* (a 1936 earthquake movie), *In Old Chicago* (1937 story of that city's great fire), and continuing on into the twenty-first century with *The Day After Tomorrow* (a global warming/new ice age cautionary tale inspired by the nonfiction book *The Coming Global Superstorm* by Whitley Strieber and Art Bell).

A fourth archetype that helped stir the pot for *Night of the Living Dead* was the apocalyptic thriller in which we see civilization as we know it crumble, often taking with it morality, compassion, and basic humanity. The novel *I Am Legend* also fits into

8. Based on a story of the same name by Daphne du Maurier (*The Birds and Other Short Stories*, 1963).

this genre and has been adapted three times (so far) to films of this kind, beginning with *The Last Man on Earth* (1964) starring Vincent Price, *The Omega Man* (1971) with Charlton Heston, and most recently *I Am Legend* (2007) starring Will Smith. Oddly, both the Heston and Smith versions change the nature of the plague so that instead of vampires the bulk of humanity is transformed into mutated humans—though they did have an aversion to sunlight. As a purist and huge fan of Matheson's original story, I disagree with this choice. Vampires are scarier than albino humans with sunglasses. Much, much scarier. At least with the Will Smith version, there was a fairly obvious attempt to riff off of the success of movies like *28 Days Later* (2002) and its sequel *28 Weeks Later* (2007), which used the zombie film model but with diseased humans rather than living dead.

28 Days Later is largely credited with rebuilding the zombie genre and, along with the comedy *Shaun of the Dead* (2004), bringing it to the moneymaking cinema mainstream. But without *Night of the Living Dead* there would have been no *28 Days Later*; but without the book *I Am Legend* there almost certainly would never have been a *Night of the Living Dead*. So . . . *Legend* influenced *Dead*, which in turn influenced *28*, which then influenced the newest film version of *Legend*. There's something curiously inbred about all that, or is that just me?

The Romero Effect

This was the pool from which Romero dipped to create the basis of his new horror film; but Romero was an innovator in his own right and wanted to tweak the model to fit his own dystopian vision and to carry his own brand of wry social commentary. He changed the vampires to flesh-eating ghouls and, instead of starting his tale after the fall of man, he chronicles the actual plummet by focusing on a small group of survivors holding out against an undead invasion.

Shot for pocket change ($114,000), *Night of the Living Dead*[9]

9. During the scripting and production phase the movie was known as *Night of the Flesh Eaters* and *Night of Anubis*.

revolutionized horror forever, created a new monster paradigm, launched a lot of careers (actors, effects people, other directors, etc.), inspired many a sleepless night, and influenced film, TV, fiction, art, poetry, music, and even toys. The full impact of the "Romero Effect" cannot be calculated.

In his films, Romero does not make any direct reference to religion or organic chemistry, and we're always left wondering just how exactly these zombies came into being. In *Night* he suggests that a space probe (never seen and only obliquely mentioned) has returned to earth contaminated with an unknown form of radiation. Is this why the dead have risen? The talking heads seen on TV screens in some of the scenes float this as a theory, but no definitive statement is ever made. No attempt is made to explain the process, but the cause is less the point than how society reacts to this new threat. They rise, we fall . . . and one way or another it's all our fault. Romero is not known for his enthusiastic optimism for humanity's higher values.

In *Dawn*, Romero only lightly touches on religion and vodoun, and even then it's clear this is not his message. The SWAT officer Peter (Ken Foree) makes the comment: "When there's no more room in hell, the dead will walk the earth." He says that it was one of his grandfather's sayings, from *Macumba*, which is a Brazilian slang name for vodoun/voodoo based on the Bantu word for magic.[10] The issue is not explored and is never mentioned again.

With the rise of the living dead, we suddenly have a new kind of horror storytelling. Instead of the thinking monster (vampires, demons), or the semi-intelligent but equally threatening supernatural beast (werewolves, mummies), or radioactive giants (*Them!*, *Godzilla*), we have something that borrows the best elements of each. We have a horde of nearly unstoppable, flesh-hungry dead who are, by their new nature, both fearless and relentless.

This new horror prototype became instantly successful, and this little indie flick raked in 30 million worldwide. Thirty million may sound like chump change considering the amounts pulled in by

10. Macumba is also the name of a Bantu deity and a Bantu word for musical instrument. When used to refer to vodoun, it is only used by nonpractitioners of that faith, suggesting that Peter is merely quoting his grandfather but not endorsing a point of view.

Brian Keene on the Zombie Effect

"Zombies are the new vampires. You know what I'm talking about. Remember, just a few short years ago, when you could stand in the horror section of your favorite bookstore, close your eyes, and your finger would land on a vampire novel? Well, there are still vampires—but their numbers seem to be dwindling under this new zombie epidemic. Zombies have invaded pop-culture; everywhere from episodes of *Aqua Teen Hunger Force* to a clothing line at Hot Topic. It has been suggested to me that some of this is my fault. You're welcome."

modern summer blockbusters, but when you consider that it made back its production costs *214 times over* you can see why even the jaded film moguls started paying attention. Since 1968 there have been hundreds of zombie films, both big budget and total backyard camcorder junk. Even the junk is popular (and some of it is good).

In his nonfiction book on the horror culture, *Danse Macabre,*[11] Stephen King suggests that zombies have become a new horror paradigm, as complete and valid as vampires, ghosts, demons, and the rest. Fantasy author C. J. Henderson, who has penned a number of zombie short stories, agrees: "In his last film, Romero moved the zombie to the same status of any other monster icon. In *Land of the Dead,* he completely reverses the audience's sympathy. Let's face it—it's the first zombie film ever where the audience rooted for the zombies to kick everyone's ass. Look at the story—poor zombies just want to go through the motions of being human. Not good enough for the rich—they have to descend from their ivory towers and steal and disrupt the wretched zombies' way of life because, as usual, the rich are parasites who always victimize those less financially fortunate rather than put their wealth to good use. Screw 'em, said the audience. Let's face it, we all wanted Dennis Hopper dead in that film, the same way we want to see

11. Published 1983 by Dodd Mead and Company.

Zombie Films You Never Heard Of (but Need to See) — Part 1

- ***Battlefield Baseball (Jigoku Koshien)*** **Japanese director Yudai Yamiguchi's 2003 madcap baseball and zombie romp. Over the top and hilarious.**
- ***Bio Cops*** **(Sheng Hua Te Jing Zhi Sand Shi Ren Wu). This superior sequel to *Bio-Zombie* (1998) features slapstick humor that foreshadows some of the stunts in *Shaun of the Dead.***
- ***Blue Sunshine.*** **A weird little mix of hippies, social consciousness, politics, conspiracy theories, and the living dead. Released in 1976.**
- ***Chopper Chicks in Zombie Town.*** **A 1989 Troma Studios mishmash of entertaining weirdness featuring a guest appearance by a then-unknown Billy Bob Thornton.**
- ***Come Get Some!*** **Released in 2003, this zombie comedy is better than most and surprisingly entertaining. Worth a look.**
- ***Dead & Breakfast.*** **A 2004 zom com so funny it'll make you pop your autopsy stitches.**
- ***Graveyard Alive: A Zombie Nurse in Love*** **(2003). You have to give this points just for being a feminist zombie film. And it's pretty good, too.**

these scum-sucking CEOs who feel they're perfectly justified in stealing the retirement programs of their employees because the billion-freaking dollars they already have salted away for their retirement just doesn't look big enough."

21st-Century Zombie Mojo

The popularity of the genre has waxed and waned, and for a while the unquiet dead seemed to have settled back down for their eternal rest. Vampires became trendy again, and the day of the dead

Zombie Clothes

***Zombie T-shirts* by J. N. Rowan**

Zombie T-shirts are enormously popular, thanks to conventions, movie marathons, zombie walks and crawls, and all-night keg parties. Among my favorites are these from J. N. Rowan's collection.

seemed to be over, or at least to have peaked in terms of cinematic potential. In fact, a few years ago if someone told me that a zombie novel would hit the hardback best-seller list and that Brad Pitt would make a movie based on it, I'd have either laughed or thought it was a sign of the apocalypse.

Turns out, however, Brad *is* making a big-budget zombie flick based on the best-selling *World War Z* by Max Brooks (son of Mel). So, yeah, sign of the apocalypse.

Zombies are back . . . and zombies are *hot*; and even though the "z" word may not have been consistently on everyone's personal radar, a vast pop culture movement has been out there, growing steadily and growing in all sorts of unexpected directions. Not just in feature films, but in fiction, role-playing and video games, TV, direct-to-video movies, comics, toys, music, and art.

Zombie films have made a huge comeback. *Shaun of the Dead* showed that flesh-eating ghoul movies make good date flicks.[12] *Dawn of the Dead* was remade with quality actors—Sarah Polley, Ving Rhames—and did very well at the box office. The king of the undead himself, George Romero, has returned to making new undead films like *Land of the Dead* (2005) and *Diary of the Dead* (2008). The video game *Resident Evil*[13] has been translated successfully into novels and big-budget, highly successful movies. Zombie-esque thrillers like *28 Days Later* and its sequel *28 Weeks Later* have been international hits, winning critical acclaim as well as audience praise. All three of his original films, *Night, Dawn,* and *Day* have been given bigger budget remakes. New zombie flicks are being hustled through development. Zombies have risen from the dead, and this time nothing seems to be knocking them down again.

Understanding the Zombie Threat

So what makes a good zombie story?

For the most part, the zombie stories in film and fiction follow a basic pattern:

12. Another sure sign of the apocalypse.
13. For more on the *Resident Evil* films, see Chapter 11.

Raw Footage — Why We Love Zombies

"Zombie movies are horrific on every level—they bring up the fear of the paranoid (having the ones you love turn up against you), they bring up our fears of carnivores (being eaten), and they bring up our fear of disease (becoming a zombie ourselves). There's no other movie monster that works on so many levels of the mammalian psyche. We're hardwired evolutionarily to be scared green of zombies."—James Gunn, Screenwriter for the 2005 remake of *Dawn of the Dead*[14]

1. Something happens (radiation, plague, etc.) that causes the recently dead to rise.
2. The risen dead have little or no intelligence and operate on a kind of reduced sub-animal instinct. This instinct drives them to attack living humans.
3. The dead murder humans and consume their flesh.
4. In the face of this plague of zombies, civilization quickly crumbles.
5. A few remaining humans hole up in a (fill in the blank: deserted farmhouse, shopping mall, underground complex, etc.).
6. The humans bicker, and ultimately one or more of them is responsible for the dead breaking in and chomping on the last survivors.
7. Often at least one good-looking man and woman escape, but the future of the race as a whole (sex appeal notwithstanding) looks pretty grim.
8. Welcome to the zombie apocalypse.

14. Michael Tolkin and Scott Frank contributed to the screenplay for *Dawn of the Dead.*

But is that how it would actually happen? Let's revisit what we talked about in the Introduction:

- If, for whatever reason, the dead did return to a semblance of life and begin attacking the living, would society immediately and irrevocably come apart at the seams?
- Would all the infrastructure fail its citizenry?
- Would medical science be unable to find a cure in time?
- Would the police and military truly be overwhelmed?

Personally, I don't think so. And I *like* apocalyptic fiction.

Having worked at various times in my career with law enforcement, the medical field, and in the sciences, I have a fair amount of faith that the technology, organization, process, and courage of the system would be up to the task.

In *World War Z*, the author takes the middle view on the issue. He holds that the zombies would overwhelm mankind, largely due to the inefficiencies of the global political system and basic human greed and stupidity. However he further postulates that humanity, pushed to the edge of extinction, would find a way to work together and fight its way back from the brink to win the zombie war.

Romero, the godfather of the subculture, takes a far dimmer view. In *Night of the Living Dead* the ghouls are ultimately (it seems) defeated, even though it's at a dreadfully high cost in human terms; but in his 1978 sequel, *Dawn of the Dead*[15], he predicts that the plague will continue to spread and more aspects of society will break down. By 1985's *Day of the Dead*, Romero predicted a total societal collapse. However, when he picked up the series again in 2005 with *Land of the Dead*, he seems to have either softened a bit in his dim view of civilization—because in that more whole cities have survived[16]—or taken a bigger picture view and granted that not everyone on earth would turn out to be

15. The original title, according to Romero's script, was *Dawn of the Living Dead*.

16. His fifth film, *Diary of the Dead*, does not continue this "future history," but instead jumps back to tell another story that occurs at the same time as *Night of the Living Dead*.

Art of the Dead – Frank Dietz

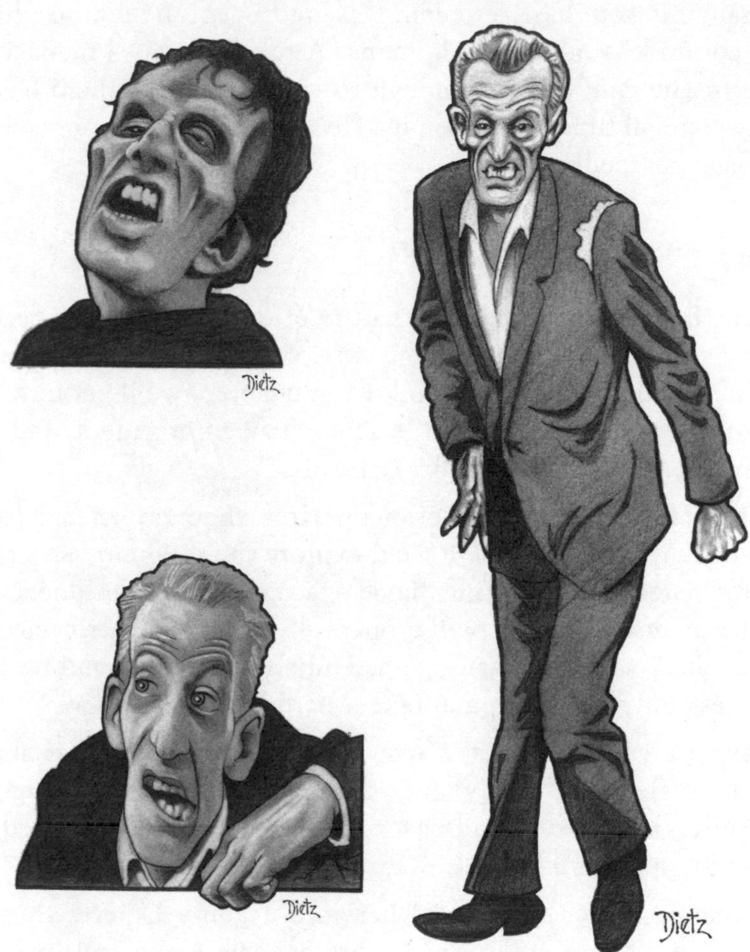

The Living Dead

"*Night of the Living Dead* is iconic, a truly landmark film. There have been *better* zombie films made, but there will never be a more important or influential one."

a gutless, backstabbing jackass or a failed hero. In that film both the humans *and* the zombies seem to be evolving to a higher level, though truth be told more of the zombies display admirable qualities (ranging from basic problem solving to genuine remorse for a fallen comrade) than do the humans. A few good guys manage to escape in the end; but few enough to suggest that Romero hasn't exactly gone all fuzzy-bunny on us. He's still the ruling monarch of dystopia.

Zombie CSU

So, now that we know the basic nature of the beast, let's go deeper into the science to understand the *why* of zombies, and the *how* of stopping them. In each of the following chapters we'll get into the nuts and bolts of how forensics, science, law enforcement, and the law operate. Each chapter is broken into:

- *Just the Facts:* These sections present the hard science from the real world, and here we'll explore the different aspects of forensics (fingerprinting, blood spatter, gunshot residue, etc.); learn how modern police operate; probe the intricacies of medical science; discuss guns and ammo; report on how the press covers a story; and take a hard look at the law.
- *Expert Witness:* This is where the experts speak out about their fields of study and their insights. I have a great collection of world-class experts in every field related to crime and punishment.
- *The Zombie Factor:* And here we ask my experts to play "what if" and apply their years of experience and insights into how science and the law would react and respond to a zombie uprising.
- *The Final Verdict:* A brief recap of the facts, evidence, and decision based on what they have told us.

Buckle up . . . it's about to get a little weird.

1

The Murder Book

Investigating an Alleged Zombie Attack

Confronting the Undead **by Kevin Breaux**

In police parlance a "Murder Book" is a three-ring binder in which all the pertinent facts of a case are kept. This book, also called a case file, includes autopsy and forensic reports, crime scene photographs and sketches, transcripts of investigators' notes, and logs of witness interviews. The Murder Book starts as soon as police begin investigating a homicide and concludes with the arrest of a suspect.

Let's start building our Zombie Murder Book together . . .

Just the Facts

The Scene of the Crime

To understand how police handle a crime, we'll use the following scenario, which will help us set time, place, and other details necessary to create a platform on which the police will build their case. For the most part, and especially in the early stages, the police procedures will be the same for any kind of serious crime (even those that *don't* involve the living dead).

Zombie Attack Scenario

Time: Early evening on a weeknight.

Location: A medical research center in the suburbs of a large city. A two-lane blacktop road runs past the truck delivery gate of the research center. The research center has a chain-link fence, an electric gate, and a small guardhouse. The lot is big, with delivery trucks of various sizes parked and locked. The building is locked and dark, closed for the evening. Several light poles cast some light, but large portions of the parking lot are in shadows.

Traffic on the road is infrequent.

Witness: Sheila Wilson, 49, a new accounts manager for a local branch of a regional banking chain. Ms. Wilson drives a 2006 Ford Explorer and receives a cell phone call from a realtor. She pulls to the side of the road opposite the research center fence in order to write down some information. She hears something that sounds like firecrackers and then turns to witness what she believes is a violent attack inside the fence. One man falls, and a second staggers off, apparently injured, crosses the road, and vanishes into the woods across from the research center. Ms. Wilson disconnects her call and dials 911.

JUST THE FACTS

The 911 Call

The transcript that follows is from a 911 call received by Romero Township Emergency Services at 7:16 A.M. on Wednesday in late August.

DISPATCHER: 911, state your emergency.
CALLER: Oh my God, I just saw this man come out of nowhere and attack someone. He looks like he's hurt. I think he's dead. God! Please hurry. Okay? This man just came out of nowhere and attacked him!
DISPATCHER: Slow down, ma'am. Tell me your location.
CALLER: I was just driving home—
DISPATCHER: What town are you in?
CALLER: Um . . . Hinzman, I think.
DISPATCHER: Are you in Romero Township?
CALLER: Yes. In Hinzman. On Argento Road, near Liberty Street. You need to *(inaudible)*.
DISPATCHER: Is this a private residence?
CALLER: No, it's that big research center on Argento Road. The one by the canal.
DISPATCHER: Can you see a sign?
CALLER: Um . . . yes, Martin Medical Research.
DISPATCHER: Please remain calm, I have police and an ambulance already on the way.
CALLER: Hurry, please! He had a gun—
DISPATCHER: Tell me what happened. Has anyone harmed you?
CALLER: No, not me—the guard. I think I heard a shot? Maybe a couple of them. And then this man came staggering across the—
DISPATCHER: I need you to try and calm down, ma'am. I need you to tell me what happened.
CALLER: He's just lying there on the ground. I really think he's dead. Or *(inaudible)*.
DISPATCHER: I didn't hear what you said. Your cell phone's cutting out.

CALLER: The guard's just lying there. I can see a lot of blood. I can't tell if he was shot. Oh my god! What should I do?

DISPATCHER: Ma'am, are you hurt?

CALLER: No, I just pulled over to make a cell call and I saw—

DISPATCHER: Are you in any immediate danger?

CALLER: No, I'm still in my car.

DISPATCHER: Did you see a gun? Did you see anyone fire a gun?

CALLER: N-no . . . but I heard some sounds. Like pops. It didn't sound like a gun, not like on TV.

DISPATCHER: Do you see the person who attacked him?

CALLER: No . . . he ran away.

DISPATCHER: He's not anywhere around your vehicle?

CALLER: No . . . I don't think so. He went the other way. Into the woods. Is the ambulance coming?

DISPATCHER: Can you tell me what he looked like? Was he white or black—

CALLER: Um, he was white. Really pale, with dark hair. Short hair.

DISPATCHER: What was he wearing?

CALLER: I don't know. Maybe a T-shirt and light pants. Like doctor's pants. Scrubs, like that. He was barefoot, too.

DISPATCHER: Was he alone? Was there anyone else?

CALLER: No, he was alone . . . just him and the guard. That poor man—

DISPATCHER: Ma'am, is the assailant anywhere in sight?

CALLER: No . . . he went across the street into the woods. I can't see him at all. I think he ran away.

DISPATCHER: Ma'am I want you to get out of your car and go over to the guard. Can you do that for me?

CALLER: Okay . . . I'm with him. He's really bad. There's so much blood.

DISPATCHER: Now listen closely, and I'm going to tell you what to do—

At this point a lot of things have happened. As the dispatcher takes the information from the witness, she's doing several things at once. The questions she asked gave her a snapshot of the events and the location of the crime. She has a physical description and an idea of the direction in which the suspect fled. While talking to the witness, the dispatcher would be typing the information into her computer and requests would be sent to patrol units and emergency medical teams. Often they'll arrive while the 911 call is still in progress.

The next thing she did was to assess whether the scene was safe—relatively speaking—for the responding officers and EMTs. This will determine how those professionals perform upon arrival.

While these units are rolling, the dispatcher may also have the witness go to the victim to assess his apparent condition.

Expert Witness

Fredericka Lawrence, a 911 operator for Bucks County, Pennsylvania, says, "We talk the witness through an assessment. We ask about the types and locations of the injuries, and whether they're actively bleeding. We ask them if the victim is conscious and responsive. If they are not immediately responsive, we ask them to try painful stimuli, which means they pinch the back of the upper arm. If the victim is conscious on any level, they'll react to that. Sometimes the witness is asked to provide first aid. For a badly bleeding wound, we'll ask them to apply direct pressure with a clean cloth; and I can't tell you the number of times I've talked a witness through CPR. Sometimes the witness is a real lifesaver."

"When calling 911, it's essential that you cooperate with the dispatcher," insists Cass Brennan, who worked dispatch in three different Ohio counties in the 1980s and 1990s. "That means that you should be as calm as possible and listen to their questions and provide the best answers you can. Don't argue, and don't make a fuss if they insist that you answer their questions, even if it means having to repeat information. 911 operators are trained to ask very specific questions and to keep the caller as calm as possible. They also want to keep witnesses in place so they don't leave, don't panic, and don't compromise the crime scene."

The operator enters all the pertinent information into the computer so that a permanent and easily accessible record of the incident is always available. All 911 calls are recorded, and every call is given an incident number. It's useful to ask for the incident

Zombies . . . Fast or Slow? Part 1

Few topics are debated quite as heatedly as that of the speed of the living dead. Romero had them move slow, and for most fans of the genre that is tantamount to the word of God. Upstart directors like Dan O'Bannon (*Return of the Living Dead*) and Zack Snyder (*Dawn of the Dead*) like their zombies to be more fleet-footed. I polled some key players in the world of zombie pop culture to see where they stand:

- **"Sssslllloooowwww!"—Max Brooks, author of *World War Z***
- **"For me, slow. . . . although I was pleasantly surprised by the *Dawn of the Dead* remake and its Olympic sprinters. But I like slow ghouls—they seem a little more elegant and there's a nice sense of inevitability in them catching up with the living. No matter how fast you run away, Death will always get you. Eventually."—Jamie Russell, author of *Book of the Dead: The Complete History of Zombie Cinema* (FAB Press).**
- **"I think slow zombies are scary as hell en masse, but I wanted the zombies in the remake to be scary individually as well.**

number in case you lose your connection or have to call back for any reason. The dispatcher will generally not offer this number but will provide it when asked. Tapes and/or transcripts of 911 calls are available on request—they're not confidential and are a matter of public record. If you're involved in an incident, you can request a copy of the tape. If you've witnessed a zombie attack, then that tape will probably get you on *Larry King* (but it is illegal to try and sell it on eBay).

Once the 911 call has been made, the central dispatch will contact the specific unit whose patrol route covers that location. "In rural counties," Brennan says, "one dispatch center is often used for all of the surrounding towns. Computers and radio reports track the general movement of available units. If the car that would normally respond is handling another complaint, at lunch, doing transport or any of the thousand other jobs that police officers routinely

The first thing I wrote in the movie was the first sequence in the movie—that of Ana's husband being attacked by the little girl, Vivian (which was actually the name of the little girl who lived next door to me at the time). Maybe I made her fast, because a slow little zombie girl in the morning light just didn't seem as scary. Whatever, I liked the idea of her jumping up and racing down the hall."—James Gunn, screenwriter for the remake of *Dawn of the Dead*:

- **"As a veritable disciple of Romero, the slow is the way to go. The idea of smashing slow zombies with a bat still appeals to me. However, I do believe there is a place for the fast zombie. Very intense and very frightening, the speed and relentlessness is very scary. *28 Weeks Later* illustrated that with perfection in the opening scene on the British countryside, when the protagonist was running from the hideout and the creatures were close to cutting him off from the hills at the angle they were taking. Very scary."—Bowie Ibarra, author of *Down the Road: A Zombie Horror Story* and *Down the Road: On the Last Day* (both from Permuted Press).**

handle, then the request for responding units is broadened. In very serious crimes this might result in units responding from several neighboring towns."

For violent crimes, like the one reported here, and one where the suspect is believed to still be at large, a fair number of cars would roll.

According to Greg Dagnan, CSI/Police/Investigations Faculty—Criminal Justice Department, Missouri Southern State University, "The dispatcher will keep the caller on the phone while emergency responders are in route. This process also encourages the caller not to hang up in case police can't find them or some other unexpected event occurs. Police are usually the first to enter a scene like this even if others (fireman, ambulance) beat them there. Police must ensure that responders will be safe while lifesaving measures are performed."

911 operator Fredericka Lawrence adds, "The constant contact between operator and witness not only saves lives, but it keeps the witness on the scene, which means that the officers and detectives will have someone they can interview. That speeds up the entire process."

The Zombie Factor

The scenario we're using to make our examination of the zombie outbreak is one seldom ever shown in the films. We're working with the actual *patient zero*, the central or "initial infected person" in an epidemiological investigation. If patient zero is stopped in time, then there will be no plague to spread; if he's stopped too late, then every person he bites becomes a potential disease vector.

The good news is that in the real world these things often start small. One zombie out there and a whole police force against it, with all the might and technological resources that can be called to bear, should be able to do the trick. It would be less dangerous than, say, a group of hunters trying to subdue an escaped lion or tiger. Dangerous, yes, but doable.

The bad news is that the zombie has to be seen and identified as a disease-carrying hostile vector. That's not going to happen quickly or easily, and probably not at all during this phase. Diseases are invisible, so the police will likely react as if the assailant is either mentally unstable or whacked out on drugs. Or both. This isn't necessarily a bad thing, because suspects demonstrating odd and irrational behavior are treated as if they are very dangerous. Extra caution is used, more backup is called, and greater safety protocols are put in place. On the level of one (or at most a few) of the slow, shuffling zombies, the police department is more than ready to meet the challenge.

In our scenario, our witness has seen a strange and apparently drunk or stoned individual attack someone else and then stagger off in to the woods across the street. We don't yet know why the zombie fled leaving a victim still alive. We don't know if the sight of the witnesses's car, or the smell of its engine frightened off the zombie. Can we even use the word *frighten* in connection with

Art of the Dead – Rob McCallum

Patient Zero

"I'm old school so prefer my zombies to be slow. The fast ones are pretty scary too but I just don't see dead bodies being able to run for too long before bits of them start to give out and fall off!"

zombies?[1] We don't know if something attracted it; or perhaps *called* it. All we know, based on the eyewitness's testimony, is that the zombie attacker has fled.

The novels *The Rising* and *City of the Dead* by Brian Keene,[2] *Dead City* by Joe McKinney, *Dying 2 Live* by Kim Paffenroth, and *The Cell* by Stephen King explore the possibility that some other force, being, or hive consciousness was able to control large groups of zombies. In *Land of the Dead* the chief ghoul, Big Daddy, seems capable of directing the actions of his fellow "stenches." However in Romero's original zombie films, *Night, Dawn,* and *Day,* the zombies were antonymous, their actions being directed by whatever constituted their postresurrection set of instincts. As such (and although they do seem to gather wherever one or more humans are hiding), they do not appear in any way organized, any more than flies are organized even though masses of them gather around a corpse. Even if we grant a certain degree of unpredictability due to the police initially having insufficient evidence, we are still looking at a situation in which the suspect will not be actively hiding (and will, by nature of its reduced intelligence, be incapable of this), and a suspect who will take no effort to prevent the leaving of evidence. There will be a lot of evidence to collect—fingerprints, footprints, blood spatter, trace DNA, witnesses, possible video surveillance from the location of the attack, and more. Once the police and crime scene unit arrives and the evidence collection begins, the hunt for our undead suspect will begin in earnest.

Help is on the way.

Just the Facts

First Responders

A crime scene is a tricky thing. It seldom has clear boundaries like you see on TV. In some cases the crime scene expands to include

1. Though in *Night of the Living Dead* the zombies certainly appeared to be frightened of fire; so fear, at least on a very basic level, may be a factor.

2. *The Rising* (2004) and *City of the Dead* (2005), Leisure Books; *Dead City* (2006) Pinnacle Books; *Dying 2 Live*, Permuted Press; *The Cell*, Scribner.

the planning and staging areas, the routes taken to and from the "primary scene," and even a recovered vehicle associated with the crime. Clues and evidence may be found at any or all of these.

The primary scene, however, is where the real action takes place. (For us it's the research center on Argento Road in Romero Township.)

The first police unit to arrive at a crime scene has a lot of responsibilities to handle, and even a two-officer car will be kept very busy. As the first responder unit rolls up, the officers have to assume that the situation is still active and dangerous. Assuming otherwise could be highly dangerous to everyone involved. Just because a witness says that the assailant has left, that doesn't make it so. And there is the consideration of the wounded victim. All of this is in their minds as they pull up to the scene.

But their first task is to observe the situation, noting the physical layout, the presence of objects (buildings, trees, vehicles, etc.) that could provide cover for a suspect or limit their assessment of the scene. They have to note whether any vehicles or persons are entering or leaving the scene. This includes identifying the presence of all persons (living or dead) and making very quick judgments about each person: Are they stationary or fleeing? Are they injured or dead? Are they actively engaged in a struggle? Are they lucid, raging, crying, etc.?

The first responders have to locate the scene, which isn't always as easy as it sounds. Witnesses, especially phone-in callers, are seldom clear and concise, and these callers may be unfamiliar with the location of the incident. Once they find the right spot, they have to secure the scene to prevent contamination of evidence. Much will depend on how well the first responders handle this.

As the officers get out of their unit, they have a chance to take sensory impressions of the scene. What do they hear? What do they see? What do they smell? Often these first impressions are crucial to the development of an effective investigation of the crime.

If the suspect is in view, he needs to be contained and detained, then cuffed and placed in the back of one of the responding vehicles.

The officers have to locate and assess the victims. Backup and

Zombie Films You Never Heard Of (but Need to See) — Part 2

- ***The Happiness of the Katakuris* (2000): A Japanese zombie musical. Weird, not very well done but absolutely watchable if alcohol is involved.**
- ***I, Zombie: A Chronicle of Pain* (1998): Granted, it's pretentious, but it's clear some real thought went into this British zom film. Give it a chance.**
- ***Io Zombo, Tu Zombi, Lei Zomba* (1979): An Italian zom com with a witty sense of humor. Very hard to find, but worth it.**
- ***Kung Fu Zombie* (1981): Hilarious Hong Kong zombie comedy. The plot doesn't make much sense, but you're laughing too hard to care.**

ambulances are typically called at this point, even before the officer gets out of his car. In our scenario the victim is comatose and badly injured with what looks like bite wounds and other lacerations. While waiting for this, the officers provide any necessary first aid the situation requires. Police officers are trained to do this and, sadly, very often have way too many opportunities to practice it. Prophylactic measures, such as latex gloves, are now standard for most police departments in the United States, which significantly reduces the risk of infection from welling blood and open wounds. In zombie attacks, of course, first aid can get dicey, since the infection rate from fluid exchange is estimated at 100 percent.

The first responders have to establish a beachhead for the invasion of other specialists who will collect and process the evidence and investigate the crime. Witnesses need to be located, identified, and detained so that they don't slip away with the words "I don't want to get involved" ringing in their heads. Safe and easy access for emergency vehicles has to be established and identified.

As they get a handle on the situation, the first responders contact dispatch, which in turn notifies the correct follow-up detective unit so that detectives can make the scene. Detectives from the

- ***Let's Scare Jessica to Death* (1971): A true "lost classic" that deserves to be found and watched. Creepy, subtle, and nicely twisted.**
- ***The Living Dead at the Manchester Morgue* (1974): Also known as *Let Sleeping Corpses Lie*, this one has the makings but never quite found its audience. Dig up a copy.**
- ***The Living Dead Girl* (1982): There's a good argument on both sides as to whether this is a zombie flick or a vampire flick; either way it's an interesting study into addiction, codependency, need, and love.**

violent crimes[3] division are requested. In violent crime, especially when there is an injured victim and the perpetrator is not only at large but also possibly armed and still in the vicinity, a lot of police support is sent. The idea is to put enough feet on the ground so that the presence of overwhelming force neutralizes any further criminal activity, and because the more eyes there are on a scene the more can be discovered.

The first responders also have to look for obvious evidence (a bloody knife, footprints, shell casings, etc.). Again, in our scenario, the officers also find the victim's gun, a Glock 23C automatic pistol. They look for and identify ejected shell casings and determine that at least three shots have been fired.

Expert Witness

Joe McKinney, a homicide detective in San Antonio, Texas, and the author of *Dead City* (Pinnacle Books, 2006), a cops versus zombies novel, observes: "On my department—and from my experience, police work is more or less the same all over—detectives

3. The name of this division may vary from one jurisdiction to another.

Art of the Dead – Ryan Allen

Unusual Suspects

"My first experience with a zombie movie was watching the Romero classic, *Night of the Living Dead.* I was just a kid when I saw it, and I recall not really knowing what I was watching. It was just some black-and-white movie I happened onto late one night. By the end I was scared and wondered where my dad kept the lumber and nails. You know . . . just in case."

respond to scenes after the uniformed officers working patrol have the situation locked down. Patrol officers, you see, are basically jacks-of-all-trades. Their job is to respond to a situation first and contain it. Once the situation is contained, the patrol officer calls the appropriate follow-up unit that has been trained on all the particulars a given situation presents. For example, a murder, or a dead body found under suspicious circumstances, would warrant the officer to call Homicide. If the officers make a disturbance call in a fleabag motel and find a homemade meth lab, they call the Narcotics Unit. The key to police work in large and medium-sized departments is specialization."

According to Sgt. Dennis Miller, a recently retired Los Angeles police officer, "We have all sorts of specialized detectives all the way up to our elite Robbery/Homicide dicks. Sometimes a case is passed up the chain of command because it's going to become a 'hobby,' meaning that it's going to take a lot longer than the regular detectives have time for. Most detectives are handling a lot of cases and luckily a lot of these get closed quickly because we're not talking criminal masterminds here. Some bozo bashes his friend over the head with a golf club and then hides the club in his garage . . . that's a quick close. But if the case gets political, or it gets big—a serial murder, something involving a celebrity, or something where there's going to be a lot of forensics and a long court case, then RH steps in and handles it."

But as Greg Dagnan points out, "Ninety Percent of the agencies in the U.S. do not have homicide units. Among those that do, this policy varies around the country. The best and most common prac-

Hard Science: Weapon of Choice

Though Glock is regarded worldwide as a manufacturer of superior firearms, the research center guard's choice of model 23C is a questionable one. This version of the gun is a "compensated version," which means that it is designed to have additional gas/flame venting to reduce recoil so that the shooter can bring the gun back to the point of aim more quickly. For daytime shooting this is a superb choice, but since the gas flame is vented by two ports on the topside of the slotted barrel, which can blind the shooter, it's not the best bet for a nighttime guard.

tice is that those who initially investigated the crime know the most about the case and they should finish it. However, on a high-profile case with a lot of media attention, homicide may insist on taking over."

The Zombie Factor

Everything starts with the crime scene, just as in the hunt for the cause of any kind of plague you need to go to the source. Our zombie assailant was described as wearing hospital scrubs, a

---

Michael Kelly – CJ from "Dawn of the Dead"

In the remake of *Dawn of the Dead*, there are a number of reluctant heroes—the thief turned zombie hunter, the cop who just wants to find his brother, the guy who sells TVs at Best Buy, the nurse who just lost her husband—but one of the most complex and interesting, and indeed the *most* reluctant hero of the film is the security guard, CJ, as played by Michael Kelly.

I asked Michael what makes CJ tick. "The character of CJ was built mostly on two things: his loneliness and insecurities. Throw in a little drinking problem, childhood abuse, and a very bizarre love of video games and you have someone who has no intention of becoming a hero."

And yet he does, several times saving the lives of the people he first tried to drive away from the shopping mall sanctuary where CJ is head of security.

Being in the remake of one of the most beloved films of the genre was a great career opportunity, but it also put the cast and crew in the hot seat. "Every remake is gonna catch shit. Before ours came out, the lash was relentless. I think fans' minds were changed as soon as they saw ours, and if they weren't then I would have to say perhaps they were diehards and stubborn, and it didn't matter what we did. People would have bitched if we did an exact remake as well. You can't please everyone, and when making a film you should stay true to yourself and your vision anyway. Everyone sees things differently."

T-shirt, and no shoes, and the attack happened in the parking lot of a medical research facility. Connections will be drawn.

As we go, we're going to raise and then knock down a number of favorite zombie plague theories. The "radiation from a space probe" idea won't hold water, as you'll see; and though toxic waste contamination holds a little promise, it's most reasonable to expect that the cause of the plague will, in fact, be a plague: a pathogen of some kind, and once the assailant has been found and examined, and the forensic evidence collected and analyzed, attention is very likely to turn back to some kind of medical source.

So our scenario, though not drawn from any specific zombie movie or book, is based on a "most likely" premise.

The first responders are on the scene; the process is in motion.

Just the Facts

Securing the Crime Scene

Once the call has been made for backup and experts, the first responders still have work to do. Officers check all routes and ways into and out of the crime scene. This is necessary for several reasons, but principally to identify any route by which the suspect may have entered or left the scene by vehicle or foot and to make sure that all emergency routes will be available. At the same time the officers need to determine if there is any visible evidence on a route that could be contaminated or destroyed by responding official vehicles. Tire tracks, footprints, blood trails, shell casings, and other evidence is surprisingly fragile, and if the evidence is contaminated it can not only become useless (or suspect) as evidence useful for identifying the suspect, it can also become tainted and, therefore, useless in court.

In addition to police and forensics teams, others respond to crime scenes—violence will eventually draw crowds of reporters and rubbernecking civilians, all of whom are a threat to the integrity of the evidence and the process of investigation. Responding officers need to either erect barricades (generally using rolls of yellow crime scene tape) or arrange for wooden barricades to be brought in.

Some evidence is vulnerable to wind, trampling, precipitation, and other natural phenomena, so to protect and preserve the evidence, officers need to consider covering the evidence with plastic sheeting or other materials until the forensics team can get to it.

Responding officers start a log of the crime scene. This log includes as precise a chronology as possible that notes the location of the victim, witnesses, and (if any) suspects; information on the environmental conditions (rain, humidity, available light,[4] etc.); the location of other objects (buildings, vehicles, etc.); visible possible evidence; location, identification and type of any arriving vehicles; ditto arriving personnel; and sketches of the crime scene that includes measurements and diagrams.

The officers set aside an area free from areas of evidence but close enough to serve as a base of operations for the crime scene. This area will always be within the barricaded restricted zone. One of the two[5] responding officers will act as a *point officer*, which means that he or she will brief incoming officers and specialists and work to limit the number of people crossing the evidence barrier lines. Not all police who arrive at a crime scene are permitted past the barriers because of the great need to protect the evidence.

A growing number of police departments around the country have begun issuing small but powerful digital flash cameras to all units in their areas so that the first responders can take photos of a completely pristine crime scene. This is especially useful when non–police emergency teams have to cross into the evidence area (firefighters, EMTs, etc.). The digital files can be quickly downloaded to the detective and forensic teams' laptops and compared with the photos later taken by the official crime scene photographer.

If any evidence is removed by officers prior to the arrival of detectives and CSU teams, then each item would be put into a labeled bag and registered in the log along with precise notes indicating where the object was found.

As the CSU and detectives arrive, the first responders release

4. If the crime scene is indoors, officers generally leave the AC or heat on, windows open or closed, etc. to preserve the condition of the scene as it was during the incident; lights, however, are turned on, but the condition of the lights are generally noted before changes are made.

5. In cases of a single-officer car as the first responder, this officer may serve as a point officer, or an officer from the next-in car may take this job.

the scene to the specialists. Part of this process is to provide detailed information to every person who has a need to know.

Expert Witness

Criminal Justice Professor Greg Dagnan discusses[6] how a crime scene is secured: "Here is how your agency can insure crime scene integrity while conserving manpower and budget dollars. First, level containment: The most basic and superficial containment, this is the crime scene tape that surrounds the crime scene itself. The first level is usually determined by responding patrol officers and perhaps modified slightly after the initial chaos dies or the investigators show up. Properly done, this level of containment surrounds all places where evidence might be, with a bit more for extra insurance. Make sure to remember possible areas of entrance and egress by the suspect as these are the most commonly forgotten when containing a crime scene. Regrettably, first level containment is all the protection most crime scenes get. As illustrated earlier, this just doesn't cut it for the big scenes because everyone does everything inside the tape.

"Secondary containment: Though taking security to a higher level, this is not as complicated as it sounds. When crime scene processing officers arrive, they put up a second barrier of crime scene tape that completely surrounds the first level making a buffer zone. The secondary level solves several problems: Officers and Command staff have a place to meet where they cannot be bothered by civilians. Equipment can be stored in this secondary area and even makeshift desks made from folding tables can be erected. If you have some sort of crime scene vehicle it can be parked in this area and the area can serve as an established place for taking breaks and for crime scene trash. Your crime scene log is kept in this area and signed only by those who enter the first level or it can be signed by officers as they enter the second level. The latter option is still advantageous, as officers will not have to leave

6. Adapted from the article "Increasing Crime Scene Integrity by Creating Multiple Security Levels" by Greg Dagnan, and reprinted with the author's permission from his website. For the complete article, go to www.crime-scene-investigator.net/MultilevelContainment.html.

Zombie Films You Never Heard Of (but Need to See) – Part 3

- ***Night of the Comet* (1984): Not a great flick, but with Paul Bartel and Mary Woronov on hand to overact and Catherine Mary Stewart to look cute, this is definitely a good flick for a slow Saturday afternoon.**
- ***Versus* (2000): Ultraviolent gangsters versus zombies versus time-traveling samurai ghosts. Better than it sounds.**
- ***Night of the Living Dead* (1990): A lot of folks dissed the Tom Savini–helmed remake, but I'm not one of them. Tony Todd and Patricia Tallman turn in excellent, layered performances that turn the roles around so that it emerges as a tale of male bravado and obsession and female empowerment. Give it another shot.**
- ***The Night of the Seagulls* (1975): The last of the Blind Dead series, with some of the best character development and emotional content to come out of the Italian zombie horror genre.**
- ***Premutos: Lord of the Living Dead* (1997): A fallen angel raises an army of the dead and wages a very, very bloody war against mankind. The humans don't have an angel on their side . . . but they do have tanks. That, apparently, is enough.**

the scene for equipment and breaks, so there will be a lot less signing in and out. Hopefully there will be no evidence discovered in this level if the first level was properly placed. However, if you do find something (like a footwear or tire impression) outside the first level but still inside the second level, having it within a protected area could still save officers considerable explanations in court. If you cannot completely surround the first level with a second level, don't worry; the idea is that you find some place that adjoins the first level for you to cordon off for your purposes. As long as the first level of containment is well secured, a small adjoining secondary level could meet your needs without it having to completely surround the first.

- ***The Resurrection Game*** **(2001): An ultrarare shot on 16 mm, backyard zombie flick. It has lots of plot flaws and no budget, but it's earnest, and it was shot in Pittsburgh, which earns it some points right there.**
- ***Return of the Living Dead Part III*** **(1993): I know a lot of zombie film buffs hate this movie, but I thought it has the makings, and almost has the performances. Melinda Clarke does a surprisingly good job of eliciting sympathy as she fights the change from girlfriend to ghoul.**
- ***Sex, Chocolate & Zombie Republicans*** **(1998): One of the rare "wacky title" horror comedies that is both funny and a decent flick.**
- ***Stacy*** **(2001): A weird and disturbing little film about a disease that causes teenage girls to become murderous zombies. Funny, absurd, sad, and violent.**
- ***They Came Back*** **(2004): A French social commentary zombie film that's truly about trying to be part of a society that is no longer your own. Disturbing more than frightening.**
- ***Veerana*** **(1985): A song-filled Bollywood zombie film. Absolutely worth watching even if the plot makes no sense.**

"Perimeter Containment: This third level is where manpower and vehicles come in to play. Perimeter containment is done at most scenes to varying levels. This perimeter is created with barricades and police vehicles set up around the secondary tape. Roads are blocked to keep unauthorized vehicles away from the crime scene and foot traffic routed elsewhere. This level may be tighter if you have media trucks trying to get as close as possible and civilians trying to get right up to the crime scene tape. Manpower needs vary depending on how much foot traffic and unauthorized vehicles you are trying to keep out and how many access points that you have for authorized vehicles. The point of perimeter containment is that you keep your first and second level of containment more secure by insuring that unauthorized personnel will not be close enough to intrude on your crime scene."

The Zombie Factor

For our zombie hunt, one of the most critical factors during the process of establishing the crime scene is determining likely points of escape. Zombies don't hide, they don't climb fences, and they don't hop in cars and drive off. Any road or path leading away from the crime scene is likely to allow searchers to track the killer.

Footprints are particularly useful here, as is scent, and K-9 units are often called in to track suspects over all sorts of terrain. A slow, shuffling zombie can't walk farther or faster than a determined and coordinated pursuit.

Why Zombies?

- **"Modern apocalyptic zombies (as opposed to voodoo zombies) represent Armageddon at the most primal level. Doomsday, in which the last remaining humans must fight to survive on the most primal level. Hand to hand. Face to horrifying face. Against overwhelming odds."—Joe Augustyn, screenwriter for *Night of the Demons* (1989) and *Night of the Demons 2* (1994).**
- **"Zombies are us; humans stripped of our souls and denied final rest; left to wander in an Earth bound purgatory (and depending on your Director—motivated by terrible desire to eat human flesh.). They are truly one of mankind's most terrible fantasies and fears."—Andy Bark, screenwriter for *Dark Waters* (1994).**
- **"Because they give us a chance to hold up the mirror to all of society. Monsters like Frankenstein and Dracula were useful morality tools, but limited in certain way. Zombies, as a mass, as a section of a culture, can be used to stand in for all of society."—author C. J. Henderson**

Just the Facts

The Witness

When a witness makes a 911 call and remains on the scene (like in our example), one officer will conduct a short interview with her. He'll make sure she's not injured. He'll make an initial determination as to whether this person was in any way involved in the crime (if she's sitting there reloading her pistol, that could be a tip-off). And he'll ask her to recount what she saw, going over it several times to make sure he has every detail. Witnesses are often upset and highly emotional, but an officer trained to elicit information knows how to calm the witness down, and knows the kind of questions that will pluck out all the previously unspoken details.

What a victim sees and can later accurately describe is dicey at the best of times. Time, distance, available light, movement, shadows, obstacles, angle, and clothing all conspire to make easy positive identification tricky. With five days' worth of beard, new glasses, a woolen cap, and sunglasses Brad Pitt could probably walk down Broadway and few people would recognize him. Celebrities count on being able to make a few subtle costume changes to their appearance as a way of dodging throngs of fans and hordes of paparazzi.

So, given all these variables, we have a woman who witnesses a crime while driving. She pulls over across the street. County roads in industrial areas are generally 24 to 30 feet wide. Add to that a 48-inch shoulder, 42-inch-wide single-block sidewalk paving, a chain link fence, and a 26-foot-wide stretch of parking lot. That leaves the witness with a total minimum distance of 57.4 feet. This was in late afternoon/early evening and the quality of daylight will certainly affect vision. Dusk is one of the worst times for accurate witness descriptions. The eyes have not yet adjusted to darkness, and the light values play tricks on even the most eagle-eyed observer.

So, the interviewing officers will know that the information they get from the witness may not be 100 percent reliable. All cops know this; but it gives them a starting point and allows them to broadcast a BOLO (be on the lookout) with as much of a physical description as possible. The physical description of our attacker, based on the witness description, is as follows:

> All units be advised. In connection with a possible aggravated assault, witness describes a white male, six feet, one-seventy, with short dark hair wearing light colored pants, possibly hospital scrubs, and a white V-neck undershirt. Pants and shirt possibly stained with blood. No shoes. Suspect is described as extremely pale, with injuries or possibly bloodstains on his face and arms. Suspect is described as walking erratically like he was drunk. Last seen crossing Argento Road heading into woods across from Martin Medical Research. All units use caution when responding.

This visual description will be updated with any new information as the case progresses. Much later, if the suspect is not apprehended, a police artist will do a sketch—either freehand or with an identikit.

Expert Witness

I asked Professor Greg Dagnan to comment on the process of interviewing witnesses at a crime scene: "The responding officer should have identified any witnesses and separated them from everyone else. Nothing makes a detective madder than seeing all his witnesses in a huddle discussing the case. The witness is then taken to a quiet place and interviewed in what is hopefully a neutral, fact-finding manner. Witnesses can be easily swayed so questions like 'Was the gun black?' are not acceptable, as it gives the witnesses only the option of yes or no. If the gun was black with a chrome slide, an investigator who does not know how to interview a witness will never discover this information."

The Zombie Factor

Let's face it, the first few people who report zombie attacks are going to fall into two categories: those who will think they're seeing something else that doesn't involve zombies and those who report seeing a zombie and aren't believed.

The first kind will be the most common because the phrase "hey, I think that's a zombie attack" just isn't likely to pop into

Why Zombies?

- **"Because we can identify with zombies so easily. If we sit in front of the television, we're zombies. When we work at a repetitive job we become robotic zombies; when we wait in lines we feel like cattle or zombies, when you get tired you feel like a zombie . . . eyes glazed over . . . it's late . . . I am a zombie . . ."—Dan McConnell, comic book writer, penciler, and inker who has worked on *The X-Men, Captain Universe,* and *Zombies of Liberty***
- **"Why Zombies you ask? And I say why not? I'm not sure why people are so fascinated by zombies but I'd have to say that it has to do with man's innate fear of death. In a way it allows him to see death *after* death, and that is a scary thing. Sort of like letting someone walk into a morgue to see a body under the sheet and asking them if they want to pick up the sheet and take one quick peek at the body. I think that most people have a sick enough sense of curiosity that they would want to take just a peek."—David A. Prior, writer/director *Zombie Wars* (2006).**
- **"Zombies are a blank screen onto which we can project whatever fears we are having as a society. Zombies can represent our unease over terrorists, super-viruses, nuclear war, crime or civil unrest. And often in zombie stories, only a few humans are left to fight the zombies off, and I think that taps into something universal as well—our fear of being left alone. Or perhaps a fear of those closest to us dying, leaving us alone to fend for ourselves in a hostile world. As a society, we also place a high importance on the physical body. In missing persons cases or murders, we often hear people talk about the need to find the "remains" and give them a proper burial. But in a zombie story, it is that physical vessel—the human body—that refuses to rest easy. There is no closure after death in a zombie story. I think that's terrifying."—David Jack Bell, author of *The Condemned* (Delirium Books, 2008).**

Art of the Dead – Lisa Anne Riley

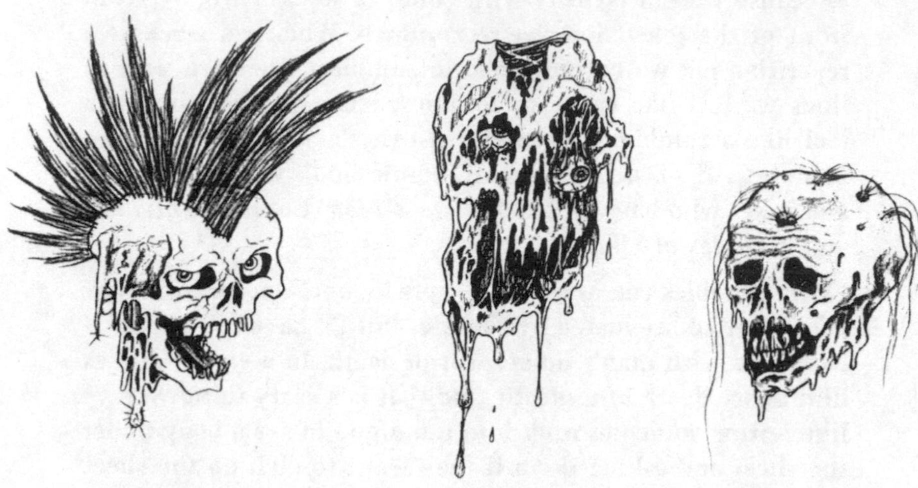

Dead Heads

"I like to see more about the zombies' view on things. Even with primitive brains they must have some form of thought regarding what has happened to them. Did they leave an 'afterlife'? Are they upset over leaving it? Does it physically hurt to be dead? Emotionally? Can they still feel any range of emotion?"

most people's heads. Even if we see a vicious fight and someone is getting bitten, the assumption will very likely be: Some crazy person is attacking that guy. Maybe followed by "I'd better call this in," or "I'd better mind my own business," or even "I'd better get the hell out of here."

The credibility of the witness in such a case will always be in question until overwhelming corroborating evidence is brought forth. And even then there will be resistance to the idea. Even the integrity of the individual witness doesn't really help the case, not in matters of the fantastic. Information even from a so-called "reliable witness" is not taken as proof positive until there is actually positive proof. After all, President Jimmy Carter filed an eyewitness account of a UFO sighting with NICAP,[7] which was made public while he was governor of Georgia; and in October of 1973, Ohio Governor John Gilligan also made headlines by reporting having seen a UFO. Many people claim to have spotted the Jersey Devil, including Commodore Stephen Decatur (the famous American naval hero), who insisted that he fired a cannonball at it while at the Hanover Iron Works in 1803; and Joseph Bonaparte, the former king of Spain and brother of Napoleon, saw the creature when he was hunting in the Pine Barrens near Bordentown, New Jersey, where he was living in exile. A couple of years ago, CNN ran footage of a sea monster[8] in Lake Van, Turkey. While these reports, and the thousands more made by less famous witnesses, are fascinating and make a lot of people go "Hmmmmm," they have not resulted in a change of belief by the masses or a call to action by the authorities.

For our zombie hunt, we are going to need solid forensic evidence.

Just the Facts

Watching the Detectives

Detectives are specialists whose job is more complex and far less glamorous than what you see on TV. Most of them aren't like Sherlock Holmes, able to recognize the fifty different kinds of dirt by visual observation alone. Nor are they the boneheaded slobs who can't solve a crime unless a wisecracking private investigator shows them how to use both hands to find their buttocks. They aren't loose cannons who drive quarter-million-dollar sports cars; they don't trample on the Constitution and the Bill of Rights to solve their crimes; they're not a pack of cynical hard-drinking womanizers who have noirish internal monologues playing in their heads; and they don't kick the tar out of suspects just because they

7. The incident occurred in Leary, Georgia, on the evening of January 6, 1969, and was reported to NICAP (National Investigations Committee on Aerial Phenomena), a now-defunct civilian organization.

8. To view the news clip, go to www.cnn.com/WORLD/9706/12/fringe/turkey.monster.

can. They also don't use shtick: no rumpled Columbo trench coats, no lollipops or hand-sewn Italian Kojak suits; no pastel Crockett and Tubbs jackets or cigarette boats.

Real police detectives are smart, highly trained, deeply experienced investigators who use science, process, and routine to collect evidence, build cases, conduct investigations, form theories, and arrest suspects. Sherlock Holmes, entertaining as he is to read about, would be a freak.

I've always been impressed by the presentation of detectives in the better police procedural books and movies. The gold-standard for these being the 87th Precinct series by the late (and very much missed) Ed McBain. His detectives were workmanlike, dogged, imaginative, and relentless without being obsessive. He also showed that detectives varied from mediocre (Andy Parker of that series) to very, very good (Steve Carella and Meyer Meyer); and they all relied on the use of established process and procedures rather than sudden intuitive leaps.

"The only true to life portrayal of police that is on today is the HBO series, *The Wire*," says Detective Mike Buben of the Lower Makefield Township Police in Pennsylvania, "Probably due to the fact that the creator is a former police officer from Baltimore."

"*Fort Apache, The Bronx*[9]; *The New Centurions*; and *The Choirboys*[10] are hands down the finest motion pictures about street cops out there; realistically portraying all that is both good and bad about police culture," says Detective Joe McKinney. "The detective's job, so far as I've seen, doesn't get portrayed with much realism on the big screen." But he concedes, "On TV, *The First 48* did a great job of showing how a case grows and takes shape. *Law and Order* tends to have too many rich, glamorous suspects to claim any sort of realism, even though they claim to rip their plots straight from the headlines. Real police work is about eighty percent junkies, thieves, and prostitutes, and I think the public would view the kind of people we normally deal with as more monstrous than any fictional monster I've read."

When detectives arrive at our crime scene they have two imme-

9. *Fort Apache, the Bronx* (1981).
10. *The New Centurions* (1972).

diate concerns: identifying, preserving, and collective evidence; and apprehending the suspect. Since our attacker is still at large, the lead detective will coordinate with the supervising patrol sergeant to begin a search of the area. K-9 dogs would likely be called in, and police departments in surrounding areas would be notified.

The detectives then do a walk-through during which they try to reconstruct the events leading up to and following the crime. Once they have a good sense of what's what, they can make decisions on which kinds of evidence are likely to be of use (though often much more is collected than is actually used), and for a while they yield the floor to the crime scene technicians.

Expert Witness

"Ninety percent of departments do not have a 'typical' Crime Scene Unit," observes Greg Dagnan. "Detectives, investigators or specially trained patrol officers collect evidence at crime scenes. For those agencies that do have specialized units, they usually have enough people that at least 4–5 persons can respond to a major crime scene, while they may go to smaller crime scenes in groups of two. Crime Scene Units are civilian employees who do the collection while investigators are interviewing people, conducting a neighborhood canvas, etc. Some are officers that have transferred into the crime scene department from other divisions within the department. Generally each department must decide how to configure their unit according to crime rates, resources and community perception. I have trained departments that only have one official Crime Scene Investigator, but that person coordinates, and is assisted by, Patrol and Detectives. Bottom line is that each agency does something a little different."

San Antonio Homicide Detective Joe McKinney gives this rundown on how detectives manage a case: "Detectives handle incidents (like the attack on the research center guard) as a team, dividing up responsibilities. Later, when one detective gets the report responsibility for the incident, he or she collates all the material generated by the team and puts them together into a document called a Prosecution Guide, which the District Attorney's Office uses for trial. But when the incident is still fresh, one or two detectives will make the scene, speak with the handling officers and their supervisor, request an evidence technician (the CSU guys) and tell the evidence tech what, specifically, they need. Every crime scene is unique and there is almost always something in particular above and beyond the normal tests and evidentiary protocol a detective wants to get. Then the detectives at the scene will arrange for witnesses to be transported to Headquarters for statements. Detectives at the office will receive and interview witnesses. Suspects will either be arrested and taken to jail or returned to the detective's office for an interview—again, this depends on the specific arrest, search, and seizure issues surrounding the case."

Detective Michael Buben of Lower Makefield, Pennsylvania, comments on the differences in the way big and small town cases are handled: "Larger departments have Violent Crime Squad detective and/or homicide units. In local departments such as ours, any detective working would respond, as well as some off duty detectives called in to assist. Detectives from the District Attorney's office also are used to assist in such investigations, as well. There are a lot of experienced investigators who can be brought in to handle a major crime."

Who responds, and when, depends on a variety of factors. "The normal response time depends on whether detectives are on duty," says Buben. "In small towns this might not be the case 24/7. If so, they usually respond with—or within minutes of—patrol officers. Otherwise, it may be the time it takes a detective to respond from home to the station, then to the scene, but in any case usually less than an hour."

The Zombie Factor

So far the police are going to be completely within the realm of known crime scene procedure and science. Cursory examination of the victim will show bite marks, but that is not all that rare in violent crime. There's nothing yet that screams "zombie!"

Since a witness provided a description, the detectives will begin their search for the assailant while at the same time overseeing the collection of evidence from the crime scene.

Hard Science: Cadaver Dogs

Just as there are specialties for police officers, there are specialties for police dogs. Some sniff out bombs, some sniff out drugs . . . but there is one kind specially trained to sniff out human remains.

Cadaver dogs.

These dogs were used heavily during the search for remains following the collapse of the World Trade Center towers. They're used in mine collapses, avalanches, the search for remains in wooded areas, and in a variety of ways. What a human might overlook a dog will find. In training, special chemicals are used to simulate the smell of rotting flesh.

These dogs don't dig up remains. They locate and then alert their handler by a prearranged signal—sometimes a bark, sometimes by just sitting at a spot where something is buried.

These dogs are used instead of search and rescue (S&R) dogs because S&Rs are used to locate *living* humans. Cadaver dogs locate decomposing flesh.

JUST THE FACTS

The Manhunt

In cases where a witness has been able to provide a physical description and a general direction in which the suspect has fled, an immediate search will be launched. In our scenario, the search extends to a wooded area across from the research center, though the grounds of the center will also be searched thoroughly in case the suspect doubled back, or if there is another possible witness or victim, or if the suspect had a confederate.

In large cities, officers may be called in from elsewhere in the precinct or from adjoining precincts. In the suburbs and more rural areas, officers from neighboring towns will likely join in, and the state police may lend a hand. If available, local or state police helicopters may be requested, and if the wooded area is part of a state park system, then some forest rangers may be brought in or consulted. K-9 units will almost certainly be requested for a search in the woods, and police dogs can track through all sorts of conditions, even in rain or snow.

A blood-covered suspect, on foot, walking in a jerky erratic fashion will not have covered a lot of ground, and unless a vehicle has picked him up, it's very likely the manhunt will find him.

Expert Witness

The success of a manhunt depends on a variety of factors, including time of day, weather conditions, manpower, and available resources; and this will vary greatly from department to department.

San Antonio Detective Joe McKinney offers this insight into a rural manhunt: "If it's a small town, there simply won't be that much manpower available to conduct a full-blown search. A town of, say, ten thousand people, may have, at most, a police department of 90 or so officers . . . and that's officers of *every* rank, not just street officers. If you consider that a department of that size may have 15 or so officers on the street at any given time, you get an idea of the kind of resources they would be able to deploy. Another thing that would limit the scope of the manhunt is that the suspect in this case is probably known. If he broke out of a hospital (or was a test subject at a research center), chances are they have his name and date of birth and other information on file already. Every police department is going to initiate a manhunt, given the violent crime committed; however, the sense of urgency is minimized if the suspect is known beforehand. The reason is because it is much easier to file an at-large arrest warrant for the individual and transmit his information to police agencies across the region using NCIC (National Crime Information Center) so that the combined weight of many agencies can be brought to bear on the suspect."

Joseph Sciscio, a detective with the Bensalem Township Police Department in Pennsylvania, adds: "Considering this is a small suburban town I would expect everyone from the chief on down to be involved along with the solicitation of other agencies including local sheriffs, surrounding jurisdictions, even fire, police and public works departments for less involved tasks of traffic control."

"If the search area is anywhere near a waterway," adds Chief

Art of the Dead – Ryan Allen

Help Is on the Way

"I think that fast zombies are a lot more scary and dangerous. But, I'm afraid that if zombies were real, they'd be slow. You have to consider that they're rotting away. Having your meat and organs decaying into fetid pulp would really put a kink in your sprinting ability."

Ken Coluzzi of Lower Makefield Police in Pennsylvania, "then the marine search units will be called in as well as helicopters. The search will be expanded when additional help arrives. Additional personnel usually begin to arrive within ten minutes or so."

McKinney says: "Let's assume that this department is bringing all available resources to bear in this case. First off, the street officers responding to the scene will call in the suspect's description and any other relevant pieces of information. A supervisor will almost certainly make the scene and will order officers in the area to set up a quadrant around the suspect's probable location. In this case, officers will set up along the boundary of the forested land. The supervisor might order officers to park along the roadway next to the forest. Those officers would remain at their posts until dismissed by the supervisor. The supervisor will order his or her communications personnel to contact neighboring jurisdictions and the suspect's information would be forwarded to them. They would be responsible for mobilizing their own response. Beyond that, the key concept here is officer safety. Unless the officers responded to the scene soon enough to see the suspect going into the forest, they would never blindly charge in after him. Witnesses may state that he is not armed, but suspects are always treated like they are. That's just sound tactics."

Small towns, however, are not as isolated as they once were and help is often just a phone call away, as Michael E. Witzgall (a former member of Marine Corps Force Reconnaissance, who served with SWAT in Dallas, Texas, and now works as a tactical training consultant) points out: "Most small towns have inter-jurisdictional agreements of cooperation with neighboring cities. A request for help in the search would be sent out and those that could help would show up; however, due to manpower constraints and vicarious liability, many of those agreements are no longer observed. The requesting agency is in charge."

"A small town would be forced to call upon multiple outside resources," agrees McKinney. "They may call upon the County Sheriff's Office, who would be able to provide additional personnel, and possibly even a helicopter. If a helicopter were available, then that would become the primary search tool. It would search the area with heat-sensitive cameras, etc.[11] Another resource would be the state police. Troopers are generally in short supply, though. They respond to any agency requesting assistance, but it may take them several hours, at the earliest, to get any sort of presence in the area. If the search continues beyond a few hours, the state police would definitely have helicopters, dog teams, and professional trackers available. Still another resource would be the game warden and the Forestry Service. In most states, both of these entities have police powers, and they are highly qualified to search wilderness areas. The trouble is, there are very few game wardens in any one region, and so you may only get one or two officers to

11. If zombies are dead or, as some of our medical experts theorize, working on a reduced metabolism, their body temperature may be so low that thermal scans may either miss them or get confused readings.

respond. However, the best resource for a small town (like the one in our medical research center scenario) would probably be a nearby large city, and a large city would have all the resources the state police have, and probably even more. Also, a nearby large city police department could deploy their personnel within thirty or forty minutes of being called. They would certainly have a helicopter unit, and also multiple dog teams. If the forested area goes into the large city's jurisdiction, they would also have personnel specifically trained in how to operate in that environment."

According to Chief Coluzzi, "Civilians may be used in situations where there is clearly insufficient police staffing. Many towns have CERT[12] Teams (Citizen Emergency Response)."

I asked my experts to explain how the search itself unfolds.

"The first step is to get people in the area," advises McKinney. "You have to have people assigned to the crime scene itself, and others to interview witnesses. What you have left over, you assign to the quadrant. Once the quadrant is established, it basically turns into a waiting game for most of the officers involved. If a helicopter is available, they do the majority of the search. If dogs[13] were to be used, all other personnel would back out of the affected area. Believe me, you don't want to meet up with a search dog off its leash. Ouch!!!"

Ted Krimmel, a sergeant with the South Central Bucks County Emergency Response Team (SERT) adds, "A biting incident could be classified as an aggravated (felony) assault. It being a felony, more resources could be brought in for the search."

Witzgall lays out the steps used to manage a pursuit: "First you establish a chain of command and a command post location; and then inventory all available materials and assets. You break down all manpower resources into teams and appoint team leaders for each team . . . and you make sure all teams have radio or cell phone communications."

McKinney adds, "Now, in this zombie situation, if the manhunt gets huge, and county and state police agencies get involved, the largest jurisdictional entity would usually assume ultimate con-

12. Not to be confused with SERT, which is a regional version of SWAT.
13. For more on K-9 cops, see Chapter 5.

trol. For example, between county and state agencies, the state would be the larger entity."

"Most searches of this manner are based on terrain denial," Witzgall says, "Meaning that while you have people (and dogs) in pursuit you also want to get officers in front of the suspect to cut off his advance. If the on-scene commander knows his stuff, he will break the area down into grid squares (or use a military 1:25000 topographical map) to cover the search area. Each team (or several teams) would be assigned a grid square to search. All roads (improved or gravel) would be monitored. Once the suspect is sighted several things can happen. Teams may be jumped ahead of the suspect. Dogs and mounted units may be redirected toward the suspect. Trailing teams will be told to speed up and, if possible, surround the suspect. And aviation assets will circle the suspect to maintain visual contact."

Sgt Krimmel describes how the actual takedown would be handled: "If the subject were spotted, he would first be given verbal commands, typically first 'Police! Don't move!' followed by commands to either kneel or lie on the ground. The officers would also notify the command post or dispatcher of their location (if they know) and situation. If the subject obeys commands, he would be approached by a contact officer and handcuffed in what cops call 'an arrest without incident.' Failure to comply would be met usually with OC spray or K-9 application (both are usually very effective). In Pennsylvania officers are required to use the minimum level of force necessary to effect an arrest. Failure of the OC or K-9 might result in TASER use or baton strikes to effect the arrest. If the subject were to attack the officers or K-9s, obviously the officers would defend themselves and the dogs bite, of course. Once again, you might see combinations of OC, K-9, Taser, and baton strikes. Officers work within a concept called the 'use-of-force continuum.'[14] In a nutshell, the practice is to always approach a suspect with the next level of force up from what they are using. If a suspect comes at you with a knife, you use your gun. If the suspect comes at you barehanded, you use one of the established intermediate, or less than lethal, force options."

14. For more on the force continuum, see Chapter 5.

But less than lethal force is not the only option, as Chief Coluzzi explains. "Officers can use TASERs, batons, pepper spray, beanbag rounds, hand gun 40-caliber automatic or AR15 commando rifle." However he adds a serious note of caution. "If officers spray the subject with tear gas that has an alcohol base and then they use the TASER they could light the subject on fire. Officers are taught not to use TASERs in these situations."

Also known as a "flexible baton round," the beanbag round is actually a small cloth sack filled with #9 lead shot. Though intended as non lethal, there has been an average of about one death per year from these rounds. I asked him to discuss their use. "In Lower Bucks County South, patrols carry shotguns loaded with less lethal rounds. These may also come into play in a situation like this. I can tell you from seeing these rounds used operationally, they will break bones and definitely slow somebody down. The less lethal rounds are usually deployed at areas with lots of fatty tissue (thighs, buttocks, upper arms) to cause maximum pain, with minimal injury. If used at close range, they will break bones and occasionally penetrate skin."

And if the beanbags didn't work? McKinney says, "Cops are usually pretty inventive. If they were to run into a subject who was attacking them and their dogs and usual police defense techniques weren't working, they would try something different. Many police use of force policies cover 'weapons of last resort.' If the weapons and techniques being used were not getting the job done, the officers are encouraged to 'improvise, adapt, and overcome.' In the situation based on your zombie scenario, the subject (zombie) hasn't used a deadly weapon, nor displayed one. The subject has done nothing that would authorize deadly force that the officers know of. A tactical retreat may be in order. Calling for more officers to assist, while maintaining visual contact with the subject (from a distance) may be another. Unfortunately, in my experience as a cop, once the fight starts, it doesn't stop, until it's resolved. There won't be a chance to back off in a tactical retreat, let alone fight until additional officers arrive. In my experience, especially during my days in uniform, the people in the fight initially are usually the people at the end of it. A lucky cop will have backup with him before the fight starts. Usually, they are over quickly. As an aside,

I have had people try to bite me as I was arresting them more than once. I was able to dodge the bite every time. A zombie biting or attempting to bite cops might not register with them as uncommon, at least not at first."

Detective McKinney adds, "Officers are not forced to remain within this continuum if the circumstances don't allow it, or it isn't practical. A 90 pound female patrol officer forced to arrest a violent WWF wrestler or NFL linebacker is justified, for example, in going straight to the gun to effect an arrest. No one would reasonably expect her to try to subdue such an individual with her baton. So . . . when dealing with a dead body, intermediate force options probably won't work. In that case, the gun is going to come out sooner or later."

The Zombie Factor

When closing in on the zombie, the officers are not likely to put themselves at any risk, even if the suspect is believed to be unarmed or out of his mind. As Witzgall sees it, "Because this person may be mentally ill—at least in the officers' minds—they may treat this as a dangerous situation; but differently than a murder suspect. Therefore dog handlers would not turn the dogs loose on the suspect (they would always be on the leash). More than likely, officers would make contact from a distance to avoid further agitating the suspect. They might even bring in a negotiator, though in this scenario that won't be effective," he admits. "More than likely transport after arrest—because the police believe him to be mentally ill—would be done by ambulance to a county hospital. If the suspect tries to bite, we generally put something over his head."

Sgt. Krimmel adds, "I have seen hoods and shields placed over biter/spitters' heads to avoid injury. Most cops feel that spitting on them puts them at increased risk of contracting disease and possibly taking it home to their families. As far as transport is concerned, most police vehicles have Plexiglas shields between the front and back seats to avoid physical contact or spitting from the arrestee."

So the idea of an infected zombie biting cops and hospital workers is a bit less likely.

The danger in our scenario would come from a secondary

source: the victim. The guard was bitten and transported to the hospital. It's doubtful the guard would die en route unless he had arterial damage—and the 911 operator coached our witness through first aid. More likely the guard would die after being admitted to the hospital; and Romero establishes that this takes quite a few hours, since the little girl in *Night* was bitten hours before Barbara and Ben get to the house and doesn't die and reanimate until either very late at night or, as is suggested, close to dawn. The real threat would come with how hospital protocols are handled, and we'll explore that in Chapter 3.

So, getting back to our patient zero, finding him in the woods was not particularly difficult. There is so much technology, so much skill, and such well-practiced procedure that finding the suspect was a good bet, and apprehending him is not likely to be difficult. We'll see why in Chapter 5 as we examine the techniques, technologies, and tactics modern police can use to arrest, detain or—at need—destroy zombies.

The Final Verdict: Scene of the Crime

In just about any scenario where infection starts from a single source, there is a solid chance that the cops will keep this thing from going haywire. If we're talking slow, shuffling Romero zombies caused by a plague, then the disease will spread with relative slowness and it will be noticed, witnessed, investigated, and dealt with appropriately.

Once the victim and the suspect were both at the hospital, the fact that this is a plague would begin to emerge. Especially if the bite victim dies and then wakes up and starts attacking people. That kind of thing is going to get noticed very, very fast. It would ring every alarm bell built into the local, state, and federal infrastructure, and in twenty-first-century America, with what has become our natural tendency to weigh sudden violence against the yardstick of potential terrorism, there would be a strong and immediate response.

If the disease involved fast zombies (or fast-infected humans) then there would be a much higher mortality rate and, very likely, a lag time in situation recognition and response—but the world

Dan O'Bannon: Prankster of the Living Dead

You have to give the devil his due. If George Romero is the King of Zombieland, then Dan O'Bannon is somewhere between the royal scribe and the court jester. He's a writer, director, and computer animator (he worked on the original *Star Wars*), and he's been a major creative force in some of the most important and influential horror and/or science fiction films of all times.

In 1979 he teamed up with Ronald Shusset to pen the screenplay for *Aliens*, arguably one of the great science fiction films of our time. In 1982 he stepped very quietly into the world of the living dead—not with flesh-eating ghouls, but with dead brought back to a semblance of their former lives. His script for *Dead & Buried* is widely considered to be one of the true "lost classics" of the genre. Thoughtful, character-driven, and cerebral.

Then in 1985 he turned to a more destructive side of the living dead with the script (very loosely based on a Colin Wilson story) *Lifeforce*, directed by Tobe Hooper. It's a wild mishmash of a story involving space aliens, London overrun by life-sucking zombie/vampire hybrids, and plot holes you could drive a star freighter through—but aside from all that, the film is totally watchable.

Then in 1985 he struck gold with his first outing as director of the now legendary *Return of the Living Dead*. Hilarious, irreverent, violent, and over the top. More importantly it introduced the first *fast zombies*, and the most notable post-Romero *talking* zombies.

Whether he takes another shot at the zombie world, O'Bannon's place is assured.

isn't going to crumble. At some point, even if we lose a city, the disaster response protocols hardwired into our police and military is going to kick in and the response will be severe, it will be overwhelming. Cities may be sacrificed to stop the spread of infection. In the 2007 film *I Am Legend*, bridges were blown up to prevent the spread of disease: That would happen.

Worst case scenario would be that the infection spread until a kind of "firebreak" could be established, which would probably be a river or a mountain range, at which point the forward press of infection would be slowed by terrain that could be defended. It's the same basic premise as digging a moat around a castle. Maybe that moat would be the Mississippi or the Delaware or the Colorado River . . . but it would be a matter of "this far and no farther," and then the counterattack would begin.

But that is worst-case scenario, and it depends on too many things occurring that are just not likely. It requires a disease that instantly spreads throughout the entire bloodstream, and continues to spread even in a murder victim in whom, presumably, blood has ceased to flow. It requires a disease of such virulence that conscious thought is instantly eradicated, which is unlikely in diseases where the body is not materially destroyed (say with a neurotoxin).

With the spread of a plague that follows some of the rules of infectious diseases, there would be a slower rate of spread than is shown in most genre films. Much slower. The police—who are seldom seen in these stories, and seldom shown to be intelligent, resourceful, or effective—would become involved; since they are intelligent, resourceful, and effective, the death rate of a zombie plague is very likely to be small. Larger if the plague happens in a densely populated urban area, much lower if in a rural area.

Bottom line: If you see a zombie, call a cop.

The Crime Scene Unit

Collecting the Evidence After a Zombie Attack

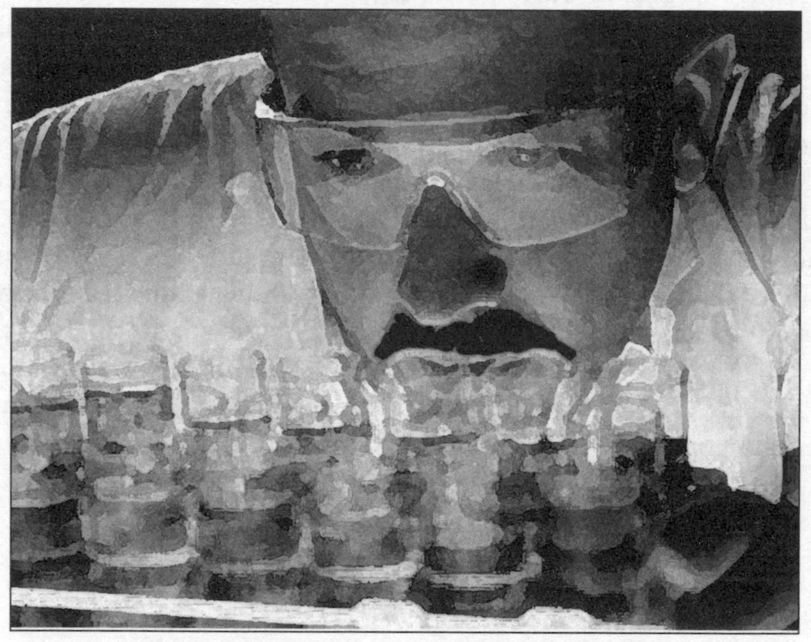

Laboratory Analysis **by Jonathan Maberry**

"The identification, preservation, collection and analysis of crime scene evidence is an absolutely crucial step in the investigation and prosecution of major crimes."

While the manhunt starts, the victim is transported and the witness is interviewed and the crucial phase of evidence collection begins. *Forensics* means "belonging to the forum" and refers to the gathering of information that will have a legal bearing. Generally speaking many forensics fields use the phrase *medico-legal evidence*, as not all evidence will turn out to have a legal use.

This process involves identifying potential evidence, gathering it in ways that protect its integrity (for both testing and legal purposes), documenting each item (including a description of it and the exact location where it was found), transporting the evidence to the lab, tracking the movement of evidence through a paper trail called a "chain of evidence," and properly storing each piece of evidence so that it is protected and preserved. A break in any of these steps could lead to evidence being destroyed, contaminated, or legally useless.

Evidence collection is often a shared responsibility between the crime scene unit, patrol officers, and detectives. In high-crime areas where the CSU is constantly in demand, this job may fall largely to uniformed officers, and all of them receive some degree of evidence handling training.

Greg Dagnan, former detective and assistant professor of criminal justice at Missouri Southern State University, comments on the frequency with which forensic experts are invited to a crime scene. "Not as often as they should. As a result we are trying to train officers in our part of Missouri to be mini experts. Usually a forensic specialist is only called out of desperation. At a guess, I would say a forensic specialist is called to the scene in less than a third of the cases and consulted in less that half of the cases."

Dr. Edmond Locard (1877-1966)

Locard, a criminologist and professor of forensic medicine at the University of Lyon, was often referred to as the "Sherlock Holmes of France," and justly so. He is the father of forensic science and the founder of the very first forensic laboratory, the Institution of Criminalistics, in 1910. Locard argued that "every contact leaves a trace," which has become the credo of modern forensics worldwide.

Just the Facts

Bite Marks and the Science of Forensic Odontology

Forensic odontology, the study of teeth, has been used in a variety of ways, not just in solving crimes and convicting criminals. It was used to positively identify the remains of Adolf Hitler; it helped scientists verify that victims of old mass graves found in Europe actually died of the Black Plague (through identification of the bacterium *Yersenia pestis* found in dental pulp), and it has been used to identify the remains of thousands of victims of Hurricane Katrina.

The presence of bite marks on the body will heighten the awareness of the crime's severity. Biting generally indicates extreme aggression and great anger. This further suggests that the assailant is (or at least was at the time of the attack) in a highly agitated state. Officers will be very much more on the alert.

Expert Witness

The presence of bite marks is suggestive of a savage attack. Bryan Chrz, D.D.S., diplomate ABFO and past president of the American Board of Forensic Odontology, had this to say about the force of a human bite: "Most agree that about 68–150 pounds per square inch in chewing and intentional clenching can be generated by the average adult. Some have reported up to 1200 pounds per square inch during subconscious nocturnal *bruxism* (grinding or gnashing of the teeth). The biting mechanism used during a frenzied attack or defense would most likely fall somewhat between the two values. Bite marks can come from light marking all the way to total tissue avulsion (tearing away of the flesh)."

J. Curtis Daily, chairman of the Bite Mark and Patterned Injury Committee of the American Board of Forensic Odontology adds, "Male adults bite with more force than adult females; both with more force than children." In Warren Harvey's excellent textbook[1] there is a discussion about volunteers biting human volunteer vic-

1. *Dental Identification and Forensic Odontology,* published by Klimpton, 1976.

Art of the Dead – Ken Meyer, Jr.

Island Zombie

"The original *Night of the Living Dead* is the granddaddy of all of them for me, but mainly for the poignancy of the characters, but not for the zombies. I thought the treatment in *28 Days Later* was much more exciting. Let's face it . . . the slow, lumbering zombies of the past are laughable, but have a certain charm and history to them. *28 Days Later* have helped to add a real element of horror to the whole idea."

tims. The victims were anesthetized. The 'biters,' even after goading, essentially could not generate a bite sufficient to leave a significant bruise. This speaks to the 'rage' state of mind that overcomes all reservation, ethics, morals, etc., and allows the biter to leave significant bruise patterns on their victims. We actually know almost nothing about the microscopic events that lead to the visual damage (i.e., bruising pattern). I would guess your Zombies are not burdened by 'ethics, morals, etc,' so this may allow their bites to be more savage."

Are bite patterns as useful as fingerprints? Daily says no with a degree of frustration. "I am the primary proponent in the USA that a police bitemark database should exist, but for now the ego of many forensic odontologists will prevent them from contributing former casework." He feels that this would result in the unnecessary scrutiny of their work by lesser-qualified colleagues.

The Zombie Factor

Unless the zombie is actually caught or if he is seen attacking another person in a way that pretty much says: "Oh yeah, that there's a zombie," the evidence that is collected won't create much of a sensation until it's brought back to the lab and analyzed.

This includes the bite marks. In zombie films there is a very common inconsistency relating to the zombie's physical capabilities and what is shown for dramatic effect. Consider: Romero and most of his followers clearly establish that zombies are not as physically strong as human beings. Their primary threat is in their numbers and in the infectiousness of their bites. If a zombie is less strong than a human of the same age, size, and weight, then its bite would also be necessarily weaker. Dr. Chrz observes: "The act of biting through skin and actually avulsing or tearing out a piece would require forces at the high range of the human biting force. Animals tend to do a better job due to the sharp canine and incisor teeth and meat cutting shearing edges of posterior teeth (molars)."

So, zombies aren't likely to tear out large chunks of a person as they do very easily in the movies, a point on which Daily agrees. "It is only in the rarest of bite mark cases that flesh is actually torn off. Usually this is from a weak and vulnerable piece of anatomy (e.g., a nipple). It is likely impossible to rip a chunk of muscle from the bicep area of the arm, for example."

Another factor to consider is the age and state of decomposition.

Hard Science: Take a Bite out of Crime

When serial killer Ted Bundy went to trial in 1979, it was the distinctive bite marks on a victim's buttocks, which matched Bundy's teeth, that put Bundy in the electric chair. There are 23 known victims of this madman, but it is believed that he murdered more than 35 people between 1974 and 1978.

A "fresh" zombie will be physically stronger in both limb and bite capability; but the more they decay, the weaker they'll get. Dr. Chrz agrees: "Teeth are not fused to bone but rather are attached to the bone by a ligament system. As decomposition occurs this ligament breaks down and releases the teeth. Morphology of the tooth root will sometimes cause them to be retained in skeletal remains, but the cone shaped roots of the incisors tend to make them more prone to postmortem loss."

Again Daily concurs, "Teeth become rapidly loose with decomposition. The periodontal ligament that holds the tooth to the bone socket decomposes just like the rest of the body."

But to the observer at this stage of the game, a bite is a bite. So, to this point the police still don't know what they're up against and are following their time-honored procedures. Or is there still a clue left to find?

Daily says, "If the Zombie infection is based by a bite, wouldn't that organism (whatever it is) be detected? There are studies—from the dental school in New Zealand I believe—that show/prove the 'bacterial burden' (i.e., the collection of bacteria in a biter's mouth) can be identified from saliva deposited in the bite. However, logic tells me decomposing bodies that bite would leave a universe of organisms. You need your zombie bacteria to be a *super bacteria* that feeds on the other bacteria on/in the human host. That way, you could avoid this issue."

Or, perhaps something else is involved, such as . . . *prions.*

If that word doesn't give you chills yet . . . wait until you read Chapter 3.

Gregg Winkler's[2] Decaying Zombie Quiz, Part 1

- **The zombies in the *Resident Evil* series of video games continue to mutate due to the presence of the T-Virus in their system. If a zombie is not decapitated or incinerated, what is the name of the creature it mutates into?**
- **What is the name of the short story in which a cannibalistic mortuary worker and a congregation of undead geeks engage in a bloody holy war?**
- **What is the name of a creature in Norse mythology that comes back from the dead, smells of decay, devours the living, and has an unusual resistance to conventional weapons?**
- **What is responsible for the zombification of the world in Stephen King's "Home Delivery"?**
- **Which 2003 novel is largely credited with kick-starting the new wave of zombie fiction?**

(See the Appendix for answers.)

Just the Facts

Crime Scene Photography

Before evidence is removed, the entire scene needs to be completely documented. Even though a detailed and measured sketch is made of the crime scene, nothing is as telling as a complete set of high-resolution photographs.

Crime scene photographers come in all shapes and sizes, from freelancers hired by departments on a per-case basis, to contracted civilian photographers, to police officers, to photographic experts working in law enforcement. Many police departments still use film cameras, and there's some good arguments in favor of this since digital photos can more easily be manipulated than can film negatives. Retouching via computer software (Photoshop, etc.) is

2. Gregg Winkler writes for www.horror-web.com.

Art of the Dead – Ryan Allan

Rot and Ruin

Photo evidence of the living dead would be crucial in establishing that zombies exist—especially in the absence of *living* witnesses.

easy; retouching a photographic negative or print is much harder and easier to detect, especially if the negatives can be produced for court purposes. However digital is making inroads, and often both are used. Digital cameras used in crime scene documentation tend to be higher-end, with large files in excess of five megapixels (often considerably larger) so that the images can be viewed in minute detail without actually intruding into the secured physical scene.

Flash photography is often used to eliminate shadows that might hide crucial details; though many photographers prefer to take flash and nonflash photos for later comparison. Just as a flash can reveal something in a shadow, it can also wash out details already clearly lit in bright sunlight or under bright artificial light.

Photographers take photos of the scene of the crime and then document the surrounding area, including roads, doorways, vehicles in nearby parking lots, nearby woods, and so on. The rule of thumb being that it's better to have too much documentation than

Zombies . . . Fast or Slow? Part 2

- **"I grew up with the traditional voodoo zombie in the horror comics and movies I loved, so in my mind zombies are magical creatures. There are too many problems to overcome when telling stories about science-based zombies—how do they move with rotting muscles, where do they get the energy to move if they can't eat and digest food? They're closed systems, and they should cease functioning in a short time, a few days at the most. You don't have those sorts of problems with magical zombies. Plus, magic comes from the shadowy realm of the unknown, where science belongs to the world of cold hard facts. Magic—the dark kind found in supernatural horror—has a greater potential to be scary in fiction."—Tim Waggoner, author of *Darkness Wakes* and *Like Death*.**
- **"If I have to outrun them, then I like my zombie's slow. But that scene in *28 Weeks Later* when Bob Carlisle is being chased from the farmhouse by the Zombie International Olympic Sprint Team is at once scary and cool. As long as fast**

not enough. When possible photographers will take overview photos, either from atop a platform (car roof, leaning out of a window, etc.). Photos are taken from multiple angles as changes in perspective can bring otherwise unnoticed items to light.

Photos are taken of the victim, ideally before transportation to the hospital. Photos of the wounds prior to their being treated and dressed are very useful in court; and sometimes follow-up pictures are taken during surgery and, if the situation turns even nastier, during an autopsy. Photo evidence of all marks such as bruises, bumps, lacerations, bullet wounds[3], and in our case bite marks, help detectives form a clearer picture of what happened during the altercation. Some criminals have known patterns of attack, and

3. Generally the most serious wounds are photographed at the hospital since emergency medical treatment at the scene of the crime naturally prohibits the taking of such pictures.

zombies chase someone else, I'm all for them."—Weston Ochse, winner of the Bram Stoker Award for Best First Novel, *Scarecrow Gods*.

- **"Well . . . that depends on if they've eaten."—Steve Alten, author of *The Lock*.**
- **"Slow is better. I don't mind fast, really . . . as long as they're not superhumanly strong . . . which I think really defeats the purpose."—Robert Kirkman, author of *Marvel Zombies* and *The Walking Dead*.**
- **"Slow . . . then you can get away even if you are not a good runner or are ambushed!"—Patricia Tallman, actress and star of *Night of the Living Dead* (1990) and *Dead Air*.**
- **"In my book, *Deadlands,* I put forth the thought that it depends on the age and rate of decay of the zombie. A new, fresh zombie would be able to move much faster than one that was being held together by rotting tissue and strings of flesh. As they begin to rot, their speed decreases. As their brains turn further and further into mush, they lose all but the basest of animal instincts."—Scott A. Johnson, author of *Deadlands*.**

this can be used as another piece of evidence to either help build a profile or match the attack to a known modus operandi.

Many crime scenes are videotaped these days as well, and guard stations and entranceways of warehouses and facilities are often fitted with digital recorders. The age of videotape is fading. A photographic evidence expert can easily remove the disk or drive from the recorder and download it, or sometimes use cables to download directly from the recorder to a police laptop.

Expert Witness

According to Daily, "photographing bite marks with the digital camera and the ability to have what amounts to a darkroom in your computer have allowed us to view images in different ways in real time. The patterns typically continue to change for up to a few days. That is why we suggest our Forensic Photographers take serial photographs (i.e., new pictures each day until the marks stop changing). Think of the body as the crime scene with new evidence appearing each day. Decomp often short circuits the process described."

According to best-selling author and forensic expert Andrea Campbell,[4] view differs somewhat: "Photography is hand-in-glove with forensic art, all aspects of it. For example, you cannot haul a completed clay bust around from location to location so you take photographs of the recreation and those are put into the newspaper (or at the post office) when seeking identification. Photography is also what 2-dimensional or superimposition is all about. Imposing a graphic against a real skull and matching: proportions, features, dimensions."

The Zombie Factor

Though still photography of the crime scene will not, at this stage of the game, do much in our zombie hunt, the files from the research center's digital surveillance camera will. Once the management of the research center is notified and permissions secured, the digital files can be downloaded onto laptops so the detectives can examine them to see if any of the crime was taped.

That's where the first big break comes in. Though the slow pan of the camera, which is mounted on a pole over the guard shack, does not record anyone entering through the gates, the audio track does capture the sound of the guard noticing someone already inside the compound. We hear the guard call out for the intruder to identify himself. The only reply we hear is a low moan and then the sounds of the guard shouting and a scuffle. There is the sound of three gunshots and then more moaning—this time of a different pitch, which is determined by the detectives to be the injured guard moaning in pain.

The real payoff comes when the suspected attacker comes lumbering into frame as he staggers out through the gates and crosses the road. Footage of that kind would later help with identifying

4. Andrea Campbell is the author of *Detective Notebook: Crime Scene Science* (Sterling, 2004) and *Forensic Science: Evidence, Clues, and Investigation* (Chelsea House Publications, 1999).

Art of the Dead – Steve Hester

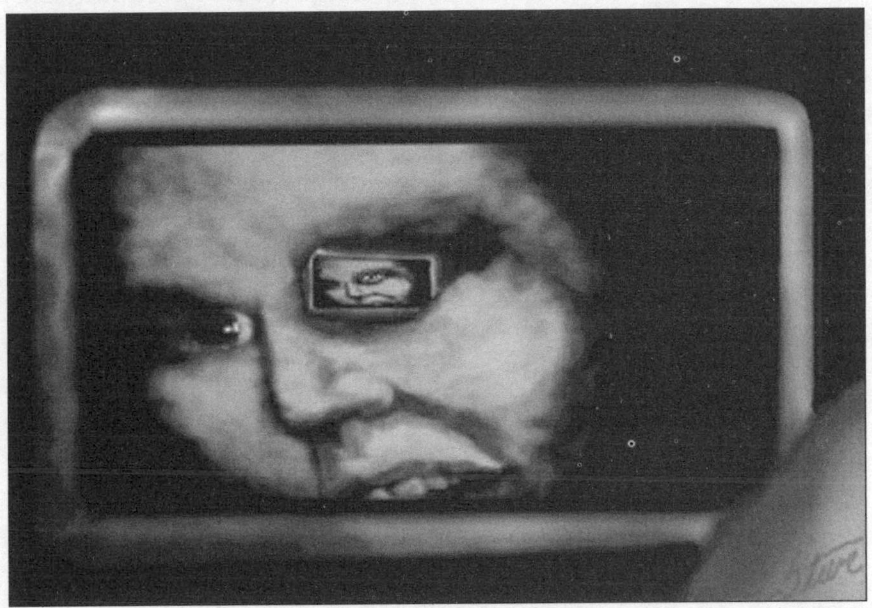

Death in Focus

"Artists see the world a little differently . . . some of them have the courage to look at the darker things—pain, madness, death . . . capturing the essence of each on canvas or in print, illuminating the mysteries for all the world to ponder."

the suspect and backtracking him to his connection with the research facility.

Just the Facts

Forensic Podiatry and Footwear Evidence

Forensic podiatry is the science of applying clinical podiatric knowledge to the task of identifying evidence associated with crime. Forensic podiatry was developed in the early 1970s, mostly in the United Kingdom and Canada, before filtering down to the

United States. Because of the vast number of shoe manufacturers—from hand-sewn Italian loafers to cheap Dollar Store flip-flops—it is virtually impossible to maintain a complete and accurate database of all styles and brands. Therefore the experts in footwear evidence are more concerned with matching specific impressions or castings taken at a crime scene with shoes found in the possession of a suspect.

Forensic podiatry also extends to include identifying walking patterns, or "gait forms." These patterns are determined from analysis of the shoe impressions and also from video evidence. The science also examines the foot impressions inside the shoe and matches it against the foot of a suspect to make an I.D.

Expert Witness

According to Dwane S. Hilderbrand,[5] CLPE, CFWE, CSCSA, "Footwear evidence and forensic podiatry are two completely different and separate disciplines. Footwear deals with the shoe, the outsole and podiatry deals with the human foot. Footwear deals with the impression left by a shoe in examining and comparing a shoe to determine if that shoe made the impression. Podiatry deals with bare feet."

I asked Dr. Hildebrand that, considering all of the shoe manufacturers out there, from top-of-the-line footwear to cheap sneakers, how can an expert determine which brand of shoe left the mark? Or is it just a matter of matching patterns found at the scene with shoes in the possession of a suspect?

"There are a few methods," he says. "There are computerized databases[6] on the market where a footwear impression from a crime scene can be searched through to determine its brand or model. There are some examiners that have trained themselves to recognize various logo and or trademarks to determine the brand name."

Do footwear specialists typically visit crime scenes? Dr. Hildebrand says no. "Normally a footwear expert will not go to a crime

5. www.ronsmithandassociates.com.

6. Such as SICAR, a standalone system that works in conjunction with Solemate, a database of over 8,000 shoes from 300 manufacturers.

scene. Crime scene investigators are trained to properly document, collect and preserve footwear evidence in all forms. The footwear specalist performs the examination and comparison between the crime scene print and the suspect's shoes."

He does point out, however, that, "there are many examiners trained in gait patterns recognition," who might be called to a crime scene and could possibly provide assistance with our zombie case. This, however, is unlikely to happen in the first few hours of a case.

According to technology sales representative Daniel Conklin, there is also highly specialized hardware and software systems for analyzing the collected evidence. "Many departments—at least the bigger labs and some of the private labs—have something like the Raman spectrometer, which can provide valuable 'fingerprints' for comparing and differentiating footwear materials.[7] Raman spectroscopy using the Foram685-2, is fast, non-destructive, can be performed on materials in situ and requires minimal operator training—an ideal technique for the examination of forensic evidence."

The Zombie Factor

Matching footwear impressions to a zombie who is later captured or killed is not hugely important. Determining the identity of the zombie, especially of patient zero, is.

If the manhunt lasts more than a day, an expert in walking patterns may be called in. A zombie walks with a distinctive shuffling gait. That will leave equally distinctive footprints on the ground. Zombies are also indifferent to hiding their tracks, which means that they'll walk over (rather than around) anything in their path, including mud, puddles, dust, and other surfaces that will take a useful impression. In the absence of K-9 trackers, the foot impression expert can often assist the police in identifying the attacker's gait and provide useful details for officers to track that person.

7. Information provided by Foster & Freeman—www.fosterfreeman.com.

Tracking the Undead Predator

Though K-9 trackers wouldn't need to rely on footprint evidence, human trackers would. The tread patterns of shoes or the shape of bare feet are distinctive enough to the trained eye.

The skill of tracking is not something a person can usefully learn from a book. It requires a good coach as well as good senses, acute observation, concentration, patience, perseverance, alertness, physical fitness, a good memory, an analytical mind, an understanding of nature, intuition, and a creative imagination.

Just the Facts

Dactylosocopy—The Science of Fingerprinting

Fingerprinting is one of the oldest reliable methods of identification. Fingerprints have been used for thousands of years as a method of identification. The ancient Chinese used prints as signatures as early as the thirteenth century. In 1685 anatomist Marcello Malpighi of the University of Bologne identified the patterns found in fingerprints, describing them as loops, whorls, and ridges—terms still used today. In 1858 a British civil servant, Sir William Herschel, began requiring residents of Bengal, India, to use handprints for identification; and many years later discovered that the patterns of palm and fingerprints did not change as people aged. In 1880, Henry Faulds, a physician practicing in Tokyo, determined that fingerprints were unique enough to be used as positive identification of individuals. It was a fairly short step from that to the 1892 publication of Sir Francis Galton's book *Finger Prints*, which became a landmark textbook on the subject, and in which Galton reinforced Malpighi's use of whorls and grooves as unique identifiers. Nine years later Sir Edward Henry created a classification system based on five distinct types of prints—a system that informed the fingerprinting identification methods still used in Great Britain and the United States.

Perhaps the most significant landmark, though, was the 1910 trial of Thomas Jennings who became the first person in the

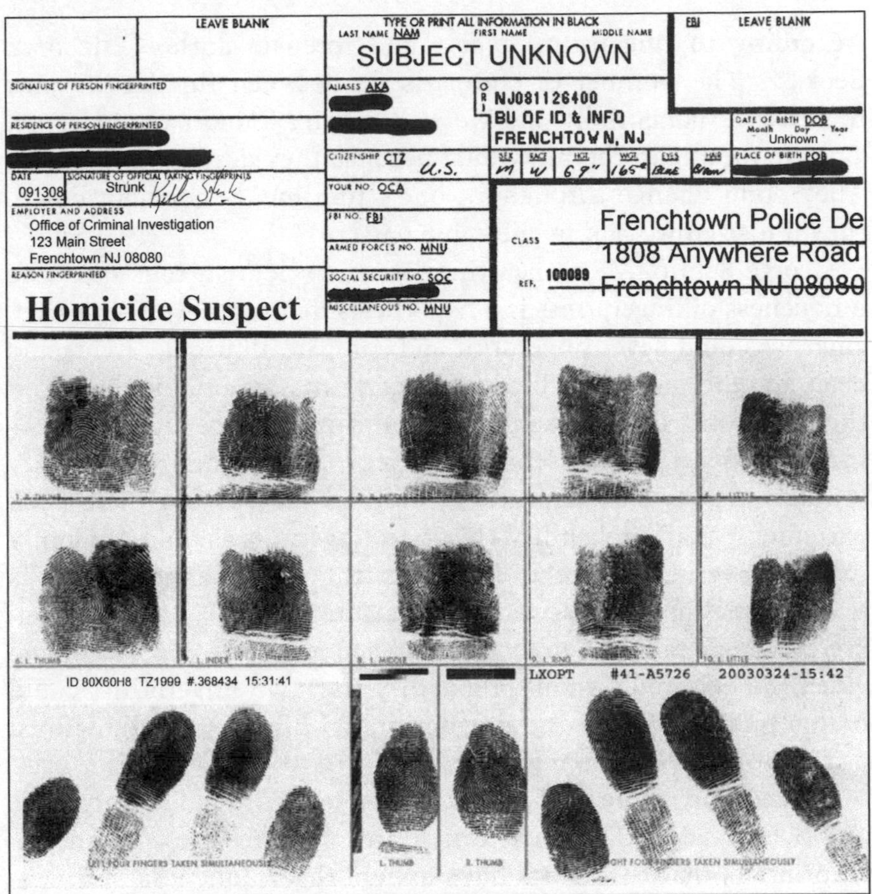
LEAVE BLANK

TYPE OR PRINT ALL INFORMATION IN BLACK

LAST NAME NAM FIRST NAME MIDDLE NAME

SUBJECT UNKNOWN

FBI LEAVE BLANK

SIGNATURE OF PERSON FINGERPRINTED

ALIASES AKA

ORI NJ081126400
BU OF ID & INFO
FRENCHTOWN, NJ

RESIDENCE OF PERSON FINGERPRINTED

DATE OF BIRTH DOB Month Day Year
Unknown

CITIZENSHIP CTZ U.S.

SEX	RACE	HGT	WGT	EYES	HAIR
M	W	6 9"	165	Blk	Brn

PLACE OF BIRTH POB

DATE 091308 SIGNATURE OF OFFICIAL TAKING FINGERPRINTS Strunk

YOUR NO. OCA

EMPLOYER AND ADDRESS
Office of Criminal Investigation
123 Main Street
Frenchtown NJ 08080

FBI NO. FBI

CLASS

Frenchtown Police De
1808 Anywhere Road
Frenchtown NJ 08080

ARMED FORCES NO. MNU

REF. 100089

REASON FINGERPRINTED

SOCIAL SECURITY NO. SOC

Homicide Suspect

MISCELLANEOUS NO. MNU

ID 80X60H8 TZ1999 #.368434 15:31:41

LXOPT #41-A5726 20030324-15:42

LEFT FOUR FINGERS TAKEN SIMULTANEOUSLY

L. THUMB

R. THUMB

RIGHT FOUR FINGERS TAKEN SIMULTANEOUSLY

Fingerprint Card **by Jonathan Maberry**

"Even zombies were human once. There's a very good chance of identifying the zombie through fingerprints, which could aid police in tracking the plague back to its start."

United States to be convicted of a crime based on fingerprint evidence. Even when appealed, the guilty verdict was upheld based on the overwhelming evidence that fingerprints are unique.

Expert Witness

According to fingerprint expert and forensic author Elizabeth Becka,[8] "The number of comparisons between fingerprints has increased exponentially and we *still* haven't found two the same. They're unique to the individual because they develop at random. They don't change throughout one's lifetime. Sand them down, they'll just grow back in the same pattern."

George Schiro, MS, consulting forensic scientist, tells us, "The uniqueness of fingerprints is a hypothesis that can never be proven, since we could never fingerprint and compare all people, living and dead, to determine if individual fingerprints are unique. Based on the embryonic development of fingerprints and the studies showing that identical twins have different fingerprints, it is highly unlikely that two fingerprints would be identical, but there is an extremely small probability that two fingerprints could randomly match. Given the context of a crime, the next question to ask is how many people had access to the crime scene. Based on the relatively small number of people that had access to the scene, and given the extremely small probability that two fingerprints could match randomly, then the fingerprints within that small, defined population would be unique."

I asked why there was so much fuss built around fingerprints, and Schiro said, "The most important thing to know about fingerprints is that the courts have upheld the uniqueness of fingerprints. Fingerprinting is also the least expensive and best means of human identification. Information from a fingerprint can be quantified and digitized, prints can be placed in a database and searched. And the most important things to know about fingerprint evidence collection are that print collection at a crime scene should be a top priority, and the surface on which friction ridge prints have been deposited should be tested with a known print, prior to attempting to lift the evidentiary print. Prints might have to be photographed prior to a lift attempt. The crime scene investigator should also know how to develop latent (invisible) prints using a variety of techniques from a variety of surfaces. All rele-

8. Elizabeth Becka is the author of *Trace Evidence*, Hyperion, 2005.

vant areas should be examined for latent and patent (visible) prints. Finally, other evidence at the crime scene must not be ignored."

He warns us, however, "Whether or not a surface takes a print depends on numerous factors, including the type of surface. Just because a person touches a surface, it doesn't necessarily mean that an identifiable print can be recovered from that surface. Typically, rough or textured surfaces can take a print, but an identifiable print may or may not be recovered from that surface. Other factors can determine whether or not an identifiable print is left on a surface. These factors include, but are not limited to, the following: the physiology of the individual, the activity of the individual prior to touching the surface, the humidity, the temperature, the absorbance of the surface, the pressure used in touching the surface, movement of the finger while touching the surface, whether or not there is an intervening material between the surface and the finger, and the cleanliness of the fingers."

Becka agrees. "Whether or not you find a fingerprint on an item depends on the amount of oil and water on the person's hands, the item's surface, the climate, and about a million other things. Contrary to TV, you don't *always* find prints on this or that and you don't *ever* find prints on this or that."

Even so, science marches on and there have been several significant advances in fingerprinting over the last few decades. According to Becka, "The biggest advance is, of course, computerized database searching. I can mark the points of minutia in a latent print collected at the scene and the computer finds possible matches for me. This means I don't have to search card files for matching prints and die of tedium. Note that the computer does not decide *if* someone is a match or not, it only summons the prints with the most similar pattern of points."

One point of clarification: *fingerprint* is used somewhat loosely here—as it is in all pop culture. According to Martin Leadbetter, FFS RFP BA (Hons), international fingerprint expert and chairman of The Fingerprint Society, " 'Fingerprint' is usually used to describe inked impressions taken for a specific use, e.g., recording prisoners' fingerprints, elimination fingerprints, cadavers etc. The terms, *latent*, *latent mark* (or *mark*, as used in the UK) always refers to impressions found at crime scenes or on forensic exhibits." He goes on to explain the different kinds of prints:

- Rolled ten-print impression (U.S. and international terminology) sometimes referred to as inked impressions or inked fingerprints in the United Kingdom: This is an impression whereby ink has been placed onto the ridged skin of the fingertip and then subsequently rolled onto a ten-print card or form in order to record an exact image of the finger's pattern and ridge detail. Upon the arrest of a suspected person, this procedure is repeated for each of the ten digits in order to produce a ten-print card.
- Slap prints (or in the United Kingdom, plain impressions): Slap prints are also recorded on the ten-print card and are used to check that each of the rolled ten-prints has been taken in the correct order. The four fingers of each hand are inked by being placed flat on an inked surface and then placed simultaneously onto the ten-print card. The two thumbs are dealt with in the same manner. (As a general rule, the term *slap prints* is not used in the United Kingdom.)
- Palm prints: These are inked impressions recorded the same as ten-prints.
- Latent palm marks, palm marks: These are palm marks recovered from crime scenes or forensic exhibits.

As technology increases, the reliability of fingerprints also increases. "The data sharing between computer databases holding vast collections of fingerprints has only increased the realization that fingerprints remain totally unique," he says. "With the rapid searching of fingerprint databases no instance of two impressions taken from different fingers, thumbs or palms have been recorded. All claims within academia and the media that fingerprints are unreliable or unsafe are purely unsubstantiated and in some instances, mischievous. It should also be remembered that when referring to fingerprints the same criteria also belong to palms, toes and soles. Furthermore, all 187 species of primate possess fingerprints and share the same pattern types with humans. All instances where it has been reported that 'two people have the same fingerprints' or an error in identification has occurred are the result of poor forensic work or worse, conspiracy to pervert the course of justice."

According to Leadbetter, different people need to know different things about fingerprints. "If you are a juror, then you need total confidence in the fingerprint system of identification, its uniqueness and the integrity of the fingerprint experts. If you are a detective you will know that fingerprint evidence, provided it leads to useful evidence, is the very best evidence you can ever hope for. The overriding issue here, is that fingerprint evidence, due to its unrivalled uniqueness is still the most conclusive and infallible of all the forensic sciences."

This need for unique perspective holds true for the process of fingerprint collection. "Jurors would need to have confidence in the scene examiner, as indeed would all the officers of the court," says Leadbetter. "For the scene examiner it's a matter of knowing where logically to look and to find those fingerprints which will later assist in proving guilt."

Leadbetter tells of another recent development that is helping police in the United Kingdom and America: "There is also *Live-scan*. This is a process whereby arrestee's finger and palm prints are recorded electronically without the need for ink and paper. Once recorded, Live-scanned prints may be sent electronically to the computer system. As *Live-scan* devices have built-in 'aliveness' sensors it would be intriguing to know whether prints could actually be captured from zombies." And, he adds, "It is also possible to retrieve DNA from latent prints, although again this would not be possible from all latents due to the factors previously mentioned."

Forensic consulting scientist George Schiro tells of another new technology on the rise: touch evidence. "DNA recovered from touched evidence has a great impact on the development and collection techniques associated with latent prints. In the past, if a smudged print was developed, then that smudge had no value. Today if a smudge is developed, this smudge could be swabbed using a sterile cotton swab and a solvent, usually sterile water, deionized water, or an ethanol solution. This swab can then be air dried and eventually analyzed for a DNA profile. Also, surfaces such as rough or textured surfaces, typically not as good for recovering identifiable prints are better suited for recovering identifiable DNA profiles. Of course, in collecting this DNA evidence, crime scene investigators must take added measures to reduce the potential of DNA cross contamination between samples collected."

The Zombie Factor

On the topic of zombie fingerprints, Schiro says, "A person who had only recently died then became reanimated would probably leave an oil based print for only a few hours after death. After that, the oils would probably not be replenished and the skin would dry out. An investigator would be better off looking for prints based in something the zombie had touched (blood, body fat, etc.) prior to touching the surface. If the corpse has been dead for a while or is reanimated in an advanced state of decomposition, then it is highly unlikely that usable prints would be recovered."

Zombies, whatever else they are, were people first. A large percentage of our population has had identifying information recorded. If our patient zero had ever been convicted of a crime, then his prints would be on record. Just as they would if he had been in the military, worked for any of the more highly classified organizations, been part of certain drug testing programs, been a government employee, held a driver's license in certain states (such as in California, Georgia, etc.), been registered with any of the child-tracking services, and so on. Bottom line is that there are a lot of people registered in the various law enforcement and military fingerprint databases. Though not all of these databases are shared,[9] there is enough information out there that a hit from a collected print is fairly likely.

Beeka believes that this would help us find our zombie, providing he's one of the millions who have been printed. "Prints are not deleted, usually, from a database if the person dies, so a dead person's prints would most likely still be in the file. And if they indulge in gore a lot, they'd be leaving plenty of prints in blood."

Schiro has a lot of confidence in the growing database of prints,

9. The U.S. military currently does not share its fingerprint database with law enforcement except under very special circumstances.

and says, "Fingerprinting would most likely be helpful in identifying the living dead who were reanimated shortly after their death for two major reasons. The first is that the recently deceased would be less likely to have their prints removed from the AFIS system, if indeed their prints are even in the AFIS system. Only a small percentage of the population is actually in the AFIS system and this small percentage is comprised mostly of people who have been arrested and booked into jail. The second reason is that those zombies reanimated shortly after death would be more likely to leave behind an identifiable print."

"The human body decomposes at varying speeds depending upon a myriad of factors," Leadbetter says. "For example . . . is the body inside or outside? Is the temperature high or low? What is the humidity? Is it immersed in water? Has it been burnt? Has it been subject to any contaminants? How did it die? Is it skinny or obese? Now in *zomboid* terms this raises a very interesting question. Bearing in mind that the skin on the hands and feet is often the last part of the human tissue to decompose, it must really be asked how quickly did the zombie regain its *undeadness*? If this was fairly soon after natural death, it could be that hardly any fingerprint detail had decomposed. If however it was the reverse, then there may not be any detail at all. In either scenario, the factors listed above will have to be considered."

Schiro concurs: "And what about a zombie in an advanced state of decomposition? That would complicate things." According to Schiro: "At some point decompositional changes will render fingerprint analysis useless. How the decompositional changes affect the fingers depends on many factors including the environment the body was exposed to prior to reanimation. Bodies exposed to the environment are going to decompose at a more rapid rate than bodies that have been embalmed or refrigerated. Bodies found in water are going to decompose differently than bodies not found in water. Insect and animal activity on bodies exposed to the elements could also affect fingerprints. Depending on the environmental conditions, the extremities (fingers and toes) could dry out and wrinkle, rendering them useless for leaving behind identifiable prints. Bodies undergoing decompositional changes in water or in humid environments will tend to slough off the outer layers of skin. This would also make it difficult to recover prints from touched surfaces."

"An interesting point is whether or not zombies perspire," says Leadbetter. "It they do, then it would be quite feasible that they would be able to leave fingerprints. Should it be that they do not perspire, then they would always be capable of leaving fingerprints in soft substrates such as chocolate, excrement, blood or toothpaste for example provided that the fingerprint detail did not break down before they joined the zomboid world. It would be interesting to note here, that due to the awkwardly articulated gait of the average zombie, the quality of fingerprint deposited by them would doubtless be subject to smudging and excessive distortion."

Just the Facts

DNA Testing

There are two primary kinds of forensic DNA testing: RFLP and PCR. RFLP (restriction fragment length polymorphism), is the more accurate of the two and is often called "DNA fingerprinting" or "profiling"; and this involves the examination of sequences of base pairs in a section of a DNA strand. Since each DNA strand is unique, the identifiers in two samples will either match up (indicating they came from the same source) or they won't, hence the reference to "fingerprinting," which also matches specific patterns believed to be unique in each person. Though this is a very accurate test, RFLP has a downside in that it requires a fair amount of collected sample cells, such as large spatters of blood or several strands of hair. These samples also have to be fresh, undamaged, and only recently dead. The other downside to RFLP testing is the time involved: which is anywhere from two weeks to three months.

The PCR (polymerase chain reaction) test is less accurate, but police can get an answer in as little as a few days; this DNA does not have to be recently collected or fresh.

Expert Witness

"DNA testing has done a lot of good for the legal system," says Georgia Stanley, a DNA testing technician for an independent New Jersey testing firm. "Not only is it contributing to the arrest of more criminals—and with a higher degree of certainty that they *are* the actual perpetrator; it is also helping to free persons wrongly convicted of crimes. Naturally courts would prefer the RFLP results because of their much higher degree of mathematical accuracy, but on the level of police work the less accurate but much faster PCR is very often used. The advantage there is that police can often identify a lead suspect and focus their investigation. Later, more elaborate testing may be ordered by either prosecution or defense."

Donna Sims, another technician at the same firm, explains the range of DNA testing. "We get all kinds of test requests, not just crime. Over the last eight years that I've been here I've done testing to identify suspects based on DNA found at a crime scene; to identify plane crash victims; to identify animals on the endangered lists in the Jersey Pine Barrens; to exonerate people wrongly jailed for crimes they didn't commit; to verify blood relations as part of an estate settlement; and to match organ donors and recipients."

The Zombie Factor

The zombies in a more advanced state of decomposition would be less likely to leave behind identifiable prints, but DNA touch evidence would still be useful. Examining its DNA through computer sequencing can identify any type of organism. Identifying unique individuals within each species is a bit less precise, but nowadays human DNA samples can be matched to the level of mathematical certainty. DNA testing may not be much help in the first hours of a manhunt, but once the zombie has been captured or killed, its DNA can provide information to investigators that will help them identify the person the zombie formerly was and then backtrack his movements, hopefully to the source of the contamination.

In the longer run, scientists and doctors will examine the zombie DNA in order to understand the nature of the disease and/or mutation that created this flesh-hungry monster.

Just the Facts

Bloodstain Pattern Analysis

Violence happens, blood spills. Bloodstain pattern analysis (BPA) is a hot topic in forensic science. Blood spatter[10] is crucial evidence in many cases in that it can often help police positively ID victims and assailants. Advancements in DNA analysis have given this aspect of forensics a major boost, and along with blood typing and other tests, it provides law enforcement and the courts with potent weapons for apprehension and conviction.

BPA is the science of examining the distribution, locations, and shapes of bloodstains at a crime scene. Properly done it allows the expert to accurately determine the sequence of events during the commission of a violent crime.

This field encompasses many other areas of science and medicine, including biology, chemistry, math, physics, anatomy, and others.

The blood spatter expert has a complicated job and will attempt to:

- Locate all individual stains and patterns.
- Calculate the angle of impact for each stain in order to determine the direction from which the blood was traveling. (Remember, a bloodstain may be present when the victim and/or assailant is not.)
- Describe each through notes, photos, and other recording methods.
- Determine the approximate number of blows.
- Determine the likely sequence of events.
- Determine the mechanism that created each stain. Blood from a torn artery will be different from blood spray from a baseball bat to the head.
- Determine the number of people present at the scene during the attack.

10. Not *splatter*.

- Determine the position of the victim and/or assailants during the attack. This takes into account any objects on the scene that a person may have encountered, touched, collided with, etc.; and objects that might have altered or interfered with the trajectory of blood.
- Determine the probable weapon used in the attack (knife, gun, teeth . . .)
- Determine the source of each bloodstain.
- Locate wounds on the victim and/or assailant that correspond with spatters.

On average there is about 4 to 6[11] liters of blood in the human body, which accounts for approximately 8 percent of total body weight. A blood loss of 40 percent or more of the total volume will produce irreversible shock and death. This includes loss from external wounds and internal bleeding. Losing 1.5 liters will usually incapacitate most adults.

There are three categories for bloodstains:

1. *Passive*: These are bloodstains caused by gravity, as with blood dripping from a wound. They are categorized as clots drips, drops, patterns, and pools.
2. *Projected*: These are bloodstains from any exposed blood source that is under some pressure, such as an open artery; or wounds that are subjected to an action or force greater than the pull of gravity. This includes gushing blood, arterial spurts, cast-off stains (from someone shaking blood from their hands or weapon, etc.); and impact spatters. Each of these can be further broken down into subcategories of low, medium, and high velocity.
3. *Transfer*: These are created when a wet, bloody surface (such as a blood-smeared hand) makes contact with another surface (such as a wall). Transfer bloodstains include bloody footprints, contact bleeding, swipes, smears, wipes, and smudges.

11. Women have about 4 to 5 liters; men have about 5 to 6 liters.

Expert Witness

I asked Consulting Forensic Scientist George Schiro to comment on whether the type of weapon used in a crime can be deduced from blood spatter evidence. He said, "The only way that a type of weapon can be deduced from the bloodstain patterns is if there is a bloody impression of the weapon at the scene or if there is a void (a bloodless area) in the shape of a weapon on a bloodied surface. Blood spatter can sometimes indicate the nature of the injuries received. This can also be indicative of the type of weapon used. For example, a misting, fine spray of blood spatter might indicate a gunshot wound. Larger drops with directionality might indicate blunt force trauma or a stabbing. The bloodstain pattern analyst must be very cautious in attempting to determine the type of weapon based solely on blood spatter. Other information, such as an autopsy report, must be taken into consideration."

I asked Schiro to comment on how temperature and other variables affect the collection of BPA: "A timetable for blood changes after spattering would be very difficult to determine. The changes depend on numerous factors including, but not limited to the individual's physiology, the humidity, the temperature, wind speed, the absorbance of the surface, the surface texture, and the volume of blood deposited. In most cases, a small volume of blood will typically dry within several hours. The blood dries from the outside in and changes from red to a reddish brown color as it dries. Over time, large volumes of blood can also undergo serum and blood cell separation as the blood clots and dries."

Since the responding officers in our research center scenario could not be sure if the bloodstains at the scene belonged just to the victim or to the attacker as well, I asked Schiro to comment on that. "Each individual stain isn't necessarily documented in every case. The overall patterns can be documented using dictated or written notes and video. Photography is the primary tool for recording overall patterns and individual stains. Measurements in photographs may also be necessary when trying to determine the location of origin of a bloodstain. Sketches are also useful in demonstrating potential origins of bloodstains within a scene."

If a biting attack were suspected, however, Schiro says that would make a difference: "The type of bloodstain patterns left by someone who savagely bit the victim depends on the location and severity of the bites. There would definitely be drip patterns. There may also be spurt patterns if arteries or lower leg veins are breached. If there was also savage clawing at the victim, then spatters showing directionality may be present at the scene."

He then commented on the directionality of blood spatter evidence, which provides crucial evidence to the investigators: "Directionality of a bloodstain is determined by the shape of the bloodstain and sometimes the wave cast-off associated with bloodstain. Bloodstains striking a smooth surface at 90 degrees perpendicular to the surface typically leave a circular stain. The greater the angle, the more elongated and ovoid shape the stain becomes. Based on these shapes, the angle that the blood drop struck the surface can be estimated. If the stain has a wave cast-off or tail, then an imaginary arrow can be drawn originating at the wave cast-off through the most elongated part of the stain to indicate the location of the bloodstain's origin. An arrow in the opposite direction shows the directionality of the bloodstain."

The Zombie Factor

One thing none of the experts could agree on is whether zombies would bleed. Certainly in the Romero films zombies bleed . . . sometimes. When shot, most of them just take the wounds without dripping blood, while at other times they bleed quite freely.

One scene, in *Dawn of the Dead*, even made a good solid argument for zombies having a very active circulatory system. One of the two SWAT officers, Roger, was attacked in the shopping mall's department store and was tackled to the floor. In the struggle he drove a screwdriver into the zombie's ear, which then welled with bright blood. Blood wells only when there is blood pressure, and there is blood pressure only when the heart is beating.

This scene was echoed in the 2005 remake of *Dawn of the Dead*, when the character of Michael used the broken handle of a croquet mallet to impale a zombie's head. Blood poured downward. Okay, so you could make a case that in the remake the blood was pouring downward, which only proves gravity not blood pressure;

but a lot of the zombies bled in that film. And in all the zombie films. Just not all the zombies.

So, would zombies still have blood in their veins, pumping or not? If the skin was intact and a zombie got up, the blood should settle into the legs, which would look bloated and squashy. Forensic expert Schiro observes, "Typically, body position and gravity will dictate where the majority of blood will be found. Livor mortis or lividity occurs when the blood stops circulating and gravity causes the blood to pool in the lower areas of the body. If someone dies while lying on their back, then the blood will pool in the capillaries on the back. If they are reanimated and upright within about eight hours, then gravity will cause the blood to pool in the legs and arms. If they are reanimated after about eight hours, then the blood will become 'fixed' and remain stationary in the back."

Another theory, supported by yet another special effect in the zombie films is that the blood thickens in the veins. How likely is that? George Schiro says that it's not very likely. "Decomposing blood would not typically be thickened unless other decomposing elements were present. Decomposing blood actually tends to be thinner due to *hemolysis*—the breaking down of the blood components. The blood also takes on a bad smell and it goes from red to a greenish brown over time. Thinner blood would tend to act more like spattered water. Transfer stains would also be less distinct and more diffuse. Spattered stains would also tend to run more and not keep their original shape. Thickened blood would be more congealed and hold its shape longer in transferred stains. In either case, due to the altered properties of the blood, experiments would have to be conducted, just as they were in the early days of bloodstain pattern analysis, to determine the flight characteristics of decomposed or decomposing blood. Without this data, proper interpretation of living dead bloodstain patterns is not possible."

And what would happen if anomalous blood was recovered at a crime scene? "If this type of blood was recovered at a crime scene, it would initially be perplexing and perhaps indicate that someone was using putrefied blood from a dead person to stage a crime scene," Schiro insists. "As more incidents of its recovery occurred, then a pattern would be noted and it would be apparent that the dead were walking the earth and attacking the living."

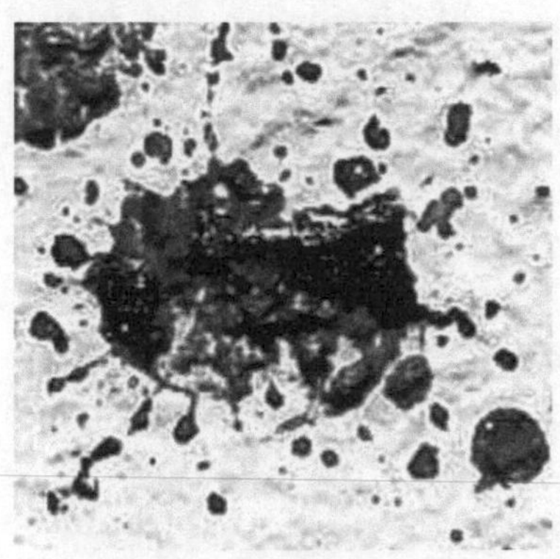

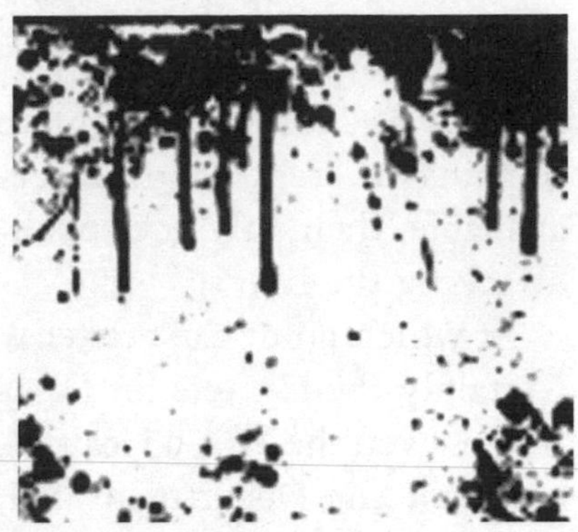

Human Blood **Zombie Blood**

Blood Spatter Evidence **by Jonathan Maberry**

"If (anomalous) blood was recovered at a crime scene, it would initially be perplexing and perhaps indicate that someone was using putrefied blood from a dead person to stage a crime scene"—GEORGE SCHIRO, consulting forensic scientist

Our research center guard took a couple of shots at his attacker. Would there be any blood spatter from a walking corpse? Schiro believes so. "There would be blood spatter from a walking corpse, but only certain types of patterns would probably be present. For example, spurt patterns require circulating blood and expirated blood requires a cough reflex, so these types of patterns may not be present. Other bloodstain patterns may be found at a crime scene. The same trajectory process would hold true for zombies. Typically a BPA specialist is used to interpret the evidence. A crime scene investigator would be the one who documents and collects the blood, although a BPA specialist could also document and recover this evidence."

What about blood tissue collected from a zombie crime scene? Would it be bloodless and therefore more anomalous? "I wouldn't necessarily expect the tissue to be bloodless," Schiro speculates, "although I would expect the tissue to be in a state of decomposition. The expert would collect the evidence and perhaps examine it him- or herself. Because of its nature, the tissue samples would probably be sent to a forensic pathologist for further evaluation. Initially it may be thought that someone is using decomposing remains to stage a crime scene. As more information becomes available, then only one conclusion would be possible: zombies are attacking the living."

At which point the matter would go to SWAT or even higher up. Certainly the Centers for Disease Control would be contacted, and maybe even the World Health Organization. It's not even inconceivable that the Department of Homeland Security (DHS) would be brought in, especially if there was some fear that zombies were the result of some kind of biological attack with a weaponized pathogen.

Michael Sicilia of California's Office of Homeland Security (the state division of Homeland) comments, "OHS is different from DHS in that we are the State Homeland Security folks, a focus on California issues, and send the federal money to the locals. For this purpose, I'll refer to DHS. Advances have been made in detection of anthrax, plague, and other bio-threats and there has been a lot of new technology deployed that can detect minute amounts of trace bio-threats in the environments. Some of these are mobile, and can be deployed to mass gatherings like the Superbowl; some are in city streets. In California there are four regional threat assessment centers that mirror the FBI districts in the State. They are staffed with local police, fire, hazmat and public health professionals as well as FBI and DHS."

When asked how DHS/OHS might get involved with a health crisis, Sicilia says, "As to when we would become involved, that depends on the nature of the event. There would need to be criminal intent that the attack was designed to cause terror to forward a political agenda, i.e., causing panic that would allow zombies to take over. OHS wouldn't get involved otherwise."

OHS/DHS would not, he tells us, just come in and take over as is often seen in movies. "Public Health officers would take the lead. If criminal activity were suspected, then the OHS would confer with the CDC on the federal level, and local public health officers would be in the lead role, because they have credibility with the public."

But first let's talk about those inconsistancies in zombie physiology that we've just discussed. Zombie films and books tend to play fast and loose with their own mythology in a number of ways, and one of the biggest areas for literary license is whether zombies are truly animated corpses. If we stay strictly in the realm of "well, it's just a story" then we don't have to come up with any logic; but readers and moviegoers are less credulous than they have been in previous generations. We've become jaded because we've seen way too much implausible nonsense, and what we want is a damn good reason to suspend our disbelief. To be fair, it's not asking a lot.

Just the Facts

Gunshot Residue

For the most part gunshot residue (GSR) forensics doesn't appear to play into our zombie scenario. Or does it? This case began with an attack on a security guard at a medical research company in western Pennsylvania. If this is the first reported attack or, better yet, the very first attack, then we are close to locating the source of the contagion. But what if by the time the police catch a zombie there are more than one of them? How will they be able to tell one from the other? This is when police rely on evidence that directly matches the suspect to the crime scene. Fingerprints, blood spatter, and DNA samples are all useful; but often the presence of these can be explained away. The suspect can claim (if he wasn't a brain-dead zombie) that he was a witness to the events rather than a participant and was wounded because he got too close to the action. Remember that in court reasonable doubt is the key to a criminal defense.

GSR, on the other hand, more clearly ties the suspect to the crime. If a person fires a gun, there is residue and powder burns on the hand, wrist, and forearm (or sleeve). The attacker who was shot at by the guard, since the fight was at close quarters, will have telltale residue on his clothes, even if the bullets missed.[12]

12. Which, as we'll discover later in this chapter, they didn't.

Oh, Come On Now!

In films we are willing to suspend our disbelief, but in return we should expect at least an attempt on the part of the filmmakers to use as much logic as possible. Give us a reason (even a mediocre one)! Some films step way over the line and abuse our credulity. I called on my friends on the PhillyGeek Yahoo! group for their input on films that just break too many rules of science:

- ***Independence Day* (1996): "The odds of being able to interface with the computers on an alien spaceship are astronomic. Having someone cook up a computer virus (within a couple of hours) that will then wreck those alien computers is just too much."—Shelley Handen**
- ***Godzilla* (1998): "In the Matthew Broderick remake there's a scene where 'Zilla runs through the streets towards the Hudson River and makes this graceful dive into the river; the thing is, that part of the Hudson isn't that deep, and half the body should have been sticking out the surface of the water."—Pete Hynes**
- ***Alien: Resurrection* (1997) (a.k.a *Alien 4*): "Even if you grant the whole 'cloning Ripley to get the Alien queen's DNA out of her,' how could that queen give live birth at the end?**

Expert Witness

Elizabeth Becka, forensic specialist and author of *Trace Evidence* and *Unknown Means*, says, "GSR can refer to two different things—gunshot residue that blows back[13] from the gun onto the shooter's hands, which is residue from the primer compounds and usually contains barium and antimony, and gunshot residue that flies forward from the barrel onto the victim, the victim's clothing, or anything else in the vicinity, and is gunpowder, containing nitrites."

I asked Becka how distance was measured in GSR. "Usually

13. Not to be confused with *blowback*, which is blood and tissue flying into the barrel from the victim.

She'd need all new reproductive/endocrine/nervous system organs."—Dena Procaccini

- ***The Last Mimzy* (2007): "The little girl can put her hand even her face in a force field where her molecules are jumbled, and yet there is no physical effect and she doesn't suffer from oxygen deprivation even though she has no means of breathing. And then there is the kids' affecting the power grid even though they are not plugged into it?"—Danielle Ackley-McPhail**
- ***Star Trek* (1966–present): "I love it, but it's riddled with ridiculous science, but one part stretched even their stretched physics: There are theoretical maximums to faster than light travel for the space vessels, but broadcast communications have zero lag."—Steven Feldman**
- ***The Black Hole* (1979): "Emotional robots and people breathing in outer space. Oh, come on now!"—Lynn and Bill Koehle**
- ***Return of the Living Dead* (1985): "All of the zombies have perfectly fine eyes with not a single indication of rot. Really, take a look. And then there's Linnea Quigley not having a mark on her after hordes of zombies had chomped on her. But I'm not complaining about that. An intact naked zombie Linnea Quigley is better than a ripped to pieces zombie Linnea Quigley."—David Christman**

through a Griess test, using treated photographic paper to demonstrate the nitrites present around the bullet hole in clothing. The gunpowder leaves the barrel in an expanding cone, getting wider the further from the barrel the particles travel (until they fall off entirely at around 3 feet). The smaller and denser this circular pattern is, the closer the end of the barrel was to the target. This can be determined with great accuracy if you take the same gun with the same ammunition and do test firings at six feet and twelve feet etc. and do the Griess test on the test targets as well as the article of clothing, then compare."

She says that the test is different when looking for GSR on human flesh: "On skin—it used to be via atomic absorption, which involved picking up the samples with moistened swabs; this would tell you if barium or antimony or both were present. Now it's done with stubs with sticky tape on the end and they're run through a scanning electron microscope, which can not only tell if barium and antimony are present but also if the particles are in a telltale spherical shape."

When asked how long GSR evidence will linger, she says, "On clothing forever if not disturbed, I suppose. On living skin (will natural oils affect this) we generally don't bother collecting if it's been more than 4 hours since the shooting, or if they've thoroughly washed their hands in the meantime."

The Zombie Factor

I asked if GSR would adhere differently to the skin of a corpse as opposed to living flesh? "You can think of GSR as very fine dirt or dust," Becka says. "It doesn't adhere well to dry, clean skin, sticking better to sweaty, oily or sticky hands. So it would depend on how long the person has been dead, and/or if he's been cleaned since death (such as at the morgue or funeral home), and/or if he's got something sticky on his hands, blood, mud, soda pop. On dead skin it will last forever if not disturbed, though dead skin would always be disturbed eventually by the decomposition process."

This means if the zombie is caught it can be tied to the crime scene, and if this zombie is our patient zero, then the medical research company and the surrounding area become the center point for the search for the origin of this zombie plague.

Just the Facts

Forensic Anthropology

Forensic anthropology combines the study of the culture and physicality of humans throughout history—with the criminal investigation. These investigators have a detailed knowledge of osteology (skeletal anatomy and biology) and a working knowledge of the requirements of law enforcement. Their research, evidence analysis, and findings often aid in discovering the cause of death of skeletal remains, and in the identification of the victim. Quite

Gregg Winkler's Decaying Zombie Quiz, Part 2

- **Folk-rock singer Jonathan Coulton did a song about zombies that was a major hit on YouTube. Name the song.**
- **Who is the only actor to reprise a role in Romero's zombie series?**
- **What is the incantations Bart and Lisa used to return Springfield's zombies to their graves in *Treehouse of Horror III*?**
- **What Japanese zombie movie has a television commercial selling "Bruce Campbell's Right Hand 2"?**
- **Who infects Spider-Man with the zombie virus in the *Marvel Zombies Versus Army of Darkness* miniseries?**

often they are called in to excavate remains using precise archaeological techniques.

Across the United States there are a number of outdoor field labs, called "body farms" where forensic anthropologists train, such as the Anthropological Research Facility operated by the University of Tennessee Knoxville, a facility founded in 1972 by Dr. William Bass—a pioneer in the field.

Expert Witness

According to private investigator and forensic anthropologist Bryon Morrigan,[14] "Just about the first thing a forensic anthropologist (FA) is going to want to do is remove all of the 'soft tissue,' so any work on the skin or other organs is going to need to be completed prior to the forensic anthropologist getting his/her hands on the body. If the body is severely decomposed, then an FA is probably going to be the one doing the examinations, but those are often limited to establishing time of death, which is going to be hard to figure on a zombie."

14. Bryon Morrigan is also the author of *Haunted Clearwater* (Schiffer Books, 2008).

Zombies . . . Fast or Slow? Part 3

- **"Definitely slow. Zombies aren't cheetahs, you know? They're not particularly smart (they're dead, after all), and the muscles are slowly dissolving, but if those bastards get hold of you, you're zombie meat."—Nate Kenyon, award-winning author of *Bloodstone* (Leisure Books, 2008) and *The Reach* (Leisure).**
- **"Damned fast!"—Nancy Kilpatrick, author of *The Goth Bible* (St. Martin's Griffin, 2004).**
- **"Slow zombies will always have their place but I think the fast zombie even if it isn't intelligent is a far more frightening thing. With slow zombies you have a chance even if you're unarmed and vastly unnumbered whereas with fast zombies, they will take you down even if you're armed to the teeth and a highly experienced combat veteran."—Eric S. Brown, author of the zombie novel/novellas *Cobble* (Mundeniz, Press, 2005), *The Queen* (Naked Snake Press, 2006), and *The Wave* (Naked Snake Press, 2006).**

He adds, "A good FA, with access to a full skeleton, ought to be able to tell you the body's sex, age, and race with no problems. They can also give good information about damages to the body. For example: You find a gunshot wound in the skull, but the FA finds a certain amount of healing has taken place, leading the FA to believe that the wound was not fatal, and the person lived for some time after the wound."

Retired Canadian forensic anthropologist Martin Schöenfeld adds, "Forensic anthropology is as much about preserving remains as it is about discovering who this person was. I've worked some cases high in the mountains where a bone was exposed by soil erosion, and as we began excavating the site we determined that the skeleton was broken up and scattered by weather and by scavenging animals. If the reconstruction had been attempted by anyone but an expert FA some valuable information may have been missed. As it turned out we determined that the bones were not from one body but from two—young twins that had gone missing a number of years before. We had 15% of one body and 11% of the other and we were able to determine the approximate age of the victims and even a cause of death. It went a long way to solving the case."

The Zombie Factor

So how would forensic anthropology help our manhunt for a zombie?

"In the early stages it won't," says Schöenfeld, "at least not in the initial stages because this is not a fast science. Forensic anthropology is slower because it requires very precise care in recovering even a single fragment of bone. There's site mapping, photography, and all manner of precautionary steps needed to preserve both the integrity of the site and the actual remains. However. . . . if it turns out that the zombie disease is the result of some older incident, perhaps contamination from an old toxic disposal site, or a contamination from improperly buried medical wastes—or even the grave of a person who had died from an infection years before, then we can help."

I asked him to explain. "There are incidents in folklore that hint at zombielike creatures," says Schöenfeld, who is currently writing a book on anthropology and folklore. "The *Ghul* of Arabic legend, the *Blutsauger* of Bosnia-Herzegovina, the *Brahmaparush* vampire of India, and the *Craqueuhhe* of France—all of these were flesh eaters according to legend, and since many people believe that there is a connection between myth and truth, then we could stretch the point to say that a zombie plague is a disease that has occurred from time to time throughout human history. It is a much more plausible and workable hypothesis than demonic possession or alien radiation. The pallid face, the diminished mental capabilities, the unnatural hunger—each of these symptoms can be individually explained by medicine. Why would it be so outrageous to postulate than a single disease, perhaps a mutated strain of rabies, cropped up now and again in different places around the world and caused zombielike behavior? If such a thing turned out to be the case, it would be either a forensic anthropologist or, perhaps, a forensic pathologist, who might make that discovery, and from there we might find a line of research leading to a cure."

Jikininki: The Flesh-Eating Ghosts of Japan

Zombies aren't a 20th-century invention nor are they uniquely American. Ghouls of one kind or another pop up all through history. In Japan, for example, the *jikininki*, whose name literally means "man-eating ghosts," are greedy sinners who return to feed on the flesh of the living. Unlike domestic zoms, the *jikininki* are smart and resourceful, and use verbal threats and even bribes to keep officials from hunting them down. The *jikininki* are in torment, however, because they actually don't *want* to eat human flesh . . . but a curse is a curse.

JUST THE FACTS

Forensic Art

Forensic art is widely used in the identification, apprehension, or conviction of suspects. This science includes a variety of disciplines including composite art, image modification, age progression, postmortem reconstruction, and demonstrative evidence. Of these, composite art is the most commonly used form of forensic art.

The forensic artists use witness statements and other information (including fuzzy video images) to create a reasonable likeness of a suspect. Having a likeness greatly increases the likelihood of identifying and then apprehending a suspect because the old saying really is true: One picture is worth a thousand words.

Artistic ability is only part of what it takes to be an effective forensic artist; of equal importance is the skill of interviewing a witness to bring out even the smallest details. Witnesses are seldom experienced with being able to usefully recall details, but with the right interview technique an almost miraculous process occurs where the image from the witness's spotty memory becomes a reality on the sketchpad.

Expert Witness

Becoming a qualified forensic artist takes more than art school, according to best-selling thriller novelist and artist Jonathan Santlofer[15]: "The trend seems to be that the best forensic artists take the Quantico intensive forensic art program where they learn everything from anatomy to profiling. I'd say that the best are also psychologically trained or have an understanding of how to make a witness trust them and feel comfortable. My forensic artist protagonist, Nate Rodriguez, also has a sort of sixth sense when it come to sketching a face; he really gets inside the witness's head and sees what they see!"

15. Jonathan Santlofer is the author of four novels including *Anatomy of Fear* (William Morrow, 2007); and has been a visiting artist at the American Academy in Rome.

I asked Santlofer how and when forensic artists are invited into a police case. "When a witness or victim has seen a perpetrator and a sketch needs to be made," he says. "Many forensic artists see more cases than any homicide cop will ever see in a lifetime sometimes producing as many as five sketches a day."

When asked how much computer work is involved in forensic art, Santlofer remarked, "There are many (commercial forensic art) computer programs but the major complaint against them is that they are expensive and difficult to master. And of course there are only a set number of features available as opposed to the total spectrum that a forensic artist can create with pencil or charcoal. I'm for the old fashioned method because it creates a bond between the artist and the witness. It's really hard to warm up to a computer program."

The Zombie Factor

So, how would forensic art help police catch a zombie, or identify one so that police could backtrack to the possible source of the infection?

"If the zombie had been seen but not caught," advised Louis Michael Sanders, a forensic artist from San Diego, "then a forensic artist would likely be called in to sit with the witness and interview them in order to create a likeness of the suspect. If the police are unable to find the suspect by canvassing the area immediately following an attack the availability of a police sketch will greatly increase the chance of locating that suspect. It can be sent via Internet, fax, TV broadcast, and photocopy handout. The police can blanket the area with these pictures and then everyone—official police and civilians alike—become spotters. Especially when you have a zombie staggering around someone is sure as hell going to see him. That's when the cavalry come a-running."

Forensics expert and author Andrea Campbell adds, "Advanced decomposition and re-creation depends on a couple factors. If there is enough of a skull, we can glue the jaw back on, take our skin tissue depth charts, cut vinyl pegs to match 26 key points on the skull and work up several pounds of clay to meet those levels, creating a 3-dimensional bust. Then the eyes are set (we set acrylic eyeballs, very life-like and expensive), lids placed carefully; features such as the nose, lips and ears are fashioned (ears are especially difficult) and, add some messy Zombie hair (I do prefer clay hair versus a wig) and we have it. That's called Forensic Reconstruction Sculpture."

She explains, "If the zombie's face is eaten away, we can rely on video, computer-aided, or photographic superimposition. This includes techniques for positioning, matching relative size, adjusting for distortion, features used for comparison, and defining the limits for a possible match. In other words, proportion is the key. What happens here is that a photograph of the victim antemortem ('after death') is positioned over a skull that is rotated to the approximate identical position in the photograph. This overlay goes through a series of steps to blend the photo and the skull into one matching image."

Santlofer says, "If there was no one who had ever seen the zombie then the best way would be to unearth the zombie's skull, let bugs gnaw off the flesh then put it in an acid bath. After that a forensic artist would get to work reconstructing the zombie's face out of clay on top of the skull. It's a slow process of figuring out tissue depth and careful measurement of bone. My guess is that a zombie's head would be a lot less fleshy than a living breathing healthy human being so that would have to be taken into account."

Forensic artist Louis Michael Sanders says, "Outbreaks involving violence of this kind—savage attacks, biting, infection—these would get a lot of attention very quickly. Very, very quickly, and there would be a lot of resources applied to the situation. Long before the authorities either realized or released information that the dead were rising they would know that the disease caused disintegration of the skin and disfigurement *similar* to that of postmortem decomposition. Now, your scenario of an attack near a suburban medical research facility would at least *suggest* a connection between the location of the attack and the nature of the business itself. On-the-job contamination would immediately be suspected. Many companies these days have employee records on their computers that include photo IDs. One of the first things that would be done would be to get someone of authority to check employee records for someone who fits the description of the attacker. If we're talking a white male of such-and-such a height and weight, that will eliminate a lot of the employees—all of the women, the shorter and thinner employees, the ethnic employees. If the remaining photo images were given to detectives they, with or without the assistance of a forensic artist, could make a connection."

What if the zombie in question already had significant facial decomposition?

"That's not that much of a problem," Sanders says, "because there are certain things that won't change. It's the same when considering a suspect wearing a disguise, or even one that has had *some* facial reconstruction. Generally the ears will be the same, and if not exactly the same due to damage or surgery, then their exact position on the head relative to cheekbones, eyes, and other referential points. It's a matter of math and geometry to come up with certain markers that we can rely on. Plus, a forensic artist can take a photo or description of a zombie and fairly easily de-zombify them to get an approximation of that person's pre-infection face. If we can reconstruct the faces of three thousand year old mummies a zombie is a snap."

Campbell agrees. "We can also take the original photo of an employee who fits the basic description and *zombify* him. This technique for aging is often referred to as 'fugitive updates,' when the police have a mug shot that is 5 or 10 years old and the case is renewed, the artist needs to 'age' the photo in a drawing. Knowledge of cranial facial growth is necessary."

Sanders sums it all up by saying, "Considering that finding the 'patient zero' is key to saving the planet, this is one of those times where forensic artists could well be the heroes of the piece."

Just the Facts

Forensic Toxicology

Toxicology is the study of the adverse effects of chemicals on living organisms; and forensic toxicology takes that a step farther to see how it applies to crime. The forensic toxicologist uses analytical chemistry to locate and identify foreign and presumably hazardous chemicals and substances in the body. These substances, or toxins, can be anything that poses a threat to health or life. Toxins include poisons, cleaning products, spoiled food, insect bites, pesticides, medicines, industrial chemicals, and many others; and these may have been inhaled, ingested, introduced via a wound, or absorbed through the skin.

Many of the zombie stories raise the possibility of contamination by toxic waste to be the cause of zombie reanimation. Discovering the identity of a toxin of this type is complicated. Not only will the zombie be uncooperative (just try to get one to pee into a cup), but many substances change once they are in the human body. If the zombie was created by a person becoming contaminated by one or more chemicals, then by the time that human had undergone the process of mutation or change the original substance may no longer be detectable; or may no longer be detectable as the culprit.

As you'll see, there is some scientific evidence to support the *possibility* of a toxic zombie; but the problem is that this toxic effect would not be transmissible through a bite.

Expert Witness

According to Dr. Charles Amuzzie, a consultant associated with the African Society for Toxicological Sciences, "Do not confuse toxic effects with side effects. They are not the same thing. A side effect is not life threatening. Itchy skin, dry mouth, blurred vision—these are side effects. When you are talking about life-threatening symptoms you are talking about toxic effects, and these are most often produced by a dangerous metabolite of the substance being activated by an enzyme. Or perhaps by biotransformation, which is when enzymes cause a chemical alteration of a substance within the body. There are three kinds of toxic reactions: *Genotoxic*, which create benign or malignant tumors (called neoplasms); *Pathological*, which cause injury to the liver; and *Pharmacological*, which adversely affect the central nervous system (CNS)."

He points out that, "Toxic effects are destructive to the CNS, and for your zombie scenario you are probably looking for

All the World's a Toxin . . .

***Toxie Ghoul* by Peter Mihaichuk**

In his book, *The Archidoxes of Magic,* Swiss physician and alchemist Paracelsus (1493–1541) wrote: "All substances are poisons; there is none which is not a poison. The right dose differentiates a poison and a remedy."

something that super-activates the CNS. A toxin can certainly kill, but it will not resurrect the dead."

However Raymond Singer, Ph.D., a nationally known expert witness on cases involving neuropsychology and neurobehavioral toxicology, says that there might be some basis for the suspension of disbelief in zombie films that have a "toxic waste contamination" plot. "It's not a bad theory. People with this type of poisoning are alive in some senses, but dead in the finer aspects of being a human. Depending upon the case, they could go into states of automatic rage. I kinda doubt cannibalism—unless that is or was part of their culture."

When I asked Dr. Singer to provide any examples of toxic chemicals turning someone into a soulless monster, he provided this anecdote. "I served as an expert witness in a murder trial of a confessed mass murderer, who heinously slaughtered a mother and her children while they were sleeping in their bedrooms. The prosecution wanted the death penalty—which if applied anywhere, could have been applied in this case most deservedly. After carefully reviewing the killer's background and history in depth, and examining him personally in the maximum security facility, I concluded that his long history of exposure to toxic chemicals, including playing many idyll days as a youth in 'Shit River'—eponymously named because of widespread pollution from toxic waste—led to the creation of a monster, a zombie, who lacked the normal human ability to control hateful impulses.

"Toxic waste and other chemicals can damage the nervous system, leading to disruptions in the ability to control, plan, manage and judge—what neuropsychologists call 'executive function.' In this case, his executive function failed to control his hatred for the woman and her children. Basically, he was insane and deranged, in part from toxic chemical poisoning of his youth. The jury took my words into consideration, and gave him life without parole. The killer was animated when he committed these crimes, but he had been dead inside."

Now that's frightening.

The Zombie Factor

In order for "toxic zombies" to work, the contamination would have to do more than alter behavior. It would have to shut down most of the body's functions while isolating and preserving a few (minimal brain, heart, and lung activity, etc.). Toxins are dangerous, but they are not parasitic; and though contamination can be passed on, it diminishes in strength with each contact and would not be something that could be passed on through a bite. A major outbreak would require a large number of persons becoming similarly contaminated at the same time and exhibiting behavioral changes at about the same rate, which isn't as likely. Similarities in symptomology occur more often in disease pathogens.

Just the Facts

Forensic Entomology

One of the creepiest (or perhps *crawliest*) fields within evidence analysis is that of forensic entomology, which is the study of insects as they relate to police work. Many insects are necrophageous (meaning they "eat corpses"), and the study of them can help to establish the time that has elapsed since death, or the PMI (post mortem interval).

Forensic entomology is an old science, dating back to at least thirteenth-century China; however it's become a very widely accepted science mostly over the last twenty years or so. Though there are a number of subspecialties within forensic entomology, medico-legal forensic entomology is the specialty involving the study of insects as they relate to criminal and legal matters.

A forensic entomologist is generally called in for cases where the decedent is believed to have died at least seventy-two hours ago, which is when insect presence is significantly seen and the age of newborn insects (such as maggots) from eggs laid on the body postmortem can help the entomologist begin his or her calculations. Flies typically arrive within a few minutes of death, attracted by protein-rich body fluids and to lay their eggs. They lay eggs and their maggot hatchlings feed on the necrotic tissue. As the process of decomposition kicks in, the body releases a variety of chemicals, including *putrescine* and *cadaverine*, both of which contribute to the ripe odor of decaying flesh and act as attractants to the insects that form such a necessary part of the natural breakdown of organic matter. Without this process no corpses would ever decay and we'd be hip deep in the unrotting dead. Necrophageous flies include blowflies, fleshflies, houseflies, coffin flies, sun flies, black soldier flies, and cheese flies.

Mites often come along next, feeding on the drying flesh and also dining on the fly eggs. If there are enough mites on hand and they consume a considerable portion of the fly eggs, there will be fewer maggots and, therefore, less tissue consumption, which can significantly interfere with the forensic entomologist's attempts to estimate the normal rate of decay and hence the length of time the body has been dead. Establishing approximate time and date of death is often a crucial factor in police work.

Beetles prefer drier flesh and usually come along after the decomposition process is moderately far along. These include rove beetles, hister beetles, carrion beetles, carcass beetles, hide beetles, scarab beetles, and sap beetles.

Moths often attend the feast, dining on human hair. It's mostly clothes moths that do this (which is something to think about next time you find one in your closet).

Other critters often found on corpses include bees, ants, and wasps. These creatures are not there to feed on the corpse but are predators who attack and eat the necrophageous insects. Just as with the mites, this can interfere with PMI calculations.

The forensic entomologist is an expert on the life cycle of these insects and by evaluating the apparent age of maggots, beetles, and mites, he or she can often make a determination of how long the body has been dead.

Expert Witness

Forensic entomologist Dr. Robert Hall, associate vice chancellor for research at the University of Missouri, discusses how the presence of these insects helps in establishing time of death: "There are two basic approaches. First is the temperature dependent development of flies (the warmer it is, the faster they develop, within limits). Knowing that blow flies arrive very soon after death, if the temperature prevailing at the crime scene can be inferred from proximate weather stations, then knowing the species of blow fly and the stage collected, it's possible to calculate how long it would have required for the species in question to progress from the stage the female deposits on the corpse (egg or first instar larva) to the stage collected. This represents the 'must have been dead at least as long' estimate called the 'minimum postmortem interval.' The second approach is to collect all insects associated with a corpse; these 'assemblages' of arthropods may then be compared with decomposition studies conducted under similar environmental and geographic conditions and the time-since-death inferred from a 'presence or absence' analysis that refers to the aforementioned studies."

Occasionally the type of insect can give clues to where the body might have been—as in cases where a victim is killed in one state and the body carried across state lines for burial—a tactic sometimes used by serial killers. Dr. Hall gives us an example. "Some blow fly species are found only in the far southern U.S. When a corpse is found in, say, North Dakota, and infested with a southern species, it's pretty significant evidence that corpse was dead within the southern range of that species and subsequently transported north. Although this doesn't happen often, it does occasionally."

Insects don't set up camp on a corpse by accident. They're actually part of nature's process of decomposition, as Dr. Hall explains. "Maggots are a powerful eating machine. 'Maggot mass' refers to

Maggot Therapy

For thousands of years healers (licensed or not) have used the placement of maggots on wounds as a method of preventing gangrene. Maggots will not eat healthy living tissue and will feed only on dead (necrotic) tissue. Soldiers in war would sometimes apply a poultice of maggots to a festering wound to clean it up. In more controlled circumstances, the maggots were disinfected first.

the large number of writhing maggots that actually—by friction—generate heat above ambient temperature. These squirming maggot masses consume tissue and can disarticulate skeletons. They're the 'buzzards' of the insect world."

The Zombie Factor

Italian horror director Lucio Fulci (and many of his peers) was fond of using masses of maggots in his zombie flicks. In *House by the Cemetery* (1981) a zombie "bled" maggots after being stabbed. I wondered if insects would colonize a dead body that was walking around and put that question to Dr. Hall.

"I have no idea whether zombies 'decay' as human corpses do, but the medical condition called *myiasis*[16] refers to infestation of a living body with the blow flies normally associated with corpses. Most living humans move, and thus movement itself is not a complete barrier to blow fly females laying eggs."

This isn't that big a stretch when you consider that humans typically wave flies away, and a zombie would be indifferent to their presence. They could very easily land and lay eggs, and the hatching maggots would have plenty of necrotic tissue upon which to feed. It would be the undead equivalent to a dinner cruise, or maybe an ambulatory "meals on wheels."

The Final Verdict: The Crime Scene Investigators

The amount of information that can be collected is amazing, and all that the forensic investigators can glean from that evidence is truly staggering. Because we live in a computer age and the Internet is a reality of our lives, investigators can share information via databases and e-mail, they can instantly contact with other experts around the world, and they can bring to bear such a weight of technology that our poor mindless zombies don't seem to have much of a chance.

Fingerprints, blood analysis, bite mark analysis, forensic art and

16. Myiasis is a disease of animals or humans caused by fly larvae feeding on the host's necrotic tissue.

anthropology, toxicology and entomology, footprints, and gait patterns . . . any one of these elements might identify our patient zero and help investigators backtrack to a possible source of contagion while at the same time hunting down the zombie/vector.

This is an area seldom if ever addressed in zombie fiction, as if there would be no time to use forensics and nothing to be gained even if there was time. Slow, shuffling zombies are just not going to move faster than science geeks. Not going to happen.

On the Slab

Medical Science Examines the Living Dead

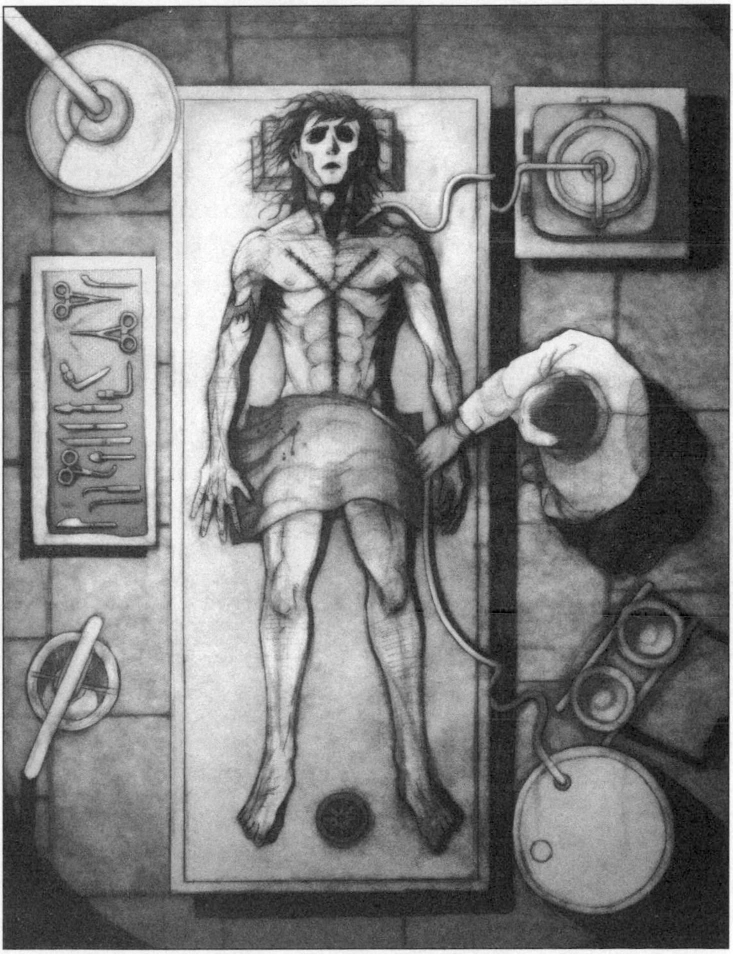

Zombie Autopsy by Zach McCain

Science cannot exist in the absence of logic. Science depends on both theory and evidence. If the recent dead came back to life, there must be a reason, and that reason will have to be grounded in science.

In *Night of the Living Dead* Romero insists that "something" has caused all the recent human dead to return to life. He includes in this buried corpses, subjects of autopsies, accident victims—the works. Whereas this is extremely cool and cinematically very threatening, it makes no scientific sense at all. In order for humans to move, certain parts of the central nervous system *have* to be working. Any other explanation is magic, and Romero never intended his films to be supernatural.

So, we're going to make a couple of deductions. First, if the dead rose, then this would have to be the result of some kind of pathogen. No other explanation really stands up to scientific scrutiny. Epidemics start from a source, are spread by a vector, and then increase exponentially as long as the vector(s) continue to make infectious contact with victims.

In later films and books of the genre, the other storytellers recognized the logical need to address this and established that the plague is spread through direct infection, specifically through the exchange of fluids during a bite. And this is necessary in order for the films and books to continue to be frightening, and indeed to become even more frightening. Otherwise it's fantasy, and we're much too jaded these days to get spooked by something that has no possibility of ever coming true. We need at least some measure of plausibility.

The burden is on the filmmakers and authors to create a framework on which a plausible story can be built. Throw the audience a bit of a bone, logic-wise, and they'll allow for a lot; insult the intelligence of an audience by denying them *any* reasonable scientific structure, and their mood gets ugly real fast. And I don't blame them one bit. There are whole books written on the inaccuracies in classic and beloved shows like *Star Trek, The X-Files, Buffy* . . . and online message boards are ablaze with postings about everything from continuity errors (like Han Solo's now-you-see-it, now-you-don't vest in *Empire Strikes Back*), to technical flubs (the entire crew leaving the *Sulaco* to go down to the planet in the film *Aliens*), to outright scientific impossibilities (*Daredevil* doing gymnastics and intense fighting after having been stabbed through the shoulder—he has heightened senses, not a mutant healing factor!).[1]

Most monsters can be scientifically understood, at least to some degree. Werewolfism—overactive hair follicles notwithstanding—has been heavily documented, particularly in court cases involving a person tried for werewolf murders. Anyone who understands abnormal psychology and who reads the many transcripts of those trials will see a clear pathology indicating sociopathic behavior. What the courts called a "werewolf" four hundred years ago would very clearly be called a serial killer today.

The legends of a mysterious invisible night-predator sneaking into the bedrooms of children by night and stealing their breath is what our ancestors called vampires but which we call sudden infant death syndrome. The belief of a soul-stealing old hag who comes in the night to torture men is now understood as sleep paralysis. Granted, not all the things that go bump in the night have been (so far) explained away, but someone grounded in science and using an open mind can work up a really good set of explanations for *most* of them.[2]

Zombies, though they are creatures of fiction rather than folklore, can also be reasonably understood. Except for a twitch here and there, Romero did a solid job of giving us a set of guidelines to understand the zombies. He is a very smart man and a terrific storyteller, and though he's not a scientist, he did try to make sure scientific plausibility existed within the framework of his undead world. In his films it's established that:

- Zombies are not alive. They are the recent dead brought back to some kind of semblance of life, but they are definitely corpses.

1. For more on this topic see the sidebar, "Oh, Come On Now!" in Chapter 2.

2. Admittedly, I personally hope that there are some spooky legends that are *never* fully explained.

- Zombies don't breathe. Maybe some of them have been shown to have throats torn away, gaping chest-cavity wounds, etc.
- Zombies don't think. Not (at least) until the third movie, and then more so in the fourth. This suggests that a process of change is ongoing in the zombies and that cognitive powers may be returning to them.
- Zombies can't be wounded (only killed). Lop an arm off, riddle their bodies with bullets and you get bupkiss. Put a round through the brainpan and the ghoul goes down.
- Zombies can be killed only by severe trauma to the brain. This suggests that the central nervous system functions to some degree.

For this chapter I approached a number of experts in various medical and scientific fields to see if we can get a better scientific view of what zombies are and what makes them do what they do.

Just the Facts

Neurology and the Living Dead

The first problem to solve is: Are zombies truly dead, partly alive, or something else? Personally, I'm leaning toward "something else," some state between clinical death and actual life.

Let's discuss death. It's not just an end to life—which is both a medical and philosophic issue—death is also a process during which the body undergoes remarkable change. The dead are by no means static, they're not frozen in time. Death begins the instant the heart stops beating. Without blood flow no oxygen goes to the cells. The brain cells are one of the first to die in the absence of oxygen, and the skin cells are among the last. Depending on temperature, the presence of insects, and other factors, this process may occur at different speeds. When the heart stops beating, blood no longer flows and begins to settle, draining from the highest points to the lowest point due to gravity. The upper skin surface is pale as blood drains, and the lower parts of the body darken as that blood collects. The now inert cells no longer produce the molecular movement needed to energize the biochemical processes in the muscles. Calcium ions leak into the nonenergetic muscle tissue and prevent them from relaxing normally, and therefore stiffen. This muscular rigidity is called rigor mortis and it kicks in about three hours after death and will keep the body as stiff as a statue for about thirty-six hours. As more and more cells die, the body's capacity to fight off destructive bacteria fails; and then the enzymes in the muscles, coupled with the now uncontrolled bacteria, begin to decompose the muscles, which ultimately cause the muscle integrity to fail, and the body becomes limp again.

During this time the body's temperature steadily cools. On average it takes about twelve hours for a corpse to become "cool" to the touch; and a full day for it to cool all the way to the core.

Are zombies dead? Do they fit the criteria? If we take the Romero zombies as the basis for our discussion, we have to assume that some aspects of reported zombie behavior must be dismissed. For starters, there is no way an embalmed corpse will rise. Nope, no way. I'm going to mark that down to bad reportage from hysterical and therefore unreliable witnesses.

I posed the question of zombie reanimation to my experts. They weren't as dismissive of the whole idea as you might think. In fact, they collectively built a pretty strong case for how a zombie might operate. Strong enough to be deliciously creepy.

Let's start by discussing the anatomy and function of the human brain, which is essentially an electrical and chemical machine, weighing only three pounds and containing about 100 billion cells. Most of these cells are called neurons and serve basically as on/off switches to conduct electrical impulses. Neurons are either transmitting signals (on) or resting (off). Each neuron has a cell body, a kind of conducting wire called an axon, and a pump for shooting out neurotransmitters that cross a gap between neurons (called a synapse) and are received by a receptor (called a dendrite), where the neurotransmitter triggers the next neuron to continue sending the signal. Different neurons use different types of transmitters, including epinephrine, norepinephrine, dopamine and others. Collectively, the electrical charge from these billions of axons generates a charge equal to a 60-watt lightbulb (give or take). Devices

PMI: Calculating the Postmortem Interval

The timetable for the process of death and decay is important to all aspects of murder investigation. It unfolds like this:

- ***Algor mortis*: (Latin: *algor*—coolness; *mortis*—of death) The process a body goes through after death during which the body cools to ambient temperature. Temperature drops at approximately 1 to 1.5 degrees Fahrenheit per hour.**
- ***Rigor mortis*: (literally "death stiffness") The stiffening of the limbs following death as muscle cells decay.**
- ***Vitreous humor changes*: There is a clear gel that fills the gap between the retina and the lens of the eye. Following death the potassium levels in this gel increases at a measurable and predictable rate, which allows forensics experts to use it to measure time elapsed since death.**
- ***Entomology*: Insects always appear on a corpse and are crucial to its decomposition.**
- ***Autolysis*: (literally "self-splitting") This is the process of post-mortem cell disintegration.**
- ***Putrefaction*: The decomposition of proteins by anaerobic microorganisms called putrefying bacteria.**

such as the electroencephalograph (EEG) can track and measure this electrical activity.

Most of the cranial cavity is filled by the cerebrum, a large rounded structure divided into two hemispheres, and each hemisphere is further divided into four sections, the frontal, parietal, temporal, and occipital lobes. The two hemispheres are primarily linked to the corpus callosum (a very large bundle of nerve fibers) through which the two "half brains" communicate with each other. This commissure transfers information between the two hemispheres to coordinate localized functions. The cerebrum controls a variety of functions (motor, sensory, and higher mental functions,

Zombie Oops!

"Using the mythology Romero put forth I realized there is a small problem. In both versions of *Night of the Living Dead* Johnny (brother of the female lead, Barbara) dies by his head being crushed. This would have damaged the brain, and since that is how to stop a zombie in the first place it makes you wonder how he came back in the first place."—Damien Rogers, zombie movie fan

such as thought, reason, emotion, and memory) and integrates their actions. It consists of both gray and white matter. The gray matter is mostly composed of neurons (cell bodies) while the white matter primarily contains axons (nerve fibers). The majority of the cerebrum consists of white matter.

Each hemisphere has an outer layer of gray matter called the cerebral cortex. The motor cortex is the part of the cerebral cortex in the brain that controls the actions of voluntary muscles; different parts of the motor cortex control different specific muscle functions. It can be presumed that in zombies there is some function of the motor cortex. The jerky movements and (in some cases) apparently dead limbs are indications of damage to this center of the brain or perhaps the cerebellum.

In the cerebrum, there are fifty to one hundred thousand neurons; information is sent from place to place like a telegram. The neuron cell bodies would be the telegraph machine itself while the axons would be the wires connecting it to other machines.

The right hemisphere organizes or sorts information; the left hemisphere analyzes the information collected by the right.

Certain mental functions (e.g., mathematics, logic, language) are lateralized in the brain, meaning they are located in either the right or left side of the brain. Generalizations are made about these functions (e.g., logic, creativity), but they need to be treated carefully because popular lateralizations are often distributed across both

Art of the Dead – Kelly Everaert

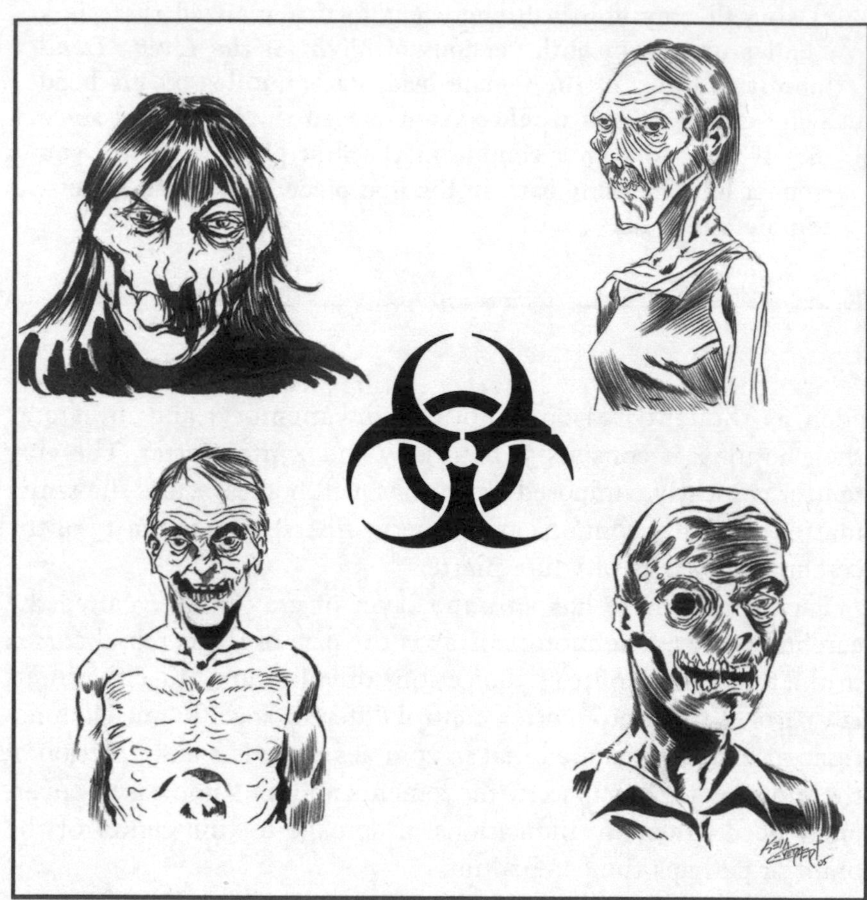

Zombie Biohazard

"*Night of the Living Dead* scared the crap out of me. I was probably ten or eleven watching the late night movie on Halloween after a night of trick or treating. At least one channel played this classic movie every Halloween and I've watched it every year since."

sides. Lateralization of these functions also depend on whether or not the person is right-handed versus left-handed. Since the majority of people are right-handed, the distribution of mental functions (see the sidebar, "Brain Function") is done with that in mind (in a left-handed individual, the lateralization is usually located in the opposite hemisphere from that of someone who is right-handed).

Brain Function

Left Hemisphere Functions	*Right Hemisphere Functions*
sequential	**simultaneous**
analytical	**holistic**
verbal	**imagistic**
logical	**intuitive**
algorithmic processing	**algorithmic processing**
perception of counting/ measurement	**perception of shapes/motions**
present and past	**present and future**
grammar/words, pattern perception, literal	**intonation/emphasis, prosody, pragmatic, contextual**

The best example of lateralization for one specific ability is language. Both sides contain major areas in language skills, but each have separate properties. Linear reasoning functions of language (e.g., grammar, word production) is lateralized to the left hemisphere while holistic reasoning (e.g., emphasis, prosody) are lateralized to the right hemisphere.

In general terms, the left brain deals with logic and analytical ideas while its counterpart deals with imagination and abstract ideas. (If one side of the brain is injured, it affects the other.) So, someone with an injury to the right hemisphere of the brain might not be able to make correlative thoughts: They might see a wall and not comprehend that they need to find a door to get through it, and instead they try to walk through it. Injure the left side of the brain, and a person might lose the ability to solve complex problems.

Human movement is controlled by a part of the motor cortex called the motor strip (or precentral gyrus). Often stroke victims will have some damage to that portion of the brain and lose function in certain parts of the body. Injure the left hemisphere, and the right side of the body will be affected, and vice versa. This is why half of a person's face sometimes droops following a stroke.

The cerebellum, a cauliflower-shaped structure located just above the brainstem, is the part of the brain governing the higher functions of motion, including posture, balance, and coordination; there is some research indicating that it contributes to some nonmotor functions such as active thought (cognition) and emotion. This part of the brain comprises only 10 percent of the brain's total mass but contains half of the total neurons.

Damage or dysfunction to the cerebellum can result in cerebellar ataxia: ataxia (gross incoordination of muscle movements causing jerky rather than smooth muscular movement), hypotonia (poor muscle tone), asynergy (lack of coordination), dyschronometria (difficulty in measuring time), dysdiadochokinesia (inability to perform rapid, alternating movements), dysmetria (impaired ability to regulate the distance, power, and speed of an act), gait disturbances (abnormal walking patterns), abnormal eye movements, and dysarthria (poor articulation). Kind of sounds familiar, doesn't it?

Different abnormalities manifest themselves depending on which cerebellar structures are damaged. Vestibulo-cerebellar dysfunction presents with postural instability; the person tends to separate his feet on standing to gain a wider base. Spino-cerebellar dysfunction presents with a wide-based "drunken sailor" gait, characterised by uncertain start and stop motions with unequal steps. Cerebro-cerebellar dysfunction presents with disturbances in carrying out voluntary movements (e.g., intention tremors), writing difficulties (e.g., large, unequal lettering with irregular underlining), and dysarthria (slurred speech).

The brain stem is the portion of the brain that connects the spinal cord to the forebrain and cerebrum. It consists of the medulla oblongata, pons, and midbrain. But it's more than just an organic coaxial cable; the brain stem relays specific categories of movement commands from the motor cortex. If the cortex wants the arm to wave, the brain stem transmits the message and coordinates the movement. Processes such as mastication are directed by the brain stem, and if you aren't up on your Latin, mastication is the act of chewing. One thing all zombies do is chew.

The cerebrum is vital for perception and conscious action, but it's the brain stem that runs the body in the absence of artificial life support. Even if everything above the midbrain is destroyed or shut down, the brain stem will sustain a living body. This is not, of course, "life" as we know it.

Collectively the brain and spinal cord are known as the central nervous system. It is reasonable to assume that for zombies to be animated some parts of this complex system need to be active. Minimally active, to be sure, but somewhere there are some organic switches in the "on" position.

Zombies . . . Fast or Slow? Part 4

- **"Slow, absolutely. They're dead; their muscles have atrophied, so none of them are going to run the hundred-yard dash in under forty seconds. Jeez!"—Gary A. Braunbeck, Bram Stoker Award winner and author of *Prodigal Blues* and *Mr. Hands***
- **"I prefer the slow, plodding variety—to me, their mindlessness is their appeal. If they were intelligent, they would simply round up humans and breed them like cattle instead of mindlessly eradicating their food supply. Though their cookbooks might prove interesting." —Scott Nicholson, author of *They Hunger* and *The Home***
- **"I prefer both slow and fast zombies, so I can race them like the Tortoise and the Hare and see who catches my grandma first."—D. L. Snell, author of *Roses of Blood on Barbed Wire***

Expert Witness

"We see limited and reduced brain function fairly frequently," says Russ Hassert, MS, a wire service medical news reporter. "I contributed to a number of stories after the Brookhaven National Laboratory released a couple of studies showing that methamphetamine ("speed") users demonstrated reduced motor and cognitive functions. The studies conclusively showed that methamphetamines taken in amount consistent with habitual abuse reduces the function of the dopamine transporters. Granted, these are not zombie stories, but they establish that there are ways that the brain's functions can be reduced and the person still be able to function on *some* level."

Dr. Andrea White, an infectious disease specialist formerly with Doctors Without Borders, adds, "There are studies ongoing that have established a link between patients seropositive for human immunodeficiency virus type 1 (HIV-1) and reduced motor function. Other pathogens can similarly affect cognitive and motor functions. We know that prions produce a lethal decline of cognitive and motor function. Some unkind writers have drawn parallels between advanced Alzheimer's and Parkinson's patients and zombies because these diseases reduce or remove cognition and communication skills while still allowing some degree of ambulation and the ingestion of food."

Nurse practitioner Helen Poland says, "In order for a zombie to exist it must be, on some level, alive. Corpses don't walk, and they don't eat. But if we consider a disease, possibly a prion disease, that shuts down most of the brain and most of the organs and retains just the minimum amount necessary to accomplish a primal need—that of feeding—then you can at least construct a theory. No, it won't hold up to the closest scrutiny, not in science as we know it today; but look at prions. Give a prion to a doctor in the 1960s and he'd be just baffled." But, she adds, "The human body is remarkably adaptive, which is both a good thing and a potentially bad thing."

The Zombie Factor

According to neurologist Peter Lukacs, "There are twelve cranial nerves that control certain functions, and some share functions. The optic nerve controls vision, but the abducent, trochlear, and oculomotor nerves control different aspects of eye movement. The trigeminal nerve controls mastication and the vagus nerve controls swallowing. The cranial accessory also contributes to the swallowing and talking functions. The vestibulocochlear nerve controls balance and hearing. We know zombies can walk, however awkwardly, and they can hear. You also have the olfactory nerve that controls the sense of smell, and a number of movies and books suggest that zombies can smell unspoiled living flesh. The cranial nerves (with the exception of the olfactory and optic) originate in the brainstem, which includes the midbrain, the pons, and the medulla oblongata."

So we're still back to headshots?

"Put a bullet through the brainstem and you switch off your zombie," Lukacs insists. "The same holds for a sword or axe cut, or sufficient blunt force trauma. However, if you inflict minor damage to the brainstem you may remove some of the zombie's functions—he might be unable to bite or unable to maintain balance. The bottom line here is that the real "off buttons" for a zombie are the brain stem and the motor cortex. Those, I think, would be interesting areas to explore in stories: zombies who have limited functions even for them. A zombie who can't eat, a blind zombie . . . the story possibilities are endless, and they could be funny or tragic."

Just the Facts

Emergency Care

When the zombie is brought to the hospital he is not going to be an immediate threat to anyone. Having been forcibly subdued by police, he will be examined by EMTs. The handcuffs and biting mask will eliminate any risk there, but when the EMT takes the suspect's vitals a lot of people are going to get a real shock to their system.

Almost no heartbeat. Minimal blood pressure. Reduced body temperature. Possible signs of rigor mortis. And evidence of at least one wound where the security guard shot him.

Samples of blood would be taken while the victim is still in the E.R., and as the disease began to take hold and the staff saw how fast the patient was succumbing, a rush request would be put on those tests. Specialists would be called, and at the very least, the patient would be put in limited or total quarantine. Once the outbreak had taken hold to epidemic proportions, the CDC (Centers for Disease Control and Prevention) professionals would be contacted and quarantines issued, probably to the point of including all hospital staff as well as patients.

The suspect would be brought to the hospital in restraints and would be secured firmly to the motal rails of the bed. Since the suspect would continue to try to bite anyone who came near, the bite mask would be kept on, and at need a more potent "Hannibal Lecter" style mask could be obtained. Even in the world of the living there have been enough cases of dangerous biters so that protocols are already in place and would be followed to the letter.

So what would happen when the zombie was brought into the hospital?

Expert Witness

G. Harris Grantham, a retired hospital administrator from Oakland, California, was very clear on how things would be handled. "The first thing we focus on is the safety of our staff. That's paramount. The patient's safety comes second, always. The reason is basic common sense: if the staff is being injured or are at risk, they either can't or won't provide any care. They are not paid to be injured."

According to Dr. Lukacs, "From my own experience (with violent or disruptive patients), there is usually a male nurse or male orderly (unusually strong from rolling and lifting heavy patients every day) that can be initially called to help out. The female nurses are also pretty tough (they have to be to do this job). If that is insufficient for an extremely violent patient, security will be called in (they are usually only called when a patient has a weapon or is considered a physical threat to himself or others). The worst-case scenario would be that a 'mob' of staff members would pile on top of the guy and subdue and restrain the guy. Plus they would try to sedate him with some tranquilizers (good luck in finding a viable vein in a pulseless zombie), which of course would have no effect. It only takes a good bear hug from behind to pin down someone's arms to their sides, zombie or living. Just stay away from the potential biting."

One potential complication is that it's going to take hospital staff a very long time before they think "zombie," especially at the very beginning of an outbreak. On the upside, hospital staff are quite used to dealing with violent patients. They would not, as has been shown in some books and films, attack the patient if, for example, he started to bite. "The medical staff is there to try and save lives. It would never cross their minds to physically hurt someone on purpose for *any* reason," insists Dr. Lukacs. "They would try their damndest to try and save this poor soul (do zombies even have souls?) at any cost. They would never consider injuring a patient just because he's being violent. If that were the case, how many hyperactive patients from cocaine would make it to the hospital? Ever see *Scarface*? When Al Pacino is doped out of his mind on coke and gets riddled with bullets but still won't go down? It's a fairly realistic scenario to a certain point . . . these people don't feel pain and think they are indestructible. Ask any police officer who has tried to subdue an unarmed violent crackhead. That's what hospital staff would think they're dealing with, and they would call in as many staff members as possible to restrain the person."

Once the patient is secured and restrained to the bed, the next step is evaluation. "If the patient was presenting with the symptoms you've described," says Grantham, "unusually low BP, low body temp, low pulse, etc.—then we'd kick into high gear. Anomalous symptoms of that level of severity are going to suggest a disease of some virulence. Once the staff had collected samples—blood, EKG, EEG, x-rays, etc—and these were in the lab we'd call in consults with specialists in each field, and we'd probably get someone from infectious disease there stat. The patient would be immediately quarantined and specialists would be called in, and at some point we'd be talking to the CDC."

And what about the bitten guard?

"We would want to take a look at anyone who had come in contact with this person, and certainly someone with whom there had been a body fluid exchange."

Dr. Chandra Singh, a surgical resident at the Salvator Mundi International Hospital in Rome. adds, "If the patient presented with gunshot wounds, then he would be rushed into surgery. Our surgical staff would take note of the atypical vitals and would call in specialists. It may be that the low vitals would be interpreted as a form of shock, in which case the staff would take steps to stabilize him, and if the placement of the bullet wounds was not life-threatening, surgery might be postponed at that point. If, on the other hand, the bullet was in the torso and damage to an organ was feared, then we would cut. And that, I'm afraid, having seen too many Lucio Fulci films, might literally be 'opening a can of worms.' "

And what about the security guard in our scenario? He's typical of the early victims in a lot of zombie stories: an unconscious and unresponsive patient brought to a hospital after being bitten by an unknown assailant. The victim presents with a rapidly spreading infection and lapses into a coma, demonstrating severe respiratory difficulty.

We know, having seen these films, that the victim is going to die and then reanimate as a zombie: and in these films the hospital is likely to become a slaughterhouse. But would that really be the way things played out?

The Zombie Factor

"You have to understand," says Harris Grantham, "that no one at any point would be thinking 'oh, this is a zombie' or 'this is supernatural.' Even with the most bizarre and extreme symptoms we would all be reacting as if this is a standard medical crisis. Certainly it would have its unique and disturbing features, but everyone—and I mean *everyone*—would be treating this incident as if it were a disease, which is certainly what it would have to be."

"New diseases and mutations of known diseases are regularly discovered," says Dr. Natalie Mtumbo of the Word Health Organiza-

Art of the Dead – Kelly Everaert

City of the Dead

"Vampires being the previous number one monster have become a kind of boring pompous nonmonster in the last few years, whereas zombies on the other hand are the downtrodden of the monster kingdom. They're the average walking stiff, just trying to get by."

tion. "I think it would be fair to say that even with all of the stress and pressure on the doctors and staff to try and understand this disease and determine a strategy for treatment there would be some doctors who would be viewing this as a ticket to a Fellowship, a grant, or maybe the Nobel Prize. This would be history in the making, and everyone in that surgical theater would know that."

Grantham agrees wholeheartedly. "That's not really as cynical a view as it sounds; not when you realize how much research depends on both grants and notoriety. If something big comes along it can draw in enough money to not only support the research but to stabilize the financial well-being of the entire hospital. Nobody comes out a loser in that scenario."

Dr. Mtumbo adds, "Every single person exposed to the infected patient would be quarantined, and that includes the police, the witness, the tracker dogs—everyone. This would be too dangerous to allow for the slightest slip. We've *seen* what happens when a disease is not taken seriously. Visit Africa, look at the millions with AIDS and the firestorm that is tuberculosis. We've all made mistakes—doctors, health organizations, governments—and we have damn well learned from them. Never in history has the world's medical professionals been so united in their stand against the spread of infectious diseases. And, yes, terrorism factors into that; this is the 21st century, so of course it does. So, what I'm saying here is that if a zombie plague happened then anyone who is even remotely suspected of being infected would be rounded up, isolated and studied. Very deeply studied. I doubt they would be going around biting people and spreading the disease."

I asked my experts to speculate on how this scenario would play out if the disease spread as quickly as it does in *28 Days Later* and the remake of *Dawn of the Dead*.

Grantham was adamant. "Not going to happen. I could buy a reduced metabolic rate and some organ shutdown, which means I could *almost* buy the *Night of the Living Dead* zombies with some medical exceptions. At a stretch I could make a case for it; but the other plague doesn't follow pathogenic spread patterns. It isn't logical enough even to compete with the plague scenarios in the George Romero zombie movies.

"I never saw the American zombie films," says Mtumbo, "but I did see *28 Days Later* in London, and I saw *28 Weeks Later* in Cape Town, South Africa. Though they were very frightening films, there were too many things in there that did not fit with what we know of science. In Cape Town, during my first year of residency, I went with some of my mates to a cinema that was showing *Shaun of the Dead*, which my friends said was very similar in many ways to the American zombie films. The dead in that were slower and it was clear that the infection required several hours to spread through the body before a person became a monster. Though I can still poke holes through that, it—at least—obeys some of the rules of disease pathology."

This does bring up a new and potentially disastrous wrinkle. If the plague does not spread as quickly as it does in the more recent films, then there is actually a greater chance of it spreading farther before it's detected. Dr. Lukacs explains, "I have to disagree that the outbreak would be contained within hospital walls. Every disease has an incubation period where the patient is asymptomatic. Even the common cold takes 2–3 days before making someone sick. For every patient admitted, there would be several infected patients still at large. And in this modern day, people can travel to just about any part of the globe within 24 hours."

Grantham reluctantly agrees with this view. "I guess it depends on where you stand in terms of the zombie scenario. If we discount the ultra-fast spread of the disease as impossible, there are a couple of ways this could go. If the guard was brought into the hospital in a coma, *and* if the patient zero zombie was caught, then we might have nipped this in the bud. But the math gets complicated here, because if the zombie remains at large and continues to bite people, and if any of those people survive the bites and are not so severely injured that they fall into a coma, then they will be the most dangerous plague vectors. They might go to the hospital, receive treatment for the bite, and be released. The plague would be working inside of them, and if alarming symptoms don't present quickly then they could potentially infect others. A kiss would probably do it, as would sexual contact. Possibly preparing foods, depending on the nature of the infection. If more than one person was similarly bitten then we could see a frightening pattern emerging. Not an aggressive attack like in *28 Days Later,* but a more quiet and insidious attack, like we saw with the spread of HIV."

And if the zombie was caught?

"Once we had the zombie at the hospital, or in the morgue, that's when useful alarm bells would ring. The physical examination and lab tests would show that we were dealing with a very dangerous and probably unknown disease. Having tried to bite the arresting police and hospital staff, and having already bitten a security guard, someone would be making the connection between bite and infection. The CDC would definitely be on speed-dial by this point, and we would use police and the media, as well as database searches of patients presenting to emergency rooms complaining of being bitten."

Would that be enough?

Dr. Mtumbo is less optimistic on that point. "Well, there is a risk of a much greater spread. Not everyone listens to TV news or reads the paper, and many would miss the public service announcements. Not everyone would go to a hospital; and some who had been in for treatment and then went home might be unreachable. They could be going on a vacation or a business trip. They could go to bed and lapse into a coma; and if they died early enough in the night and reanimated early the next day they could attack their families, neighbors, or other people."

"If we miss that early patient," Grantham says, "then there would be a bigger spread of the disease and a greater potential for infection. But I'm still optimistic about our chances of getting ahead of the spread."

Investigation of the source would be a top priority, he says. "One of the things I personally would want to know was where this initial patient came from and how and where he contracted the disease that was now in my hospital. If there was a disease of that level of virulence I would leave no stone unturned to find out. The fact that the man was brought in following an attack outside a medical facility would tell me a lot, and our own infectious disease investigators would be shoulder to shoulder with our lawyers as we tracked down who owned that facility and what the hell they were testing there. We'd call in Homeland Security and maybe FEMA. In short we would raise holy hell to find out what the hell they were testing out there that caused something like this. And if there was even the slightest whiff of cover-up we'd file ten kinds of suits against them and sue them back to the stone age . . . and the Fed would have our back, too, providing they hadn't already kicked down the door. Something like this smells like bioterrorism if you sniff it the right way, and I can just imagine how much OHS[3]

3. Office of Homeland Security.

would want to put something big in their 'win' column. Global pandemic? Not on my watch, and not on the watch of anyone at OHS who wanted to stay employed. Wrath of God would be nothing compared to what would hit that research center, believe me."

Just the Facts

Mad Zombie Disease

So . . . what then could both destroy higher brain functions while at the same time keeping the central nervous system and some minimal organ functions operating? Ah . . . now that is the question.

Most of the zombie stories talk about a virus or bacteria. In Max Brooks's *Zombie Survival Guide* and *World War Z* it's *Solenum*; in *Resident Evil* it's the T-Virus; and according to Sean Michael Ragan, a biochemist from the University of Texas at Austin, it's "the Romero-Fulci Disese."[4]

Many of my experts came to the same conclusion, that prions would be a likely culprit in this kind of crisis.

Prions are very nasty little pathogens believed to be the driving force behind a variety of neurodegenerative diseases called transmissible spongiform encephalopathies (TSEs). They're proteinaceous infectious microscopic particles, meaning that they are proteins similar in some ways to a virus, but prions have no nucleic acid. These diseases slowly attack brain tissue, often leaving spongelike holes (hence *spongiform*).

Mad cow disease (*bovine spongiform encephalopathy*) or BSE, is a prion disease affecting cattle. In 1986 an outbreak of BSE was diagnosed in England during which some 178,000 cows were believed to have been infected from a protein feed supplement that contained rendered remains of scrapie-infected sheep brains. Scrapie is a prion disease that affects sheep.

Prion diseases in humans can cause (among other things) loss of balance, disrupted coordination, blindness, dementia, sleep disor-

4. From an admittedly fictional paper, *Etiology of Romero-Fulci Disease: The Case for Prions*, published in the fake-but-should-be-real *Journal of Zumbie Science*, 2005, 1519–1523.

ders, among other symptoms. All known prion diseases are invariably fatal.

The theory of disease-causing protein particles was established in 1982 by Stanley Prusiner, a neurologist at the University of California at San Francisco, who coined the term *prion*,[5] and who went on to win the 1997 Nobel Prize in Physiology and Medicine for his discoveries.

There are three forms of TSEs affecting humans: sporadic, familial, and iatrogenic.

1. Sporadic cases strike about one person per million; the cause is unknown, and no treatment for it exists. At the moment these account for close to 85 percent of all TSE cases.
2. Familial cases, which account for 10 percent of TSEs, are passed down through bloodlines in ways not yet understood since inherited traits are genetic and prions have no DNA. There's even a version called fatal familial insomnia (FFI), an ultrarare disease found in only a couple of dozen bloodlines worldwide, and in which the victim cannot ever fall asleep, not even when medicated. The victim becomes delusional and erratic, and lingers in a living hell of unending wakefulness until, months later, exhaustion and brain damage causes death.
3. The remaining 5 percent are *iatrogenic* cases, which result from the accidental transmission of the causative agent via contaminated surgical equipment or as a result of cornea or dura mater transplants or the administration of human-derived pituitary growth hormones.[6]

The body's immune system does not react to prion diseases the way it does to other diseases. The immune system doesn't kick in and the disease spreads rapidly. Once it takes hold, there is no treatment.

And killing a prion is incredibly difficult. In labs, where growth

5. *Prion* rhymes with *aeon*.
6. Courtesy of the World Health Organization.

Art of the Dead – Chad Michael Ward

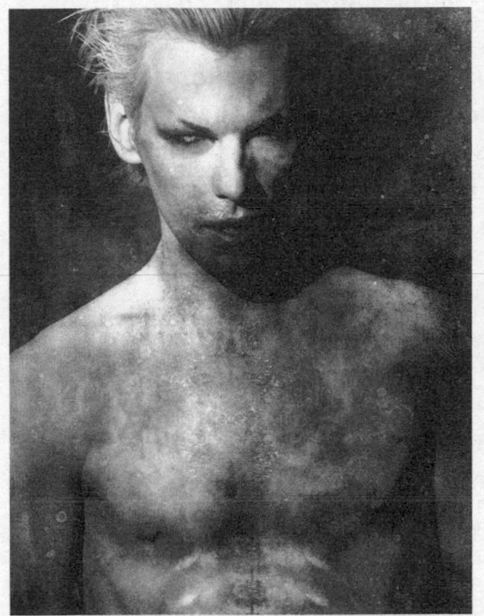

Rate of Infection

"I think zombie culture speaks to people on a primeval level and people can't help but be drawn to it. Most zombie tales tend to be end of the world fables and that's something that's permeated our culure forever. I've always loved the slow, shuffling zombie—very apocalyptic, but the new fast versions cropping up in recent movies bring the fear to a whole new level. In the end, I think I'd have to go with fast."

Prions and Cannibalism

One prion disease, *kuru*, found in the South Pacific, has a frightening link to eating human flesh. Among one tribe in the eastern highlands of Papua New Guinea it was the custom to show respect for deceased family members by eating them. Unfortunately this transmitted the disease from the organs and flesh of the dead to their living—but doomed—relatives. This practice has since been stopped and no further infections have occurred.

hormones are cultivated from extracted pituitary glands, solvents of various kinds are used to purify the tissue; these solvents kill everything . . . except prions. Even formaldehyde won't kill them. Radiation treatment and bombardment with ultraviolet light doesn't kill them. Scientists have tried just about everything, including treating diseased brain tissues with all manner of chemicals including industrial detergent—and the prions endure. They don't even die with the host organism. Bury a corpse with a prion disease and dig up the bones a century later . . . and the prions are still there. They are, after all, just proteins.

One of the many prion-related areas that has not yet been fully explored is the effect of radiation on prions. If it turns out that radiation in one of its many forms can mutate this disease, then we might be back with Romero's space probe from *Night of the Living Dead*. So far, luckily, no evidence supports this.

Prion diseases in animals include:

- *Bovine spongiform encephalopathy* (BSE) in cattle (mad cow disease)
- *Chronic wasting disease* (CWD) in elk, moose, wapati, and mule deer
- *Exotic ungulate encephalopathy* (EUE) in nyala, oryx, and greater kudu
- *Feline spongiform encephalopathy* in cats
- *Scrapie* in sheep
- *Transmissible mink encephalopathy* (TME) in mink

Prion diseases in humans include:

- *Alpers syndrome*, an autosomal recessive, mitochondrial DNA depletion disorder
- *Creutzfeldt-Jakob disease* (CJD) and its varieties:
  - *Iatrogenic Creutzfeldt-Jakob disease* (iCJD)
  - *Variant Creutzfeldt-Jakob disease* (vCJD)
  - *Familial Creutzfeldt-Jakob disease* (fCJD)
  - *Sporadic Creutzfeldt-Jakob disease* (sCJD) is the most common prion disease in humans
- *Fatal familial insomnia* (fFI) is an autosomal dominant inherited disease
- *Sporadic fatal insomnia* (sFI) a noninherited type of fatal insomnia
- *Gerstmann-Sträussler-Scheinker syndrome* (GSS) is associated with autosomal dominant inheritance
- *Kuru*—the word *kuru* means "trembling with fear" in the language of the Fore people, trembling is a symptom of dying brain tissue

Expert Witness

Dr. B. Burt Gerstman, an epidemiologist from San Jose State University, remarks, "Prions represent unknowns . . . and people fear unknowns. Prions are strange creatures—they have no DNA but are capable of replication (not reproduction). We still know very little about prion transmission and pathogenesis. We do know they are resistant to routine disinfection and can withstand harsh environmental conditions. I believe they can even survive autoclaving, which is sort of the standard for aseptic technique. These are strange creatures . . . no DNA yet capable of self-replication under circumstances which we understand relatively little about."

According to Dr. Pawel P. Liberski[7] of the Department of Molec-

7. Dr. Liberski is also the author of *The Enigma of Slow Viruses: Facts and Artifacts* (Springer-Verlag Telos, 1993) and *Light and Electron Microscopic Neuropathology of Slow Virus Disorders* (CRC-Press, 1993)

ular Pathology and Neuropathology at the Medical University of Lodz, Poland, "Prions do not have DNA. According to the prion hypothesis, a prion is a protein (our own) encoded by a cellular gene. In normal situations—you and me for instance—our prion gene (PRNP) encodes for a normal protein called PrPc (from a cellular isoform[8] of prion protein). In abnormal situations, this PrPc changes the shape (technically speaking it is *misfolded*) into 'scrapie' isoform (PrPSc). In people with mutations within the PRNP gene this misfolding occurs spontaneously. If you eat the brain (as in cases of *kuru*) or you get injected (as in Creutzfeldt-Jakob disease after human growth hormone), the abnormal protein (PrPSc) acts on a normal protein and the normal one is transformed into abnormal protein. It's a domino effect. How the disease, as in the case of Mad Cow Disease, mutated in humans into variant Creutzfeldt-Jakob Disease (vCJD) nobody really knows. Perhaps passage through an organism (human) different from the original host (cow) somehow change it."

Dr. Bruno Vincent of the *L'Institut de Pharmacologie Moléculaire et Cellulaire*[9] tells us: "Prions are strongly supposed to be exclusively composed of one protein named PrPsc (for PrP scrapie) that is an abnormal form of the cellular prion protein (PrPc) which is produced physiologically by mammals and non-mammals—and even yeast and fungi."

Dr. Vincent adds, "Numerous mutations (that occur randomly) associated with this gene have been reported that lead to the development of spontaneous prion diseases. They confer to the mutated prion protein the ability to form aggregates more efficiently and more rapidly by complex molecular mechanisms. These mutations are rare and account for the so-called inherited prion diseases (genetic forms that are transmitted from parents to children) which represent less than 5 percents of prion pathologies. The remaining cases are either infectious (ingestion of bovine infected meat or

8. An isoform is a protein that has the same basic function as another protein but which has been encoded by a different gene and may, therefore, exhibit differences in its sequence.

9. Part of the Centre National de la Recherche Scientifique/Universite Nice Sophia-Antipolis in Valbonne, France.

Scrapie

Scrapie is a painful and fatal prion disease that attacks the nervous system of goats and sheep. This transmissible spongiform encephalopathy (TSE) is similar to mad cow disease and other related maladies. Scrapie was first recorded in 1732 but to date has not been known to be transmissible to humans.

This TSE disease gets its name from one of its symptoms: Infected animals will frequently rub or "scrape" against fences, rocks, or trees to alleviate an unbearable itch. Other scrapie symptoms include erratic gaits, compulsive lip-smacking, and convulsions.

Scrapies, which has been recorded in England and North America, is incurable, and the only "treatment" is to destroy and cremate the infected animals.

cannibalism) or sporadic (that account for 90 percents of prion diseases and for which the cause of PrPc/PrPsc conversion is unknown). The notion of 'strains' (several infected brain tissues display distinct incubation times and pattern of neuropathology when injected to mice) is even more puzzling if we referred to the 'protein only' hypothesis. This is not due to PrP mutations and is currently under intense investigation in numerous laboratories."

I asked Dr. Bruno to speculate on whether a prion disease of this kind could be combated. "Numerous pharmacological agents have been shown to slow down or reverse PrPc/PrPsc conversion. Most of these compounds display anti-aggregate properties and prevent the beta-sheet structure of PrPsc. However, the most promising therapeutic against these pathologies is undoubtedly vaccination. Considerable progress has been made in this direction, and, optimistically, a vaccine against prion diseases should be available in the forthcoming fifteen years. Another strategy that could prove useful is to target the cellular prion protein (PrPc) with either PrP RNA antigens or small double-stranded RNA (also called RNAi). In either case, the normal protein is extinguished and the abnormal

PrPsc form can no longer replicate because of the lack of the 'matrix.' "

I asked Dr. Gerstman to help us understand what a "plague" is: "The term *plague* is used in various ways. There is a specific zoonitic disease called plague—the disease that wiped out half of some European populations in the Dark Ages. With this said, I think 'plague' is also used loosely to refer to an epidemic that incites fear." He goes on to discuss the popular view of what an epidemic is. "This depends on the nature of the epidemic. The term *epidemic* is general. An 'HIV epidemic' is quite different than an 'epidemic of teen pregnancies.' However there are many highly contagious diseases. When environmental conditions are right, just about any contagious disease can spread rapidly."

If it spreads too fast, it's an epidemic; if it crosses national lines, it becomes a pandemic.

The Zombie Factor

If zombies could come about as a result of a prion disease, how could the disease be stopped? I put this question to my experts.

Dr. Liberski says, "There is no treatment. Certain drugs can interfere with the conversion of normal into abnormal protein, but they are not very efficient. But if you stop the conversion, perhaps the disease can be cured. The goal has not been achieved, however."

Dr. Vincent, however, says that there are some advances in "nonzombie" prion diseases. He explains, "The recently described human variant of Creutzfeldt-Jakob disease due to the ingestion of contaminated bovine meat as well as the now eradicated Kuru disease which emerged some decades ago in the Fore linguistic group of the eastern highlands in Papua New Guinea and was due to ritualistic cannibalism are the proofs of such a possibility. Thus, the oral route is one way to inoculate humans with prions. Injection in blood is another way to acquire prion diseases since some people contracted Creutzfeldt-Jakob disease following intravenous injections of contaminated growth hormone prepared from bovine hypothalamus. However, we must take into account that both routes in those cases carry small amounts of infectious prions that lead to disease after a long period of time."

Both doctors maintain that a cure or treatment is not certain and carries with it some considerable risks.

I asked if humans could be inoculated in some way against transmissible prion diseases, but Dr. Liberski didn't think so. "You must remember, however, that prion is a misfolded *normal* protein. A vaccine would hurt *all* forms of that protein."

Many of the zombie stories talk about an "experimental" pathogen that accidentally escapes a lab. I asked Dr. Vincent to comment on whether a prion could be modified or combined with other pathogens to form a more dangerous pathogen. "Of course it would be feasible to combine prions with other pathogens by laboratory process. However, one should keep in mind that the time-course of prion pathologies following infection could be very long (from several months to 30 years in humans). Thus, prions are far from being a short-term weapon and could at best represent a time-bomb."

In fiction we have the advantage of considering science somewhat elastic. We can speculate that a laboratory has been working on just such an advanced prion disease and our patient zero was a test subject who escaped. We can also speculate on prion research specifically designed to speed up the infection process, down from months or years to hours. That might be within the limits of possibility, but Dr. Vincent says that the superspeed infection shown in *28 Days Later* and the *Dawn of the Dead* remake are not possible. "On a scientific point of view, the immediate change observed in infected people in zombie-themed films is absolutely impossible whatever the infectious agent considered. If the contamination state (by viruses, bacteria or prion) is effective immediately, it takes time before the symptoms appear: several hours to several days for the most virulent pathogens."

This lends strong support to Romero's original vision of a death through infection that lasts several hours.

Just the Facts

Dead Stasis

Our neurologists insist that some part of the zombie's brain has to be functioning, even at a reduced level, for it to do what a zombie does. The motor functions have to be working, as well as some cognitive ability—after all, the little zombie girl in *Night of the Living Dead* uses a garden trowel to kill her mother; Bub in *Day of the Dead* is taught to load a gun, he feels grief, and even speaks a line of dialogue; and Big Daddy in *Land of the Dead* is the organizer of a very effective zombie revolt. Either these are examples of recovered memories, suggesting that the brains of the zombies are not total organic junk, or they possess the ability to learn—both from their actions and through coaching. Probably both.

The bottom line is that the brain must be preserved after death for a zombie to operate. That is one point we cannot dismiss. If total cellular death occurs, you do not have the potential for a zombie, no matter how strong the virus or other initiating causes. The zombie has motor functions, therefore, some of its brain is working.

This appears to lend support to the working theory that zombies are not entirely (or even *actually*) dead. Certainly they defy all conventional definitions of *dead*. Once a human succumbs to the zombie plague, he or she is presumed to be officially dead; but it seems more likely that he or she has actually lapsed into some kind of deep coma state in which most of the body's functions have stopped but a few (such as the central nervous system) have merely gone into a kind of stasis. There is some support for this in nature.

Expert Witness

The wood frog (*lithobates sylvaticus*) is the only frog found in the Arctic Circle to freeze solid many times a year and revive unharmed. During the winter as much as 45 percent of the wood frog's body freezes; ice crystals form beneath the skin and are scattered through the frog's skeletal muscles. As this happens, the frog stops breathing, its heart stops and there is zero blood flow. By the long-held standards of clinical medicine, it is dead. Only it's not.

Weird Science: Fido of the Living Dead

There's just no way to be surprised that this news comes from Pittsburgh, but the Safar Centre for Resuscitation Research in Pittsburgh[10] has successfully reanimated dogs several hours after inducing clinical death. The experiment is intended as a step toward a proposed method of flash-freezing severely injured soldiers so they can be transported from battlefield to surgical centers and then successfully reanimated under proper medical and life-sustaining conditions.

The Safar Center has accomplished this with dogs several times and went public with the information in late 2005.

Granted this isn't the same as reanimating all the dead dogs in the pet cemetery, but when someone in Pittsburgh starts bringing back the dead, anyone in the post-Romero era is going to take notice (and possibly take flight).

"The wood frogs regularly undergo freeze-thaw cycles in the lab between 20 and a potentially infinite number of times," says Dr. Kenneth Storey, a professor of biochemistry at Carleton University in Ottawa, Canada. "In nature they go through it about twenty times a year without harm. You can't kill them with the normal temperatures; but if you froze it to the temperature of dry ice[11] you'd kill it for sure."

Can this process happen in humans? Storey, who also has the Canada Research Chair in Molecular Physiology, says, "No way. Frogs have a set of genes that we don't have that allow them to undergo this process, and while it's happening their bodies are producing huge amounts of cryoprotectant sugars. Normal levels are between about 4 and 8 mmol/L[12] (70 to 150 mg/dL), and during the freezing process the frogs' sugar level jumps to 400 mmol/L (7200 mg/dL). Humans go into a coma at 600 mg/dL. The human body

10. Part of the University of Pittsburgh.
11. -78.5 °C (-109.3 °F).
12. Millimoles per liter.

can't produce enough sugar to protect from cell and organ damage from the ice."

I asked Dr. Storey how this might apply to zombies. "I'm afraid that's not your answer. Freezing is fine for organs harvested for transplants. We use it to preserve sperm, eggs and embryos . . . but it won't make a zombie or preserve a body that has become a zombie. Granted, in the lab we can introduce the gene from the frogs into a human cell and then freeze and thaw that successfully, but that's a single cell. Try and duplicate that in a whole mammal and you destroy the mammal. Massive tissue destruction. In fact cold is used to destroy tissues, such as in the process of injecting frozen materials into tumors to destroy them, but that's the reverse of a process that will reanimate a body. Can't happen that way."

That eliminates one possible theory, but it still leaves the question of hibernation. Could the infection cause the victim's body to lapse into a hibernative coma so deep that it is virtually impossible (outside of a laboratory) to detect life? Ground squirrels appear dead when they're in hibernation . . . why not humans?

"Understand the difference between hibernation in humans and that of some other animals such as the ground squirrel," cautions Dr. Storey. "When a ground squirrel hibernates its metabolic rate drops from 100% to about 1%. When a human hibernates—say when a Swami goes into deep trance—the metabolic rate drops from 100% to only 99%. We're a long, long way from inducing hibernation significantly deeper in humans."

But the possibility still exists; and for our quest to find the scientific possibilities in the zombie this is an exciting lead. It's a stretch, sure, but don't forget that according to the physics of aerodynamics, a bumblebee *cannot* possibly fly. Science is exact, but it's not yet complete.

This process of hibernation, both natural and induced, is being actively studied. At Seattle's Fred Hutchinson Cancer Center scientists have been experimenting with hydrogen sulfide to temporarily convert lab animals from warm-blooded to cold-blooded, which is what happens during natural hibernation. It is not an *unnatural* process, and we know from our studies of all aspects of science that nature loves variation and mutation.

Hydrogen sulfide is a naturally occurring chemical in the body that buffers our metabolic flexibility. Among other things, this chemical regulates our body temperature at 98.6, regardless of whether you're in Haiti or Nome. At the Hutchinson Cancer Research Center scientists have already induced hibernation in mice. The researchers hope, among other goals, to be able to induce hibernation in patients waiting for organ transplants. The process is known as metabolic hibernation.

Military science views this as one of several possible methods of preserving soldiers injured in the field until they can be transported to proper military facilities. Researchers see it as one possible way to induce hibernation for long-distance space travel. Doctors hope that it will be a lifesaver for patients with dangerously high fevers, and oncologists are looking to this as a way of temporarily eliminating oxygen dependence in healthy cells to make them less vulnerable targets to radiation and chemotherapy.

There are even some military experiments ongoing to determine if it would be possible to totally exsanguinate[13] a wounded soldier, (see the box, "Weird Science: Fido of the Living Dead," on p. 149). There is some supporting material on this in animal testing, though the issue of cellular damage from oxygen deprivation, especially to the brain, has not yet been solved. Even so, it does contribute another splinter of plausibility to the concept of a body that has received massive trauma, has suffered blood loss, and has had a severe metabolic drop still being technically alive.

The Zombie Factor

It's even more plausible if zombies are the result of a disease that mutates the molecular physiology during the infection process and dramatically lowers the metabolism. Outside of practical science? Sure, just as induced metabolic hibernation is currently outside of practical science. Outside of possibility?

Not at all.

13. Exsanguination is the process of removing all blood from a body.

Just the Facts

Raising Hell

What on earth would make the dead rise and attack the living? What sparks the reanimation process? What drives the hunger for human flesh, or in some cases, brains? What is the driving force behind this enduring and expanding mythology of zombies?

The simple answer is that there *is* no simple answer. There are almost as many theories as there are films and books in the genre, including radiation, plague, toxic spills, demonic possession, and even wrath of God. Granted, some of these theories are so absurd and unlikely that even the most die-hard zom fan (like me) have an impossible time suspending disbelief; while other theories are chillingly close to "possible," according to modern science.

The zombie message boards and forums buzz constantly with discussions over which theory is the most valid; you hear it debated at genre conventions, book signings, or other events. So here are the leading theories on the cause of the zombie uprising, with some comments by a variety of experts.

Expert Witness

"The body is designed by evolution to have natural redundancies," explains neurologist Dr. Peter Lukacs. "Without these redundancies we'd never survive injury or illness. For example you only really need about 10% function of the liver, and about 20% function of one kidney. If certain other functions were online, and the zombie possessed the ability to seal wounds, we would have as reasonable an understanding of how they work as science allows. And it's not that far outside of science."

To answer the question on which parts of the brain are required to make a zombie undead, it depends on how "human" the zombie is. Does the zombie have a pulse and/or breathes for example?

"A basic zombie's functionability," Dr. Lukacs explains, "is that it can walk and move its limbs. For this to happen, it would need the motor cortex—this is located bilaterally (both sides of the brain) near the top part of the brain and curves to the outer curvature of the brain—to be at least minimally functioning. The right motor cortex controls the left side of the body, and vice versa. The central part of the cortex moves the legs while the arms and mouth are located on the outer curvature. Actually, I would love to see a 'stroke-like' zombie shown in a film who has had a localized blow to one side of the head who drags one side of its body. Without a functioning motor cortex, a person is completely paralyzed."

Considering the odd twitching and staggering of individual zombies in different films, it's reasonable to assume that we *have* seen stroked-out zombies.

Dr. Lukacs adds, "Now consider the cerebellum, which is located near the base of the skull (lower part in back of the head). The basic function of the cerebellum is the coordination of movement. For example, in order to reach for an item, the arm muscles need to move smoothly so as not to under- or overshoot the item. If the cerebellum is damaged, the muscles work in a jerky fashion (causing ataxia). Without a functioning cerebellum, there is movement, but it is in a very jerky fashion (much like many zombies) though it makes it very difficult to walk but not impossible."

So it would seem that a zombie needs to have at least a partially functioning brain. What else needs to be in operation?

We know from zombie movies that they moan, which means they either breathe, however minimally, or they possess the ability to draw breath as needed in order to moan. My guess, supported by science and common sense, is that they do breathe. Not well to be sure, but moaning is created by air causing the vocal chords to vibrate. Let's take that as read, then."

We can also assume that zombies have a working circulatory system. Again, we're talking minimal function, but we've seen zombies bleed in too many films to dismiss it as a possibility. Plus, science tells us in no uncertain terms that in the absence of blood and oxygen the brain will cease to function and will soon decay so that even if resuscitative steps are taken, the brain will be so much gray goop.

So, we can also take it as read that zombies do have some kind of circulatory system, however feeble. As we've already discussed, we've *seen* them bleed in plenty of movies, including Romero's; so let's attribute the inconsistencies relative to bloodless zombies as bad reportage . . . and may Romero forgive me.

If we want to stretch medical credulity (and let's face it, we are talking about zombies here), we could consider the possibility that zombies have a hyperactive wound healing capacity. Not on the scale of Wolverine from the X-Men, who regenerates back to complete health, but more on the lines of car tires when they're filled with a can of sealant. Wounds do seal, as we know, otherwise we'd bleed out from a paper cut. Proteins called fibrins and high-molecular-weight glycoprotein containing fibronectins bond together to form a plug that traps proteins and particles and prevents further blood loss; and this plug establishes a structural support to seal the wound until collagen is deposited. Then some "migratory cells" use this plug to stretch across the wound, during which platelets stick to this seal until it's replaced with granulation tissue and then later with collagen.

So, if this process were stimulated by the same force that has reactivated the motor cortex (and other functions), and if it worked at a high-enough rev, then the zombie might be able to form seals around wounds to prevent total blood loss. If this process happened abnormally fast, then the zombie could even keep from bleeding out if shot, stabbed, or had a limb cut off. Mind you, this process would have to work at an incredibly accelerated rate, so the mutation would have to be elaborate and very complex.

And yet zombies can be killed. We know that from nearly all the stories: A bullet in the brain or severe cranial trauma seems to punch their ticket. I asked Dr. Lukacs to comment on this.

"For a zombie to breathe and have a beating heart," Dr. Lukacs observes, "it will need to have a functioning medulla oblongata and pons. This is part of the brain stem and is located in front of the cerebellum. Destroying this alone would be difficult by trauma since it is in a relatively small area near the cerebellum. A forceful blow between the back of the head and the nape of the neck should damage the cerebellum and the brain stem; which could kill a person (but not necessarily a zombie) since it would damage the respiratory and cardiac centers of the brain stem. So the simple answer of what part of the brain to destroy to stop a zombie would be to destroy the motor cortex, located on the top of the head."

So, not just any shot to the head?

"No way," Lukacs assures us. "Zombie destruction would

require a lot of accuracy. If I were to train soldiers on where to shoot a zombie in the head with a weapon that had a very localized effect (say doing damage in only the size of a quarter or nickel to a part of the brain or something like an arrow), I would advise them to shoot for the motor cortex region of the head: the top of the head, slightly below the 'pointy' part of the head. Another spot that would bring down a zombie would be to sever the spinal cord: all the connections from the brain go through the spinal cord to the lower body (arms, trunk, legs) so damaging that would paralyze everything below the part damaged. If the upper neck portion is damaged, the zombie would become a quadriplegic, versus the lower back causing a paraplegic zombie. Severing the spine will bring a zombie down but it will still have upper brain functions (if there is such a thing in zombies) meaning it can still bite people and move its head about (and have a beating heart and be able to breathe if it could before). So . . . though it requires more accuracy it's still pretty much a headshot that will bring down a zombie and 'kill' it, while spinal damage will paralyze it but not kill it."

"There are many reports of gun shot wounds to the head where the patient survived. The most impressive of these are some attempted suicides done with a firearm at point blank range. Though these cases were not fatal, the injury undoubtedly caused brain damage on some level. So, if a point blank head shot to a healthy human brain doesn't ensure death, why should it in a zombie brain with fewer working brain tissue?"

The Zombie Factor

So, the headshot theory holds water, but it requires more refinement. But in later chapters we'll also learn that a lot of other types of shots will do the trick, because killing a zombie may, at times, be far less important than merely stopping one.

Just the Facts

Radioactive Zombies Ate My Brain

In *Night of the Living Dead*, it is suggested that radiation from a returning Venus space probe may have reactivated the central nerv-

Art of the Dead – Scott Cramton

"*28 Days Later* turned the entire zombie genre on its ear. It was the end of the world, but it was brutal and fast. It was something that we really wouldn't be able to fight and THAT was scary."

Ghouls

ous system including (to a very limited degree) the brain. However, Romero never comes right out and says that this is the actual cause and instead drops hints through snatches of TV interviews and news stories.

Can radiation raise the dead?

I put the question to Dr. Eric Gressen, Assistant Professor of Radiation Oncology at Jefferson Medical College.[14] He answered, "Radiation therapy causes free radical formation that destroys DNA by slowing the repair of cancerous and normal tissue and upsetting the duplicating process. The more oxygenated the tissue the more free radicals and the more damage/irradiation effect. Dead brain tissue is lacking oxygen and hence radiation therapy will have little to no effect. Also, the more actively the tissue is growing, the quicker the effect, as the tissue regenerating process is faster and the damage to the DNA is more evident early on. Hence hair loss/skin changes are seen much sooner than in slow growing tissue that exists in the nervous system!

"Now if we give too high a dose when we irradiate the whole brain, what typically can happen is, over time, the myelin that coats the brain can break down, messing up our cross-circuitry, and we can get brain damage from as little as mild memory loss to overt dysfunction. Radiation therapy does not assist in the transmission process of information in the brain but actually ruins it by messing with the myelin and such The repair mechanisms for all DNA damage can be rather complex, but you can imagine that if we are dealing with dead tissue, the brain without oxygen is already decayed and irradiation is not going to liven things up. If anything, over time, the brain typically goes dead from lack of oxygen, hence the term brain dead from oxygen deprivation after heart attack, stroke, etc. Radiation therapy can also alter the blood vessels in the brain, assisting in stroke formation. None of the above regenerates the nervous system.

"Now I mention the chronic problems first because they are most significant to the patient. Acutely during the radiation treatment, you can get swelling of the brain. Since this is in an enclosed cranium, pressure in the brain can cause a whole array of symp-

14. Thomas Jefferson University Hospital, Philadelphia.

toms, headaches, nausea, and vomiting, etc., which are typically controlled with steroids. Squeezing the brain is not likely to wake someone up. The nervous system is a late-responding tissue and hence any effect irradiation can have on this system is going to take months to years—not immediately—so *'It's alive, it's alive'* will not occur."

The Zombie Factor

The foregoing should, I think, effectively bury the concept of radiation from a returning space probe. To be fair to Mr. Romero, he never actually *said* that this was the cause of the dead returning to life. Talking heads on TV screens in the movie speculated as to whether it could be the reason.

Just the Facts

Pathology of the Dead

Pathology (literally, "the study of disease") is the diagnosis and study of diseases through examination of bodily fluids, cells, organs, and tissues. There are two primary fields within pathology: a medical specialty in which fluids and tissues are used to obtain useful information for clinical use, or forensics; and the study of the entire disease process.

Forensic pathology is that branch of science built around the need to determine the cause of death in criminal and civil law cases. Forensic pathologists are medical doctors whose specialty is usually anatomical pathology. Many of these are board certified by the American Board of Pathology. Forensic pathologists perform autopsies to determine cause of death. Sometimes this is going to be pretty simple (guy with a knife stuck in his heart), sometimes it's complicated (guy with a knife in his heart who had taken lots of poison), and sometimes it goes into the realm of diseases, which includes infections.

Pathologists also examine wounds of all kinds, including bites. They examine tissue samples to determine the age of the wound, the presence of infectious agents, and a variety of other tests in order

Art of the Dead — Lisa Gressen

Got Brains?

"*Shaun of the Dead* appeals to my inner wiseacre. It's a brilliant parody that's very witty and hysterically funny. Not surprisingly, *Re-Animator* is another favorite. It's a darker spoof of horror films than Pegg and Wright's but still a worthy cult classic."

to create a clear picture of what caused the injury. And of course they look for the presence of drugs, toxins, chemicals, and poisons.

Naturally the pathologist works closely with the medical examiner or coroner to contribute evidence to ongoing investigations, or for court cases.

Expert Witness

"There are a couple of things to know about this subject," remarks Dr. Herschel Goldman, a consulting pathologist and expert witness. "First, if you've been in pathology for any length of time you've seen just about everything. Early in my career, I worked for nine years at the University of New Mexico hospital, and we had several plague victims come through our department. They tell you about that in medical school, but until you actually have a plague victim on your table there's a part of you that just doesn't believe it. Since then, I've worked in the States and abroad and I've seen more disease victims than you can imagine. To me this is old hat nowadays. This is thirty years in now, and I don't know how many postmortems I've done. Thousands upon thousands. I'm beyond being shocked anymore."

I asked him how jaded a pathologist would get after a while.

"It's not that you get jaded *per se.*" he says. "It's more that you become used to these extremes because there are six billion people in the world and *everyone* will die at some point. It's a perspective check when you stop and realize that everyone who has ever lived since history began has either already died or will at some point die. At first the thought is morbid, but after a while it's oddly calming because you realize just how much a part of life death is. It's a wondrous and endless cycle."

How does that view withstand global pandemics?

"That's hard, just like it's hard to see so many people die in the rush of a tsunami or a hurricane. We view discase on that scale as, yes, part of the natural world, but at the same time we've become somewhat armed against them. Just as we'll build stronger levees in the hopes of withstanding the growing strength of tropical storms we're also building stronger medicines and better processes for epidemic prevention."

The Zombie Factor

I asked Dr. Goldman how a pathologist would react to a zombie plague.

"Call me gruesome, but I'd love to take a shot at it. Discovering a new disease would be a nice thing to retire on. Of course, ideally I'd like to discover a new disease that can be prevented or treated. With plagues you often have victims before you have an idea of the pathogen, and in your zombie concept that's what we'd have. We'd have the zombie, whether he's still thrashing around in restraints or lying there with a couple of police bullets in his cranium, we'd still have a prime specimen. And if the infection from the bites is as virulent as you say it is in the movies, then we'd have the security guard, too. Two subjects presenting with two different aspects or phases of a new disease."

In the movies the doctors are often bitten or are too scared to work with the infected.

"I would doubt that these movies are written by medical doctors, my friend. I don't know a pathologist worth his salt who would back away from that. This would be the kind of thing we got into science for. The chance to learn something new, to add to the body of knowledge, to make a significant impact on medical history . . . that's why we went to med school in the first place. We all had dreams of being scientific pioneers, but the reality is that most of what we do is routine. Crucial, to be sure, but it is routine.

"Now you ask if we would be so shocked that we'd become zombie food? That's not an outcome I can ever see happening. Understand, every pathologist, coroner or medical examiner I've ever met has had weird experiences, or knows someone who has. Corpses turn out not to be dead. You unzip a body bag and there's your next door neighbor. Corpses are wheeled in with erections or big grins on their faces. You see it all after a while."

So, no panic?

"No way. If a body started moving I'd be making a lot of calls right away. I'd have staff flooding the place; and, God forbid, if the corpse tried to bite me, I'd probably flee the room and lock the door, then call security. Remember, by the time we start conducting a post mortem the body has probably been wrapped in plastic and stored in a cold room for hours if not days. That means that even if we are talking a reanimated corpse it will be a very cold, very stiff, and very *slow* reanimated corpse. I'm over sixty but I play golf and tennis and I swim. If I can't outrun a half-frozen zombie then I'm not trying."

What about the psychological effects?

"Sure, there would be some, especially as we began to explore the pathology and realized that we had, in fact, an actual zombie. Views would change, nerves would be affected. That's what therapists are for. But the big picture is that rather than be terrified of this we'd all be excited by it. It would be seen as an opportunity for a massive leap in medical knowledge. Everyone would want to book time to be in that autopsy suite. You'd have doctors flying in from every country on earth."

What about a global epidemic?

"Most of the best doctors today, the young lions of pathology, got into it because of pandemics like AIDS. You think there's a pathologist alive who doesn't hope that someday they're going to perform a necropsy and find something, some clue, some new direction that will lead to answers or to a cure? We study the diseases of the body with the hope, open or secret, of making a real difference. In forensic pathology mostly what we do is help prosecutors convict criminals. Very worthy, very important, but that doesn't change the world. If a zombie plague existed, the best—the absolute *best*—in the field would be aching to take a shot at the case. Depend upon it."

Just the Facts

The Coroner's Office

Not all bodies are autopsied, but virtually all bodies associated with violent crime are. A postmortem examination performed on a body associated with a crime (or suspected crime) is known as a forensic autopsy. If a body is presented with an uncertain cause of death, an autopsy becomes even more crucial, and the surgical exploration, the examination of the organs and tissues, and the tests performed on blood and other bodily fluids often reveal what might otherwise go unnoticed.

Eternal Lust

Zombie Love by Lisa Anne Riley

A number of zombie stories have strayed from ghouls and humans fighting to the death themes into the realm of ghouls and humans exploring a whole new (and incredibly twisted) slant on necrophilia. Ranging from movies like director Michele Soavi's *Cemetery Man* (1996) (a.k.a *Dellamorte Dellamore*) in which hero Francesco Dellamorte (played by Rupert Everett) has a torrid affair with a gorgeous zombie (played without a sign of decay by Italian supermodel Anna Falchi); to the indie cult hit *Zombie Honeymoon* (2004), directed by David Greboe, in which Danny, a young newlywed husband (Graham Sibley) is infected with the zombie plague and his wife, Denise (Tracy Coogan) tries to keep their marriage together despite the fact that her new hubby is starting to eat people.

There is zombie porn, zombie *gay* porn, zombie romantic comedies (zom rom coms, like *Shaun of the Dead*) and all sorts of twists and turns on love after death.

But here's a twisted little fact that might make you squirm next time you're at a funeral: In some cases, when a man dies facedown or vertically the blood descending from higher to lower points after the heart stops beating can sometimes engorge the penis resulting in a postmortem erection. Over the centuries some wags have nicknamed this phenomenon *angel lust*, or—as I heard it described at a horror con a few years ago—a zombie chubby.

Expert Witness

I spoke with experts at the Los Angeles County Department of Coroner to learn how this process works, particularly in connection with a criminal case. According to Lt. David Smith of the Investigations Division, "We have the best forensic doctors in the world working here. We are a teaching facility and have an extensive intern program that attracts future pathologists to study here from monthly residents to yearly interns. We have a caseload of 20–40 bodies daily and because the population is so big and diverse, there is little to nothing that we haven't already seen at least once."

How soon after a homicide does the coroner's office generally take possession of a body? "That would depend on where the person died," Lt. Smith says. "If they die at a hospital, we generally take possession of the body within 2–3 days (we have a lot of hospitals in this County and over 5,000 miles to cover to get to them). If they die at a residence or crime scene, then we pick up the same day, usually within a couple of hours of being notified of the death by police. We allow the police to conduct their investigation and recover evidence before we recover the body."

When asked which types of crime require an autopsy, he said, "Under California law, anyone who dies by means other than natural causes is a Coroner's case. Even those cases who die of natural causes but have not seen a doctor in the 20 days preceding their death is a Coroner's case. The pathologist is the person who will decide what type or level of autopsy an individual will receive. In L.A. County because of our high workload, we pick and choose which case receives a full autopsy. All homicides, regardless of circumstances will receive a full autopsy. Males under the age of fifty with no known medical condition will get one. Females under the age of sixty with no known medical conditions will get one. Traffic accident victims will usually receive a limited autopsy to include blood draw for BAC (Blood alcohol content), a drug panel, possibly x-rays and a superficial examination only (you don't have to do a full autopsy to determine that a person died of multiple traumatic injuries when you can just look at a person and make that determination). A suicide death of gunshot wound to head would get a limited autopsy if the bullet didn't exit (they would open up the head and retrieve the projectile). They would draw blood for toxicology and that would be all. Males fifty years of age and older and females sixty years of age and over with no signs of trauma and no foul play suspected would get a blood draw only and their death would be recorded as 'Arteriosclerotic Cardiovascular disease.' This is a medical determination after years of study of bodies that have shown us that individuals in this age range almost always have the disease therefore autopsy is not required to prove it."

And the turnaround time for a postmortem? "During our slower times of year, once we receive a body, normal turnaround time is 2–3 days. During our busier times of the year (holidays, Christmas and late summer), turnaround time can be as much as 2 weeks. We make every effort to accommodate homicide detectives when we can. Under California law, detectives have 72 hours to charge someone who is in custody of a crime or let them go. When it is unsure if a murder has taken place, this would be most relevant and we push these people to the 'front of the line' when we can to help out. The Coroner's office is an independent entity and does not have policy or practice dictated to it from other law enforcement agencies."

Lt. Smith adds that there are investigators at the coroner's office who sometimes participate in the investigation: "Coroner Investigators serve as the eyes, ears, nose, etc. of the pathologist who is not able to go to a scene of death. The Coroner Investigator is charged with taking scene photos, interviewing witnesses, family, detectives, police officers and anyone else who might have information related to the death of the person. Investigators collect forensic evidence at a scene to include: hair samples, fingernail clippings and scrapings, GSR (Gunshot Residue collection), weapon recovery (firearms are collected and turned over to law enforcement for storage, all other weapons are brought into the office and placed in evidence). Investigators collect personal property and search for next of kin information, as the Coroner is the entity charged under law with the obligation of notifying the family."

I asked Lt. Smith to comment on the differences between real-world postmortems and the versions portrayed in films. "You're not going to find a dark room with the single overhead light and the family standing in the room identifying a body that is pulled out of a cooler on a tray. We do not allow the families to view bodies while in our possession. If identification is an issue for us—no fingerprints on file, no x-rays, etc.—we would allow a family member to view a Polaroid facial photograph of the decedent to establish the identification."

Why the precautions? "Due to all of the contamination risks, smells, numerous bodies, etc. family members are never allowed on the service floor to view bodies or witness autopsies."

Joyee Kato, who works in the Decedent Notification section of the Los Angeles County Department of Coroner discussed the process of notifying the next of kin in a murder case. "The coroner has responsibility to identify and notify the legal Next-of-kin (NOK) of death. However in Homicides, we allow the Handling Homicide Detectives to attempt notification first. We would then follow up with them in a couple of days. If they are unsuccessful—we would take over and search for NOK on our own. If the NOK is not present at the scene, our Investigator would begin searching for NOK info immediately. If they locate information, the ideal approach would be to make the notification in person. When done in person, we would usually request PD[15] to accompany us in case the information causes the medical assistance or the notification results in violence. If NOK info is not readily available, we would continue to search for family back at the office using various resources at our disposal such as arrest history, DMV, special search websites, witness interviews, request report and so on."

I asked Lt. Smith about the scenes in films where a body is laid out with a sheet covering it—which falls off as the zombie or vampire rises. You see the same thing in the forensic-themed TV shows. It's all very dramatic, but how likely is it? Lt. Smith was very eloquent on this point: "Bodies are never just covered with a sheet. All of the bodies are wrapped in plastic when they are picked up, with a sheet overlapping the plastic. This is to protect people and equipment from body leakage. I'm sure there's probably more than what I have listed but the truth to be told is, I do not

15. Police department personnel.

watch the forensic shows—I get enough at work! And they tend to make me laugh at the way they do things. I mean . . . I wish we could solve a case in an hour, and have forensic evidence literally dripping around a crime scene for us to find and use!"

The Zombie Factor

Now the crucial question: What if the corpse turned out to be infected? "It depends on what they are infected with," advises Lt. Smith. "We have had several cases of bubonic plague come through the office (yes, it's still around). We notify the L.A. County Public Health Nurse of any contagious disease that we receive—spinal meningitis, tuberculosis, plague, etc. Anything that might be a public health risk is reported to the nurse who in turn follows up with notifying any other agencies that might need to be contacted as well as notifying family and/or friends who may have had contact with the decedent prior to the death and who may be at risk. Serious health risk cases are locked up in special refrigeration units isolated from the rest of the decedents and staff and key-controlled by authorized personnel only."

Which means a zombie is not going to get up and walk out of the morgue, as is so often seen in films.

Smith adds, "If the CDC[16] is monitoring something special (bird flu for instance) and we encounter cases with the disease, we would let them know for tracking purposes, as well as the public health nurse. Something like a plague incident does not fly under the radar."

Just the Facts

The Zombie Infection

To anyone in the health field, the word *epidemic* is guaranteed to send chills up the spine. Nothing paints a more terrifying picture than an invisible army of disease germs that spreads like wildfire.

16. Centers for Disease Control and Prevention is an agency of the United States Department of Health and Human Services. It's based at Emory University in Atlanta, Georgia.

Art of the Dead – Peter Brown

Out for a Quick Bite

"I like both fast and slow zombies. It depends on how hungry or mad they are. I consider them as formidable creatures, reacting on a primal urge to feed. Just because the body is rotted doesn't mean they are always slow to react. Considering their unnatural abilities of reanimation, why wouldn't they have unnatural strength and speed as well? Hell, if you can rise up from the dead, lose a limb after being shot and still have the ability to move around free of pain . . . you see my point."

The correct term for something like this is *pandemic,*[17] which is defined by the World Health Organization[18] as the emergence of a disease new to the population in which the agent infects humans, causing serious illness; and in which the agent spreads easily and sustainably among humans.

17. From the Greek for "all people."
18. www.who.int.

There are plenty of diseases that kill hundreds of thousands or even millions and which are not considered pandemics, cancer among them. For a disease to be a pandemic, it must be infectious or contagious. Fighting communicable diseases is tough at the best of times.

The World Health Organization classifies diseases of this kind as follows:

Interpandemic period:

- Phase 1: No new influenza virus subtypes have been detected in humans.
- Phase 2: No new influenza virus subtypes have been detected in humans, but an animal variant threatens human disease.

Pandemic alert period:

- Phase 3: Human infection(s) with a new subtype but no human-to-human spread.
- Phase 4: Small cluster(s) with limited localized human-to-human transmission.
- Phase 5: Larger cluster(s) but human-to-human spread still localized.

Pandemic period:

- Phase 6: Increased and sustained transmission in general population.

History is filled with accounts of plagues whose destructive force is truly hard to grasp. The Black Death of the fourteenth century killed seventy-five million people worldwide, including two-thirds of Europe's population! Two hundred years later the disease returned as the Italian Plague of 1629–1631, killing 280,000 people and then spread from country to country, becoming the Great Plague of Seville (1647–1652), killing 60,000 people (25 percent of Sevilla's population); then the Great Plague of London (1665–1666), which killed nearly 100,000; the Great Plague of Vienna (1679) in which 76,000 died; the Great Plague of Marseille in 1720–1722, which killed another 100,000; before moving onto

Hard Science—Pathogen

A pathogen (a.k.a infectious agent) is what causes illness in an organism. The name itself is a translation from the Greek meaning "that which produces suffering." The major classifications of pathogens includes Bacteria (such as anthrax, tuberculosis, pneumonia, etc.), Viruses (AIDS, herpes, influenza), Protozoa (malaria, cryptosporidiosis, giardiasis, etc.), Fungi (ringworm, candidiasis, cryptococcosis, etc.), Parasites (roundworm, tapeworm, etc.), and Prions. The immune system, along with "good" bacteria in the body, fights invasion from pathogens. When the immune system is compromised or weakened, pathogens can create opportunistic infections.

Moscow in 1771 and slaughtering 200,000 more. And that's just the bubonic plague.[19]

Aside from Black Plague, there have been a number of major epidemics throughout history that have torn their way through whole cultures. During the Peloponnesian War (430 B.C.E.), typhoid fever killed a quarter of all the Athenian troops, and roughly the same percentage of the overall population of Athens during a four-year period. Typhoid fever is an incredibly virulent disease that often kills its host so quickly that they don't live long enough to spread the disease, so in a sense the strength of the disease probably kept it from wiping out all of Greece . . . and maybe all of that part of the world. Talk about cold comfort.

The Plague of Galen (165–180 C.E.[20]) also known as the Antonine Plague, scythed its way through the Roman Empire. There is some doubt as to whether the disease at the heart of the epidemic was measles or smallpox, but what's not in doubt is that it cut down nearly five million citizens of the Empire, including a couple

19. Properly known as *Yersinia pestis*, a gram-negative facultative anaerobic bipolar-staining bacillus bacterium belonging to the family Enterobacteriaceae.

20. C.E. = Christian Era, a somewhat more politically correct term now in common use in modern literature; it replaces A.D. (anno Domini).

of emperors, Lucius Verus[21] (130–169 C.E.) and Marcus Aurelius Antoninus (121–180 C.E.). At the height of this plague, two thousand people a day were dying in Rome, according to the historian Dio Cassius.

The first recorded outbreak of bubonic plague was the Plague of Justinian, which lasted from 541 to 750. The outbreak began in Egypt and swept into Constantinople like a tsunami, killing ten thousand people a day. The Byzantine historian Procopius wrote that this plague killed close to half of the population of the known world. Sit with that thought for a minute.

Cholera, another killer disease, has racked up seven pandemics so far, with a body count in the tens of millions. The first of these plagues began in Bengal in 1816 and spread outward from there, reaching China and the Caspian Sea before it slackened its lethal pace in 1826. But three years later it was back, striking Europe in 1829 and then leaping across the Atlantic to America in 1834, until it again slowed in 1851. It struck in Russia between 1852 and 1860, killing over a million people; then three years later it hit Africa. North America took another hit in 1866; and a sixth wave hit Germany in 1892. In 1899 it struck Europe again, but now science had begun to catch up to the needs of the suffering population, this time the disease did relatively little damage. However, when you speak of a disease like cholera, "relatively little" still doesn't equate to a cheery outcome. For decades the disease seemed to be in retreat and then it hit Indonesia in 1961, then shot through Bangladesh, and back to Russia. Every time health experts think the disease is gone, it rears its ugly head again.

The flu, or influenza to give it its proper name, is an infectious disease caused by an RNA virus of the family *orthomyxoviridae*, and it's racked up its own disheartening kill rate. And like the other disease, it has attacked in waves over the centuries. There have been documented cases of influenza dating back to the third and fourth centuries B.C.E, but modern tracking of the disease as a pandemic began in Africa in 1510. It blossomed on the Dark Continent and then spread like wildfire through Europe.

Influenza is constantly mutating, and when a new and particu-

21. Also known as Lucius Ceionius Commodus Verus Armeniacus.

larly aggressive strain appears, the dying starts. The worst outbreak was the Spanish Flu of 1918, which killed somewhere between fifty and one hundred million people in just eighteen months. It edges out the Black Plague as the worst pandemic in human history.

By comparison the Asian Flu of 1957–1958, which killed about 70,000 people in the United States, is considered "mild." That's another thought to digest for a bit.

And there are so many other diseases that have spread to epidemic proportions: chicken pox, measles, typhus, smallpox, tuberculosis, and others. Many of these are diseases we once believed had been eradicated. It's beyond disturbing to discover how wrong we were about that. Many of these are commonly referred to as Old World diseases because they came with the settlers when the New World was discovered and conquered. It is a widely held belief among historians and epidemiologists that up to 95% of the Native American peoples were killed by these Old World diseases. Before Columbus landed, the Americas hosted a populace of many millions. Chicken pox and measles did more slaughter than bullets in conquering the West; and before you go off thinking that well, this was an "act of God"—there are plenty of recorded cases of settlers giving blankets to the Indians knowing full well that they carried infectious agents. Biological warfare has been going on for a long, long time.

Influenza has an inordinately high infection rate, somewhere near 50 percent. Imagine if a zombie plague got out there, with its 100 percent infection rate.

There are also some spookier diseases of unknown type or origin, such as the one that hit England in the sixteenth century and killed almost instantly. Known as the English Sweat, this disease seemingly struck without warning and literally dropped its victims in their tracks. The disease has not reappeared and it remains as one of several mysteries in the world of epidemiology . . . and believe me when I tell you that *mystery* and *epidemic* are not words anyone wants to hear in the same sentence.

Nowadays we have a whole slew of slayer diseases:

- *Avian Flu*: Also called bird flu, this is a new bully on the block and has been giving nightmares to infectious diseases

Art of the Dead – Graham Pratt

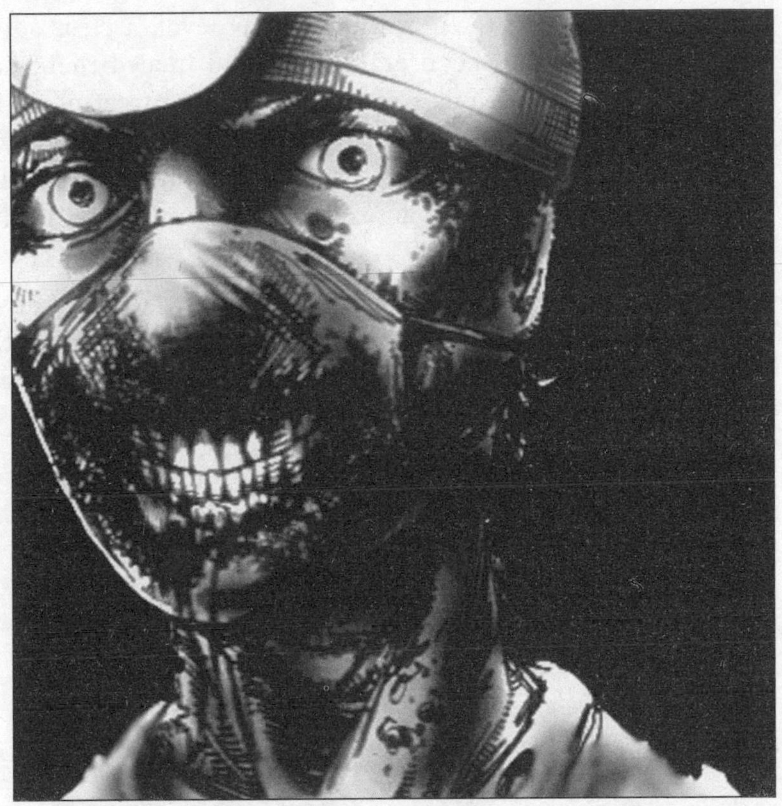

Public Health Hazard

"If there was a zombie uprising I think we would bury our heads in the sand and get bitten in the ass."

experts since 2003. This little monster is carried by various kinds of hosts, including birds, and the carrier is typically asymptomatic, meaning the host does not get sick. This makes it very hard to spot before infection occurs. Heightened awareness of the threat of the disease has been instrumental in preventing its spread.

- *Yellow Fever*: In historical novels you often read of ships flying the Yellow Jack to indicate an onboard infection of this disease, and of whole island populations being wiped out. Many people seem to think that yellow fever, a virus spread by mosquitoes, has been eradicated, and indeed there have been significant advances in prevention and treatment. But not in the Third World. In the absence of regular medical care, adequate hygiene, and other poor conditions, yellow fever continues to claim an estimated thirty thousand lives per year.
- *HIV/AIDS*: Acquired immune deficiency syndrome or acquired immunodeficiency syndrome is a global killer that went from being the disease people didn't talk about to a pan-

Zombie Child **by Ken Meyer, Jr.**

We might have a chance of stopping a zombie plague if it starts in a heavily industrialized country; but if it starts in the Third World it might spread beyond control.

demic that we can no longer ignore. Over 38 million people are infected with HIV worldwide, and to date more than 25 million have died from it. In Africa and other Third World areas, HIV is running rampant and still not enough is being done to combat it, and there is no true cure in sight.

- *SARS*: This is a severe acute respiratory syndrome caused by the SARS coronavirus that apparently began in Guangdong Province, China. Because of the aggressive action of the World Health Organization, the first SARS pandemic claimed only 774 lives between November 2002 and July 2003. In the absence of an organization like that, there would have been hundreds of thousands more SARS-related deaths.
- *Ebola*: Properly known as Ebola hemorrhagic fever, this is a nasty disease that causes organ failure. The virus has a few different known strains. *Zaïre Ebolavirus*, first discovered in 1976, is the most virulent kind, with a 90 percent infection rate and an 83 percent mortality rate. *Sudan Ebolavirus*, also first reported in 1976, is somewhat less aggressive. *Reston Ebolavirus*, discovered in 1989 in Reston, Virginia, was caught before it spread to humans. *Ivory Coast Ebolavirus*, discovered in 1994, was discovered among chimpanzee populations and resulted in one known human infection (in a doctor treating an infected chimp), but the doctor was treated and survived.

Expert Witness

"A communicable, or contagious, disease refers to any infectious disease that can be transmitted from one species to another or one person to another," explains infectious disease expert Dr. Robin Dobson. "A disease that carries with it an extraordinarily high degree of communicability—anything above 30%—is a cause for major concern. Something that carries a 100% communicability—which is luckily very unlikely—would be a potential global catastrophe."

He adds, "The issue here is complex, however, because communicability is only part of the equation. You also have to con-

Hard Science: Patient Zero

In all plagues there has to be a first case. Whether this is the person who contracted the disease from eating the wrong thing, getting stung by the wrong mosquito, cavorting with the wrong livestock, or being in the wrong place at the wrong time . . . someone has to be first.

This deeply unlucky individual is called "patient zero" or the "index patient." The importance of patient zero can hardly be underestimated because how an epidemic begins often provides clues to its origin, which in turn may lead to the best possible chance of either a cure or of some kind of prophylactic measure.

Identifying the patient zero also helps scientists in their attempts to track the spread of the disease.

Why is this person not referred to as patient 1? Well, it's because someone read it wrong back in the 1980s. When Dr. William Darrow and his colleagues at the Centers for Disease Control were studying the earliest instances of HIV, they believed they had identified the first (or at least first known) infected person. Since this person had come from California his confidential case record was designated as Patient (Out of California), or Patient O for short, O's and 0's look pretty close, and someone else read it as the number. And so patient zero came into the worldwide lingo of epidemiology.

sider infectivity, which is how the pathogen enters the host, how it survives in that body, and how it spreads throughout the body. Many diseases spread very quickly from the moment of infection, anywhere from a day or two to a few weeks. It's unlikely we would see anything capable of replicating and spreading throughout an entire host in seconds or even minutes. It would be hours at the very least."

Dr. Andrea White, a colleague of Dobson's who worked with him in South America to study smallpox, adds, "Just because an infection exists it does not mean we have an infectious disease. An infection may remain within a host, with or without clinical symptoms or impairment to the host, and it may not spread.

Sometimes a disease can be contained within a host so that the infected person does not become an active carrier."

"There are a number of ways in which the transmission of a disease can occur," Dobson says. "In general transmission refers to the process by which a disease is passed from an infected host to another person or to a group of people. This can happen through airborne transmission (if the pathogen remains in the air for extended periods of time); through direct contact between infected and uninfected, and this includes everything from kissing to sexual contact to biting; through droplet contact (from coughing, sneezing, etc.); through fecal-oral transmission (which happens often with contaminated water or food sources—you see that a lot in the Third World); through indirect contact, meaning contact with some substance that carries the contaminate; and, of course, through vector borne transmission, which means that it is carried by an animal or insect. Or, in this case, by a zombie."

"We would have to do studies," adds Dr. White, "to determine if the contaminate is something that can exist outside of the host. If this plague is strong enough to exist without the support of a living organism, which you see with some kinds of bacteria, parasites and so on, then everything the infected zombie touches is a potential source of infection."

"And," Dobson says, "you have to wonder if we have a nidus, or natural reservoir, in play. A nidus is a host who carries the pathogen but does not contract the actual disease. For example shellfish can carry cholera but don't become infected by it, just as black rats and prairie dogs carry bubonic plague and mosquitoes carry malaria. If that's the case, then you may have disease vectors other than zombies carrying the zombie infection. That would be very, very bad."

The Zombie Factor

As with all outbreaks, a zombie plague would need to be placed in its correct historical context, which means that a search would have to be done to see if a similar outbreak has occurred before. If so, the way in which it progressed, the rate at which infection spread, the methods used to identify it and then combat it are all relevant because any steps taken—successes or failures—will refine and inform the steps that doctors take to combat the current outbreak.

It's equally important to make sure we know exactly what type of outbreak is being faced, especially when faced with something new and potentially radical. Few diseases present with absolutely no historical reference, which is why keeping—and checking—exact medical records is so crucial. If a zombie plague existed, there may be some reference to it, possibly under some other name, in the world's many shared medical databases. And even if no zombie plague has previously existed, diseases with similar symptomology may serve as guideposts toward treatment, prevention, or even a cure.

Dr. Michael Augenbraun of Brooklyn University Hospital advises us to, "Compare current and historical rates of zombieism to make sure this is real and not someone's *impression*. Develop a case control study of cases versus matched controls to determine associations and possible causes. Assuming you have no preconceived notion of how one acquires this illness, this is the only way you can really impose any sort of control program."

Plagues have been used in a large number of zombie stories, and these are largely responsible for the resurrection of zombie pop culture and which stand as being among the most significant in the recent resurrection of the genre. Certainly *Shaun of the Dead*, Romero's *Land of the Dead*, and the Zack Snyder remake of *Dawn of the Dead* are all key players in the return of the dead to top pop

Zombie Bugs from Outer Space

At one point during preproduction, the story of *Night of the Living Dead* dealt with humans infected by an alien pathogen brought to earth in the ill-fated Venus probe, but this was later scrapped. The working title *Night of the Flesh Eaters* was attached to the film at this point, but Romero and his writing partner, John Russo, decided to take the story in another and far less specific direction.

culture status, but along with *Resident Evil* one other movie, also released in 2002, stands a little apart as an impetus behind the genre: *28 Days Later*.

This landmark flick, written by novelist Alex Garland (author of *The Beach*) and directed by Danny Boyle (who directed the 1998 film version of *The Beach* as well as the marvelous comedy *Trainspotting*), took the supernatural out of the zombie genre and infused it with new "life." The threat in this film is not a reanimated corpse but rather a human being infected with a virus that hyperactivates the rage impulse in the brain. The virus was being tested on lab monkeys, but a well-intentioned but misguided group of animal rights activists breaks in to a research center and liberates the chimps. It all goes to hell from there as the infection immediately spreads to humans, and once infected a person immediately succumbs to total and uncontrollable murderous rage. The infection spreads so quickly that England is virtually destroyed in four weeks; and there it is suggested that much of the rest of the world may have likewise been affected.

This idea is turned around with the 2007 sequel *28 Weeks Later*, in which NATO troops move in to England several months after the plague. All the infected are believed to have died from starvation and exposure, and the world governments (led, apparently by the United States) are attempting to repopulate London. Of course things go to hell and the infection starts again, this time definitely spreading to Europe, where it is presumed there will be no English channel to act as a barrier for a pandemic. At this writing a third film, *28 Months Later* is in preproduction.

Though, as mentioned elsewhere in this book, this theme is not original and doesn't even supplant Romero (because he thought of it first in 1973 for his film *The Crazies*), it does bring the concept to a new generation where the idea benefits from higher production values and better special effects.

The nonzombie virus is, to many, more frightening than the undead ghoul idea mainly because it's so much more scientifically plausible. Viruses are real. Out of control rage states are possible, as we learned from forensic toxicologist Dr. Raymond Singer in Chapter 2.

The rage infection in the *28* series is not specifically spread

Codename: Trixie

In his follow-up to *Night of the Living Dead*, George A. Romero went deeper into speculative fiction with *The Crazies*, in which a weaponized virus, called Trixie, is accidentally released following a the crash of a military plane. The virus gets into the water supply of a small Pennsylvania town and anyone who drinks it either dies or becomes a homicidal maniac.

The soldiers sent in to clean up the mess are almost always seen as faceless killers in white Hazmat suits; and the threat of these dehumanized, white-faced killers echoes similar themes from *Night*.

Though well-made and a cult favorite, *The Crazies* never quite found the audience it deserved, and Romero eventually returned to flesh-eating ghouls to serve as the voice of his social commentary.

through a bite, though it can be passed along that way just as it can through serum transfer, meaning any transfer of body fluids. Primarily rage is transmitted when one of the infected vomits blood at its victim. The diseased blood is absorbed through mucous membranes and open wounds. It is not, it appears, transmitted through skin absorption.

Though terrifying in concept, the rate of transmission of the rage virus isn't logical. Like the zombie virus in the Zack Snyder remake of *Dawn of the Dead*, the rage virus in the *28* movies spreads too fast. Not too fast within the population, but too quickly within the human body. Our expert witnesses have all confirmed this. The stories, as told, just don't provide enough time for the entire blood supply and all of the mucous membranes, including the mouth, to become totally infected and therefore capable of transmitting the disease.

The speed with which these hyperactive plagues spread through the host-victims is crucial to the believability of the stories, and because they are in some ways less possible than a mutation of the central nervous system resulting in the slower Romero zom-

Mad Monkey Kung-Fu

In *Shaun of the Dead*, made two years after *28 Days Later*, a quickie gag involves a newscaster commenting on the zombie plague in London and denying reports that it was caused by rage-infected monkeys.

bies, the threat becomes one of purely fictional supposition. The logic of this has created a significant division between the view of how we would react and respond to a plague that created the slow, shuffling zombies and one that created very fast human infected. If a disease could spread that fast through the host so that it is immediately transmissible, and if the infected host could move like a marathon sprinter, then it would be game over unless natural barriers such as wide rivers or, indeed, oceans, separated the lands of the infected from those of the uninfected.

Just the Facts

Forensic Psychology

Forensic psychology has gotten a lot of play on TV and in movies. Often the Hollywood view of what one of these professionals does is wildly inaccurate or clinically incorrect.

Zombies are not known to be "thinking creatures," but perhaps there are some elements of psychology that can help us predict how they'll act, which could aid in finding them, understanding how to oppose them, or even (gasp) understanding them.

Expert Witness

To understand the nature of this branch of science, I spoke with Katherine Ramsland, Ph.D., who teaches forensic psychology at DeSales University in Pennsylvania, and is the author of 31 books, including *Beating the Devil's Game: A History of Forensic Science and Criminal Investigation* (Berkley, 2007), *The Human Predator:*

Zombie Novels

Bookstore owner and genre expert Greg Schauer shares his picks for the must-have zombie novels:

- ***Among Madmen* by Jim Starlin and Daina Graziunas (Roc, 1990)**
- ***Berserk* by Tim Lebbon (Leisure, 2006)**
- ***Dead City* by Joe McKinney (Pinnacle Books, 2006)**
- ***Dead in the West* by Joe R. Lansdale and Colleen Doran (Night Shade Books, 2005)**
- ***Deadlands* by Scott A. Johnson (Harbor House, 2005)**
- ***Deathbringer* by Bryan Smith (Leisure, 2006)**
- ***Dying 2 Live* by Kim Paffenroth (Permuted Press, 2007)**
- ***Plague of the Dead (The Morningstar Strain)* by Z. A. Recht (Permuted Press, 2006)**
- ***Roses of Blood on Barbwire Vines* by D. L. Snell (Permuted Press, 2007)**
- ***The Dead* by Mark E. Rogers (Infinity Publishing 2001)**
- ***The Night Boat* by Robert R. McCammon (Avon, 1980)**
- ***Twilight of the Dead* by Travis Adkins (Permuted Press, 2006)**
- ***Xombies* by Walter Greatshell (Berkley, 2004)**
- ***Zombie Jam* by David J. Schow; illustrated by Bernie Wrightson (Subterranean Press, 2005)**

A Historical Chronicle of Serial Murder and Forensic Investigation (Berkley, 2006), and *The Science of Vampires* (Berkley, 2002). She writes features about forensics for Court TV's crime library and has also cowritten books and articles with former FBI profilers.

She gave me the basics of how forensic psychology works: "Wherever the legal system and psychology intersect, you have forensic psychology. While most practitioners (psychologists, psychiatrists, licensed social workers) are clinicians with a specialization in forensic issues, this applied discipline actually involves a

Art of the Dead – Harold M. Vincent

Flesh-Eating Ghouls

"I believe zombies are so popular because of the mystique surrounding them. People love to be scared and disgusted. I would also venture to say that people, as a whole, are inherently violent and would like to kill others without feeling guilty or suffering any consequences. Zombies, in their simple and primitive nature, also represent the essence of survival in a brutal, unforgiving world where they are the victims striving to live. In that respect many people can sympathize with their tragic existence."

range of specialties in the civil and criminal arena. These include consulting on criminal investigations, assessing threats of violence in schools or workplaces, determining the fitness of a parent for guardianship, developing specialized knowledge of crimes and motives, evaluating the effects of sexual harassment, and conducting forensic research. Whether police will request a consultation depends on what type of situation they're dealing. For the court, forensic psychologists are often asked to evaluate a person's present psychological state for competency to participate in the legal process. They may also evaluate a defendant's mental state at the time he or she committed an offense. In addition, psychologists appraise behaviors such as malingering, confessing, or acting suicidal."

When mounting an investigation, police often require some kind of psychological sketch to help them find out what kind of person they're looking for. I asked Dr. Ramsland how that works.

"Only occasionally does a psychologist do profiling," says Ramsland, "since the FBI offers this service, but some do develop a relationship with specific police departments to assist. Still, most are not experts in any type of serial crime. Profiling is basically assessing the facts one has from a specific crime scene or series of related scenes. There's no formula; it's specific to the type of crime and to what occurred. The popular but erroneous assumption that forensic psychologists track down serial killers derives from fiction, not real life. Although psychologists may interview serial killers as research or preparation for a court case, they are not detectives, and most are not profilers. Nevertheless, the FBI's Behavioral Analysis Unit (BAU) does provide training in criminal psychology to agents who will act as crime scene consultants. A good profile is an educated attempt to provide investigative agencies with clear parameters about the type of person who committed a certain crime or series of crimes, based on the idea that people are slaves to their unique psychology and will inevitably leave clues. From a crime scene, a profiler can assess whether the person is an organized predator as opposed to having committed an impulsive crime of opportunity (disorganized).

"A police chief usually decides whether or not to involve the FBI or engage a consultant, and then offers everything they have to that person to assist in the evaluation. That person then will speak to the task force involved to let them know the results. Whether they follow it or not generally depends on their attitude. A profile is just a tool in the arsenal; it does not solve crimes, it only helps to narrow down the pool of suspects with behavioral parameters, based on what's known about the behavior of a perpetrator from the crime scene. It is not a generic blueprint against which to measure anyone. it is not a science. It is an educated estimate based in probability."

When asked how a profile is constructed, Dr. Ramsland said, "To devise a multi-dimensional profile, psychological investigators examine such aspects of the crime and crime scene (usually murder but other types of crime as well) as the weapon used, the type of killing site (and dump site, if different), details about the victim, method of transportation, time of day the crime was committed, and the relative position of items at the scene. The basic idea is to acquire a body of information that shows common patterns for a general description of an UNSUB (unknown subject) in terms of habit, possible employment, martial status, mental state, and personality traits. Contrary to popular belief, it's not necessary that the offender be a serial criminal. Profiling can be done from a single crimc scene, and since 70–75% of murders are situational, developing a way to profile without reference to repeated patterns is useful. Profiles have also been devised in product tampering, serial bombing, serial rape, kidnapping, and arson."

How does information and evidence gathered at the crime scene aid the forensic psychologist? Ramsland says, "Probing for an experiential assessment of a criminal from a crime scene (or series of crime scenes) involves, first and foremost, a detailed victimology. In other words, the profiler must learn significant facts about the victim's life, especially in the days and hours leading up to his or her death. A timeline is drawn up to map their movements, and investigators study all of their personal communications for signals to where they may have crossed paths with a viable suspect. It's important to know their state of mind and their mental health assessment and history, as well as their risk level (with a prostitute's risk being much higher, obviously, than a woman in her own home).

"Once the victim's details are known, the crime scene and offender's methodology are evaluated for how best to categorize him (or her). Profilers will look at whether a weapon was brought in or taken out, the state of the crime scene(s), the type of wounds inflicted, the risks an offender took, his or her method of committing the crime and controlling the victim, and evidence that the incident may be staged to look like something else. In addition, there may be indications that the offender did not act alone."

I asked if profiles worked in all (or even most) cases. Ramsland says no, but adds, "Profiles work best when the offender displays obvious psychopathology, such as sadistic torture, postmortem mutilation, or pedophilia. Some killers leave a 'signature'—a behavioral manifestation of an individualizing personality quirk, such as positioning the corpse for humiliating exposure, post-mortem biting, or tying ligatures with a complicated knot. This helps to link crime scenes and may point toward other types of behaviors to look for. What a profile can offer that's helpful are the offender's general age range, racial identity, ideas about the modus operandi, estimates about living situation and education level, travel patterns, the possibility of a criminal or psychiatric record, and probable psychological traits. A profile may also describe a fantasy scenario that drives the person or even pinpoint an area where he or she probably resides. This is all based on deductions about the specific crime from what is already known about offenders and deviancy."

Zombies . . . Fast or Slow? Part 5

- **"That all depends on my own situation: If I were being pursued by them, then I would say slow. However, if I were among the undead legions, I'd want to move fast enough to put on the feedbag without having some grizzled, wisecracking hero shotgun me down first."—Mike Segretto, author of *Bride of Trash***
- **"Cinematically zombies are more interesting fast. Practically I prefer them slow, making them easier to kill."—Nicole Blessing, actress, *Doomed to Consume***
- **"Slow! You just got up out of your grave . . . you're disoriented, covered in dirt, trying to sort things out, and have a strange new compulsion to devour human brains. Suddenly you've become a track star?"—Monica O'Rourke, *Suffer the Flesh***

The Zombie Factor

I asked Dr. Ramsland to give us a rough idea of how profiling might apply to the zombie attack scenario we're using in this book.

"Naturally I'd need a victimology to do it right, but some of the behavioral clues indicate the following: It's likely there's mental illness involved, with the possibility of a *delusion* that the person is a mythical monster, such as a werewolf, vampire, or zombie. He could also be high on drugs, such as crack, which can trigger unprovoked aggression, and the attack does occur in the parking lot of a drug manufacturer. His obliviousness also supports a drugged state or substance abuse, as does his appearance, which indicates unhealthy eating habits. He probably lives in the area, within walking distance of the parking lot, since he walked away rather than getting into a vehicle, and he wore no shoes. His attack seems unplanned and he leaves obvious evidence that can be linked to him (bite mark, saliva), so he's probably more disorganized than organized. In that case, we would expect his residence to be somewhat chaotic and possibly not very clean. He might be responding to external stimuli, such as the moon or weather conditions. He could have a record in a local psychiatric institute, or have escaped from a prison, so these institutions should be checked. Police should also look at records of similar attacks, especially the same night, to try to pinpoint a zone of comfort for this offender."

Based on that, what questions will the police need to have answered to help them find this guy?

"Does the guard know the attacker? That would matter in a profile. What was the guard doing when attacked? What area of the parking lot? What season? What was the weather? Was the attacker larger than the guard? How long did the attack last? What time did it occur? There are many questions that need to be answered to give a more detailed analysis. I'd recommend having a dog handler track him, since the scent is fresh and he was barefoot."

I asked Dr. Ramsland to speculate on what kind of advice might a psychologist give to police/military if a case turned out to involve zombies.

"Nothing generic," she says. A lot of it would depend on what kind of zombies are involved. "How many, what happened, what's

Zombie Series

Genre bookstore owner and pop-culture guru Greg Schauer of Between Books shares his picks for the best zombies series of books:

- **Max Brooks**
  - ***Zombie Survival Guide* (Three Rivers Press, 2003)**
  - ***World War Z* (Crown, 2006)**
- **Brian Keene**
  - ***The Rising* (Leisure, 2004)**
  - ***City of the Dead* (2005)**
  - ***Dead Sea* (2007)**
- **David Wellington**
  - ***Monster Island* (Thunder Mouth, 2006)**
  - ***Monster Nation* (2006)**
  - ***Monster Planet* (2007)**
- **Bowie Ibarra**
  - ***Down the Road: A Zombie Horror Story* (Permuted Press, 2006)**
  - ***Down the Road: On the Last Day* (2006)**
- **David Moody**
  - ***Autumn* (Infected Books, 2005)**
  - ***Autumn: The City* (2005)**
  - ***Autumn: Purification* (2005)**
  - ***Autumn: The Human Condition* (2005)**
  - ***Autumn: Echoes* (2005)**
  - ***Autumn: Disintegration* (2007)**
- **The Living Dead**
  - ***Night of the Living Dead* by John Russo (Pocket, 1980)**
  - ***Return of the Living Dead* by John Russo and George A. Romero (Dale, 1978)**
  - ***Dawn of the Dead* by George A. Romero and Susanna Sparrow (St. Martins, 1989)**

their behavior, what kind of analysis is wanted, and for what purpose? The advice will depend on the situation and on what's specifically requested. There's obviously no codebook for zombie psychology. If they came to someone like me, with a pretty good background in the occult, I would suggest a strategy of containment in order to see how they act. Find out what's predictable about them, and what their strengths and weaknesses are. That will provide some answers in terms of how dangerous they are, how imminent the danger is, and what kinds of things might work to protect society. Again, their actual behavior is the key for what to do, not a generic idea."

For more on the psychology of zombies see Chapter 4.

The Final Verdict: Doctor, Doctor, Tell Me the News . . .

Are zombies likely? No. And we can all be thankful for that.

Are they totally impossible? Also no. And we can all lose some sleep over that.

Granted there would have to be some pretty radical shifts in human physiology and disease pathology for anything even close to this to happen, so there is additional comfort in the thought that Mother Nature probably isn't actually out to get us and so wouldn't craft mutations of this kind just to mess with our heads. On the other hand, Mother Nature did invent prions, so she certainly has her mood swings.

In light of the medical evidence and theories discussed in this chapter, we have to turn around and take another look at the issue of whether zombies are dead or alive. Let me rephrase that: Are they truly dead or only partly dead?

If they are actually corpses, then the process of rigor mortis could offer storytellers a reasonable explanation for why zombies are sometimes fast and sometimes slow, because with rigor mortis first the body is loose, then stiff, then loose again. Loose could equal quick and spry. Also, a dead zombie will eventually decay and fall apart. If they are somehow kept alive-ish by feeding on living flesh, there will be a point where that source will either run out or be denied to them. With no nutrients, proteins, or liquids being ingested, the bodies will decompose. It should take anywhere from a few weeks to a few months before zombies are no longer even a marginal threat (though the infection will likely persist).

On the other hand, if zombies are at least marginally alive, as my experts all seem to think, then a zombie's speed will depend on how much brain damage is present. Brain damage can certainly interfere with motor function, resulting in stiff, jerky, and uncoordinated movement.

Romero called his film *Night of the* Living *Dead*. Everyone has focused all their attention on the word *dead*; but for me the operative word is *living* but only as it impacts the definition of *dead*. *Living death*, then, would be a brand new term, a concept that fits into what we now see as a gap between truly alive and definitely dead. Given all that we've learned so far from our experts, that's what *living dead* is going to have to mean: a third designation of existence.

The Predator Compulsion

Zombie Forensic Psychology

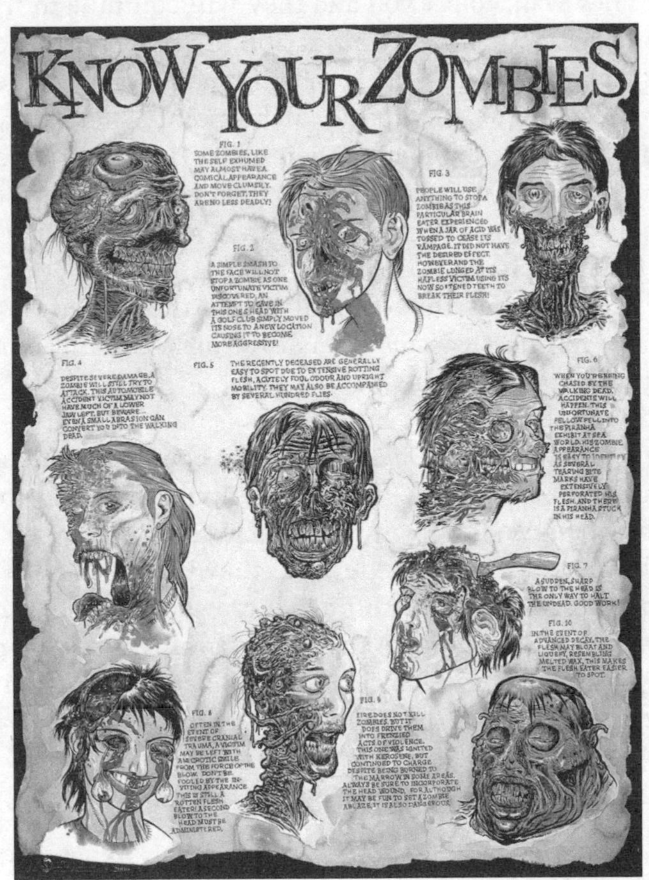

***Know Your Zombies* by Robert Sacchetto**

"I did this instructional poster for fun, around last Halloween. It was just after I finished a commission piece for a client who wanted a regular portrait of his two small kids. I think that there was some time overlap . . . I guess my brain was in a weird place at that point and I thought, 'Why not make this fun and combine the two?' and there it was!"

Just the Facts

Zombies and the Human Psyche

One thing you have to admire about zombies is their dedication to purpose. They want to eat you and they will continue to try and do so without distraction or any alteration of intent until they either get their victim, are irrevocably prevented (by, say, a bullet to the head), or until they decompose to the point where they are no longer capable of accomplishing their goal. They don't require rest, they don't succumb to frustration, they never lose interest. Theirs is a task assigned on the deepest primal level, and they will set about it indefinitely.

In the genre stories this compulsion is the source of frequent speculation, but no clear answer is ever uncovered. Having risen, why do they attack humans?

And, do they attack only humans?

In *Night of the Living Dead* one of the ghouls is seen eating an insect, suggesting that they feed on any living thing. In the *Dawn of the Dead* remake, however, the zombies clearly have no appetite for anything except human flesh, eschewing to chew on a dog, which then runs unharmed through a crowd of hundreds of them.

This is one of the elements that is never fully resolved, probably because as a plot point it brings up more issues than it would solve. Here are some of the points to consider:

- Are zombies omnivorous or just carnivorous?

- If merely carnivorous, will they eat any living thing?
  - Romero establishes that they eat (at least) humans and insects.
  - It has been speculated that it is warm living flesh that attracts the zombies' appetites, but then how do you explain the zombie who eats the insect? Insects, though certainly possessing body heat, do not possess very much of it.

  - Heat alone can't be the lure or else they would continue to feed on the recently dead, and all the movies suggest that the zombies eventually stop feasting on a corpse after it begins to cool (else there would be no new zombies left intact to rise). It takes hours for a body to cool to room temperature.
  - If zombies are attracted to warm flesh, then they should logically be compelled to feast longer on victims in warmer climates and less so on victims in cooler climates.

- If these arguments successfully deflate the belief that it is warm human flesh that the zombies crave, then what is their true desire? Is it, perhaps, some kind of energy? Perhaps *ch'i*, the intrinsic vital energy believed by many to flow through the body along pathways called meridians? If so, how does the zombie feed on the *ch'i*?
  - Does feeding on ch'i mean that they are actually some kind of psychic vampire or perhaps essential vampires? (See "Fearsome Folklore: Essential Vampires.")

- If they are not essential vampires, then what is it about humans that causes the zombies to fixate? In nature all things have an explanation, even if we do not currently understand it.

- If, on the other hand, zombies will attack any living thing (human or otherwise) can their infection be passed on?

There are endless ways to spin the zombie's predator compulsion. But there are other psychological issues at hand, such as how humans would bear the knowledge that the dead were rising, that death had been more or less repealed in the ugliest possible way; that our buried loved ones may be rising from the dead (if you go with that version of the mythology rather than the virus); that we might have to confront a zombie who was formerly a loved one, a neighbor, or a friend and shoot them; and so on.

But is there a way to crawl inside the zombie's head and understand what makes it tick?

Fearsome Folklore: Essential Vampires

Essential vampires feed on one or more of the following:

- ***Life Force, often called ch'i (Chinese), gi (Korean), or ki (Japanese).*** **This life force is believed to be either electrochemical, or made from pure energy and flows throughout the body along pathways called meridians that are laid out much like the circulatory system. This energy flow is the basis for healing arts such as acupuncture and acupressure, and it cultivated through various meditative practices, such as yoga.**
- ***Breath.*** **Many of the world's shape-shifting vampires, particularly those that transform into cats, will-o'-the-wisps, or flying insects, land on sleeping humans (usually children) and then drain away the breath leaving a child gasping or dead.**
- ***Sexual Essence.*** **Some vampires seduce their victims in order to drain away a man's potency or a woman's fertility.**

Expert Witness

A lot of writers have speculated the concept that humans, facing an unbearable situation such as their own friends and family coming back from the dead, would not be able to cope with it on a spiritual or psychological level. People would break, their emotions would race out of control and then explode like overworked turbines, their sanity would rupture, and long before the zombies won the war the humans and their fragile minds would lose it.

This is a disturbing concept, and I put it, and some related questions, to my experts on psychology, religion, and philosophy. Their answers may disturb you.

"One of the requirements for sanity," says therapist Jerry Waxler,[1] M.S., "is to develop a set of rules about life that let you predict with some sort of certainty what is normal and what is not. When the rules are broken too severely it can lead to a break-

1. Jerry's blog can be found at www.jerrywaxler.com.

Art of the Dead – Doug Schooner

After the Apocalypse

"I would like to see more artists and filmmakers explore the actual mental activity of the 'zombies.' What if the person a zombie used to be was actually still alive and conscious within the body, unable to control their actions through the loss of their free will? Trapped within a body they couldn't control, watching and feeling every aspect of the horror as they continued without rest or chance of redemption. This is the overall concept I tried to convey when painting "After the Apocalypse: Contemplating My Day in Hell." To be trapped within yourself without free will or control over your own actions. As human beings, we are trapped within our own bodies. We have conscious thought wrapped in a shell that will never "touch" another person or living creature in any aspect other than through the use of our bodies—through verbal and physical actions. Loneliness within yourself. Compound that with the loss of control over your own body (similar to complete paralysis) but while still continuing to have it function without your consent, controlled by something else. This is my concept of true hell. Loss of free will but still having consciousness to experience all the feelings associated with the 'death.' "

down. For example, soldiers in Vietnam went in assuming they were protecting their orderly, civilized way of life. Then when they found that to survive, they had to shoot women and children, it created a conflict that drove many of them to the brink. The same is true for zombies. If you discover a loved one, a family member or even spouse wants to eat you—the shock goes far beyond any ethical consideration. Your very definition of what is sane in the world becomes disturbed to the breaking point. At that point, you are casting off from the realm of psychology, and into the realm of prayer. May God have mercy on our souls."

"There is a point where what happens in the mind and what happens in the soul are part of the same process," says Kanchana Patel, Ph.D., a consultant with the University of Mumbai. "When we experience a global event such as the Indonesian tsunami we are, as a people, struck to the heart. An event of this kind is too large to allow a purely personal reaction. Our reactions are not only social, but they interact and collide in a panic as everyone else tries to both understand the *why* of the event and at the same time grasp the simple science of it. It is difficult, in the moment, to step back and say with dispassion that plate tectonics are a fact of life and there is nothing personal in it, just as there is no personal malice, no intent to harm in a volcano or a typhoon, and yet while the winds are blowing or the ash is falling we cling together and scream out 'Why?' as if the storm itself will speak an answer. When no answer comes we pray and when prayers do not appear to be answered—at least in any way we can perceive—we despair. Hot lava from a volcano may kill many people by destroying their bodies, but it is despair—that sudden, terrible thought that the universe is out to get them and that no other celestial force is willing or able to intervene. How strange it is that faith of such intensity exists at the moment of death, or in those moments leading up to a sure and certain belief in death; and how sad that this faith is the total certainty that the universe wants to murder them."

Waxler adds, "While I have never lived through a zombie attack, I have witnessed in my lifetime two national traumas, the assassination of John Kennedy, and the crashing of the World Trade Center on 9/11. In both cases, the national psyche was severely wounded. The collective pain and disruption was far-reaching, and because such severe trauma takes place outside the reach of logic, you can only understand its effects by observing its aftermath. After 9/11 we responded by collectively moving into a defensive stance. Airport security lines, and the two wars we are fighting simultaneously are direct results of 9/11. It's not quite so easy to understand how JFK's assassination affected the national psyche. One thing is that, decades later, it still feels like a knife through my heart. And I wonder if some of the craziness of the late sixties was a sort of reaction against the disturbance of the assassination. The loss of an orderly world leads to some strange behavior."

Nick Ladany, professor of counseling psychology at Lehigh University, takes a slightly different view. "People would adjust more quickly to death and go back to seeing it as more natural, rather than the sterile and removed way death is dealt with currently. In the past, the primary place for children to play was in cemeteries and it was not uncommon for bones to pop up every now and then after a storm. But because death was seen as a natural process, it was not seen as so unusual. Imagine today if a parent was with a child when a bone of a dead person popped up out of the ground."

Dr. Patel of Mumbai recalls, "My grandmother was in New Delhi the evening that Mahatma Gandhi was murdered by Nathuram Godse. Like many women my grandmother was so convinced that Gandhi would be the one to permanently change things for the better. He was for the liberation of women, for the end to untouchability, for unification of religious and social groups, and for an end to poverty. Could a man have higher aspirations or be more selfless, and yet the *Akhil Bhāratīya Hindū Mahāsabhā*[2] sent assassins to kill him, and they did kill him, using a gun to shoot down a man who would not have raised an arm to block a slap to the face. Grandmother told me that on that night, as news reports came over the radio that Gandhi was dead, that she felt some of herself die, too. She said that Gandhi, as political as he was, had brought a hopeful innocence to the world and now it was dead. I thought about that and then about what you asked me about how we would react if the dead rose to attack the living. Truly, I believe

2. The name translates as "All-Indian Hindu Assembly," a Hindu nationalist organization founded in 1915.

Art of the Dead – Seth Rose

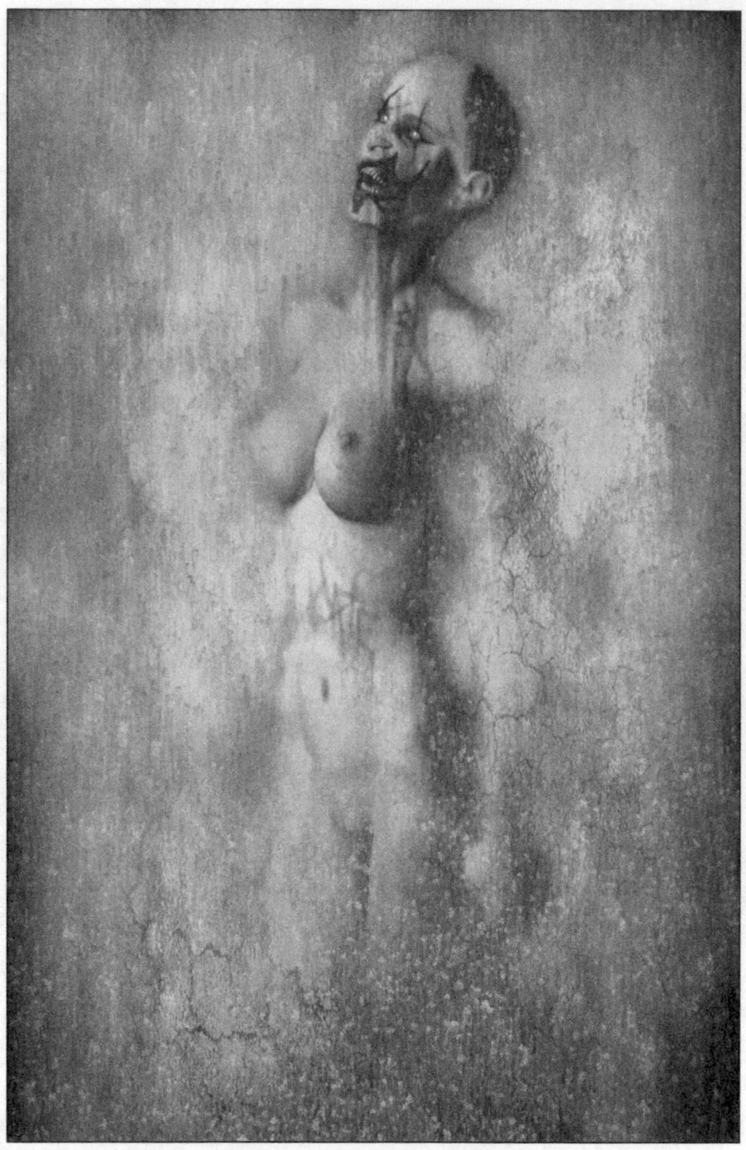

Strange Immortality

"Immortality is no gift. I can't think of anything sadder than to just continue to *exist*."

that if the dead rose, if we were at war with our own beloved dead, all innocence would die long before the battle was won by either side. I do not know that, as a people, as a race, we would psychically survive such an event; and if we physically survived it we would be a different people."

Joyce Kearney, Ph.D., an interfaith pastor and counselor at the Burlington House in New Jersey, says, "I don't think the issue of killing one's neighbors—should they become zombies—will do as much psychological or spiritual harm as killing one's family. Particularly the children. Not only would this cause rips in the fabric of the mind and soul, if the zombie menace were to continue for any length of time then no one would dare to get pregnant. There might be some desperation 'save me' kind of sex, but who would want to bring new life into a world where death ruled?"

This view, however, would come about if humanity was believed to be losing the war against the zombies. If the situation was desperate but under some kind of visible control, the deepest levels of panic might not kick in, an opinion to which my experts agreed.

"But if we were seen to be losing that fight things would go terribly wrong, terribly fast. It would destroy our ability to think about the world," insists Dr. Patel. "Not only would conception fall off, but there would be a rise of what you could call 'compassionate murder.' This would not be euthanasia of someone infected by the zombie bite; but murders of healthy children and probably of the elderly, and husbands killing wives and wives killing husbands. Why? Because people would know that to die of a zombie bite would be the practical equivalent of being damned to eternal hell and torment. Mercy killings would seem reasonable to guarantee that their loved ones would never become the living dead. This would, of course, be a catastrophe of incalculable proportions, but worse still would be what would happen if the plague was ended. Imagine surviving such a calamity knowing that you killed your family and that the zombies may never have been able to because the government was getting on top of the situation. You would see yet another round of suicides . . . so long after the last zombie was destroyed you would still be seeing new deaths."

Zombie Crawls

Zombie Jesus by Shannon Freshwater

People are funny. On one hand you have a dread of zombies, and on another you have the idea that zombie apocalypse is a keg party waiting to happen. Every year, in cities worldwide, people dressed as zombies meet their leader, Zombie Jesus (no, that's not a typo), and go out drinking.

David Christman, photographer, artist, and zombie expert, explains: "The initial idea of the creators of the Philly Zombie Crawl (Melissa Torre, Dave Ghoul and Robert Drake) was to celebrate the greatest zombie of them all: Jesus Christ."

Then the Philly crew learned that there was a Zombie Pub Crawl thriving in Minneapolis, and others popping up all over.

"We have all kinds of zombies at our crawl," Christman says, "some that go back to the Revolutionary period! In 2006, over one hundred and twenty zombies gathered at Tattooed Mom."

Rabbi Shevack, an interfaith leader,[3] believes that our national psyche would also be a victim of an uncontrolled zombie rampage. "Zombies would destroy the national psyche, just as they would destroy nationality itself. Most dividing lines would fall. Zombies wouldn't care if it was American flesh or Mexican flesh. They'd eat heterosexuals or homosexuals. Neo-cons or pandering liberals would be equal entrees. All our precious politics and national agendas would be consumed, voraciously, by zombies; as the living dead, they become the living-equalizers! And the Constitution? Well, that would just be carbohydrates."

"What would it be like to die slowly from a zombie bite?" speculates therapist Jerry Waxler. "It's just a much speeded up version of dying from life. We all start dying the minute we're born, and then we watch ourselves with varying degrees of self-awareness."

That brings up an interesting point: What *would* it be like? In zombie fiction and film we've all seen characters die, slowly or quickly, from infection, but rarely is this explored from the point of view of the infected person. Author David Wellington is one of the few who takes a shot at this, and his book *Monster Island* has some fascinating and unnerving scenes with a doctor who is going through that process.[4]

"The terror would be incredible," says Dr. Kearney. "And there would be grief, too. Not just over one's own life coming to such a tragic end; but grief of the harm a person might do after he's lost his fight and succumbed to the zombie infection. The fear of becoming a monster, something harmful to those we love, is a dreadful thing, but it's very common. You see it in victims of abuse who fear that they might grow to become abusers themselves. You see it in substance abusers who, in moments of clarity, realize the actual or potential harm inherent in their actions and yet feel powerless to stop themselves from taking that next crack pipe. The fear is similar here because these people are also being gradually overwhelmed by a process of negative change. Granted, substance

3. Rabbi Shevack is also the author of *Adam and Eve, Marriage Secrets from the Garden of Eden* (Paulist Press, 2003).

4. See the section on "But First a Word About Zombies" for more on how Wellington explores this theme.

abuse is treatable and zombie infection, according to the movies, is not . . . but the psychological process has definite similarities."

"Fear and anger toward an identifiable person/thing would be a difference," observes Professor Ladany, "but the stages of denial, anger, bargaining, and acceptance would still be there. The acceptance may not happen, however, until after the zombie state sets in. I would also suspect that the process of turning into a zombie may involve a change in personality such that dominant personality styles become exaggerated (for better or worse). For example, an angry person may become more angry, an extroverted person may become more extroverted, etc."

Dr. Gretz observes, "I think it would depend upon their religious beliefs and personal strength. If I knew I were dying and would become a threat to people around me after my death I would be emotionally distraught. However, if I were dying and knew that preparations had been made to eliminate that threat to others (such as destruction of my body after death), I would probably go through the same six steps common to all dying from denial to anger, to acceptance, etc."

"Grief," agrees Dr. Kearney, "would be a constant and terrible presence in all our lives. It would be its own kind of plague."

"Usually, grief is a very private thing," says Gretz. "We attend funerals and wakes to share our grief with others and to support the grieving. However, there are many people who find it extremely difficult to attend such events or even visit people in

---

Afterlife

Award-winning author Douglas Clegg shares his views on our obsession with the risen dead. "We're fascinated by the physical body and what happens after death to it. Additionally, with zombies, there's the sense of the dumb, destructive crowd out there that's going to somehow drive us insane or destroy us—sort of like the guy in Munch's painting, *The Scream*, with the world all around him while he exists in his own nightmare."

Horror of the Dead

"What could be more intimately awful than the most familiar person in our lives actually becoming something both unfamiliar and dangerous? It's horrifying. Thus fascinating. I remember seeing *Dawn of the Dead* for the first time as a teenager, and actually relating to the woman (near the beginning of the film) who sees her dead relative walking about and is overjoyed to find him 'alive'—only to be attacked and then partially devoured. Gah! It doesn't get much more horrific than that."—Stephen Mark Rainey, author of *Blue Devil Island* (Thomson Gale/Five Star Books, 2007)

the hospital because of mortality issues. While grief is generally private; we don't expect strangers to attend the funerals of loved ones. However in national crises like a 9/11, a Pearl Harbor, the great influenza epidemics, there is a sense that 'we are all in this together.' Following WWI and the great influenza epidemic that killed more people than the war itself, everyone either lost someone in their family or knew someone who had. There was a great sense of vulnerability and an awareness of one's own mortality. At the same time, I think that many people finally entered a mild state of denial. Think of the Cold War—when I was a young child we had practice 'duck and cover' exercises in school in case of a nuclear attack. This was particularly true around the time of the Cuban Missile Crisis when everyone thought the end was right around the corner. By the time I finished high school, we didn't even talk about it. College students were actually praising all things Russian and Che Guevara was a national hero on US campuses."

The Zombie Factor

When asked how this applies to zombies, Gretz says, "I think a zombie plague might be dealt with similarly. In locales where there were actual outbreaks, those people who saw one would become hyper vigilant—possibly to the extent that there might be real psychological damage. However, in areas where none had been seen, many would simply deny their existence and any danger (especially if admitting the danger would cause them any real inconvenience). As in most grief situations, I think religion would become increasingly important, both philosophically to explain what was happening and psychologically to help people deal with it. 'There are no atheists in a foxhole' would apply on a national level—remember how church attendance spiked during WWII and after 9/11; and I'm told that most of the troops in Iraq and Afghanistan attend services whenever they can."

And he makes a final point: "There is one more complication; during the flu epidemic, people often avoided wakes and funerals for fear of catching the flu—many of those who did attend did catch it and died. With a zombie plague, initial responses might be (1) how do I know you're not a zombie, (2) could I catch the plague from you or whatever, or even, (3) what sin did you commit for God to punish you in this way? And that will do a completely different kind of damage to our culture and our minds."

Just the Facts

Death and Undeath

What is it about dying that so deeply terrifies people? Considering that most people have, or claim to have, religious or spiritual beliefs that promise paradise after death and an end to all human suffering, it would *seem* that death should be welcome rather than railed against.

Expert Witness

"People are obsessed with death because it is the one thing they cannot at all control," says Rabbi Michael Shevack. "They can delay it, dance around it, and maybe, at times, detour themselves away from it. But, death is totally inevitable and we are all face to face with the ultimate irony of life, that we are 'born to die.' We fear it because we can't control it, and we can't control it, so we fear it. Death renders us powerless. Like the famous poem by Shel-

Chronicling the Apocalypse with David Moody

"Romero has always been my main influence. I love the bleakness and hopelessness of his stories. He concentrates as much on the living as the dead, which is something that too few zombie film-makers and writers do. Without any human involvement, zombie stories just become relentless bloodbaths.

"I have a fascination with post-apocalyptic stories and it was a natural progression for me to write an 'end-of-the-world' zombie novel. The *Autumn* story gave me an opportunity to look at zombies in a new light and take a different approach to everything I'd seen and read before.

"My other influences are more horror-specific than zombie-specific: the films of David Cronenberg, John Carpenter, Peter Jackson (before *Lord of the Rings*) and Roger Corman have all had a huge effect on my books. Cronenberg in particular. In films like *The Fly, Shivers, Rabid, Videodrome* and *The Brood* he looked at the disintegration of 'normal' human beings and their becoming something else entirely. That's one of the themes that runs through the whole *Autumn* series—what a so-called normal person at the beginning of the story goes through to turn them into a cold lump of hate-filled rotting flesh at the end?"—David Moody, author of the *Autumn* novels (Infected Press)

ley, 'Ozymandias,' we are reduced to rubble, no matter how exalted our accomplishments and egos. The fear of death is what causes the obsession with death, which includes all sorts of religious paraphernalia and psychological-projective symbols as well as a tremendous amount of cravings for it—death voyeurism—I would call it. We ritualize our fear to expiate it. And in the Jewish and Christian traditions death is always associated with sin, which is considered the cause of it. If we are born to die, it is because we have sinned in some fashion. So, there is moral-fear, and retributive-fear heaped upon its already fearful nature."

Dr. Gretz observes, "People have always wondered what happens after death. Like the old Peggy Lee song, 'Is this all there is?' " we wonder what's next. As children, we are often frightened of the

Zombie Porn

***Zombie Love Slave* by Kevin Breaux**

Over the last thirty years there has been a sub-(sub-, sub-)-genre of the living dead cinema in which zombies and their victims engage in hard-core sex. Redeeming value: zip, except as a statement of sorts about the true meaning of freedom of speech. Where these could have been fun, too many of them are fiercely (indeed, savagely) antifemale, showing not just violence against women, which has always been something of a staple in horror storytelling, but deliberate degradation, humiliation, and torture. These elements do not advance the story toward some meaningful turnaround or social statement: They are the story.

Good writers can include torture and other ghastly crimes (abuse, rape, murder) in a story and use the shock value to steer the story toward some understanding of the way in which the mind warps and the human spirit fractures. Romero did this in his films, letting the violence act as a conduit toward insight into greater social problems. Most of the zombie porn reveled in the connection between sex and humiliating death.

The kings of these films were Joe D'Amato (real name Aristide Massaccesi), who churned out trash like *Porno Holocaust* and *Erotic Nights of the Living Dead* (both 1980); and Claude Pierson, who inflicted *Naked Lovers* (a.k.a. *Porno Zombies*) on the world in 1977.

In 1982 director Mario Sicilano *attempted* to legitimize the genre by focusing more on the sex and far less on the misogynistic violence with *Erotic Orgasm,* but the damage was done.

Some of this stuff has surfaced on DVD, mostly bootleg, and with any luck it'll sink back into the unmarked grave from which it came.

dark and the unknown. Most religions answer that question with possibilities of endless light and joy or endless darkness and despair. I think the television news and the current round of increasingly violent movies and video games has also played a part. On the one hand, they bring death right into our everyday lives. Unfortunately, they also make it unreal to us. It is something that happens to others and isn't totally real because we play the same game tomorrow with the same characters. The actor who is killed in one show is in another next week. Until about fifty years ago, most children attended at least one wake and funeral for a family member, neighbor or friend before they finished grade school. People died at home rather than in the hospital and they were washed and prepared for burial at home. Only the wealthy could afford embalming. So children grew up watching loved ones slip away. They had time to say their good-byes before or after the person died and they watched as the body/casket was lowered into the ground, giving them closure. Today, we try to protect children from all that—violent movies, TV shows and video games notwithstanding, and children often never gain that closure. The result is often not only a fascination with death but also an unhealthy fear of it."

Dr. Ladany says, "Existentialists would argue that all anxiety is based on a fear of death and that people create fantasies or religions as a way to deal with, or distract themselves from the fact that we will die and there is nothing left afterwards. I don't completely agree with existentialists, however, I think people are intrigued by death because it offers an alternative to the suffering that takes place for people. Almost everyone experiences suffering on a day-to-day basis and the idea of death offers an escape plan."

The Zombie Factor

Zombie films and books have done a thorough job of exploring the different phases of psychological and spiritual disintegration that is likely during an undead attack. We've seen the gamut of human emotions, from heroism to cowardice, from self-sacrifice to murderous selfishness, from generosity to greed, and from wisdom to folly. And it isn't just film and novels that have been used to explore the topic; comics, short stories, and art also get their say, and in these forms some of the most powerful insights are presented.

Zombie Anthologies

Greg Schauer, owner of Between Books in Claymont, Delaware, provides a list of the absolute essential anthologies:

- **The Dead Collections edited by John Skipp and Craig Spector:**
  - ***The Book of the Dead* (Bantam, 1989)**
  - ***Book of the Dead 2: Still Dead* (1992)**
- ***The Mammoth Book of Zombies* edited by Stephen Jones (Carroll & Graf Publishing, 1993)**
- ***The Ultimate Zombie* edited by Byron Preiss (Dell, 1993)**
- **The Flesh Anthologies edited by James Lowder**
  - ***The Book of All Flesh* (Eden Studios, 2001)**
  - ***The Book of More Flesh* (2002)**
  - ***The Book of Final Flesh* (2003)**
- ***The Undead: Zombie Anthology* edited by Brian Keene (Permuted Press, 2005)**
- ***History Is Dead* edited by Kim Paffenroth (Permuted Press, 2007)**

Robert Kirkman's *The Walking Dead* tells of a group of survivors on the run: friends, family, and strangers smashed together by events and forced to redefine "civilized behavior" on a day-to-day basis. These black-and-white comics published by Dark Horse allow us to see the psychodynamics played out with more depth and complexity than any film can manage in two hours. Even a 400-page novel would have a hard time plumbing as many depths as Kirkman has in the hundreds of illustrated pages that comprise the series. The stark visuals give us the backdrop and set the scenes and allow the storytelling to be lean and hungry.

Short stories (the best ones anyway) have always been mini-dramas, allowing more room for experimentation than novels or films. You can take more risks in 5,000 words than you can in 100,000. If it flubs, very little of the publishing industry's money is wasted, and if it's successful, it drives sales of everything else in the genre. The 1988 anthology *Book of the Dead* (Bantam) edited by John Skipp and Craig Specter is widely considered to be the gold standard, and not just because of the caliber of writers (Stephen King, Ramsey Campbell, Joe R. Lansdale, etc.) but because of the inventiveness of the stories. This was a raw book, with stories that took chunks out of the reader; it was frightening and heartbreaking and often damn funny. The only thing it was not was forgettable.

And as for art . . . scattered throughout the book you're holding are dozens of pictures from artists around the world. Professionals and amateurs are drawn to the world of the dead through some fascination or compulsion, each with its own deeply emotional story to tell. Look at the pictures, read what the artists had to say, and see where your mind wanders. Each one of these took me to a different, shadowy and important place in my head.

Zombies will do that, you see.

Ellen Datlow Picks the Best Zombie Short Stories

Ellen Datlow, editor of some of the best anthologies of genre fiction, including *The Year's Best Fantasy and Horror* (St. Martin's) and *Omni Best Science Fiction* (Zebra), shares her picks for some of the best short zombie fiction of recent years.

- **"The Hortlak" by Kelly Link**
- **"A Sad Last Love at the Diner of the Damned" by Edward Bryant**
- **"Zora and the Zombie" by Andy Duncan**
- **"Hunting Meth Zombies in the Great Nebraskan Wasteland" by John Farris**
- **"Calcutta, Lord of Nerves" by Poppy Z. Brite**
- **"On the Far Side of the Cadillac Desert with Dead Folks" by Joe R. Lansdale**
- **"Beautiful Stuff" by Susan Palwick**
- **"Jerry's Kids Meet Wormboy" by David J. Schow**

The Final Verdict: Predator and Prey

Nature adores a predator. It's a key component to the survival of the fittest rule, and we see it in ourselves. We humans are a predator species. We are naturally violent, naturally aggressive. The growth of "civilization" has not been geared toward removing our predatory natures, but to either controlling it or focusing it. Sure, there are people of peace like Martin Luther King, Gandhi, and the Dalai Lama . . . but look at what happened there: Two of the three were murdered, and the last one had to flee the armed takeover of his country.

Does that mean that the violent and vicious outnumber the peace-loving? I sure as hell hope not.

If we are not on the battle lines, we try to become less violent, to focus on growth and values and the cultivation of civilized behavior, and a lot of people do succeed. They're well apart from the hard and gritty world of pain and damage. They're antiwar and antiviolence. And then a 9/11 happens.

Like most people, I remember where I was on that morning and what I was doing. I was still working a nine-to-five job then, doing graphic design for a law firm. When the second tower was hit, a bunch of us gathered in a conference room and watched in horror as the towers began to burn. All around me were shocked and terrified faces—the faces of people whose lives had become so disconnected from violence that its presence, even on TV, was as real to them as if someone had struck them each a physical blow. These were people to whom violence was not—or, perhaps, no longer—part of their daily lives.

The next day, when I came to work and we all stood around and talked about how we felt when we watched the TV footage of the towers collapsing, and how we felt when we heard about the plane hitting the Pentagon, and the one that went down in a Pennsylvania field, I saw on each face the civilized mask begin to slide away. I saw anger, rage. I saw hatred. I heard people—good, gentle people—say how they wished we could just kill everyone responsible; how we should find them and bomb them back to the stone age. These were people who were not particularly hawkish, people who weren't necessarily right-wing. These were just *people*; and they had been hurt. Someone had struck them—however much it was via the surrogates of the victims of the World Trade Center and the Pentagon; they were feeling it as each one of them had been hurt. And when humans are hurt, they lash out and strike back. Even babies do it.

It is in our nature. It is a decidedly uncivilized response, and it's knee-jerk, and many of those people who screamed for revenge later, when the intensity of the moment cooled, backed off from their desire to see a blood-for-blood form of redress. That's fine, that's part of the civilizing process; but in the moment, if you had put guns in their hands or handed them a remote detonator, they might have killed. Many would. Not all, of course; but many more than you or I might have previously guessed. Perhaps you would have; perhaps me as well.

We are a predator species.

In times of great conflict, it is the heart and the mind that takes the gravest wounds. If the dead rose to attack us, we would go to war with them. I believe—as do the overwhelming majority of my experts—that we would win. We would be vicious about it, too. It would become a kind of ethnic cleansing: our species against theirs. It would be genocide. So, yeah, we would win . . . but we would lose, too, because you cannot go from being a nonviolent person to being a violent person and then go completely back again. Ask anyone who has ever been in combat. You may find peace again, you may be able to willingly put down your gun and walk away from war, but you cannot ever forget that it happened, and you cannot ever remove all of the marks it leaves.

We would fight. We would get tougher by becoming more of what we naturally are: the most successful predator species to ever hold the lease on planet earth. We would not yield it to the dead. And once the last of the dead are truly dead, and once we have adapted our society to make sure the dead stay in their place, we would go back to the process of trying to evolve into nonviolent and civilized beings. We would not, however, be the same people we once were. The world will have changed for us, just as it changed on 9/11. We are marked by that event and always will be. If the dead rise and we win that war, we will be a new version of humanity. Who knows what shape it will take, or what paths

Among the Dead by Alan F. Beck

"*Night of the Living Dead* had the greatest impact on me ... but watching all of those old, moody B&W films: *The Mummy's Curse, Dracula, Frankenstein* ... they all told about life after death and were constructed to engage the imagination of the viewer."

Twilight by Jason Beam

"I enjoy being a Dark Art storyteller in my work, and digital art allows me to explore themes and concepts that are beyond ordinary media. This piece, *Twilight*, was created specially for *Zombie CSU*. It's beauty even in death."

Zombie World by Matt '6' Bahr

"My art creeps people out and makes them feel uneasy. I take that as a compliment."

Loss by Robert Papp

"I had a class in high school called the Gothic Tradition and it was all about horror . . . films and literature. The teacher introduced the subtleties of *Night of the Living Dead* to us, so it's always been my favorite as well. Besides, after painting sweet scenes for the covers of romance novels for 10 or 15 years, a little gore in my artwork doesn't hurt a bit, does it?"

Johnny Gruesome
story by Gregory Lamberson; art by Zach McCain

"The soldiers in *Day of the Dead* and the cops in *Dawn of the Dead* go through terrible depression and despair. I can understand that . . . they're the last line of defense in a war they can't win. Zombie stories have always explored those subtle layers of disintegrating emotions." —Zach McCain

Zombie Portraits by Robert Sacchetto

"So far I've done a lot of zombie portraits, ranging from Scott Ian of the band Anthrax to wedding pictures and family pets. Apparently I'm not the only sick and twisted person who finds zombies a hell of a lot of fun."

Why Zombies?

- **"I think that now, more so than any other time in history, people believe they are powerless to control their own fates, and so feel like they're living by rote: get up, move around, eat to stay alive, repeat."—Gary A. Braunbeck, author of the Bram Stoker Award-winning short story "We Now Pause for Station Identification."**
- **"On a metaphorical level, zombies represent the freedom from restraint and the breaking of ultimate taboos, i.e., breaking the bonds of life and death and indulging in cannibalism. On a personal level, it's a great way to see your ex-lovers and ex-bosses get consumed without having to do jail time."—Scott Nicholson, author of *They Hunger* (Pinnacle Books, 2007).**
- **"Because hell is full, right? Zombies combine a universal fear of death along with a disturbing loss of humanity and reason. We see ourselves in zombies, since they began as human beings, but they are a moral insult to life and the living, no more than repugnant, decomposing flesh driven by senseless and insatiable hunger. Familiar yet completely alien."—John Passarella, Bram Stoker Award-winning author of *Kindred Spirit* (Pocket Star, 2006).**

social evolution will thereafter take? Probably the only thing that you could place hard money on with a guarantee of a win is to bet that no matter what happens that man, the superior predator, will never be too far beneath the surface.

5

Drop Dead

Police, Military, and Civilian Tactics for Destroying Zombies

SWAT **by Jonathan Maberry**

"Zoms fought the law and the law won."

Forensics and medical science have shown that there are qualities of the living dead that will identify them as such and send up all the appropriate flags. Now we need to discuss how police will stop a zombie.

Zombies don't flee.

Zombies attack.

As soon as the zombie is able to detect the presence of a human, it will invariably turn and pursue that human, and when it's in range it will attack. If the human is a frail older person, a child, or someone with absolutely no sense of how to manage the rudiments of defense (parry a grab and run like hell), then the zombie's attack will very likely result in the spread of its infection. That victim, once dead, will reanimate after a period of time, and now we'll have two zombies. Each person they attack continues the infection, and we are left with a geometric spread.

In this chapter we'll explore the methods used by law enforcement to arrest and detain a violent suspect. We'll also go a step further to discuss what officers would do if that suspect was more than ordinarily difficult to control; and then go further up the line to discuss armed responses and the use of deadly force. We'll even call in a SWAT team.

Just the Facts

Arrest and Detain

If the human the zombie attacks is a police officer—even a single officer—the outcome is going to be a lot different. Modern police are not only very well trained in the skills of controlling violent or even irrational suspects, they have a variety of tools and weapons at their disposal that will allow them to respond with appropriate force.

In many of the zombie films and books, the officers who respond to a zombie attack are usually overwhelmed very quickly. Too quickly, in my opinion. Granted, verbal commands, threats, and harsh language are not likely to deter a zombie from attacking; but on the whole cops are a lot more effective, careful, and controlled than they are portrayed. A police officer is not just going to stand there with bug-eyes and a gaping mouth while a zombie rushes him or her. At most the officer will assume the person is whacked out on drugs or mentally disturbed. Remember, cops are taught to maintain a safe distance when confronting a possible suspect, and they always—*always*—prepare for the possibility of a violent attack.

Expert Witness

"Officer presence and verbal commands would be tried first," says Detective Joseph Sciscio of the Bensalem Police Department. "Though if we're talking zombies I assume we would see a very quick progression through the use of force. Considering the likeli-

---

Zombie Nonfiction Books

Between Books' store owner Greg Schauer shares his choices for the best zombie nonfiction books:

- ***Book of the Dead*: *The Complete History of Zombie Cinema* by Jamie Russell (FAB, 2005)**
- ***Eaten Alive!: Italian Cannibal and Zombie Movies,* second Edition by Jay Slater (Plexus Publishing, 2006)**
- ***Gospel of the Living Dead: George Romero's Visions of Hell on Earth* by Kim Paffenroth (Baylor University Press, 2006)**
- ***The Cinema of George A. Romero: Knight of the Living Dead* by Tony Williams (Wallflower Press, 2003)**
- ***The Undead and Philosophy: Chicken Soup for the Soulless* edited by Richard Greene and K. Silem Mohammad (Open Court, 2006)**
- ***The Zombie Movie Encyclopedia* by Peter Dendle (McFarland & Co., 2000)**
- ***The Zombies That Ate Pittsburgh: The Films of George A. Romero* by Paul R. Gagne (Dodd Mead, 1987)**

---

hood the officers would or could be getting seriously hurt, I would expect deadly force to be deployed at some point."

According to retired NYPD officer Jerome Wilson, "I've seen all those living dead films a hundred times and they state pretty clearly that individually the zombies are not that strong, not even as strong as a normal man. If one of the slow zombies came at an officer and tried to bite him, the officer would first adjust distance to allow himself time to manage the situation, and to give him more time to try verbal commands. If that failed, he has lots of things to fall back on—OC spray, baton, and nowadays a lot of departments have TASERs."

The question remains, though, as to what would happen if the zombie was able to get close enough to grapple and tried to bite. Wilson doesn't see that happening, even when the officers are attempting to put the face shield in place. "Damn, you know how people are when someone tries to bite. It's like when someone tries to kick you in the balls. People move at warp speed. It's our natural reaction, our basis instinct, a primal thing. We don't let people bite us—there's a fear reaction that amps up evasion and resistance. Now, consider the combatants in the situation. You have a slow zombie who is unsteady on his feet and a police officer who is trained for close combat, who is probably wearing a vest, who has a belt filled with tools, and who can tell that this suspect is not acting rationally. He's not going to just grapple with the zombie and let himself get bit. No way."

Dennis Miller, a former sergeant with the LAPD, agrees. "I worked riots in LA and there was all kind of fighting going on there. Things got pretty crazy as you may remember following the Rodney King verdict. Point is, there were some serious tussles and those officers involved in one-to-ones were not fighting mindless ghouls, they were fighting street kids and adults who were very tough, very fast, and very experienced street fighters. I'll put any kid over the age of fifteen who comes from South Central up against a zombie anytime, and that zombie is going *down*. Cops are even tougher. Get bit by something like they have in *Night of the Living Dead*? No, I just can't see that happening."

This is a topic on which the author is also going to speak out as an expert because when I'm not writing books about monsters I

Why Zombies?

- **"The living dead are low maintenance. They don't talk back, have simple needs, and have wisely given up the rat race for something much simpler. On the downside, they don't smell very good, and they want to eat us. But I'd still prefer hanging out with zombies than most of my extended family."—J. A. Konrath, author of *Whiskey Sour* (Hyperion, 2004) and the zombie short story "In Cold Flesh."**
- **"There is just something extremely creepy about a creature that moves at a snail's pace but is still able to catch and eat you. Every piece of logic screams that you should be able to escape the slow-moving critters . . . but you can't. I think the 'creep' factor is why I like slow moving zombies. BUT, on the other hand, a rapidly-approaching piece of dead flesh that's coming to rip your head off is equally as terrifying but in a very different way. I think it's the 'threat' factor that makes me like fast moving zombies. So, there ya have it . . . A non-answer! Why? Because zombies are cool no matter if they're moving fast of slow. Either way, they're gonna get ya!"—Jim O'Rear, actor, stuntman, and haunted attraction consultant.**
- **"Zombies blur the line between here and there, dead and not dead, and take away the finality of things. The walking dead, in any form, haunts the mortal mind, I think."—L. A. Banks, bestselling author of the Vampire Huntress series.**

am a chief instructor of COPSafe, Inc., a company that provides cuff and control workshops for law enforcement. Along with my colleagues—former Philadelphia Police Department attorney Jeffrey Scott and martial arts instructors Jim Winterbottom and David Pantano, I've given workshops to all levels of police officers, from raw recruits straight out of the academy to chiefs of police, and that includes a number of SWAT and SERT[1] officers.

1. SWAT: Special weapons and tactics is a general term used by many police departments; SERT: South central emergency response team.

In our COPSafe workshops we teach officers how to control the most aggressive and violent suspects, including those who are acting irrationally due to mental instability or drug use. The techniques in these workshops is based on martial arts: distancing, deflection, redirection, joint manipulation, and pain compliance. Granted pain compliance won't work on zombies, so any time one tactic doesn't work, the officer adjusts and upgrades his or her response.

We teach a technique used to respond to an aggressive rush, and with it even a female officer or small male officer can put a three-hundred pound PCP-cooked man down on his chest and in cuffs. It's not muscle, and it's not magic; it's applications of basic principles of physics and some common sense. Turning the hips creates, torsion which is an incredible power source (just ask any home-run hitter). When an attacker lunges, no matter how much control he exerts, he is still subject to the dynamics of mass in motion. And gravity is always there, and it's always useful to a smart fighter.

When a zombie lunges, the officer can sidestep or shift, or ideally step into the rush but with his main body mass shifted out of the line of impact. Using a simple parry-and-grab, an extended leg, and hip torsion, the attacker can be yanked into the pull of gravity and down hard on his chest. The effect on the attacker is like lunging hard to open a heavy door with rusted hinges and finding that it's made of balsa wood and the hinges are well-oiled. Down goes the attacker—human or zombie. It's a science thing . . . zombies wouldn't understand.

As soon as the attacker hits the deck, the officer can use his arm to steer his body mass and control his ability to resist, turn, or bite; and on go the cuffs. The whole thing takes about half a second. Any single officer can do this; a pair can do it more easily.

The Zombie Factor

The biggest danger in an arrest comes once the zombie is cuffed, because in some situations the officer may relax the pinning pressure and try to pull the attacker to his feet. That's when a bite is most possible. Even so, the officer is expecting trouble, and if the

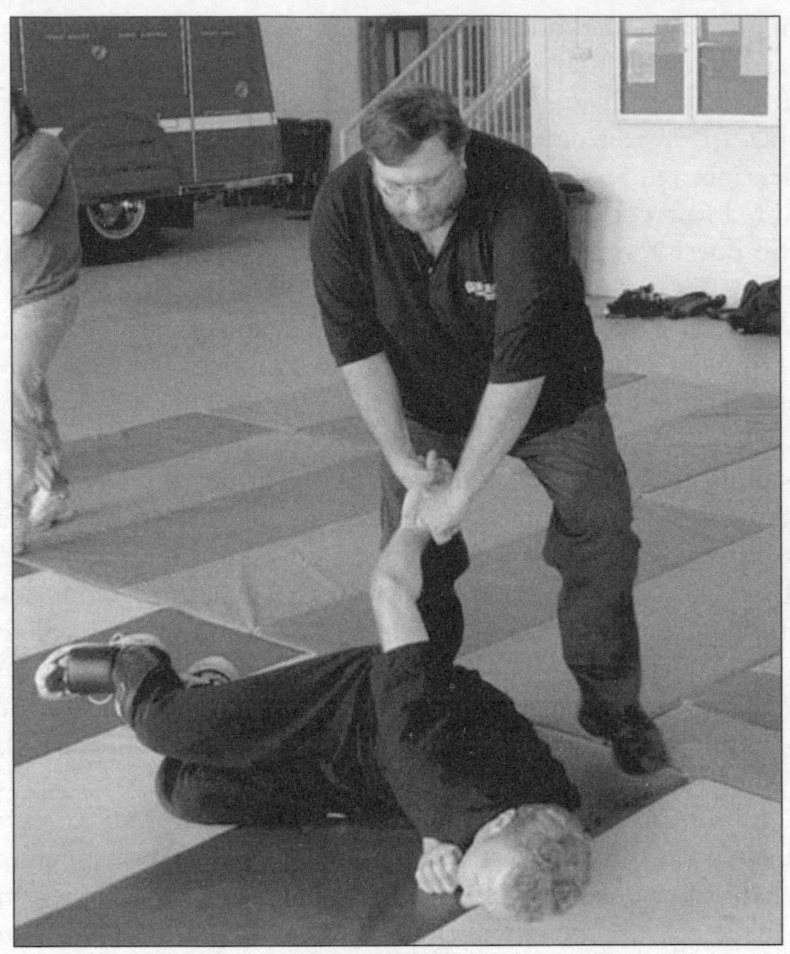

Police Arrest and Control Practice
photo by John West

Many police departments bring in specialists to offer additional training for their officers, like this advanced Cuff & Control workshop.

suspect makes a sudden and violent move, the officer—who would be maintaining a grip on the suspect's arm—could easily trip him, shove him away, or otherwise distance himself from the bite. At that point, the officer would likely resort to more and different methods of control.

According to San Antonio PD detective Joe McKinney, "Biters and spitters are usually secured with a hood, much like that used by beekeepers. Of course, patrol officers are going to use anything at their disposal to protect themselves, and if a hood isn't available, then they're probably going to toss the suspect into the back of a paddy wagon, or transport him in a patrol vehicle equipped with a prisoner transport cage."

Ultimately the zombie would be brought down, either under restraint or as a true "corpse", and then transported to jail or a hospital. In the next section we'll discuss how police can upgrade their response if the threat increases.

Just the Facts

K-9 Cops

Dogs have been used for many years by police departments all over the world. Dogs are smart, reliable, versatile, and they possess sensory abilities far beyond those of humans. Dogs have more than twenty times the number of olfactory (smell) receptors than humans do; and these receptors allow dogs to sense odors at concentrations nearly 100 million times lower than anything a human can smell. They can smell a single drop of blood in a five-quart bucket of water. They can track scents through rain, mud, and snow, and they don't need footprints to track a suspect over rocky ground and even desert sand.

A dog can also differentiate between thousands of commingled smells, which would be like a human trying to smell a single daffodil in a greenhouse filled with every flowering plant known to science.

This ultrasharp sense of smell allows police to employ dogs for search and rescue, bomb and drug detection, tracking, and even locating human remains.

Training a dog to be a professional sniffer is actually fun for the dog. The trainers and handlers use the promise of a favorite toy or play activity as a reward. When a K-9 officer locates something (drugs, bomb, whatever) it signals its handler using a conditioned response, usually barking, sitting, or pawing the ground.

These dogs are very deeply trained and in most modern departments they become both the partner and the property of their officer handlers, usually living at home with them and becoming part of the family. On the job, though, they are very focused and provide a skill set no human can match.

Expert Witness

According to Detective McKinney, K-9 units are a tremendous help in manhunts, especially if the police need to search a wooded area like the one across the street from our medical research center crime scene. "Best-case scenario would be to have multiple dog teams. The handler walks with them through the search area. The handler employs a variety of search patterns and techniques, depending on the size of the area to be searched. In a large forested area like this, the grid search pattern would probably be used. The area is divided up into grids, and personnel are assigned specific portions of the grid to search exhaustively. It usually takes ten minutes or so for San Antonio PD dog teams to get to a scene, though in this zombie scenario it might take considerably longer because the dog teams would probably be coming from the County or State Police. Response time would also be affected by call load. If this happens on a Friday or Saturday night, the dog teams might be otherwise engaged in non-related search missions."

"Typically, a K-9 handler will want a cover officer going with him," says Sgt. Ted Krimmel. "If the suspect has blood on his t-shirt and the K-9 handler has witnesses showing him where the subject went into the woods, the track should be a relatively simple affair. Even if the subject has a good lead on K-9, the dogs will either catch up, or he will eventually run into the perimeter officers. In my experience, the dogs actually have an easier time tracking in woods and over land than in urban/suburban settings. The first step after obtaining initial information on the incident, would to decide how large a perimeter to set (based on how long the suspect has been gone, direction of travel, terrain, etc.), then set it as quickly as possible. I like the use of K-9 and probably would have called to get it rolling even before the first units were on scene. The dogs are brought in from various agencies, usually local PDs. In Bucks, for example, there is no county police agency. The Sheriff's Office here does not have full police powers or training, thus no need for dogs. The deputies transport prisoners from the jail to court, serve civil papers, and make arrests for failure to appear for court. They always help the PDs if asked though. As far as the state goes, I don't think PSP has that many dogs, if any. Usually, we would use as many dogs as we can get. Timing is based on how far away the dogs are, are the K-9 officers on duty or home on call, etc."

The Zombie Factor

The Romero zombies seem to want to eat anything, human or not, and so the police dogs might be at risk during a capture. They are trained to bring a suspect down and maintain bite control over them until their handlers take over. In such a struggle, a zombie, who wouldn't react in fear of the dog and wouldn't care about the pain of a bite, might be able to successfully accomplish a bite.

The dog would likely react with increased aggression, and its handler/partner would be none too pleased. A bit of zombie stomping might occur at this point.

Whether the dog could become infected is unknown—and never addressed in the Romero films[2]—though its mouth would carry infectious materials (skin, blood) and it could, therefore, be a danger to its handler. In the earliest stages of an outbreak, this could lead to secondary infections, but once the nature of the infection was understood and the pattern of the spread of infection recognized, this kind of thing would likely not occur again.

More probably the cadaver dogs—those police dogs used to search for body parts in rubble (as in the wreckage at Ground Zero) or remains (in woods, inside the walls of a house, etc.)—might find a new role as zombie sniffers. If they're trained to bark at the presence of decomposing flesh, then they will become invaluable aids in searching for zombies. The dogs are attracted by cadaverine, a molecule produced by protein hydrolysis during putrefaction.

Should the crisis continue, it's reasonable to assume that there would be an intense push to train more and more dogs for this

2. In the *Resident Evil* films, zombie Dobermans are a common plot device.

Zombie Bit My Dog

On the subject of dogs catching the zombie virus, this has been touched on in some films, and in the *Dawn of the Dead* remake it's shown that zombies won't even attack a dog. Although we know that some diseases can be passed on from animals to man, it isn't that common, as Dr. Bruno Vincent, a world-class expert on prions, tells us: "Luckily, large-scale contamination of human population with contaminated bovine meat (as in Mad Cow Disease) seems not to have occurred since no recent cases have been reported during the last couple of years. This may be due to what we call the 'species barrier.' Transmission of prions from one species to another is by far less efficient than intra-species transmission."

job—not to find the dead, but to detect their approach so that civilians can flee and the police can prepare.

Just the Facts

SWAT on the Job

Police departments are tough, but when the ante gets upped and the standard training, arms, and equipment a patrol officer has at his or her disposal are not appropriate to the needs of the situation, there is a fallback plan: SWAT.

Expert Witness

SWAT (special weapons and tactics) is an acronym used by many police departments, and refers to a military-style approach to crime fighting. Other acronyms include SRT (special response team), QRT (quick response team), HRT (hostage rescue team), and others. Ted Krimmel is a member of SERT (South Central Bucks Emergency Response Team), and he shares a few of the differences between the film/TV version of SWAT and the real thing. "In films

***SWAT Alley Fight* by Jonathan Maberry**

Modern police officers are highly trained, heavily armed, and thoroughly conditioned to stay calm and efficient in all circumstances.

you often see the SWAT team at odds with the situation negotiator, but in reality the negotiator is a part of the team working with tactical to resolve the situation. You also see SWAT guys being all trigger-happy, but that just isn't so. In fact the life expectancy of suspects, hostages, and other involved persons rises *significantly* upon SWAT arrival."

Michael E. Witzgall, a former Dallas SWAT officer and now a tactical training consultant, agrees that the pop culture perception of SWAT is skewed. "First and foremost while we are the apex A-type personality, we are not the Neanderthals Hollywood has made us out to be. Most of us are well educated and have very stable family lives (divorce rate in SWAT is very low). Nor do we have the 'kill them all, let God sort them out' mentality."

This opinion is echoed by Walt Stenning, Ph.D., former head of the psychology department at Texas A&M University, who says:

"Generally speaking, a sound tactical operator (SWAT officer) is a very intelligent individual who performs well in an independent and/or team environment. These people must be able to think quickly and correctly without caving to exterior pressures."[3]

Sgt. Krimmel says that SWAT does, however, come prepared. "At a minimum, each officer carries a handgun (Glock or new S&W M&P in 9mm, .40 or .45), extra ammunition, handcuffs, gas mask, tactical body armor, ballistic helmet, eye protection, radio, gloves, knee and elbow pads, small tools, a good knife, a flashbang, a smoke grenade, OC spray, a small mirror, water, and a nomex hood. Depending on their assignment, they will also carry a long gun, typically a shotgun or Colt M-4 Commando machine gun (shortened M-16 variant). If not carrying a long gun, they might be carrying a less lethal shotgun, a 40 mm gas gun that fires both gas projectiles and less lethal projectiles, a pole camera, a ballistic shield or breaching equipment. Some officers carry a small revolver or pistol as a backup. Snipers carry Remington 700 sniper rifles in .308. We just got TASERs, but haven't fully implemented them yet."

The Zombie Factor

So, how then would a SWAT team respond to zombies in the streets attacking civilians? Witzgall observes, "Since I have no practical experience with zombies (most tactical commanders do not) after I changed my underwear, I would treat the situation by using our most basic operational concepts of contain, isolate, and control."

This means:

- *Contain*: Keep the zombies from spreading to greater areas.
- *Isolate*: Get zombies away from innocent people.
- *Control*: Make the zombies move where we want them to go.

3. Dr. Stenning's comment first appeared in a doctoral thesis by Dr. Kelly M. Jones, 1995, and is now used in most standard SWAT training manuals.

Bruce Bohne: Andy Takes Aim

In the remake of *Dawn of the Dead,* actor Bruce Bohne plays Andy, the owner of a gun shop located across the street from the mall. His character, who has virtually no dialogue in the film except for a wry message scrawled on a dry-erase board, nonetheless gained a huge fan following (particularly among gun enthusiasts and law enforcement officers) because of the character's superb skill with a rifle. In one of the most bizarre (and darkly hilarious) scenes, the survivors in the mall select zombies for Andy to shoot based on their resemblance to celebrities, including Jay Leno, Rosie O'Donnell, and Burt Reynolds.

I asked Bruce to comment on the significance of his role in the film. "I think the addition of Andy and his gun shop was a brilliant creative stroke for the plot. It moved some of the action from the confines of the mall; it gave the main cast hope and reason for attempting a breakout (arming themselves with Andy's guns); and it provided what many fans have told me was a favorite part of the film—the celebrity shooting."

Despite his involvement in such a landmark horror flick, Bohne says, "I've never been a huge horror movie fan, but have certainly seen my share of them. Zack Snyder's *Dawn* is the kind of horror I like best, with a great sense of humor along with the requisite blood and gore." He said he also liked the faster zombies. "It just makes it more in-your-face, amped-up, whoa-look-out-behind-you scarifying—which I like."

On the DVD release, Andy was given a far more complex backstory in a video short, *The Lost Tape: Andy's Terrifying Last Days Revealed.*

And when I asked him about seeing the original *Night*, he said, "That was almost 40 years ago. I was in 10th grade and saw it at a drive-in movie theater with a carload of beer-guzzling high school buddies, so my memory of it is a bit, um, hazy."

"To achieve my first goal of containment," says Witzgall, "I would use a series of ever tightening phase lines along each route of advancement and egress. This would mean that all streets would have SWAT teams holding the line. To keep zombies from moving into buildings, I would place patrol officers inside each building with orders to lock and barricade doors and windows. Anything making entry without contacting the officers first, would be shot. Civilians would be allowed to pass through our lines and proceed to medical & evacuation points. There would be several lines of defense. As my first phase line repels the zombies, my second line would pass through the line and pursue the zombies for approximately 50 yards. At that point the next phase line would hold as the previous line advances. By using this leap-frog method it would be hoped that I could drive the zombies into a location of my choice thus isolating them from civilians. Keeping the pressure on, we would eventually begin to control all the zombies' movement. If the terrain is used correctly—and the zombies are not allowed to break out, as my units close in an inner perimeter will gradually form. If the zombies break through or push a phase line back, that phase will egress and join the rearmost lines, tripling that line's strength."

Sgt. Krimmel's tactics are slightly different, showing the range and flexibility of this kind of response. "In response to a dozen zombies chasing civilians down the street, first I would establish they are in fact, zombies. Working off the assumption that the zombies are already dead and that the bite of a zombie will cause death or serious bodily injury, as SERT commander, I would authorize the use of any force needed to stop the zombies. I would send snipers to high ground or rooftops to deal with the zombies via head shots. On the ground, I would use SERT officers with M-4s and shotguns riding on top of our various armored vehicles, carrying as much ammunition as they can. I would set up a wide perimeter using uniformed patrol officers and K-9s. Most of our patrol officers carry shotguns and some assault rifles. They would have the same rules of engagement as the SERT officers. I'd also advise bringing personally owned axes and swords (the PD doesn't issue them), in case ammunition supplies run low. You don't have to re-load axes and swords. I'd also utilize helicopter or other aircraft if they were available."

Krimmel also commented on how SERT might handle a more contained situation. In our zombie scenario we've seen an infected person wearing doctor scrubs walking away from a medical research center. Naturally this building, being part of the crime scene, would be searched. If the zombie infection started there, then the entire building and all of its occupants would become part of a different kind of crime scene, and the tactical teams would be called in.

"Upon arrival," Krimmel says, "we would set a perimeter of SERT officers with M-4s and K-9 units and put out as many snipers as available. While this was going on, we would attempt to find out in detail what has occurred, who may be involved, how many suspects and their descriptions, what type of weapons they may be armed with, do they have hostages, backgrounds on the hostages, who might have a grudge against the business owner, what kind of hazardous materials may be stored inside, if they have security cameras inside, can we view the cameras via the Internet, and I would find the maintenance man for the building and keep him with me. Nobody will know the building better than him. We would make arrangements to have EMS treat and evacuate the injured to local hospitals. We would have fire apparatus sent to standby. At some point, we would start making attempts at communication with the occupants, find out what they want and advise them to surrender. If communication failed, eventually we would make entry in an attempt to arrest the occupants and rescue any civilians. While making entry would certainly be a last resort, we certainly would not wait too long. Waiting too long would endanger any injured civilians and possibly give the suspects a chance to fortify their position, endangering the SERT officers further. Upon entry, we would probably utilize K-9 to quickly locate any hostiles and then take necessary steps to take them into custody. Should this turn into a zombie situation, I would have to make arrangements to safely house the injured in case they turn into zombies. I would call the CDC for guidance as well as the FBI and the rest of the alphabet agencies."

I asked my experts to comment on the movie set piece of cops being overwhelmed. "The biggest thing to remember here," says Krimmel, "is we train to tactically retreat when necessary. Obviously, the whole concept of retreat is looked down on by people who have no concept how to win a fight. We look at retreat as a necessary element of eventual victory (or live to fight another day).

In the event an element of the SERT team was overwhelmed or even a single member was injured, they would notify command of their situation. Any injured members would be evacuated ASAP with available non-injured members providing cover fire. On every single mission we take, we have a Rescue Team on standby. That team is usually staffed by SERT officers and TEMS (tactical emergency medical services). We have a combination of sworn police TEMS and select members of local rescue squads. The rescue team's sole function is to go to a SERT element that is in trouble and assist as needed, particularly with respect to injured officers. We train 'officer down' rescues on a regular basis, using shields, armored vehicles, and natural cover to effect the rescues. Upon activation of the rescue team, the original mission (hostage rescue, high risk warrant) takes a secondary role to the mission of providing safety to the SERT element that is in trouble."

Witzgall has an equally high opinion of what the modern military would do when faced with this same kind of problem. He says, "A contemporary infantry squad (12 men) can deliver or has on call more munitions than a WWII infantry company (200 men). Unless ordered to DIP (Die in Place) being overrun is not very likely. An infantry unit will break contact before that is allowed to happen. As for the headshots they always talk about in zombie films. . . . If ya put enough rounds down range (as only our military can) head hits will most certainly happen. Also, you may only kill a zombie with headshots, but I would like to see him walk with his legs blown off.

"And as for panic and run scenarios," he adds, "well-trained soldiers rarely break down and run. Some will fall back without orders, only to regroup and attack. Units are trained to hold or move off a defensive point then counter attack. It is a type of self-discipline that can hardly be explained. As the old saying goes: Courage is not the absence of fear, but the conquering of fear. And in that, there is true valor!"

What would make soldiers—or police, for that matter—fight so fiercely against such frightening opponents? And what about the emotional component—after all zombies were once ordinary people, not terrorists of a foreign government. Would this take the heart out of the men holding the line? "This really depends on the circumstances," Witzgall admits. "Killing something that is trying to eat me leaves little room for discussion. Still, what if the Zombie was someone you knew or loved. That will be pretty tough going! Most SWAT/Military types deal with killing someone in their own way. It is not something we talk to outsiders about, fearing condemnation. A question that is often asked (to me) is why do we fight, especially if killing a person is so difficult to deal with. The answer is that we fight for our teammates to our left and to our right—and we fight for our friends and families so they will not have to."

And in a zombie war, the soldiers would fight so that their friends and their families—and their fellow soldiers on the line—don't fall victim to the infection itself. That kind of determination is more likely to strengthen resolve rather than cause a soldier to drop his or her gun and flee.

"We often train officers to shoot center mass," says Sgt. Krimmel, "because it is the easiest thing to hit in a high stress situation. But . . . we have taught 'body armor drills' for years in firearms training. Basically the drill simulates shots to the body that have been ineffective (due to body armor, or in this case zombies). The officer then transitions his shooting to the head.[4] We train the officers to continue firing until the threat has stopped. One thing I am a big proponent of is the concept that cops carry handguns because they are convenient (easily carried on the belt, always there), not because they are the best weapon in a fight. Handguns rarely stop a suspect with a single shot, and typically take a couple. A suspect can still hurt you while being shot. Shotguns and rifles on the other hand, cause tremendous, immediate damage to humans, typically breaking bones and causing sudden, massive blood loss. I train our officers to always take a long gun if they think a fight may be coming. A firearms writer and former cop I admire, Clint Smith, has said, the handgun should be used to fight your way to your long gun. I agree."

He adds, "In order to kill a carbon based life form with a firearm, you basically have to disrupt the function of the heart, lungs, or brain. Assuming the premise that the zombie will only be

4. Also known as "failure drills!"

killed by a head shot, a shot to the chest could potentially cause enough blood loss (hydraulic failure) to at least slow a creature down. A 12-gauge shotgun loaded with 00 buckshot (standard police load) fires 9 .33 caliber pellets at once. The tissue damage and resulting blood loss at close range is devastating. It should have enough energy to enter the chest and exit the rear of the suspect. There is potential damage to the heart, lungs, and spinal cord with such a shot. A 5.56 mm tactical, bonded round fire from an M-4 or police assault rifle will have similar effect on a human torso. Besides head shots, we also train officers to take shots at the groins and upper thighs of dangerous suspects to hit the femoral arteries or break leg bones to stop movement of the suspect. A close shot to the arms with a shotgun or M-4 should incapacitate said arm simply through broken bones and/or tissue and blood loss."

The bottom line is that in a one-to-one confrontation or in a pitched battle the officers of the law and the military would be able to hold the line.

If it started as a plague and spread, we'd take a lot of losses; but once the enemy was identified and the information relayed to the proper authorities (and, as discussed in Chapter 3 this would happen very quickly), then the response from law and military would be immediate and it would be formidable. Cops have radios and computers for communication and information sharing; they have high-tech weapons and body armor; they have armored vehicles; and they have the training and discipline to hold the line.

On the other hand if *all* the recent dead rose at once without requiring a bite to start things off, well sure, we'd be toast. But as we've already established, that's the least likely scenario. It's the plague we have to worry about, and when serums and inoculations fail, a barrage of well-aimed bullets seems to be a pretty good backup plan.

Just the Facts

Deadly Force

The use-of-force continuum is a set of guidelines established by the U.S. Department of Justice to help officers respond to the flexible nature of street encounters. The idea is to maintain control over the situation while insuring the safety of the officer, the safety of civilians (witnesses, bystanders, family members, victims, etc.) and, whenever possible, the safety of the suspect. But the suspect's safety comes last, and in need the officer can escalate all the way to lethal response.

The Department of Justice describes it this way: "When the use of force is reasonable and necessary, officers should, to the extent possible, use an escalating scale of options and not employ more forceful means unless it is determined that a lower level of force would not be, or has not been, adequate. The levels of force that generally should be included in the agency's continuum of force include: verbal commands, use of hands, chemical agents, baton or other impact weapon, canine, less-than-lethal projectiles, and deadly force."[5]

In confrontations police always start low on the force continuum ladder, attempting verbal commands first; and most often this works because rational people know that resisting arrest seldom ends happily. Noncompliance with verbal commands, however, is more common than patrol officers would prefer, and when that stratagem fails, the officer moves another step up the force continuum. This is something all police officers are trained to do, and they do it automatically.

Zombies aren't the only ones who bite; irrational (and sometimes even rational but pissed-off) humans do it, too. Long before AIDS and other communicable diseases elevated health concerns, cops were employing skills to prevent being bitten. It's disgusting, it hurts, and the human mouth is filthy.

There are a number of techniques, both unarmed and using the tools all officers carry, to deter and control someone who has gotten a little "bitey." As we've discussed, control techniques such as

5. www.usdoj.gov.

takedowns and joint locking are useful in most cases. Joint locks and attacks to pressure-sensitive spots (nerve clusters, etc.) will not, of course, work on zombies since the living dead feel no pain and will struggle even with a sprained or broken arm. And a lot of experienced officers will tell you that a crack addict or a hysterical and irrational person will sometimes continue to fight even in the presence of great pain or injury. The lack of response to pain compliance doesn't startle officers into vulnerable immobility as is sometimes shown in fiction. All this means is that there is a clear and present need to go at least one more step up the force continuum.

Chemical weapons like Mace and OC spray[6] are often employed. Zombie experts have widely suggested that zombies, though unthinking, rely heavily on sight, smell, and hearing for tracking their prey. Mace (tear gas) or OC spray will significantly blur vision and interfere with the sense of smell. This would allow the officer to cuff the zombie.

Or would it? According to Detective McKinney, pepper spray wouldn't be his weapon of choice against a zombie. "Pepper spray works because it severely irritates the eyes. As such, it is what is known as a pain-compliance tool. If your zombies are reanimated corpses, then a mere eye irritant will not bother them or slow them down in the slightest. It's a clear liquid that does not totally occlude a person's sight, but rather irritates the eyes to the point that the person can't help but close them (while writhing on the ground in pain). A corpse, I don't think, would react at all to the pepper spray."

And so we take another step up the force continuum.

If the zombie was too wild, or if there were multiple zombies, then the use of batons would be a common next step. When an officer takes a baton to a suspect's knee, that knee is going to bend. A leg that is suddenly and forcefully bent removes the structural support for the body's mass, and gravity yanks it down. Gravity is a constant, and lacking support any object will fall at approxi-

6. OC spray, also known as pepper spray, is an abbreviation of Oleoresin Capsicum, and is a lachrymatory agent, which is a chemical compound that irritates the eyes to cause tears, pain, and even temporary blindness.

Art of the Dead – George Martzoukos

Zombie Hunger

"The art of the weird and the fantastic feels like it is my second nature. I find so much beauty in it."

mately 10 meters per second. This value (known as the acceleration of gravity) is the same for all free-falling objects regardless of how long they have been falling, or whether they were initially dropped from rest or thrown up into the air. Even a zombie will hit the deck.

If the zombie is even more aggressive—or is rushing forward in such a way that the officer does not feel that the baton is the appropriate choice—there are two very serious upgrades in his potential response: Tasers and firearms.

The final step in the force continuum is the use of deadly force.

Expert Witness

Wilson says, "Shooting to the head is not standard procedure for police. We're taught to aim for the center of the body. That's where the heart, lungs and spine are. Unlike the movies cops don't fire unless they have no choice, but when they do fire shooting to wound is seldom a smart move. You don't try to 'wing' someone, you don't shoot them in the leg. Guns are killing devices. If we've drawn our service weapon then a lot of other things—strategies and tools—have failed, or the situation was too big to begin with. In those circumstances you are shooting to put someone *down*."

Former LAPD officer Dennis Miller agrees. "In the twenty-two years I worked LAPD I never fired my gun once. I used OC spray a lot, and my baton. I even did some hand-to-hand stuff. I'm a believer in the idea that guns are for killing, not for settling disputes. Sure, we may draw our weapons in order to maintain order, say while someone else is cuffing suspects or during a house entry, but having to fire is rare. And I've been in some pretty hairy situations. So I know for sure that if I had ever needed to fire my gun it would be to kill."

An active officer from Washington, D.C., who declined to be named in this book, had this to say: "Here's the problem with shooting to wound. Actually, here are a couple of problems. First, you aim for an arm or leg you could miss and that bullet is going to keep traveling until something stops it. How stupid is that on the street? Second, the bullet can easily pass through a limb and you have the same problem. Also, a wounded suspect who still has his gun can continue to shoot back, and screw that! Last, and here's a real problem all across the U.S.—you shoot some schmuck who's just popped a cap in a liquor store owner and taken a shot at you and you hit him in the arm or leg, he's going to *sue* the ass off the city and the SOB will win. I was in two shoot-outs. I guess it's my good fortune that I didn't have to kill someone, but it wasn't

Use of Deadly Force **by Jonathan Maberry**

Deadly force seems like an appropriate response to an attack by the living dead.

for lack of trying. In both cases there were circumstances that prevented me from being the one to make the take-down shot."

Though head shots may not be standard operating procedure (SOP) for most police departments, it has become common in the personal enrichment training many law enforcement professionals seek to improve their skill sets. One training exercise that has gained a lot of popularity is the "failure drill." Firearms expert Karl Rehn, owner of KR Training, a company in Austin, Texas, that teaches firearm safety, NRA instructor certification, and firearm safety instructor programs, tells us about this drill: "Failure Drill" is short for 'failure to stop' drill. It—like dozens of other terms used in relation to defensive handgun training—originated from Col. Jeff Cooper and the Gunsite Academy out in Arizona. Gunsite taught students to shoot a 'double tap' (two shots in rapid succession) to the chest of someone that was a lethal threat. If that failed, then following up with a single head shot was the next thing to do. Modern thinking amongst trainers is that firing two to the chest and stopping to assess is dangerous because often people do not react immediately to handgun wounds, even two hits to heart and lungs. Current doctrine at most schools is to fire until the threat is down rather than give the bad guy an opportunity to shoot you back. Often this results in the general public getting upset because people get killed in shootouts with cops. The reality is that it can take up to 10 seconds for a lethal wound to drop someone, and even though the first hit may have been fatal the shooter doesn't know that until the threat is down. So while the first hit is taking effect the shooter continues to fire on the threat."

The Zombie Factor

Which brings us to the issue of the effect of a gunshot to a zombie.

"Aiming for small targets such as the head or legs from any distance beyond 4 or 5 yards seems like a near-certain recipe for a miss; remember, in a gunfight, only hits count." This comes from a Vietnam War veteran and member of the Combat Handguns online group.[7] He adds, "Rather than aim for small areas such as legs, arms or head, it seems more logical to continue to aim for the center of mass, as we are now taught, and to concentrate on the lower portion of the center of mass, in particular, the pelvic area. The pelvis is a large and very strong bone but most bullets with a kinetic power level of the .38 Special +P or larger and most centerfire rifle rounds can break the pelvis. Once the pelvis is broken, the individual is not physically able to stand and mobility is limited to his ability to crawl using the upper part of his body. Now, in a real human being, the pain associated with the slightest movement with a broken pelvis is almost beyond belief so effective resistance is pretty much ended. In a zombie, pain is not a consideration but the loss of agility and movement is the same. They may be able to crawl after their intended victims, but only a very

7. He declined to be named.

slow pace. Their intended victims could simply walk slowly away and dispatch the crippled zombies at their leisure. Yeah, it's a bit gruesome, but such is the nature of the beast."

"It's also a question of sheer impact," says Miller. "In the movies everyone seems to shake off a bullet. Heroes get shot and they keep running and firing their guns, same with the bad guys. In zombie movies they get shot over and over again and, okay, they're corpses so a body shot won't hurt them, but the foot-pounds of impact is sure as hell going to knock them down. At the very least it'll knock them back. That's a reality, man. A .357 Magnum handgun bullet weighs about 125 grains and travels at 1450 fps."[8]

"The shock of impact of a gun," explains Miller, "will knock most people down, even if they're not taking a serious injury. Look at what happens when an officer takes a round in his Kevlar vest. Puts him on his ass."

But Rehn reminds us of the "failure drill," with its two-to-the-body one-to-the-head philosophy. He observes, "While this may sound overly aggressive, in reality it's been proven that this approach is the best way for the shooter to survive the incident and the fastest way to immediately stop the attack."

The Final Verdict: Deadly Forces

Cops versus zombies? Except in the presence of truly overwhelming odds, I give it to the cops. The question then becomes what constitutes overwhelming odds?

In a Romero scenario, one officer with a handgun and at least two spare magazines could probably take down six to ten zombies, and this accounts for body shots and misses. an expert shooter would do 50 percent better on average. A police sniper may be 100 percent better. In one-to-one confrontations it seems highly unlikely that a slow zombie would win against an armed and trained officer.

If we're talking fast zombies of the kind found in the *Dawn of the Dead* remake, or the fast human infection as seen in *28 Days Later*, then there will be a lower success rate due to shock value;

8. Fps: feet per second.

but as the situation becomes known, even in the midst of a crisis, the officers would bring more aggression to the game and more firepower. So round one may go to the zombies, but the rest of the fight will go to the guys with the guns.

Now the math on this changes in favor of the officers if they don't need to score a kill shot every time. Head shots are tough; shots to the centerline are easier, and a damaged spine will drop anyone—alive or dead. That's an electricity thing, and a damaged central nervous system is not going to help a zombie any more than it'll help a human. If the officers shoot to the pelvis and damage the hips, hip ball joint, or thigh bones, then not only will the zombie go down, they'll become obstacles that will slow down the attack of the zombies behind them. Again the odds turn in favor of men and women trained to use firearms.

A slam dunk? No; but the hot money will be on the boys in blue.

6

Spirits of the Dead

The Spiritual and Philosophical Implications of the Walking Dead

Hands **by Brandon Hildreth**

"This painting has a lot of personal meaning to me 'psychologically' but I'd say it represents a person that has been dragged down in the world, or someone that has been sort of killed inside and shut out, turned almost monster, but there is still a small part that begs to be let back inside; a part that still longs to show signs of a human soul."

Just the Facts

When the Spirit Moves You . . .

In *Night of the Living Dead* the zombies are just walking corpses. There is no trace of a personality in any of them. There is no love, no compassion, no fear; just as there is no hate, no malice, and no *deliberate* aggression. They are no longer human beings by any of the conventional definitions just as they are no longer "alive" by any known definition of that word.

Vampires, because they are intelligent and retain the memories of who they were before they were transformed into the undead, are a different matter. If a vampire kills a human, it is an immoral act, even if the vampire claims exemption from moral laws because those laws were created for mortal man and they are no longer mortal. The issue of a separate morality has been endlessly explored in vampire fiction and is the ongoing plot thread in all of Anne Rice's vampire novels, where her characters step back and forth across the line of "human" moral behavior and the belief that they are no more bound by moral restraint than a human is when slaughtering a cow. The vampire at least has an argument, however thin, to defend his actions, especially if he truly believes that he is now a higher being, or at very least, belonging to a separate species. This is the same view used in one way or another by centuries of humans to justify everything from slavery to eminent domain.

Zombies are not vampires. They don't think and they don't wrestle with complex issues of social and political philosophy.

Unless, of course, they possess a soul. If they possess souls, or if they retain any portion of their human consciousness or memories, then the issue suddenly becomes vastly more complex.

In *Night* there was not even an issue raised about zombies with souls, just as there was no obvious connection with any aspect of spirituality. The dead rise because of radiation. It's weird science, sure, but it's science. Then in Romero's second zombie film, *Dawn of the Dead*, hard science seems to take just a bit of a sidestep into spirituality in that it is *suggested* that planet earth has become the standing room only area for an overcrowded hell. The catch phrase is: "When there is no more room in Hell, the dead will walk the earth."[1] Just as with the first film, the cause of the zombie resurrection is implied rather than clearly explained.

Looking back, though, it seems likely that Romero had at least some kind of spiritual connection in mind when he conceived the whole series. After all, an early working title for the first film was *Night of Anubis*, and Anubis is the jackal-headed Egyptian god who served as the guardian of the dead and the overseer of the embalming process.[2] Anubis was also one of the gods who weighed the good and evil of each newly dead person and passed judgment on them. The bad souls linger in the underworld, the good ones are made into stars and cast into the heavens. The old working title implies both a spiritual link and a process of celestial judgment that has been imposed on mankind and his works. It's this latter that appears to inform most of Romero's *Living Dead* films and fits in well with his often scathing social and political commentary.

But then the rest of that second movie is played out in a way that reinforces the message that the zombies are soulless; just organic machines programmed by some totally unknown means to kill humans and eat them. There doesn't seem to be any emotional or psychological component evident; the zombes are aggressive and they're deadly, but they aren't actually *mean* about it. There's no evident personal hatred in them, no deliberate malice in their actions even though those actions are potentially lethal. If they are truly mindless and soulless, then their actions bear no more actual ill will than a hurricane, tornado, or earthquake. From that view zombies are a fact of a rather strange tweak on nature. They do, however, retain the smallest spark of memory, at least in as far as it is attached to gross motor skills. They can use simple tools (clubs, etc.), they can grab with their hands, they can make fists, they can climb ladders, and even turn door handles. Sure, you say, so can a spider monkey, but that doesn't make it a human being.

1. From the shooting script by George A. Romero.

2. In the oldest Egyptian histories Anubis was the god of the dead and the son of Ra; but in later histories he is depicted as the son of Osiris and the guardian of the dead who greets the newly dead and protects them on their journey to the underworld.

Art of the Dead – Tootie Detrick

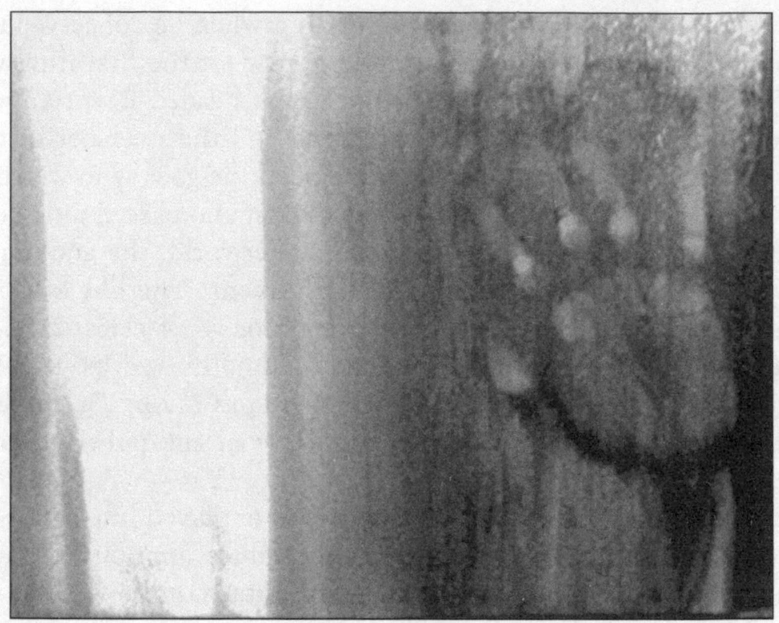

Don't Go Home

"I would like to see zombie films explore more of the connection between zombies and religion. I think that's part of our primal fear of zombies: the thought of hundreds of dead people with no souls, who don't feel pain or fear, coming after you and you are fighting to escape and stay alive. I tried to capture that in my painting, and people see it as a person reaching out for help to no avail."

In Romero's third and fourth films, *Day of the Dead* (1985) and *Land of the Dead* (2005), the issue becomes much more complicated, which further complicates any forensic analysis.

In *Day* a scientist tries to rehabilitate a captured ghoul by working to rebuild some degree of conscious awareness associated with ordinary objects (pocket combs, a paperback copy of a Stephen King novel,[3] etc.). The implication here is that pattern and object recognition might possibly stimulate active cognition and therefore some amount of reason. To a degree this works as the test zombie, known as Bub (wonderfully played by Sherman Howard[4]), seems docile toward the scientist, Dr. Logan (Richard Liberty), and even manages a single short sentence: "Hello, Aunt Alicia."

Though speech alone is not enough to establish a reasoning intelligence (just ask a parrot to explain *why* he wants a cracker), speech coming from a creature formerly capable of it is at least suggestive of the potential for a return to some level of reason.

The other side of this process is explored in Stephen King's 2006 novel *The Cell* in which a computer virus broadcast through cell phones wipes clean the mind of anyone using a phone at that moment. The wiped brains reboot into a new form—a telepathic hive mind that unifies the zombified masses. King's book discusses personality and its loss but stays away from any exploration of the soul and its connection to organic life. Romero, on the other hand, at least suggests that the soul exists and is tied to the physical body even after death.

In *Day*, after the inevitable plot turn when the humans typically screw things up through infighting and pettiness and everything goes to zombie hell in a handbasket, Bub reacts with both grief and anger when Dr. Logan is murdered. He goes hunting for the murderer, the vicious Captain Rhodes (Joseph Pilato) and kills him; but instead of doing it the typical zombie way, he *shoots* the captain. This demonstrates intelligence (however rudimentary), a thirst for vengeance, and some understanding of the concept of justice. Whereas revenge brings with it its own complex set of questions about morality, it is a decidedly *human* action. So . . . if Bub is human to some degree, does he then have a soul?

In *Land of the Dead*, the zombie Big Daddy—played with remarkable sympathy by Eugene Clark—is a hulking brute of a ghoul who is clearly functioning on a reasoning level, and who

3. And if you know that the King book in question was *Salem's Lot*, then you are a freakishly knowledgeable zombie geek . . . which means we'd probably get along pretty well.

4. Though billed as *Howard Sherman* in the credits.

ultimately leads his fellow zombies in an attack on a walled city of humans. Big Daddy's assault directly follows a supply raid by the humans during which a number of laughing, mocking humans maim and kill several ghouls. This seems to both alarm and anger Big Daddy, and he leads his "people" in a fairly clever and successful attack. During the attack Big Daddy demonstrates cunning, planning, and the use of tools. When his fellow ghouls are killed, he cries out in pain; when one is beheaded, he puts the crippled ghoul out of his misery. Each of these actions, though minimized to the barely articulate level, is human.

He learns from his actions, and he teaches other zombies what he's learned. For example, one plot device has the humans, who are raiding zombie-infested towns for food, using fireworks (called "sky flowers" in the film) to distract the zombies. For whatever reason zombies are attracted to fireworks. But Big Daddy shakes off his fascination with them and then jostles other zombies to take their attention away from the fireworks so they can focus on attacking the humans. That is reason.

He then organizes all the zombies in a raid on Fiddler's Green, the last known stronghold of humans. This is also an intelligent action; but his real moment of genius comes when his zombie army comes to the edge of the river separating his town from Fiddler's Green. Big Daddy looks out at the city across the river and then down at the water. Humans would be stopped there without the use of boats; but zombies don't *need* to breathe.[5] Big Daddy jumps into the river, followed by his army, and then they apparently walk across the riverbed to the far shore. The moment when they emerge is a riveting scene, beautifully shot . . . but more than that it establishes that the zombies not only made their way across the river but did so in a way only zombies could accomplish. That shows self-awareness, reason, and invention. It's advanced and adaptive problem solving.

Hard to imagine soulless and unthinking creatures figuring that out.

The actions of Big Daddy show more compassion and moral outrage than do the actions of nearly all the humans in the story. Just

5. According to Romero; a point our experts dispute, however.

as Bub's vengeance on Captain Rhodes shows more humanity than is shown by most of the humans involved in that story. In both cases—Bub and Big Daddy—we have a zombie with emotions and compassion; in both we have zombies with soul. If Bub and Big Daddy have souls, then we can infer that all the Romero zombies probably have souls.

Boy does that open up a can of worms, especially when you consider that we have to kill them in order to survive. So now the issue of whether zombies have souls is more complicated. Much more complicated.

Expert Witness

I asked my panel of experts to discuss these issues.

Dr. Kim Paffenroth, associate professor of religious studies at Iona College and author of the book *Gospel of the Living Dead*[6] sees it this way: "Since some people consider killing animals immoral, they would (I would assume) also consider zombie killing immoral. However, given the examples of Bub and Big Daddy, I would think that killing them would then have to be justified, especially under theories of self-defense (or, in our current troubled world, perhaps national security or an undeclared state of war). That could still be done, of course, as the killing of another person can be justified, but it would represent a huge difference from simply machine-gunning whole crowds of zombies without considering the action any further."[7]

"One cannot construe that zombies are immoral," argues Rabbi Michael Shevack. "You *can*, quite the opposite, construe that they are perfectly moral, because they cohere with their own nature, and are acting, naturally, as themselves. Theologically, the only question is whether or not zombies are an aberration of God, and therefore, by their instinctive nature, however natural it is to them, they are abominations. This would certainly be implied by

6. 2006 by Permuted Press; it won the 2006 Bram Stoker Award for Outstanding Achievement in Nonfiction.

7. Dr. Paffenroth is also the author of *Dying 2 Live*, a zombie novel published in 2007 by Permuted Press, and edited the zombie anthology, *History Is Dead*, 2008, also by Permuted Press.

Art of the Dead – Geff Bertrand

Zombie Nightmare

"The first zombie movie I saw was the black and white *Night of the Living Dead* by George Romero. I was very young and my peepers were glued to the TV because the idea of the dead coming back to life was very bone chilling. I woke up screaming many a night after that and had to sleep with a night-light."

the fact that radiation, viruses, prions, interfere with the natural course of God's Creation and therefore generate zombies. At best, zombies can be called amoral, with fairness to them, pending a serious discussion as to whether they are an aberration; but, like all aberrations, they were created out of creation, so, since Genesis has stated seven times (lest we forget it) that creation is GOOD—zombies must, in some fashion, have their right place and be part of that goodness, even in their fallen natures, if they have one. Nothing can arise unless the hand of God is in it. Including zombies. Unless of course, one believes in radical dualism, such as a competitor of Satan. I do not believe in such a radical dualism—so I believe that even zombies have their own blessed place, though what that place is as yet, I have not been able to discern."

And that brings up another and very subtle question, according to Rabbi Shevack: "Is a covenant between human beings and zombies possible? I wonder. After all, maybe they could be used to dispose of dead bodies, rather than turning what little open spaces we have now into graveyards. Maybe zombies can be harnessed as a way of getting rid of unwanted matter, and can actually be ecological-helpers. I don't know, but it's certainly food for thought."

"I'm not a fan of labeling things as moral and immoral," argues Professor Ladany, "because I think it takes away from individual freedom and cultural influence. I think of it rather as a healthy or unhealthy act. In the case of a predatory ghoul, if volition was not in his or her control, then it would be no more immoral than when any animal eats or attacks a prey or what seems to be a prey (e.g., a shark attack could be perceived as what happens when humans get in the way of sharks). Similarly, recall when Roy Horn (of Siegfried & Roy) was mauled by the tiger. People said the tiger went crazy. Chris Rock, however, pointed out that in actuality, 'the tiger just went tiger!' "

Interfaith Pastor Joyce Kearney says, "Morality is a funny thing. If you get a bunch of people together—clergy and lay persons—and ask them about the morality of killing they'll almost always tell you that it's immoral and against God's laws. They'll cite the Commandments. Yet some of them either have served in the military or are family with someone who has; some of them may have killed in war, or while on duty as police officers. Some may hold the belief that assisted suicide is a mercy rather than murder. Some support capital punishment. Some will hold that killing in self-defense, or in defense of, say, a child, would be justifiable. If zombies existed and they attacked, what they would do would not be immoral because they have no thought and no soul and are therefore not bound by Commandments or any other religious or governmental law. People would fear zombies, and they would hate them, but I can't see anyone pointing a finger and calling a zombie a sinner."

On the morality of killing zombies, Dr. Gretz says, "The first question would be, 'Would it be an illegal act?' What would the police do? The supreme court would have to rule that the zombie was not really a person and had no legal protections and not only could, but should be put down (the level of dead before that happened would be interesting). Next, is the individual's 'spirit' still residing in the body or has it left? If the spirit is gone—i.e., the person is literally dead in the religious sense—then there should be no problem once the Pope or some other authority said so. I think many people wouldn't wait before trying to 'kill' the zombies. However, many others would probably hesitate long enough to become victims themselves."

The Reverend Thomas Jefferson Johnson III, a Baptist minister from Trenton, New Jersey, weighs in on this: "If we delude ourselves into believing that we are a peaceful and nonviolent species—and all of history stands against that view—then we could never shoot a zombie even in defense because no matter what they are now they were once humans; but as I said, that would be delusional thinking at best, and at worst a barefaced lie. We are violent, and our church laws have tried, with varying degrees of success, to keep us from acting on our *nature* for the last six thousand years. As a man of God I would love to say that we are closer now than we've ever been to finally becoming a naturally moral people. But I just came back from Somalia where I was on a medical aid trip with the Red Cross. I've been in Iraq, and I said prayers over the butchered bodies of children in Rwanda. If we would do such things to each other—often in the name of God—then what makes you think we would even flinch when it comes to pulling the trigger on a zombie?"

Like most issues this one defies easy explanations.

"Consider this," says Rabbi Shevack, "Rabbi Akiba,[8] whose dictum became definitive in Judaism, says that if someone attempts to kill you, kill them first. It makes no difference if it is a Zombie at all. However, if, in attempting to kill them, you could have stopped them from killing you by simply maiming them, and you didn't just maim them—then it is tantamount to murder. In the case of Zombies one has no choice, since the maiming of them has little effect. Morally one must go for complete destruction."

Zombies . . . Fast or Slow? Part 6

- **"Slow. There is something so terrifying about the slow attack that is inescapable. Serial killers can be fast, jaguars can be fast, a train about to hit you on the tracks can be fast—but there is a more nightmarish quality to the shambling corpse whose only goal is to find the nearest living human to eat. There is something incredibly horrible about the idea of being taken down by a slow, dumb predator—we expect the smart ones to get us, but not those relentless brainless ones."—Doug Clegg, Bram Stoker Award-winning author of *The Vampyricon***
- **"For me, slow, but I have no beef with the fast ones. But slow makes more sense. They're inexorable, so why run? What's the hurry?"—Novelist and comic book writer/artist Bob Fingerman**
- **"Fast! (Unless they're after my ass!)"—Best-selling mystery novelist Ken Bruen, author of *The Guards* and *American Skin***

8. Akiba ben Joseph (c. 50–c. 135 C.E.) is considered the father of rabbinical Judaism and is referred to in the Talmud as *Rosh la-Chachomim* ("head of all the sages").

The Zombie Factor

In his excellent series of living dead novels, author Brian Keene takes a decidedly supernatural view and has a demonic force causing the dead to rise. Unlike many of the other zombie stories, Keene also has this otherworldly evil resurrect all recently dead things: animals, insects. It's an attack on all life, not just on humanity, and as such is an unstoppable force.

Keene comments, "The zombies in *The Rising*[9] and *City of the Dead* aren't your father's undead. These are not mindless, slow-moving corpses. They're smart. Fast. And very, very hungry. They can hunt you, set traps for you. Use weapons. Drive cars. In the mythos I've created for both books (and indeed, all of my novels) the bodies of the dead are possessed by the Siqqusim, a race of demonic entities, led by an arch-demon named Ob. The Siqqusim have been with us for a long time. Their cults sprang up in Assyrian, Sumero-Akkadian, Mesopotamian, and Ugaritic cultures, where they were consulted by necromancers and soothsayers. Eventually, they were banished to a realm, which is neither Heaven nor Hell, but somewhere in between. Now, they have been unleashed upon the Earth once again. After we die, they take up residence in our bodies, specifically—in our brains. Once the body is destroyed, the Siqqusim return to the Void and await transference to a new body. The process begins anew. Finally, when they have destroyed all of the planet's life forms, they move on to somewhere else, just like locusts, and start all over again. There are life forms on other planes of existence, other realities, and the Siqqusim have reign over them all."

David Wellington works possession from a different angle in his zombie trilogy, *Monster Island, Monster Nation*, and *Monster Planet.*[10] In that series of books an ancient evil force exerts its will to transform the world into a global kingdom of the dead. Of his choice to vary the model, Wellington says, "I wanted to do something different with my zombies. I didn't want to say it was a virus, or a prion, or radiation from a Venusian space probe. I

9. Winner of the 2003 Bram Stoker Award for the Best First Novel.

10. *Monster Island* and *Monster Nation* were published in 2006, and *Monster Planet* in 2007—by Thunder Mouth.

wanted to tell a story about the end of the world, too, which had to encompass all of human history, from the dawn of civilization until its final collapse."

This is not to say that the more supernatural zombie stories veer completely away from science. In fact, Wellington nicely combines the two and has a doctor who stage-manages his own transition to the zombie state in order to retain his intelligence. The doctor (Gary), knowing that he was dying of the infection, keeps an oxygen mask on as his body dies so that his brain doesn't suffer from the deteriorating effects of oxygen deprivation. This is a clever plot device that allows for the creation of a truly unique thinking zombie. "Gary's original role," Wellington says, "was simply to be an observer behind enemy lines—someone who could walk amongst the zombies and see what they did when there were no living people around. As I wrote the book however he evolved and became central to the thematic questions of the story—what is the real difference between life and undeath? And what kind of obligations last beyond death? Instead of creative freedom I think he gave the novel its direction."

Since Wellington's zombie uprising does not start with a single infection but is a truly spiritual pandemic, he lets this color his view of whether humanity would, or indeed could, survive a zombie apocalypse. "If the dead came back all at once," he observes, "if everybody that died came back in minutes, yeah, we'd be hosed. The world's military and police forces are designed around the idea of suppressing outbreaks of violence in small areas over relatively short durations. We're not ready for that kind of threat. Small groups of survivors might hang on for a few months but slowly they would starve to death—or die of various diseases once they lost the ability to control their water supply. Meanwhile the zombies would be closing in on them, every day, overwhelming them with vastly superior numbers . . . Yeah, it would be the end."

Whether an author or filmmaker takes a scientific or spiritual stance on zombies, the genre still lends itself to social commentary. As Wellington views it, "Zombies are just like us, but with any individual qualities and personality removed. They can't be reasoned with, nor can they be satisfied. They have no inner lives, nor any free will, and with just a bite they can make you just like

Art of the Dead – Zach McCain

Apocalyptic Despair

"What do you do with your life when you are the only person left in the world? The soldiers in *Day of the Dead* feel much more despair than the scientists because they are still clinging to the world that was. They consciously know that the world has fallen . . . so the subconscious process of clinging to hope is driving them insane."

they are. They don't even have to be violent to be frightening—it's their sheer anonymity that bugs us, I think."[11]

We've been primarily discussing one of two kinds of zombies: the Hollywood kind as opposed to the Haitian kind. But in truth there is a third kind, according to David Chalmers, professor of

11. David Wellington is also the author of the vampire novels *13 Bullets* and *99 Coffins*, both published in 2007 by Three Rivers Press.

philosophy at the Australian National University and director of the Centre for Consciousness. Chalmers is one of a number of world-class philosophers who have written about "philosophic zombies," or P-zombies for short. "A philosophical zombie," he explains, "is physically identical to a normal human being, but completely lacks conscious experience. Zombies look and behave like the conscious beings that we know and love, but 'all is dark inside.' There is nothing going on inside . . . it's like being a zombie."

Professor Richard V. Greene, co-editor (with Kasey Silem Mohammad) of *The Undead and Philosophy: Chicken Soup for the Soulless* (Open Court Publishing Company 2006), a book on the philosophy of zombies and vampires, adds: "Philosophical zombies are molecule for molecule identical with normal humans, but have no consciousness (i.e., no experience). They are different from movie zombies, which appear to have a variety of inner experiences. If zombies are actually animated dead what does this do for the definition of 'alive'? It's not clear. It seems like the definition (animated and dead) is merely stipulative. One pretty much has to grant that such a category exists (because if one thinks about it too much one would have to conclude that things that are animated ARE alive)."

The Final Verdict: Musing on Zombies

It comes as no real surprise that there isn't a clear-cut and definitive set of philosophic answers to whether zombies are human or not. There are too many ways to spin it, and exploring the philosophic riddles inherent in this monster archetype has been part of the fun and fascination of the genre. Even Romero seems to have a flexible view of things, shifting from the stance that they are merely mindless corpses in the first films to the far more chilling thought that they are somehow evolving in the more recent entries.

This evolution of the physical nature and of the spiritual self is in keeping with most people's view of how all beings exist: they learn, they adapt, they change. On one hand there is some hope peppered in with the dread because it suggests at least the *possi-*

Art of the Dead – Zach McCain

The Savage Dead

"Sub-genres of film rise and fall in popularity from time to time (spaghetti westerns, kaiju, martial arts films, etc.) and are revolutionized in some way or another so that they are fresh to new viewers. Whatever the reason though I hope zombies continue to be popular seeing as how there is still a lot of room for creativity and expansion in the genre."

bility that communication and understanding might one day happen. Who knows, perhaps Big Daddy might have come to some agreement to live and let live (rephrase that however you like for zombies) with the humans fleeing the ruins of Fiddler's Green in *Land of the Dead*. Maybe Bub led the zombies of *Dawn of the Dead* into the beginnings of zombie civilization and Big Daddy was a step or two further along in that process.

That's the one really comforting thing in philosophy: anything's possible.

7

Law of the Dead

Legal Ramifications of a Zombie Plague

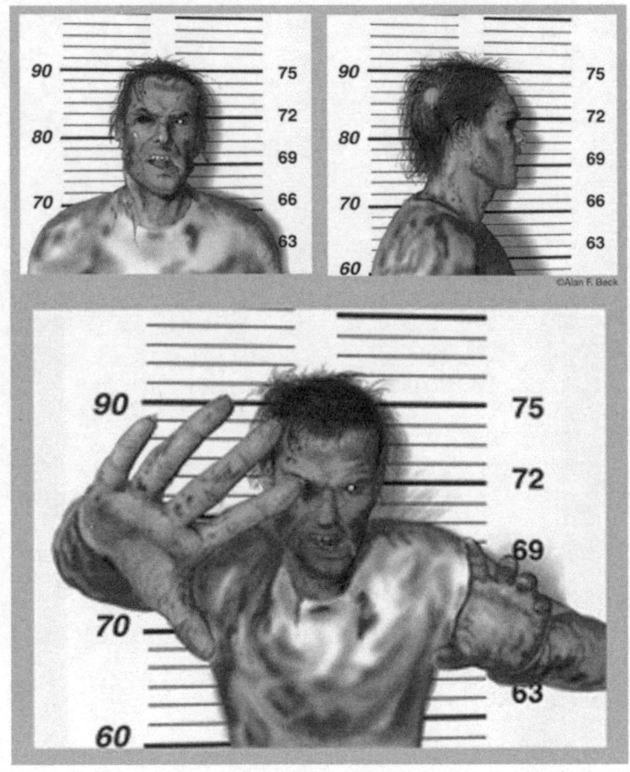

Zombie Mugshots by Alan F Beck

"Do we all hope for immortal life? Death is bad. How about a second chance. Also most zombies become one not of their own doing. They are usually victims of a curse, environmental disaster or science gone bad. They are sympathetic in a way and if it could happen to them, then it could happen to you and me. We've all been a victim of something sometime."

There are always legal issues, no matter what the situation. Unless the world is actually totally overrum by the dead and humanity is wiped out, lawyers are going to get involved. Judges and lawmakers will get involved. Laws will be changed, charges will be filed, and somebody somewhere will get sued. After all, we are talking about *people*—even if they became zombies. We're also dealing with infection, death, suicide, euthanasia, murder, self-defense, and a host of other legal issues, none of which will have been clearly defined in terms of zombies prior to the event—thus, afterward these laws will have to be interpreted.

Let's take a look at how that plays out in the legal arena.

JUST THE FACTS

Zombie Murder?

Is killing a zombie murder? Let's open a law book and see:

This definition is too vague to fit the wide variety of crimes that

---

Homicide

The killing of a human being due to the act or omission of another. Included among homicides are murder and manslaughter, but not all homicides are a crime, particularly when there is a lack of criminal intent. Noncriminal homicides include killing in self-defense, a misadventure like a hunting accident or automobile wreck without a violation of law like reckless driving, or legal (government) execution. Suicide is a homicide, but in most cases there is no one to prosecute if the suicide is successful. Assisting or attempting suicide can be a crime.[1]

---

1. All legal definitions used in this chapter are excerpted by permission of the authors from *The Peoples Law Dictionary: Taking the Mystery Out of Legal Language* by Gerald and Kathleen Hill (MJF Books, 2002).

Murder

The killing of a human being by a sane person, with intent, malice aforethought (prior intention to kill the particular victim or anyone who gets in the way), and with no legal excuse or authority. In those clear circumstances, this is first-degree murder.

may be associated with a zombie uprising. Certainly there will be killings in self-defense and legal execution (something that would be government sanctioned once zombies start roaming the streets). But in a one-to-one confrontation, we need something more specific.

This immediately gets complicated because there is some debate as to whether a zombie can be classified as a human being. Authority could hardly be given in the earliest stages of the crisis; and prior intent is not always there, especially if a zombie comes lumbering out of the dark.

First-Degree Murder

"Although it varies from state to state, it is generally a killing that is deliberate and premeditated (planned, after lying in wait, by poison or as part of a scheme), in conjunction with felonies such as rape, burglary, arson, involving multiple deaths, the killing of certain types of people (such as a child, a police officer, a prison guard, a fellow prisoner), or with certain weapons, particularly a gun. The specific criteria for first degree murder are established by statute in each state and by the United States Code in federal prosecutions. It is distinguished from second-degree murder in which premeditation is usually absent, and from manslaughter, which lacks premeditation and suggests that at most there was intent to harm rather than to kill.

Second-Degree Murder

A nonpremediated killing, resulting from an assault in which death of the victim was a distinct possibility. Second-degree murder is different from first-degree murder, which is a premeditated, intentional killing, or results from a vicious crime such as arson, rape, or armed robbery. Exact distinctions on degree vary by state.

It's doubtful anyone would be charged with first-degree murder in a zombie situation . . . unless the victim was, in fact, a child, police officer, prison guard, or fellow prisoner. And all of those are likely if the infection spreads.

Well, an attack by a zombie would certainly fit with the concept of a sudden quarrel or fight and in the heat of passion. One tends to get quite passionate about surviving a zombie massacre. But is killing a zombie a reckless act? It doesn't seem so.

This one's tricky since flight to safety from zombies certainly carries with it the possibility that zombie killing may be a factor, though it can be argued that very few people actually planned to have those deadly encounters while making a run for it. Again a clever lawyer (who, for whatever reason, wants to defend zombie rights in the post-zombie world), could argue that since zombies are slow and awkward that a reasonably healthy adult should be able to evade them or at most knock them aside or down rather than outright killing them during the escape. In cases where the zombies are thin on the ground, this is certainly true, though an opposing view would state that as long as zombies exist they are a constant threat to human life, and, therefore, violent and/or lethal attacks at any time are justified.

It's about at this point that the trial would settle down to months upon months of expert witness arguments and legal wrangling. Somebody someday will do a book or movie on The Great Zombie Trial.

This obviously doesn't apply in most zombie cases, but in films like the original *Dawn of the Dead*, outlaw bikers attack zombies

Malice Aforethought

(1) The conscious intent to cause death or great bodily harm to another person before a person commits the crime. Such malice is a required element to prove first-degree murder. (2) A general evil and depraved state of mind in which the person is unconcerned for the lives of others. Thus, if a person uses a gun to hold up a bank and an innocent bystander is killed in a shoot-out with police, there is malice aforethought.

while looting a mall. Technically so do our four heroes in that story. In the aftermath of a zombie crisis, a crafty lawyer could build a case that killing a zombie in order to commit a crime (looting, robbery, etc.) is itself a crime. Whether that case would be successful is a hard call, especially when we recall cases where burglars successfully sued homeowners for being shot while in the commission of a home invasion.

Voluntary manslaughter certainly seems to apply, since killing in the heat of passion (providing one is passionate about surviving a zombie attack) is pretty much the standard operating procedure in these cases. And there are lots of involuntary manslaughter

Manslaughter

The unlawful killing of another person without premeditation or so-called "malice aforethought" (an evil intent prior to the killing). It is distinguished from murder (which brings greater penalties) by lack of any prior intention to kill anyone or create a deadly situation. There are two levels of manslaughter: voluntary and involuntary. Voluntary manslaughter includes killing in the heat of passion or while committing a felony. Involuntary manslaughter occurs when a death is caused by a violation of a nonfelony, such as reckless driving (called "vehicular manslaughter").

Self-Defense

The use of reasonable force to protect oneself or members of the family from bodily harm from the attack of an aggressor, if the defender has reason to believe he/she/they is/are in danger. Self-defense is a common defense by a person accused of assault, battery, or homicide. The force used in self-defense may be sufficient for protection from apparent harm (not just an empty verbal threat) or to halt any danger from attack, but cannot be an excuse to continue the attack or use excessive force. Basically, appropriate self-defense is judged on all the circumstances. Reasonable force can also be used to protect property from theft or destruction. Self-defense cannot include killing or great bodily harm to defend property, unless personal danger is also involved, as is the case in most burglaries, muggings, or vandalism.

cases where zombies were hit by the cars of people fleeing the crisis. Although in *Shaun of the Dead*, Ed (played by Nick Frost) seems to definitely be going out of his way to smash into as many zombies as possible on the way to the Winchester Pub. But in most cases the killing of a zombie by car would likely be viewed as involuntary manslaughter or, possibly, self-defense.

Now we seem to be getting closer. By any rational viewpoint killing a zombie would be classified as self-defense. But what does the law have to say?

The law makes clear provisions for self-defense. According to attorney and forensic expert Andrea Campbell,[2] "The first requirement for self-defense is that the defendant must believe that force was necessary for his own protection. This belief must be qualified as a 'reasonable belief,' such that a reasonable person in the same or similar situation would have formed the same strategy."

One can reasonably assume that anyone facing a hungry zombie would have the same reaction. However the law is often a little trickier than it first appears, Campbell warns: "One other requirement as established by some states are the elements of retreat and

2. Andrea Campbell is the coauthor (with Ralph C. Ohm) of *Legal Ease: A Guide to Criminal Law, Evidence, and Procedure* (C.C. Thomas, 2002).

deadly force. For example, Oklahoma law says that, 'There is no duty to retreat if one is threatened with bodily harm.' Although the Tennessee court, on the other hand, says that, 'A person who can safely retreat must do so before using deadly force.' Now most courts do make the allotment that a person does not have to retreat in his own home."

Which also brings us to justifiable homicide.

Is killing a zombie evil intent? Not for most people. Is it criminal intent? In some cases, sure, especially during breaking and entering (almost all zombie stories involve survivors barricading themselves in a house, building, etc., that doesn't belong to them) or looting (whether for survival basics like food, or for less noble and excusable reasons).

In many of the zombie films, starting with *Night*, retreating from the ghouls is the basic plan everyone seems to be following, hence the holing up in a deserted farmhouse and the subsequent nailing of boards crookedly across the windows. It's really only after the zombies attack en masse that the humans retaliate with lethal force. In the opening scene, when the character Barbara and her brother Johnny are attacked in the cemetery, Barbara wants nothing more than to retreat. The zombie chases her, attacking her again and again. If there was ever a case of justifiable homicide that would be it.

Ben, the hero of the piece, is in the process of fleeing when his truck runs out of gas. The cellar of the farmhouse is filled with folks who have fled from the ghouls.

Justifiable Homicide

A killing without evil or criminal intent, for which there can be no blame, such as self-defense, to protect oneself or to protect another, or the shooting by a law enforcement officer in fulfilling his or her duties. This is not to be confused with a crime of passion or claim of diminished capacity, which refers to defenses aimed at reducing the penalty or degree of crime.

By any legal standard the requirements for retreating are certainly fulfilled. The zombies, however, are persistent, and the trapped humans have no choice but to use deadly force in order to survive.

"In all such cases the question of the amount of force is always looked at as well," Campbell says, "and you won't be surprised to know that there are different schools of thought here too. How much force is *reasonable* depends on the circumstances of each situation and there are two tests: the subjective standard of reasonableness, which is another way of saying, the jury places itself in the defendant's own shoes. The objective test, embraces the idea that the jury is supposed to place itself in the shoes of a hypothetical 'reasonable and prudent person.' In general though, the battered woman syndrome of self-defense is an example and has held up where women have had to use deadly force against the assaultive or homicidal offenses of men, in order to protect their own lives."

This suggests that humans trapped by zombies have a reasonable right to defend themselves. Campbell points out, however, that the issue of self-defense, especially where a horde of flesh-eating ghouls is concerned, is viewed in a bigger-picture sense by our federal government. "One only has to look to the Patriot Act to see that the United States is not going to tolerate any intrusion. I believe that Zombies would meet a clear definition of terrorists."

The PATRIOT Act states: "The Act creates new federal crimes for terrorist attacks on mass transportation facilities, for biological weapons offenses, for harboring terrorists, for affording terrorists material support, for misconduct associated with money laundering already mentioned, for conducting the affairs of an enterprise which affects interstate or foreign commerce through the patterned commission of terrorist offenses, and for fraudulent charitable solicitation. Although strictly speaking these are new federal crimes, they generally supplement existing law by filling gaps and increasing penalties."

Granted the PATRIOT Act does not mention zombies by name, it's pretty clear that terrorist atacks of any kind will not be tolerated. One particular section of the act nails this down very securely: "With respect to terrorism definitions, for example, sec-

Art of the Dead – Alan F. Beck

In the Land of the Dead

"I have always been an avid reader of science fiction, fantasy and horror novels, movies and TV. They say as an artist you should paint what you know and these worlds have been a part of my life since I can remember. It's a natural extension of my being."

tion 802 of the Act created the new crime category of 'domestic terrorism.' According to this provision, which is found in the U.S. criminal code at 18 U.S.C. § 2331, domestic terrorism means activities that (A) involve acts dangerous to human life that are a violation of the criminal laws of the U.S. or of any state, that (B) appear to be intended (i) to intimidate or coerce a civilian population, (ii) to influence the policy of a government by intimidation or coercion, or (iii) to affect the conduct of a government by mass destruction, assassination, or kidnapping, and (C) occur primarily within the territorial jurisdiction of the U.S."

Campbell is very clear on this point: "I think we can safely say that an *attack* involves dangers to human life. Hordes of zombies would apply."

Aside from self-defense the zombie films and books also describe counterattacks on zombie hordes. Max Brooks's *World War Z* details how different world governments mobilized their armies (with varying degrees of success) against the zombies. Joe McKinney's *Dead City* brings it home and shows how police officers fight back. The *Resident Evil* films, books, and games involve mercenaries and private armies in pitched battle with the dead. And most of the major entries in the genre have military, police, or civilian defense as part of the backstory, often seen in news clips on TV. In fact *Night of the Living Dead* (both the original and the 1990 remake) ended with a mixed group of sheriff's deputies and local hunters working together to systematically hunt down and destroy the ghouls. In the first movie Romero had a bit more optimism because the ending of the film *suggested* that the humans were turning the tide and would likely prevail—a stance he recanted by the time he wrote the screenplay for *Dawn of the Dead.*

None of the films have so far described a coordinated and effective military response to the zombies, though the film version of *World War Z* will touch on that since the story takes place after the zombie war is won.

Dan O'Bannon's gruesome and hilarious *Return of the Living Dead* took an approach somewhere in the middle of the issue by suggesting that the events in *Night of the Living Dead* were true and the result of a failed military research project; and the events were covered up and fictionalized for the movie. Because of a "typical Army screw-up," canisters containing bodies of zombies from that incident were shipped to a medical supply warehouse and are then accidentally opened by a couple of boneheads who work there.[3] Through a series of mishaps, the chemical from the canisters leaks out, and the dead from the nearby cemetery rise. Mayhem ensues. One of the characters sees that the canisters have a number to call if there is a disaster and he makes the call to the Army . . . who then nuke the entire town.

Though the movie is a comedy, no one I know who has seen the film thinks that the military response depicted is either unwarranted or unlikely; and it brings up a point that is both disturbing and comforting. If a disaster of this kind was happening and containment was likely to fail, then extraordinary measures, however horrible to imagine, might be justified. It's the "fire cleanses" view of national self-defense; a preemptive strike to save the whole world from being overwhelmed. In its effect it's no different than a biological research facility going into permanent lockdown if there is an otherwise uncontainable viral breech. Innocent people will die in either case, but in the absence of other options, it comes down to the needs of the many outweighing the needs of the few.

That doesn't make it any less horrible, though. Not even a little bit.

To a degree what we're talking about here is a kind of euthanasia. In zombie pop culture this concept is explored in a variety of ways because of the nature of the plague. If a person is bitten by a zombie, there is a 100 percent certainty that they will ultimately die of the disease and reanimate as a zombie.

In the first Romero films all the recent dead rose, bitten or not; but as the series continued this aspect wasn't explored and instead the bite-and-reanimation concept was given a lot of play. In many of the films and books this is also a scene of great drama and tragedy. The little girl in *Night of the Living Dead* is the model for this. We know early on that she's been bitten and is sick; though in that film we don't yet know that she will reanimate. I remember when I first saw that I was creeped out com-

3. Played with great comic timing by James Karen and Thom Mathews.

Art of the Dead – Ken Meyer, Jr.

Zombie Rot

"I think zombies forming cohesive thoughts, overrunning the living, even forming political parties, new religions and such, might be interesting."

pletely when her mother went downstairs to find the makeshift cot empty and the little girl standing in the shadows with a garden trowel. Later, when her wounded father goes downstairs (after being shot following a tussle with Ben), his daughter takes a chomp out of him.

In *Dawn of the Dead* Romero really amped up the emotion on this. He takes one of the central characters, a tough and resourceful SWAT officer (Roger, played by Scott H. Reiniger), one of the characters we were pretty damn sure was going to make it to the final reel, and late in the film has him get bitten. Unlike the little girl, who had no lines and so we empathized without actually *knowing* her, Roger was someone we got to know, came to really like, and when he got bitten, we ached for some cure. Romero, never one for a Disney ending, showed him getting sicker and sicker. And with the skillful direction, we found ourselves deeply afraid for Roger, and terrified by the choices left open to his best friend, Peter (Ken Foree): Let Roger die and then have him revive as a murderous zombie, or have Peter kill him and end the torment before it escalated beyond control? Roger swears to Peter that he is going to try not to come back, and that scene always brings a tear to my eye. I'm not as cynical as Romero—I wanted that Disney ending. But Roger dies and Peter sits there, watching him, hoping that his friend's will is stronger even in death than the virus. But this is a Romero film. Roger wakes up and Peter shoots him.

This scene is echoed in a number of films. In the remake of *Dawn of the Dead*, we have several different takes on this. First, a pregnant young woman is bitten early on and we—the audience—know what's going to happen even if the characters don't. Her husband Andre, played with tragic understatement by Mekhi Phifer, tries to keep her safe even after she dies, just as she's giving birth. Sadly the infection must have crossed the placental wall, and the baby is born as a monster. His friends, reacting in horror, shoot the zombie wife and child, but Andre, insane with despair, opens up on his friends and kills one of them.

Later some refugees enter the shopping mall where our heroes have holed up, and among them is a father, Frank, (Matt Frewer) and his teenage daughter. Frank has been bitten and Michael (Jake Weber), who is an everyman in the process of becoming a true hero, insists that they execute the victim before he can turn. Ana (Sarah Polley), a nurse and the heart of the survivors, freaks and won't allow the euthanasia, leaving it for Kenneth (Ving Rhames) to stand vigil as the father sickens, dies, and reanimates. We hear the gunshot, and we feel it in our guts.

Still later a fellow survivor—a gun shop owner named Andy (Bruce Bohne)—is infected during an aborted attempt to send provisions to him; the heroes get to him too late and are forced to kill him. As the heroes flee back to the mall, one of their numbers is injured—a broken leg rather than a bite—and the fleeing good guys are unable to drag him fast enough to escape the pursuing zombies. One of the survivors, CJ (Michael Kelly), shoots him rather than letting him suffer the pain and torment of the cannibal attack and likely reanimation. Of course when the film's resident total jackass, Steve (Ty Burrell), is bitten and becomes a zombie, Ana shoots him without remorse and pretty much everyone in the theater cheers. Compassion is relative to patience.

At the film's close, Michael is bitten during the great escape from the mall. This is a devastating moment because he's someone we really, really want to survive this mess. He helps everyone else get onto a boat and then opts to remain behind. A heroic Michael tells Ana to go with the escapees, insisting that it'll be all right.

"No," she says, "it won't." As the boat sails off into the dawn, the zombies close in around Michael and he shoots himself. Again, we *feel* it.

In *Shaun of the Dead*, when Shaun's (Simon Pegg) mother (Penelope Wilton) is revealed to have been bitten, the madcap comedy takes a weirdly tragic turn, and even the fact that the scene where the survivors are arguing over whether to kill her or not is more or less played for laughs, the surrounding humor makes the tragedy and loss more poignant.

These films all explore a variety of complex issues that, taken out of the context of the film, would amount to desecration of the dead, felony murder, euthanasia, and suicide. But within the context of the films . . . are they even crimes?

The issue touches on a number of legal areas:

- *Euthanasia*: the intentional killing by act or omission of a dependent human being for his or her alleged benefit. ("The key word here is 'intentional.' If death is not intended, it is not an act of euthanasia," points out Campbell.)

- *Voluntary euthanasia*: When the person who is killed has requested to be killed.
- *Nonvoluntary*: When the person who is killed made no request and gave no consent.
- *Involuntary euthanasia*: When the person who is killed made an expressed wish to the contrary.
- *Assisted suicide*: Someone provides an individual with the information, guidance, and means to take his or her own life with the intention that they will be used for this purpose. When it is a doctor who helps another person to kill themselves it is called *physician-assisted suicide*.
- *Euthanasia by action*: Intentionally eausing a person's death by performing an action such as by giving a lethal injection.
- *Euthanasia by omission*: Intentionally causing death by not providing necessary and ordinary (usual and customary) care or food and water.

Expert Witness

I put this question to my experts: If a person were dying from a zombie bite, and it was known to a high degree of medical certainty that once that person died he/she would reanimate as a predatory and infectious zombie, would the law permit assisted suicide?

Common Sense During the Apocalypse

One way to bottom-line this whole thing is to consider the big picture view and worry about the legal issues later and at the moment shoot the zombie who's trying to chew on your leg. Or, to put it in simpler terms: "I'd rather be tried by twelve than carried by six."

Campbell sees this as an enormously complicated issue: "This is not Holland.[4] In as far as I know, aggressive euthanasia is illegal in most of the United States. Patients retain the rights to refuse medical treatment and to receive appropriate management of pain at their request (passive euthanasia), even if the patients' choices hasten their deaths. Additionally, futile or disproportionately burdensome treatments, such as life-support machines, may be withdrawn under specified circumstances. Many States, for example, now permit 'living wills,' surrogate health care decision making, and the withdrawal or refusal of life sustaining medical treatment. At the same time, however, voters and legislators continue for the most part to reaffirm their States' prohibitions on assisting suicide."

Retired California civil rights attorney Allen Steingold believes zombies would require a change in the laws. "As the laws currently read we don't allow euthanasia, assisted or not, and we certainly consider suicide to be a crime. This is funny when you consider that old wry comment that suicide is the only crime they can't convict you for if you're successful. However, if we consider the concept of zombies—I think it would take congress no time at all to draft legislation not only legalizing euthanasia for persons infected with a zombie disease, but they would likely go a step forward and make it mandatory. Understand, that there would be a lot of tragic misuse and misinterpretation of such legislation, but it would almost certainly be drafted and passed. The only time things are done quickly in congress is during a time of crisis. Look at how quickly everyone on both sides of the aisle ratified the Patriot Act, despite some hasty and questionable phrasing."

Rabbi Shevack says, "Euthanasia of someone dying from a zombie bite, is the same problem of euthanasia in general. However, if in extinguishing someone from dying from the zombie bite one can prevent further spreading of zombieism, then such euthanasia would be warranted as an act of self-defense for the entire community."

A sticking point here is whether the victim should be allowed to die first, which would then necessitate the killing of a zombie

4. Where euthanasia is permitted under certain circumstances.

rather than a living person; or whether assisted suicide or active euthanasia would be permitted.

"There is no euthanasia unless the death is intentionally caused by what was done or not done," observes Campbell. "Thus, some medical actions that are often labeled 'passive euthanasia' are no form of euthanasia, since the intention to take life is lacking. These acts include not commencing treatment that would not provide a benefit to the patient, withdrawing treatment that has been shown to be ineffective, too burdensome or is unwanted, and the giving of high doses of pain-killers that may endanger life, when they have been shown to be necessary. All those are part of good medical practice, endorsed by law, when they are properly carried out."

Campbell insists that the general population would probably accept this. "A recent Gallup Poll survey showed that 60% of Americans supported euthanasia. Attempts to legalize euthanasia and assisted suicide resulted in ballot initiatives and legislation bills within the United States in the last 20 years. And Oregon passed the Death with Dignity Act."

Dr. Gretz brings up this point: "I think the Catholic church (and many others) would say, 'yes, it is immoral.' As long as the person's spirit is still in the body, it would be important to make them as comfortable as possible while dying and then cremate the body or something ASAP after their heart stopped beating."

And if they then resurrected afterward as a zombie?

"At that point they probably don't fit anyone's definition of human anymore," says David Chiang, a military legal advisor. "We might have to make some retroactive changes in the law once the crisis was over, but in the face of a crisis of this kind once the person has died the body—awake or not in the case of zombies—is a disease vector and not a human being. The rules would change."

If someone killed a zombie—prior to a change in the law allowing such an act—would that be considered justifiable homicide? "That depends," Campbell says, "on whether a Zombie is considered human life at this point? Probably not. It's an oddity, it's unnatural, and I think it would be treated as if killing a dangerous animal, so I don't know that this type of suit would hold up in a criminal court."

***Plague of Zombies* — photo by Elizabeth Lopez**

An attack of zombies would be viewed much the same as a terrorist attack—with an emphasis on "terror."

Steingold agrees. "A zombie is a disease vector, not a person. A lawyer could easily argue that destroying one would be in the best interests of public safety. I don't believe it would be viewed as an act of violence. However . . . if this were to happen in the earliest stages of a zombie plague, and if there is insufficient supportive evidence, either through eyewitness testimony or inarguable forensic evidence, then the person who kills the zombie might actually be charged. The same would hold if a person believed his next door neighbor to be a vampire or werewolf. If, after the killing, there was no evidence to support the claim then that person would, very rightly, be charged. Otherwise anyone with a grudge could say that the annoying neighbor next door was Dracula and that killing him was a public service. Some degree of proof is always required."

Chiang also agrees on this point. "In fact, not killing the zombie might be seen later as a crime. Of course, you could simplify the dilemma by tying up the dying so that if they reanimated they wouldn't be an immediate threat to anyone. Disposal could then be handled later when minds are cooler."

Other aspects of liability play into the situation. If a person knows themselves to be infected with a highly contagious disease (in this case a zombie virus), what is his or her legal responsibility? Does he or she have to inform others? Is he or she required to turn themselves in to authorities?

Steingold says yes. "Such a person has a moral and legal responsibility to inform the authorities, either medical or legal . . . if possible, depending on the circumstances."

"We only have to look to the most recent debacle with the TB carrier traveling on an airplane," Campbell says, "and the mad hunt for him, the rounding up of people he had contact with, and his subsequent commitment to a hospital. This is also not technically criminal law but I think would be under a federal code for endangering the public."

"In the event of a zombie plague—or even a potential zombie plague," Steingold adds, "there is also the potential for imposing martial law. The government would be very forceful in its efforts to prevent a mass epidemic."

"Martial law," Campbell explains, "is government by military authorities when the normal machinery of civilian administration has broken down as a result of disaster, invasion, civil war, or large-scale insurrection. It is not to be confused with military law. Any trial of civilians held by military authorities under martial law would not enjoy the status of a court martial. This is a federal mandate and supersedes other state laws. Martial law may also be established within a state itself in substitution for the ordinary government and legal system during serious disturbances. Again, in this event, justice is administered by military tribunals. Usually while the military authorities are restoring order, their conduct cannot be called into question by the ordinary courts of law. After the restoration of order, the legality of the military's actions might well be theoretically capable of examination."

Would the government act quickly enough?

"Well," says a skeptical Steingold, "we have a spotty record with that. I think that our national intentions are almost always for the best, but between knowledge and action there is bureaucracy and that can slow things down to a crawl. Or in the case of zombies, slow it to a shuffling walk. Sometimes we're right on the mark with rapid response, and then we have something like Katrina and the FEMA debacle."

Jason Broadbent, a civil engineer from Baton Rouge, takes a surprisingly more optimistic view. "Katrina was a total bureaucratic mess no doubt; but all of us are learning from it: The people, the local and state governments, and the Feds. We're going to be looking at the Katrina thing for years. Laws will be written and rewritten because of it. Nothing in U.S. history has ever painted the government as clumsier or more ineffectual. Even the delays and screw-ups in the response to what was happening during 9/11 pale in comparison. And yet . . . I honestly believe we're learning from that. God forbid anything else hits us again—be it planes flying into skyscrapers, hurricanes or the living dead—but I think the Feds would step up and do a better job."

In many of the zombie stories, the culprit is some testing facility—a lab[5] working on a new virus, some toxic waste being mishandled. I asked my experts to comment on what kind of legal response would ensue.

Campbell says, "This is a federal CDC function but I would imagine that the offending institution would be up the creek without a paddle."

"Every administration loves a scapegoat," says Steingold. "We're very, very good at going after them like the Mongol Horde. If a crisis of this kind occurred, and we survived it, someone would have to pay. It would strengthen the government—and to a very real degree increase its effectiveness and the trust in which the people place in it—to have a non-governmental institution be at fault. The entire weight of the government, backed by intense public outrage, would smash them flat. I'll bet you'd even have the liberal left calling for public executions."

And if it turned out to be a runaway experiment from a government testing facility?

Campbell's view of this is understandably dim: "Hey, the American Veteran's Association is *still* trying to figure out why there is a history of experimentation at their facilities."

Steingold believes such a revelation would be traumatic. "In that case I think every American, right or left, man, woman and child, would suddenly find themselves embracing the concept of anar-

5. Like the medical testing facility in our scenario.

chy. That would be far worse than any mass of zombies. That would be a civil war to end all civil wars; and we'd probably get the most severe kind of sanctions from other countries."

How severe?

"Think 'nukes,' " Steingold warns. "And who could blame them?"

The Zombie Factor

Zombie pop culture takes a mighty dim view of how the government and law enforcement would handle the crisis. Cops are usually shown as inept, undertrained, and unable to properly respond to the situation. For the most part, government officials are not even included in zombie stories, except as brief talking heads on a TV. One thing that's fairly consistent in the pop culture view of the government handling of a crisis is that they would bungle the job or somehow use the crisis to further some dark agenda.

In his books *Down the Road: A Zombie Horror Story* and *Down the Road: On the Last Day*, author Bowie Ibarra paints a dismal view of how FEMA and similar organizations would handle things. As he sees it, the government has not, in fact, learned from their mistakes. He says, "Look at how forces controlled by the government have responded in critical situations: the WTO protest in Seattle; in my opinion, government-sponsored anarchists were sent in to disrupt the peaceful protest, trash the place, and then were led away, providing the excuse for the storm troopers to come in and rough up the peaceful protesters. Then look at Katrina. Not only was it an example of government incompetence, but an example of how humans would respond when holed up in a large space with little to no supplies or supervision (i.e., child rapes, fights, murders). There is a conspiracy claim that most of FEMA's budget money is actually spent on creating prisons/camps for future use. REX-84[6] is an interesting piece of legislature. Bottom line, the government forces would be told to try and secure citizens by any means necessary. The zombie infestation would only be half of the problem."

6. Rex-84 (Readiness Exercise 1984) was a U.S. government plan to test their ability to detain large numbers of American citizens in case of massive civil unrest or national emergency.

Author Tim Waggoner takes a different stance. "I think that—assuming the zombie contagion spread fast enough to create multitudes of zombies—that there would be a lot of chaos and a temporary breakdown in society, but the apocalypse wouldn't occur. Humans would adapt to their new circumstances quickly, learning how to prevent the spread of contagion, disposing of dead bodies quickly and efficiently, and learning how to protect themselves from zombies through barriers and shelter. Plus, humans would go out hunting zombies. How many animal species have humans hunted to extinction without even trying? We'd wipe the zombies out in time and, even if the zombie contagion still existed, we'd learn to prevent any mass outbreaks. I wrote a story called 'Provider' in the zombie anthology *The Book of Final Flesh*[7] which deals with some of these ideas."

Horror movie actress Nicole Blessing (*Doomed to Consume*) sees things as dim but hopeful. "There are so many instabilities in the world at play already. Power politics suggests that many nations would attempt to use a zombie uprising to leverage their status in the world. Society as we know it would fall, but all empires are destined to fall given time. We wouldn't be completely obliterated. Humanity is very resilient, and once we managed to adapt to the threat, what's left of humanity would survive."

"Certainly some cultures would be more successful at dealing with a zombie holocaust than others," suggests Bram Stoker Award-winning author and screenwriter Lisa Morton, "but we've become so globally interdependent that no country would withstand it completely. Here in the U.S., I think we'd separate into small barricaded city-states, each with its own food production and resource gathering."

THE FINAL VERDICT: THE LAW OF THE DEAD

If zombies rose, the laws would change. Laws that permit self-defense would be reevaluated and probably strengthened. Laws limiting the ownership of guns would certainly take a hit. Curfews would be imposed, and martial law would almost certainly go into

7. Eden Studios, 2003.

effect until well after the crisis was over. In heavily infected areas, it's not unreasonable to assume that martial law might, to one degree or another, be kept in place indefinitely.

Once the crisis had passed and things had either gotten back to normal or settled into what would be the new version of "normal", the lawsuits would start. Lots and lots and lots of lawsuits. If there was even a smidgeon of evidence to suggest that the plague had started in a laboratory somewhere, then anyone adversely affected by the disaster would file major class action suits against the companies, personnel, and stockholders involved. If the government had been in any way involved, as in the scenario of a military bioweapons program gone awry, administrations would fall, heads would roll, cover-ups would be attempted, and monies would be spilled all over the place.

There would also be some major litigation within families and neighbor to neighbor. Figure if the son of one family turns zombie and bites his buddy next door, the surviving family members will go to court over it. No doubt about that. If there's anything we are more than predatory it's litigious. There will also be tragically complicated suits built around euthanasia, as survivors have their lawyers try to settle the rightness or wrongness of killing the infected. Expert witnesses will get rich collecting fees to try and determine at which *point* a person is considered legally dead and at which point an infected person—alive or dead—became enough of a threat so that shooting them is justifiable. Within two years, there will probably be college courses on zombie law; within ten there will be degree programs. Even though much of the economy may receive mortal wounds, the legal and legal education systems will flourish.

Oh, and *ambulance chaser* will take on a whole new set of meanings.

Dead Aim

The Zombie Fighter's Arsenal

Dead Aim **by Jonathan Maberry**

"You got to bring enough gun for the fun, son."

—Old U.S. Army catch-phrase

n Chapter 5 we discussed how law enforcement and the military might respond to a zombie attack. Now let's discuss the weapons and equipment they could bring to the game.

JUST THE FACTS

Firearms

Mike Witzgall, former Force Recon Marine and former Dallas SWAT member, thinks that the standard SWAT weapons would do the trick. He says, "Weapons are broken down into 3 categories. Primary Handgun, Backup Handgun and rifle or Sub-gun. The Primary Handguns carried by SWAT teams vary from team to team and sometimes, from teammate to teammate. Most teams have now standardized what the team carries. 9mm, 40 caliber and 45 caliber are weapons of choice, though makes and models vary from team to team. I personally preferred the 9mm Beretta (Italian made) 92F for close in surgical shooting on hostage rescues (headshots). Most people that have the higher caliber weapons are not secure in their marksmanship skill. Remember, if ya cannot shoot for crap, a higher caliber ain't gonna help."

What about backup guns? "Backups," Witzgall says, "are rarely carried in SWAT—when they are it is usually something like a compact Glock 9mm or a 9mm Beretta 92FC."

And long guns? "The choice of which sub-guns and rifles to use opens up a major can of worms," Witzgall says, "because most SWAT teams cannot decide what they want to carry. Here's a little history: Back in the mid 1970's I was in Marine Corps Force Reconnaissance. We carried the Colt (223) C.A.R 16 which looked like a little M16. This weapon was the mainstay for Special Operations for many years. Around 1982 the H&K 9mm MP5 sub-machine gun came out and everyone loved it (it really is a very good weapon). Problem was, it was a 9mm that was great for close in fighting; but had poor range and poor knock down/stay down. Eventually the H&K 40 Cal. MP4 came out. Better range, better knockdown/stay down capabilities; but still had poor range. Then the bad guys started wearing ballistic vests and carrying AK's. SWAT teams then adopted the M4 (223) Weapons System. Which is the C.A.R 16 revamped and made of better, lighter materials. So, until something new and nicer comes out, we are using the M4 Weapons System. In case you are wondering about the name 'Weapons System,' the M4 is just an M4 until you start adding a bunch of way cool (but useless in my opinion) dodads to the weapon. Laser targeting, range finders, night enhancement scope and lights."

I asked him about the weapons used by SWAT snipers. "That's almost always the sniper's choice. Most carry a bolt action 7.62. Make and Model is up for grabs. I always liked the Remington 700 Police Sniper System. Straight out of the box, it's about one of the best around. A skilled SWAT sniper could drop one zombie every five seconds = 60 seconds per dozen. There is generally one sniper element (two men—a sniper and a spotter) per each SWAT team. In Dallas SWAT, we had eight primary snipers and at least another five or ten SWAT officers that had the skill and training." Put that kind of skilled manpower on some rooftops and it would truly be a shooting gallery.

For advice on how to choose a handgun, I asked Vincent DeNiro, movie weapons armorer and defense industry consultant.[1] "People that are not familiar with handguns believe what they see on TV; and many TV shows and movies are produced and directed by people that are not familiar with guns. In reality people don't fly back ten feet when shot, guns don't shoot forever without reloading, and no one shoots two handguns at the same time. Now, for picking an appropriate handgun, here are some things to consider:

- *Size:* Compact guns (in full-size calibers like 9 mm, .40, .45) are very popular now as concealed carry is allowed in every state except IL and WI).
- *Feel:* The gun must fit the hand.
- *Weight:* Polymer (plastic) frames are very desirable and metal-framed guns have now taken a back seat to Glock, Beretta Px4 series, Springfield XD, and Smith & Wesson M&P models as weight is a big consideration.

1. Visit him online at www.exoticarms.com.

Hard Science: "Fire . . . Good!"

Let's take a second look at the Glock 23C used by the security guard in the scenario described in Chapter 1 and match it against what we know of zombies. Romero clearly established in *Night of the Living Dead* that zombies fear fire (if *fear* is the right word). They shy away from it.

Though all handguns emit some burning gasses when a shot is fired, compensated guns such as the 23C have two slotted ports on the topside of the barrel. We can presume that the shots were fired during the struggle. We also know that something spooked the zombie and made it run away. Since it's doubtful that the arrival of the witness's car had any real effect (though under other circumstances it would be like a pizza delivery to a hungry ghoul), we can deduce that the additional flame—repeated during the three shots the guard fired—are what made our zombie flee. Otherwise he would have lingered to feed on the guard.

- *Caliber:* In years past, the .22, .25, .32, .38 Special, and .380 were considered sufficient stopping power, but this gave way to the 9 mm. Although the 9 mm is about the same strength as a .38 Special, it has the high-capacity fast reload feature, which the .38 doesn't have. Over the past fifteen years, the trend is to go stronger than the 9 mm and calibers like .357 SIG, .40, and .45 are very popular now.
- *Action:* Semiautomatics or pistols have taken over revolvers as the choice for handguns since the 1980s. Semiautomatics allow for fast reloading with some pistol magazines holding 30 rounds. The revolver tends to have a much slower reloading time, and the user only gets to reload five, six, seven, or eight rounds. However, the advantage of the revolver is that revolvers can handle much more powerful ammunition like 454 Casull or 500 S&W. There are even revolvers that fire the big game rounds like the 45–70, which was a popular buffalo cartridge.

- *Firing Mode:* Double action is the mode in which a revolver fires: there are also pistols that are double action. Double action is when the trigger is pulled, the hammer is drawn back and then released when the trigger reaches a certain point. Single action is when the hammer is back, the trigger only has to be pulled lightly and has little travel, which causes the hammer to fall resulting in more accurate firing. Many models combine both whereby the first shot is double action and all the following shots are single action. Single-action 1911 style .45 pistols are prized for their accuracy. These should only be used by experienced shooters."

Expert Witness

I asked Witzgall to discuss what the military could bring to the fight that could turn the tide even against a horde of zombies. "It all depends on what collateral damage I have to be worried about," he says. "We know bullets work to the head; but so would shrapnel tearing a zombie's head and limbs off or blasting him into a thousand little pieces. If I did not care about leaving a building standing (but could not nuke 'em) I would use a Napalm air strike and incinerate the zombies. Failing air strikes, an artillery strike would do just as well. I would send in tanks (with flame throwers) and the infantry as mop up."

Captain Dick Taylor, U.S. Army (retired), agrees: "It would take a lot of zombies to overwhelm the military. We could send in a tank division and simply roll over them. It's not like we would be taking return fire. All we would need to do is make enough noise to attract the zombies and then they're ours."

What kinds of tanks would we use? "Let's start with the Mobile Gun System," advises Taylor. "That's an armored fighting vehicle rolling on eight-wheeles and mounting a 105 mm tank gun. This is a thinner vehicle, just shy of nine feet wide, which means that it's better for urban deployment. You could use noise or whatever to lure a bunch of zombies into a side street and then sic a Stryker on them. Between the fire capability and the weight of it just rolling over them, you'd damn soon clear the street with absolutely no risk to the personnel inside. Zombies are not going to chew through 14.5 mm armor."

Taylor is enthusiastic about the Stryker's stopping power. "Well, the 105 mm gun is a great crowd pleaser. Since you're not taking fire you can let the hostiles close to point blank, though afterward you'd better have a hose crew with a strong stomach. Then you have the M2 Browning .50 machine gun. These fifty-cals kick out 500 belt-fed rounds per minute at 3,050 feet-per-second and they're effective at up to 1,800 yards. Guns like that don't care about headshots: they'll chop the zombies into pieces. Pieces aren't a threat." He adds, "If you're out of 105's then the Stryker has an Mk 19 Grenade Launcher belt-fed automatic 40mm grenade launcher, which has a sustained firing rate of 40 rounds per minute. That'll put grenades into a crowd of zombies at a range of 2,200 meters. Though if you want to do pinpoint shooting you're good at 1,500 meters. That's close to a mile. If you need to create a real hell zone, the Mk 19 is man-portable, which lets a team take it to a secure firing position separate from the vehicle."

The Stryker is just one tool of modern military combat. Another equally effective weapon in the war against zombies would be the attack helicopter. "If you've ever seen attack helicopters really open up then you understand what putting the fear of God into your enemy is really like," says Taylor. "It'll just park there above the zombies' heads and then hose them with an M197 Gatling gun capable of a cyclic rate of fire of 730 rounds per minute. And, if things get tight, it can open up with Hydra 70mm rockets. All of our helos carry more firepower than you'd think. Even the old AH-1 Cobra's have a couple of 7.62mm multi-barrel Miniguns that'll chop up a whole crowd of zombies without risking a single casualty. If the Army gets called to war against the zombies, then the zombies had better wake up and find religion."

"If the zombie's body is desiccated," mused Rick A. Shay, owner/moderator of the Combat-Handguns Yahoo! Group, "I'd choose a weapon with a heavy projectile—like a 12-gauge shotgun slug. An impact by such would have the greatest physical footprint as it goes through the man-sized target, transferring its momentum to all it touches, and destroying anything in its direct path. If the zombie's body is moisture laden, then a more-or-less standard

Art of the Dead – John Worsley

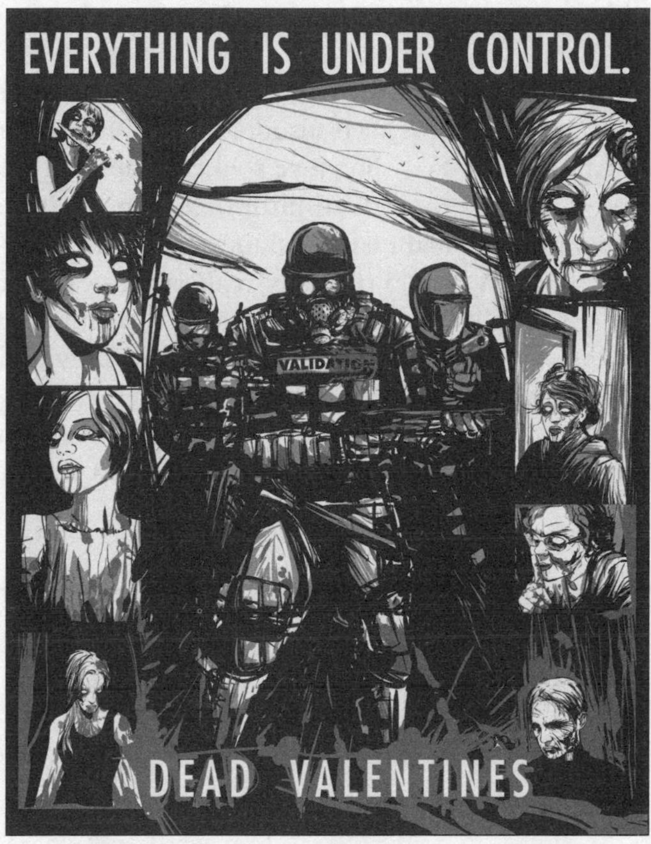

Dead Valentines

"*Dead Valentines* is the story of the Office of Dead Validation, a quasi-military branch of the Portland Police Department dealing with the aftermath of an abortive apocalypse. Most undead stories exist at one of two extremes: The Isolated Incident, and The End of the World. I wanted to explore what might happen socially, at both the personal and macroscopic levels, after a potential epidemic of undead is actually gotten under control by competent, organized emergency action. What happens to the survivors? How does society respond? And how do the undead ultimately, as you know they must, adapt?"

hunting bullet like a .30 caliber Hornady V-Max would do. Fast delivery of kinetic energy would be the best bet in that case. The projectile would lose its energy to the target in as fast a manner as possible, taking out any and all bones and connective tissue it may encounter."

Gun safety range owner Karl Rehn cites NRA safety and is less optimistic about head shots: "Headshots with a pistol? Only effective if you can hit a 2" × 4" box (eye socket zone). Maybe 10% of pistol shooters can do that given unlimited time at a stationary target past 3 yards. Typical pistol distances are 0–15 yards. Maybe 3% of pistol shooters can do it in any realistic time frame against a moving target. Basically only SWAT team guys and competition shooters in the top 25% nationally and even then only at distances less than 10 yards." His advice: train. A lot.

But this doesn't mean that everyone should start packing a piece just in case Romero turns out to have been a prophet rather

***Armed for War* — photo by Jonathan Maberry**

"Zombies may not feel pain but they are not indestructible. In the end technology will overcome savagery."

than a filmmaker. Rehn insists that everyone who goes near a gun should memorize the NRA rules for gun handling: "ALWAYS keep the muzzle in a safe direction. ALWAYS keep your finger off the trigger until ready to shoot. ALWAYS keep the gun unloaded until ready to use." He adds, "Rule #3 really doesn't matter if you obey rules 1 and 2. The key is the word 'ALWAYS' which is where most people screw up. Gun safety is not hard. It just requires consistent discipline and just enough fear of the consequences of a gun accident that you never get complacent. 'Experts' and cops are the worst about making gun safety errors. I put 'experts' in quotes because most gun owners that believe themselves 'experts' are not. Reading lots of gun magazines and being a mediocre shooter that owns a lot of guns does not equate to expertise."

The Zombie Factor

Guns have been a favorite weapon against zombies since *Night of the Living Dead*, but as we've learned from neurologist Dr. Peter Lukacs, it isn't just any shot to the head that will drop a zombie; and we've learned from gun experts that good shooting is more than just a matter of pulling a trigger.

Gun expert Constance Link insists that it isn't how powerful the gun is, but where you place your round: "Stopping a perp or a game animal is like buying real estate. Three things matter above all else, location, location and location. Where you put the bullet is paramount. No amount of power will work if you miss a vital area or miss entirely."

Just the Facts

Shock the Zombie

Tasers are a type of nonlethal weapon that administer an electric shock strong enough to disrupt superficial muscle functions. Since zombies, no matter how they are created, rely on a whole or partly functioning central nervous system, the Taser will drop them in their tracks.

Zombie Squad

Zombie Squad Posters

"We make dead things deader!

"Zombie Squad (ZS) bills itself as the world's premier nonstationary cadaver suppression task force. They aren't joking. (Well, not entirely.) ZS is an honest-to-God disaster preparedness organization that uses the "Zombocalypse" as a way of teaching folks how to prepare for actual natural or man-made catastrophes (hurricanes, earthquakes, terrorism . . . you name it). All the money they collect goes right to charity. I asked Kyle Ladd, one of the brains behind ZS, to give us the lowdown on the group:

"It started several years ago by a group of disaster preparation minded zombie horror fans in St. Louis, MO, who enjoyed getting together to review bad zombie flicks and plan for a theoretical end of the world. We later discovered that there are lots of

other crazies like us out there so we took the initiative to try and organize them in a way that may do some good. We discovered that there is, in fact, a rather large number of philanthropists in the zombie horror fan culture.

"We have three official chapters as of today, but we have several in a probationary status around North America. We have strict standards on what a chapter must do to uphold the ZS name. Chapter members must be dedicated to community involvement and promoting the mission of the Zombie Squad organization.

"As far as membership goes, it is not mandatory to buy a membership in order to be involved in ZS. We have lots of people involved with us who are not paying members, so it's not easy to get an exact number. There are thousands of members on our Internet forum but right now we only have around 300 active card-carrying members. Our members come from all walks of life and bring a vast array of experience to the table ranging from disaster response professionals like police officers and EMTs to comic book store clerks and zombie book authors.

"We organize different types of charity and disaster education events but the difference is that we make them fun. Some of our more popular charity events are the BBQ Blood Drives, movie festival canned food drives and zombie/apocalypse themed trivia contests. The Zombie Survival seminars are popular at the sci-fi conventions, and we are regularly invited by conventions, schools, and other organizations to present it. Our more popular events are camping gatherings (Zombie Con and Wintergeddon) when ZS members from all over North America get together for several days."

Why zombies?

Kyle explains, "It's the perfect metaphor for disaster. Zombie Squad believes that if you're ready for the downfall of society caused by the flesh eating risen corpses of your friends and neighbors you're ready for anything."

He adds, tongue seriously in cheek, "Of course if the dead do ever rise . . . we'll be ready."

Zombie Squad can be found at www.zombiehunters.org.

Tasers were developed in 1969 by inventor Jack Cover, a long-time science fiction buff who nicknamed his device the "Thomas A. Swift Electric Rifle," taking the name from the sci-fi character Tom Swift who was originally featured in a series of adventures[2] published from 1910 through 1941.

The Taser model most commonly used by modern law enforcement is the Taser X26,[3] which uses a replaceable cartridge containing compressed nitrogen to deploy two small probes that are attached to the Taser X26 by insulated conductive wires with a maximum length of 35 feet (10.6 meters). The Taser X26 transmits electrical pulses along the wires and into the body affecting the sensory and motor functions of the peripheral nervous system. The energy can penetrate up to two cumulative inches of clothing, or one inch per probe.[4]

Expert Witness

Joe McKinney, San Antonio Homicide: "The TASER works through electricity, and that might change things slightly. Muscles, even reanimated dead tissue, might react to electricity. There have been experiments with dead frogs, for instance, in which the frog's legs twitch when hit with electricity. Maybe you could temporarily immobilize a walking corpse with a TASER."

"I like the idea of the TASER for use against zombies," agrees Dr. Michael Pederson, a pathologist from Toronto, Canada. "Electricity should effectively and efficiently short-circuit the central nervous system, and that's what will stop any living thing, and we can extend that definition to zombies because they *must* have an operating CNS if they are moving."

2. The first books were outlined by Edward Stratemeyer and his Stratemeyer Syndicate, and the actual stories were then written by ghostwriters under the house name of Victor Appleton.

3. The U.S. military employs the M26 model.

4. Taser specs provided by Taser, Inc., Rick Smith, CEO; Tom Smith, chairman. www.taser.com.

Art of the Dead – Matthew "Six" Bahr

The Undead Are Coming for You

"Fast zombies are scarier . . . especially at the beginning of an outbreak. But I'm a little old school and the slow zombie is my pick. A horde of slow zombies is scary because they won't stop . . . you can run but eventually they're going to get you."

Art of the Dead – John Worsley

Zombies Everywhere

"They're versatile, they're simple, and they're terrifying. Through their silence, zombies are a great vessel for a variety of villainies; they have no necessary agenda but hunger, and there's something

hauntingly ineffable in their blank-eyed stare. George Romero showed that with the right elements surrounding them they can neatly parallel social ills and mindless consumerism."

The Zombie Factor

One of the things humans have going for them in any war is technology. Zombies, should they rise, will have numbers, they'll be infectious, they never tire, and they don't feel pain . . . but a ninety-year-old woman in a wheelchair could take one down using a Taser.

However, if Romero and his followers have taught us one thing, it's that the human element is too often the weakest link in the chain of defense. Technology will give us an edge, no doubt, but focus and cooperation will keep us alive.

The Final Verdict: Armed Response

The reason we're not living in caves while bears and tigers snarl outside is because we learned how to fight. We developed fire, which allowed us to harden the sharpened points of sticks into spears sharp enough to pierce the hides of animal predators.

Once out of the caves, we learned to sharpen stones to make even better spears and to make knives. We paid attention to which woods made for the best clubs. We learned to throw rocks, and after a while we learned to throw our spears. By observing the resiliency of certain woods, we came up with the concept of the bow and arrows. Then the sword, the catapult, the cannon, the match-lock, the wheel-lock, the flint-lock . . . and so on up to the laser-guided missile.

We're *good* at that sort of thing. Give us an enemy we really, really don't like and give us a ticking clock so that we have to develop something right now, and watch the process happen. It's like magic. Remember, the nuclear age was born during America's struggle to beat Germany and Japan in World War II. Space exploration was born from military rocket science.

Give us a horde of zombies and you'll see just about everyone reach for a gun. Sadly, pacifism would be *consumed* during the plague. Zombies do not respect nonviolent ideals, and they don't have a Geneva Convention.

If the plague lasted more than six months, there would be a technology boom as researchers, engineers, designers, and builders would conceive new products based on need. Urgency would bring these products to market with incredible rapidity. Arms dealers would pop up everywhere, as would training centers for armed and unarmed response. New weapons would be developed, new technologies invented, and even in the face of a massive attack, there would be battles won with new weapons, and the counterattack would spread out from there.

9

Zombie Self-Defense

A Guide to Kicking Undead Ass

Self Defense Against the Undead
by Jonathan Maberry

"Even against the undead a human being is never totally helpless."

In Chapter 5, we discussed how armed police and military could take down zombies, and along the way we've shared a lot of views about armed civilian response; but what about *unarmed* defense?

In most zombie stories, humans are unable to adequately defend against zombies. Sure, in the films with slow shufflers the humans barge through them, knock them down, kick them, and even smash them in the face with pies.[1]

But what about a sophisticated physical response? After all, four thousand years of martial arts development have pretty well established that the human body is a fierce weapon. I mean, could you imagine zombies giving Jet Li or Steven Segal much of a problem? In TV and film, unarmed fighting has been shown to be pretty effective against the undead. *Buffy the Vampire Slayer* and *Blade* were both built around martial arts themes. Even Chuck Norris, who's pushing 70, could probably still kick undead ass.

Science is an ally here, too. In the face of terror and undeniable physical threat, the human body produces adrenaline, which kicks in the "fight or flight" instinct that was hardwired into us before we even climbed down from the trees. Most of us opt for the flight option, which is generally the smartest course of action. The saying "He who fights and runs away lives to fight another day" is an enormously practical view; but what if your instinct was to fight? Or, what would you do if running away were no longer an option?

It's been established that zombies are attracted to sound. Guns are noisy, and unless you have enough bullets to chop down every zombie who comes running after it hears a shot, you're in trouble. When faced with a zombie while running for cover, it's best to pick a response that will get the job done as quietly as possible, and the human body is a virtually silent weapon.

Not all martial arts are based strictly on unarmed fighting, however. Many teach the use of staffs, clubs, chain whips, spears, knives, and swords. None of these weapons run out of ammunition

1. No, really, Romero had some fun with this in *Dawn of the Dead*.

(although swords will blunt after you've chopped a few dozen necks); and they are relatively silent. Of course they require skill, and unless we already know there are zombies on the loose, it's not likely we'll just happen to have our lucky samurai sword with us the day the dead rise.

Just the Facts

Fighting the Dead

As a martial arts instructor, I advocate self-defense training for everyone—and that has nothing to do with any fear of the dead coming back to life with an appetite.

There are thousands of different martial arts, and these arts teach both armed and unarmed skills for defense and attack. Every country has had some kind of native art. The process of development and proliferation as we understand it from a historical perspective got its start in India thousands of years ago and then spread slowly through China and from there into Korea, Japan, and Okinawa . . . and then around the globe. And over the last hundred-odd years, the martial arts have split into three distinct categories: sport (boxing, fencing, judo, wrestling), esoteric (tai chi, some forms of kung-fu, aikido) and combat (anything self-defense oriented).

A case can be made that all martial arts have a combative element, but really many of the most popular sport arts need significant modification to be effective in life-or-death combat. Judo and wrestling rely on throws and pins; boxing is based on pain and tissue damage; contact karate and kickboxing are mostly point-driven. Zombies never submit to holds, you can't choke them out, they're dead so what do they care if they get a broken nose, and they're not likely to weep over being outscored in a fight. A boxer might get eaten; a mixed martial-arts grappler who takes his undead opponent to the floor is probably going to become a picnic snack for the zombie's friends. The arts that would flourish during a zombie crisis would have to be those focusing on structural damage and killing.

From the point of view of technical philosophy—the logic behind the development and implementing of combat kills—even

Art of the Dead – Kevin Breaux

Subway Zombie

"If the dead rose then martial arts will save more lives, at least during the outbreak phase, than guns will. Most people don't carry guns, but millions study—or have studied—martial arts. I know that if a zombie came at me on the street, or in the subway, or some ordinary place . . . I'd be ready."

most of these more lethal combat arts need to be adjusted for use against the undead. Some of the most popular skills would be eliminated out of hand. The two-knuckle punch, though capable of breaking bones and rupturing internal organs, is a poor choice against a zombie; as is the tiger-claw slash across the face, the elbow to the solar plexus, and the good old-fashioned kick to the balls. Against a mugger, rapist, or thug, these are fan favorites, but zombies tend to shrug them off. But a side-thrust kick to the knee will take a ghoul down, no question about it. Living dead or not the zombie still depends on its skeleton, and we've already established that skeletons are designed by nature to resist the constant pull of gravity. They are in effect scaffolding. Break a knee and gravity will pull the zombie down, simple as that. Yes it can still crawl; yes it can still bite . . . but it can't crawl faster than you can run; and while it's crawling along the floor, you have time to go pick up some handy blunt instrument and bash its skull in.

Zombies . . . Fast or Slow? Part 7

- **"Quick answer: slow. Slow answer: These dudes are falling apart at the seams. Even I can't go very fast some days. Imagine how the average person feels the day after a rugged workout and multiply it by 100 or 1000. That's the sort of physical condition I attribute to zombies. Their muscles are detaching from the bones. It's a wonder they can move at all."—Bev Vincent, author of the Bram Stoker Award-nominated book *The Road to the Dark Tower* (NAL, 2004), the authorized companion to Stephen King's *Dark Tower* series.**
- **"I like slow zombies but it's all about the story that's being told. I've seen fast zombies done right and they're just as scary, just as effective, as shamblers and twitchers."—David Wellington, best-selling author of *Monster Planet*.**
- **"I kind of like the fast zombies only because there is a greater sense of urgency to their approach. They seem more human, and thus deceptive. You may have to get up close to one to tell if it's an actual zombie, and then it may be too late. But I think a proper mix of the fast and slow type of zombie is probably the best. The slower ones can be the ones that have been dead and rotten a lot longer."—Zombie portrait artist Robert Sacchetto**

Expert Witness

"There are few techniques more reliable than the side kick," observes Rene Sampier, an 8th-degree black belt instructor of Shorin-Ryu Karate-Do from El Paso, Texas. "Even a fair-sized kid can break a grown man's knee. The technique is pretty simple: you pull your knee up above the waist and tilt your hip so that the flat of your heel is aimed to the thin spot just above the kneecap, the base of the femur. There's very little muscle there and by stamping sideways and down you knock the attacker's leg straight and then it breaks. It's about as easy as standing a cheap broomstick against a wall and breaking it with your foot."

Australian women's mixed martial arts champion Jane Dalkieth agrees. "The adult male knee breaks at about twenty PSI when hit just above the knee. Just a side kick of even reasonable speed (anything above fifteen miles an hour) will crack the bone My grandmother could at least sprain a man's knee, and if you piss her off enough she could probably break it."

Jim Winterbottom, a teacher of Jeet Kune Do (the style developed by the late Bruce Lee), has this to say: "As much as the human body is built to be enormously tough there are always built in vulnerabilities. Otherwise only the strongest would ever have survived, which we know isn't the case. Martial arts taught us that smart trumps strong because the smart fighter knows where the body is weak. Even a bruiser like the Rock has weak spots. The knees, the elbows, the small bones in the foot, the ankle, the neck . . . all vulnerable. Zombies have those same structural weaknesses and they don't dodge, evade or block. You don't even have to be a great fighter to score the shot."

"I had steel-reinforced hockey pads on my knees, covered with double-thick foam," remembers Sean Gallagher, a former assistant in the Personal Defense for Women program at Temple University, "and even with all that I had my leg sprained a couple of times. If it hadn't been for the steel struts in the knee braces I'd be in a friggin' wheelchair. And these were just women—some of them as small as five foot tall and a hundred pounds soaking wet. And I was *trying* not to get kicked. Some friggin' zombie would go straight down, no questions asked."

The kick to the knee is the easiest, fastest disabling technique for zombies. A slightly less effective but still highly useful skill is the sweep. "There are two basic kinds of sweeps," explains Sensei David Pantano, fourth-degree black belt and owner of Counter-Strike Kenpo Karate in Philadelphia. "You have the footsweep and the leg sweep. The footsweep needs more timing and is used to knock aside an attacker's foot just as he's taking a step forward. With the foot knocked aside the body is still committed to the forward motion and down he goes. The leg sweep, on the other hand, doesn't rely on such precise timing but it does require more muscle. With that you launch a kick—wheel, roundhouse, whatever—at the attacker's lower leg; anything from the back of the knee on down. Basically you're kicking out his support, and again down he goes."

Other useful kicks include the back kick and some of the lower, more powerful turning kicks including the front thrust. "A front thrust or shuffle side thrust isn't going to do any kind of damage to a zombie," warns semipro kickboxer Calvin Watson, "but it'll knock their ugly asses away from you, maybe clear a path, maybe knock the sonsabitches into a ditch or down a flight of stairs. You use them to buy time to move, and then you damn well *move!*"

"Snapping kicks will not have the effect that we would desire," advises Damian Gonzalez, an Aikidoist and instructor of Nami Ryu Kenjutsu. "Avoid all of the snapping kicks, front, side or snapping round kicks, either to the body, face, or groin. They work by generating pain and we are dealing with something that wouldn't feel pain."

Hand strikes are a different matter. Body punches would serve little purpose, but the jaw, eyes, neck, and legs are still viable targets for well-placed, fast, and powerful blows. "I would think their (zombies') motor functions and dexterity would be greatly impaired," observes Raymond Hook, a sibak (assistant instructor) of Kajukenbo[2], "therefore the balance of a zombie would be almost

2. A hybrid martial art (developed in 1947 by Adriano D. Emperado, Joe Holck, Peter Young Yil Choo, George "Clarence" Chang, and Frank Ordonez) that combines karate, judo, jujutsu, kenpo, and kung fu. The name is an acronym for: *ka* ("karate"), *ju* ("judo"/"jujutsu"), *ken* ("kenpo"), *bo* (Chinese and American kickboxing).

non-existent. With this in mind, striking from a distance would be my best bet. I think low strikes to the legs and knees could be just what the *witch doctor* ordered. With limited motor skills a broken leg or separated knee would be hard to maneuver with. Also, weapons would do great. I would most likely want to use something with a bit of length, and something that might be lying around. I'm thinking a shovel, something that's practical and easily accessible, and nothing fancy."

The Zombie Factor

Zombies don't fight. They just grab and bite. Singly they are easy to defeat and easy to escape. A punch or forceful blow—with hands, feet, or a handy blunt object—that just knocks them off balance will allow a human to run past them.

The danger comes when the zombies are in groups, or if there are a lot of them spread out along the human's route of escape. While fatigue won't affect a zombie, a human can eventually tire and slow down. That could get ugly.

Just the Facts

Edged Weapons

Swords and knives have worked pretty well for the last several thousand years, and if somehow zombies became a concern for modern man, I think we'd see a pretty quick return to the way of the blade. As has been pointed out elsewhere in this book, zombies can probably hear, and gunshots are noisy. Attracting more zombies when trying to deal with the one at hand is not a great solution if you don't have a lot of ammo and are a reliable marksman. Though finesse in swordplay takes years of exacting practice, the basics of swinging a sword are fairly easy for anyone to grasp.

Like all forms of combat, however, the nature of zombies does require that the sword be used with some degree of precision. Slashes to the body and stab wounds are (pardon the pun) pointless. Swords would have to be used to decapitate (ideally), or failing that to literally "disarm" the attacker and cut at least one leg out from under him.

When possible it's preferable to cut off a zombie's head. Most swords are capable of doing this, and anyone from a midsized adolescent boy (or average-sized woman) can manage that, once they learn how to use the hips rather than muscular arm strength to power the cut. Muscles may fatigue quickly but hip torsion provides easy and virtually inexhaustible power. The motion would be similar to that of a ballplayer swinging a bat. This does take practice, and requires a sword sturdy enough to cut through meat, tendon, and bone; or one slim enough to cut like a scalpel. Heavy-bladed swords, like European longswords, sabers, and cutlasses are fine, but they depend on considerable physical strength. Most Asian swords such as the Japanese *katana* are lighter and designed to take a finer edge. This is my favorite weapon of choice.

The *katana*, with its sleek and elegant single-edged blade is the samurai's traditional weapon, and these swords are considered to be the sharpest weapons ever devised. The samurai treasured their swords, and eventually formed such a devotion to them that it was believed the sword was the embodiment of the samurai's soul. The *katana* is so sharp and the cut it makes so fast that it is estimated that it can sever the head from the neck in one hundredth of a second. Even fast zombies are no match for that kind of speed.

The samurai had many different types of swords and knives, including the *tachi*—great swords, which were four feet in length; *katana*—thirty-two inches; *wakizashi*—fourteen inches; *tanto*—a dagger of varying length; among others. The samurai were trained to use these and many other weapons through practice of various specialized weapon arts such as *kenjutsu* (swordplay), *naginata-jutsu* (art of the halberd), *kyujutsu* (archery), *tanto-jutsu* (dagger fighting), *hanbojutsu* (art of the short stick), to name just a handful of their weapon arts.

Despite the antiquity of the Japanese sword arts, it's easier to learn the use of those arts today than it is the use of more modern European sword skills. Many martial arts teach weapon use—and the sword is very popular—including jujutsu, aikido, aikijutsu, ninjutsu, as well as those schools dedicated expressly to the sword: kenjutsu and kendo, iaijutsu and iaido.

There are a number of useful swords in the Chinese martial arts, many of which are taught in the various styles of kung fu. The *dao* is a tough single-edged saber ideal for chopping and useful to modern zombie fighters because its use is so common among practitioners of kung fu and wu shu, which means that there are—at a conservative estimate—ten thousand Americans who have a fair working knowledge of its use. The heavier *dadao* and *piandao* are also reliable, though fewer people are skilled in it; and the *pudao*, known as the "horse cutter sword," is very powerful, but its use is almost entirely unknown in the West. A *guandao* is an excellent weapon (once mastered) but cumbersome for a beginner. It's a pole weapon with what looks like a heavy curved blade on the end, similar in basic concept to the European halberd.

If we enter an age where zombies are a reality, then the way of the sword would make an even more substantial comeback. Bet on it.

Expert Witness

Jujitsu sensei Rick Robinson, chief instructor of the Yamabushi-Ryu dojo in Fort Washington, Pennsylvania, agrees that the sword will, quite literally, give humans an *edge* over zombies: "There is a cut that is drawn in an are from left to right that hits the forward forearm of the attacker, and continues to hit the orbital socket with the kissaki,[3] that would turn the head away, the sword is brought around a second time to take the head. This prevents an initial grab and then beheads the zombie. If you use the hips for the cut rather than the arms the movement takes almost no energy and can be utilized many, many time without tiring. That would be very helpful with groups of zombies. There are techniques meant to sever the legs, but with zombies they would be more useful with *naginata*[4] or *nagimaki*."

"I would want to have either a *wakizashi*, or *katana*—one of the thin-bladed swords," says kenjutsu expert Damian Gonzalez," so that I can cleanly cut through necks or hit them right above the bridge of the nose to remove the tops of their heads. Cutting off the arms and legs is useful when trying to escape."

3. The *kissaki* is the tip or point area of a Japanese sword.

4. The *naginata* is a long pole weapon with a sword-like blade at its tip; excellent for long-distance fighting; the *nagimaki* is a shorter version of the same weapon.

Harry Matsushita, a fourth dan[5] in the Cleveland Toyama Ryu Iaijutsu sword school, says, "If we have a problem with those ghouls from the movies people would flock to our *dojos* (schools) to learn how to fight. We'd be able to meet that need, too, because we wouldn't have to teach them the full art of iaijutsu or kenjutsu. After all, they wouldn't need to learn formality and ritual, they wouldn't have to learn how to block. All they would need to master are a very few basic cuts. Taking the leg, taking the outstretched arm, taking the head. We could crash-course them through a lot of that in a day and refine it for practical application in a week."

"Ninjutsu swordplay would be pretty useful," insists Bernardo Gutierrez, a fifth dan in that art. "Ninjutsu isn't about ritual swordplay or duels—it's dodge, evade and kill. The big thing would

***Zombie Mutations* by Ken Meyer, Jr.**

"Zombies are frightening but they're no match for skilled fighters."

5. *Dan* is the Japanese term for an advanced degree or step, hence a fourth dan would be a fourth-degree black belt.

be to reinforce in practitioners the need to take heads off rather than cut throats or slash open the body, but that's just a matter of some focused training."

And what about other edged weapons?

"I'd bet my life on the effectiveness of the kukri knife," says Tapaswi Dhamma,[6] a practitioner of the Burmese martial art of Bando. "It's a great bone cutter, it's heavy enough to lop off an arm or sever a head but light enough to be mighty damn fast." The kukri, or *khukuri,* is an ancient weapon from Nepal that is favored by the *Gurkha,* a hardy people from Nepal and parts of North India. This long knife has a 20-degree bend in the blade that allows for a combination of chopping and cutting.[7] "If zombies ever attacked a *Gurkha* village," Dhamma reflects, "even our kids would make short work of them, slow or fast."

"I think you'd find that there are a lot of people out there who know how to use a sword," insists Brady Howard, a sword and arms trainer for Renaissance combat performers. "Sure, we don't practice with sharpened blades, but we train to be good swordsmen; and most of us own new or historical blades that will definitely take an edge. If zombies start coming after us we'll sharpen up and be ready."

Smaller knives would be a bit less useful because they require far more precision and would really only be of value in attempting to blind a zombie (very risky), darting in to cut hamstrings or ankle tendons (also risky), or in stabbing up into the slot at the base of the skull where a knife blade could rise up to pierce the brain. Whereas this technique, favored by knife-wielding assassins and military special forces, would dispatch a zombie, it's doubtful anyone but an expert would be able to pull it off.

The Zombie Factor

The bottom line is that one-to-one an armed person should be able to kill a slow-moving zombie. In films we've seen zombies dispatched with screwdrivers, the broken handle of a croquet mallet,

6. No relation to the monk of the same name.

7. Milla Jovovich uses one pretty effectively against zombies in *Resident Evil: Extinction* (2007).

clubs, tire irons, and a variety of blunt objects and edged weapons. They can be destroyed.

The difficulties come from mustering the courage to go mano a mano with a ghoul, being competent in close-quarters fighting, remembering where to hit, and avoiding blood spill during the fight.

Swords, spears, long-range clubs, a chain mace, baseball bats—all of these are practical for fighting zombies while at the same time keeping out of biting reach, and avoiding contamination.

The Final Verdict: Zombie Chop-Socky

In a world where zombies were a real threat, martial arts would become an even bigger business than it is now. Everyone would be learning how to throw a few basic kicks and to swing a sword.

Zombies . . . Fast or Slow? Part 8

- **"I don't care as much for the newer zombies. The fast ones. They're cartoonish. It's too much. Adding speed to zombies is overkill."—Tony Todd, star of the *Candyman* movies and *Night of the Living Dead* (1990)**
- **"Zombies are slow but relentless. That is scarier than fast." —John Lutz, Edgar and Shamus Award-winning author of *Single White Female* (Pocket, 1992)**
- **"I want both, if I can. The old school part of me enjoys the slow, relentless march of the slow zombie, a force as inevitable as the tides, society itself lumbering along making victims randomly, the sheer numbers (not one individual) finally overwhelming you. That said, I have to admit, the fast zombies in 28 DAYS LATER were frightening as hell. Each presents a different dynamic."—Paul G. Tremblay, author of the short fiction collection *Compositions for the Young and Old* (Prime Books, 2005) and the novella *City Pier: Above and Below* (Prime, 2007)**

In a few of the zombie stories, there's been a twisted little subplot of "zombie games." including gladiatorial combat of humans against zombies (e.g., the cage fights in *Land of the Dead*). Though these scenes are played either for laughs or to make a cynical statement about the extent to which the entertainment industry would go, I don't think they're all that far from what might happen. Whether legal or illegal, there might actually be some cage fights with zombies; and some of the folks I've talked to about this think it would actually be "cool."

Josh "the Viper" Gallagher, a practitioner of mixed martial arts and avowed lover of all extreme sports, had this to say: "If there were zombies and people could capture some, they'd be like the ultimate X-game challenge or maybe 'Z' games. Imagine the stones it would take to go into a ring with a zombie. You got nothing, no weapons, no armor. Just you and one of *them*. Man, I'd sign up for that right now. I mean right this minute."

A colleague of his, who preferred that I used only his competition name of "Ratt," adds, "You'd have rich guys buying zombies on the black market and setting up illegal safaris. Think about it: a guy with a pistol and maybe one bullet and having to get out of a cave or off an island or whatever that has a zombie on it. What a rush that would be. You want to try and tell me that people wouldn't pay big bucks for a chance to try something like that! Are you nuts?"

On behalf of most of the human race, let me just say: "Yikes."

Live Feed

Reporting the Apocalypse

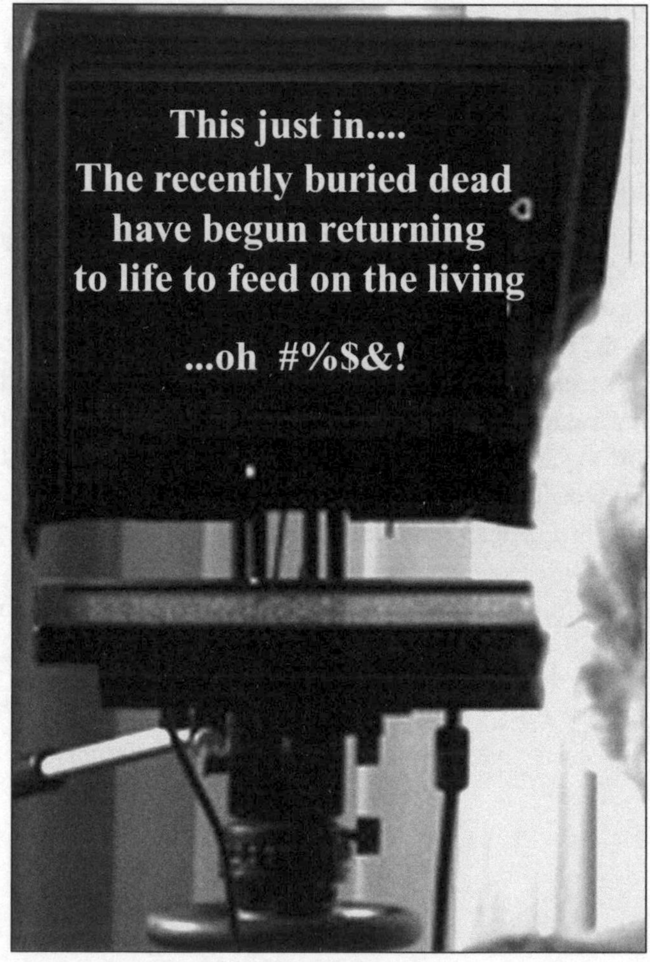

Live Feed by Jonathan Maberry

"The apocalypse *will* be televised."

There's an old Chinese curse: "May you live in interesting times." On the surface that doesn't sound too harsh; even sounds kind of nice; but if you take a big picture view of the world and consider the "interesting" events that fill up our history books and—more to the point—every single newspaper headline and TV news broadcast lead story, well . . . you get the point. If you're the person to whom these interesting events are happening, then to use a popular catch phrase: "Sucks to be you." If you're the reporter who is working on one of these stories, then the appropriate comment is: "You hit the jackpot." It's all relative.

For reporters a major calamity is very much hitting the jackpot. Careers are made by it. The Kennedy assassination put Ted Koppel on the map. Vietnam (the first "TV war") and Walter Cronkite are inextricably linked. Watergate made superstars of Woodward and Bernstein. Desert Storm turned Wolf Blitzer into a household name. Hurricane Katrina transformed Anderson Cooper into the news equivalent of a rock star.

I remember on my first day of Introduction to Journalism at Temple University, way back in the 1970s, my cynical journalism teacher wrote these words on the blackboard: "News is entertainment." After he let us digest that for a few minutes, he picked up the chalk and added: "So bloody well be entertaining." And added a half dozen exclamation points.

Just the Facts

Live from the Apocalypse

If the dead rose, the news media would not be deserting their posts and heading for the hills as they did in *Dawn of the Dead*. No matter how bad things got, they—like just about everyone else—would assume that this, too, will pass and that if they keep right with the story, right there at the front lines where things get hot and bloody, then they will get that story (or for photojournalists—that *picture*) that will make them a star. They'll get the scoop, or the exclusive. They'll land the story that will be the hook and the headline. Their names will get printed above the fold in the paper, or they'll get a shot to do a live stand up from the field. They will become the story, and we will want them, specifically *them,* to be the ones to keep us informed. I mean . . . you don't think reporters ask to be embedded with combat troops because of the size of their paycheck. I've worked in the field . . . the paycheck isn't that hot, and certainly not big enough to risk being blown up. No, the reward is career advancement or a place in history, or for the idealists it's that rare "great story." It will be a long time before the general public and the history books forget Cronkite, Koppel, Woodward and Bernstein, Blitzer, or Cooper. Hell, they're still talking about Edward R. Murrow, and he died in 1965.

This rising of the dead would be a massive story, maybe the biggest ever. Careers would be made, immortality would be assured for whomever got the best footage or was able to report the story from as close to the front lines as possible. The cops and military would have to spend half their time pushing reporters out of the way of marauding zombie. But man oh man how *well* that story would be covered.

"If the dead started rising," observes Jack Spangler, a freelance feature writer and former Chicago TV news reporter, "I'd be there with my photographer up to the point where it started trying to take a bite out of us, and even then I'd have my tape recorder in his face trying to get a sound bite out of his unearthly moans. You couldn't chase me off a story like that. No way, José."

In *Day of the Dead*, there's a terrific scene in which a newspaper blows down the deserted street of a town that we think (hope) is deserted. The paper blows up against a wall, and we can read the headline: "The Dead Walk." Soon after that, we start hearing the moans of the living dead as they stagger out into the street. It's an absolutely compelling moment. Years later the film *Resident Evil* built a scene around the main character, Alice (played by a marvelously vicious Milla Jovovich), walking through a ruined and deserted city street where terrible violence has obviously raged. She walks past a newspaper with the same headline. In both cases, there is the suggestion that reporters were following the story all the way up to the end. They are, in fact, reporting the apocalypse.

In the zombie movies, there is a standard plot device of showing us snippets of TV news coverage of the growing disaster. The directors never give us the full story because in film less is more when it comes to exposition, especially early on . . . and besides it's a wonderful tease. I always loved those TV news snippets. I always wanted more coverage. I wanted to know what the reporters were saying—right or wrong. In the remake of *Dawn of the Dead*, there is an almost comedic parallel storyline early on where Ana (Sarah Polley) keeps walking past radios and TV screens, distracted by her duties as a nurse or later during lovemaking with her husband, so that she never hears the coverage of the developing catastrophe. It makes us wonder how she might have otherwise acted had she known—and that's great movie storytelling because it means we've been drawn into the creative process by imagining the what-if scenarios.

From a reporter's view, however, it shows that the story is being followed everywhere it goes; but since the new *Dawn* deals with the fast zombies, which results in a lot of sudden attacks, we also see reporters becoming a bit too much a part of the story.

Let's explore how real-world reporters work and what they say about reporting the raising of the dead.

Expert Witness

In *Night of the Living Dead*, the story starts in rural Pennsylvania, somewhere near Pittsburgh, which means that it would probably fall to small-town newspapers to begin the coverage. Nancy Barr, author of the *Page One*[1] mystery series and former journalist explains how stories are developed by small-town papers: "Most small newspapers get their news tips one of four ways: The standard issue press release; an anonymous person calling or writing a reporter or editor; someone calling, walking into the office or e-mailing the newspaper; or the reporter attending a meeting where something of interest is mentioned. Let's say someone called a reporter or editor and said, 'I heard from someone over at the hospital that three people have died in the last week of some bizarre illness. How come there's been nothing in the paper?' The reporter would try to get some more details such as who the people were, how old, when it happened,

1. *Page One: Hit and Run* (2006) and *Page One: Vanished* (2007) are both available from Arbutus Press.

The Worst Zombie Films of All Time, Part 1

- ***Plan 9 from Outer Space*** **(1958): The plot has something to do with aliens, a vampire, the rising dead, and . . . apparently a total loss of storytelling sense. Ed Wood—may he live forever!**
- ***The Dead Pit*** **(1989): Slow to get started, slow to build a story, and slow at the end.**
- ***Die You Zombie Bastards*** **(2005): Great title. That's it, just a great title.**
- ***Flesh Freaks*** **(2001): Devious worms from out of space turn people into zombies. Starring no one you ever heard of.**
- ***Ghosts of Mars*** **(2001): John Carpenter, who should have known better, gives us Martian zombies in what appears to be a weird rip-off on *Road Warrior*.**
- ***Gore Whore*** **(1994): I'll say this once: It's about a penis-slicing zombie prostitute.**
- ***Hot Wax Zombies on Wheels*** **(1999): Another example of a title that has all the good stuff and a movie that has none.**
- ***The Incredibly Strange Creatures Who Stopped Living and Became Mixed Up Zombies*** **(1963). No.**
- ***Junk*** **(1999): Calling your movie *Junk* is asking for it. There's nothing original here, and what is there . . . is, well . . . junk.**
- ***The Laughing Dead*** **(1989): Not a chuckle, not a shiver.**

what type of symptoms, etc. Realizing all this could be nothing but a silly rumor, the reporter would then call the hospital for confirmation. If she dead-ended there, she'd call the local health department, then the CDC, and the local university for background. Hopefully, if there is any truth to the story, someone will be able to go on the record. Taking this a bit farther, an enterprising reporter will find out at least one of the victim's names and then contact the family, etc. An editor is going to be very concerned about causing a panic, so confirmation from several sources on something like this would be of the utmost importance."

According to Joe Student, editor for *Philly EDGE* (newspaper) in Philadelphia, "A story (such as the attack on the research center guard in our scenario) would most likely have its genesis through the 'cops' reporter's monitoring of the local police scanner. If it was a full-out zombie attack, since there would ostensibly be multiple victims and an apparent homicide, the reporter would be sent to the scene with other crime-beat reporters added as the case/story became bigger. On the most local level, the decision to run the news of a murder would be instantaneous; the decision to associate the attacks as zombie-related would have to come from someone within law enforcement or the coroner's office suggesting and substantiating the claim."

Gregg Winkler's Decaying Zombie Quiz, Part 3

1. **The Cranberries' 1994 single, "Zombie," is a song protesting what?**
2. **What 1941 movie depicts an Austrian doctor-turned-spy using newly created zombies to obtain war intelligence?**
3. **What was the name of Peter Jackson's zombie movie?**
4. **Which of the following will not make a zombie?**
   - **a. The bite of a zombie**
   - **b. A voodoo ritual**
   - **c. Drinking a zombie's spit**
   - **d. Combine rum, crème de almond, sweet and sour, triple sec, orange juice, and 151 proof rum into a Collins glass over ice.**
5. **Tetrodotoxin, which is a potentially lethal toxin said to have been found in relation to Haitian vodoun practices that can leave a person in a "state near death," can be found in all but which of the following?**
   - **a. Puffer fish**
   - **b. Starfish**
   - **c. Jellyfish**
   - **d. Some flatworms**

I asked these reporters how this process might change if an outbreak was suspected. "Even small newspapers have someone who is particularly interested in health stories and has the contacts," Barr says. "That person would probably break the story. However, if the story is of a large enough magnitude, the entire staff would be put to work covering various aspects of an outbreak (financial, health, society, etc.). Associated Press would likely send someone to the area to provide coverage to the entire state and beyond if the outbreak is large. Again, the reporter would check with hospital officials, doctor offices, the local health department, local university (they might have students impacted or the faculty might be able to speak about diseases and their impact on society, i.e., how people react), even the person on the street. In a small town, the best news tips are found in the local diner. The police would play a secondary role, perhaps keeping the peace at the hospital. I imagine a larger community would have a bioterrorism unit within the police department. The state police in Michigan have such a unit that might be called into action."

Student adds, "Most likely whichever reporter covers the town/area in which the event happened, the more significant the outbreak, the more reporters assigned. Also, if it had a national scope, AP and other national, and international agencies and press could potentially send staff. Of course, there would be some vetting because there is a health risk; it would be more similar to the coverage of the Iraq War than the 9/11 attacks. Not every reporter would just be sent in to cover news as it happens."

When asked how reporters know what's reliable information and what's hearsay or gossip, Student observed: "Insiders at hospitals, in municipal government and public safety offices. Not those giving the press releases but those talking directly to people at the scene. Some rumor and exaggeration makes it through, but a good reporter can check it out before alleging something outlandish in print."

"There would be some doubt about a story with zombies," says Elaine Viets, a novelist[2] who reported for the *St. Louis Post Dispatch* for twenty-five years. "If a story just sounded too fantas-

2. Elaine Viets is the author of the Dead-End Job and Mystery Shopper mystery series from Penguin.

tic a reporter would need more than one source because there are plenty of folks, even experts, who will say anything just to get into print. Good reporters get at least two sources before they put their name to the story."

Outbreaks and epidemics are newsworthy. At what point, however, does the story get moved to the front page? Student remarked, "It's all about the size of the story, or how big it might get. Scope, immediacy and interest are all factors, but once casualties can be counted, the story is played larger. Best example is the 2004 tsunami in Indonesia. If the wave had claimed as many lives as the 2007 Minnesota bridge collapse, the story probably doesn't make the first page in the U.S., but as a result of its scope it goes above the fold; the bridge story was as significant domestically though there were less lives lost because of its developing nature. This story had great potential because it had a local angle in nearly every U.S. community where there was a structurally deficient bridge."

Barr says, "In a small town, it would probably start below the fold on the front unless it was clear we were dealing with a serious outbreak. In that case, it would be top story and would remain above the fold until the crisis was on the decline."

In fiction and film there's always talk about "preventing a panic" when a truly epic story is about to break.

"Simple," says Student. "What do we know to be accurate? Journalism is a de facto public service, so it needs to transmit information without exaggeration. Of course . . . the economic impact of a sensational story could conceivably tempt some editors to hype findings more. Are the killers at-large? Are they capable of killing again? Are there any leads? Is the tornado on the ground? Will more tornadoes hit? Are more storms on the way? And so on. That's info that people *need* to know. People can find out that they were zombies, or an F-5 tornado, later."

"The editor's first concern would be avoiding a panic," says Barr, "which is why it would be so important to have reliable sources providing real information and tips for people to follow and then insure that information is disseminated to the schools, major retail outlets (Wal-Mart, etc.) and major employers in the area. This is really more the responsibility of the local health department,

***Documenting the Dead* by Jonathan Maberry**

"If it's a crisis, it's a story."

where effective leadership would be imperative to avoiding a full-scale panic. A newspaper must report the news responsibly. That does not mean covering things up, though, simply because some government official is hesitant to go on the record. It's a delicate balance."

In pop fiction, reporters and law enforcement are always at odds. How does this relationship work in the real world?

"Depends on the individuals," Student muses. "Both groups have a job to do and can hamper or help the other's work. It comes down to trust and how the relationships are built. If it is antagonistic, it's hard for it not to remain that way. Ultimately though, just like a cop has to write a ticket, serve papers, etc. reporters have to report a story."

Barr says, "At small newspapers, it is up to the reporter covering the cops and courts beat to develop a symbiotic relationship with law enforcement. In most cases, reporters and cops get along

The Worst Zombie Films of All Time, Part 2

- ***Lord of the Dead*** **(2002): A spectacularly bad piece of crap. This is no joke: One of the "demons" in the movie is actually a hand puppet. And it's *not* supposed to be funny.**
- ***Curse of the Cannibal Confederates*** **(1982): I'm all for historical zombie stories, but for god sake give us at least passable makeup effects, a story, characters we care about, good lighting, above nineth grade acting . . . I'm not asking for all of this. Any single one of those would have helped.**
- ***Biker Zombies from Detroit*** **(2001): A demon recruits bikers for his gang of zombies. I think that sentence was the entire script before they started shooting.**
- ***Bloodsuckers from Outer Space*** **(1984): Texas farmers become zombies. Neighbors fail to notice. We're supposed to laugh; but we don't notice.**
- ***Bloody Bill*** **(2004): One of those movies that more or less "remakes" a film (*Ghost Town*), which didn't deserve a remake. Not surprisingly it tanks.**
- ***Zombie Nation*** **(2004): It's just pure crap. There's nothing nice you can say about a film whose zombie makeup consists entirely of too much eye shadow. It's also dreadfully misogynistic.**
- ***Dead Heat*** **(1998): Well before he became TV's Mr. Warmth, Treat Williams was slogging through a lot of really bad movies. This one's about zombie cops trying to solve their own murder. Yeesh.**

just fine as long as they respect each other's boundaries. There are certain things cops can't reveal and there are certain things reporters have a duty to report. Having said that, if the reporter is any good at all, she will have developed at least one or two law enforcement sources in the community that she can call and get the story off the record. That off the record information can then be used to track down information on the record. It can sort of provide road map for what questions need to be asked of the 'officials.' "

In some countries, the authorities can control what the press says and what (and when) they can report certain news. In Great Britain, a D-Notice (also called DA-Notice) is often issued for stories tied to national defense.[3] In criminal trials, the press is advised not to run stories once a case is sub judice (or, under judgment) based on the belief that public comment such as newspaper articles may influence the fair process of the trial. In America, the First Amendment, signed into law by Lyndon Johnson in 1966, allows for freedom of the press (except in matters of security), and the Freedom of Information Act requires that government information be made available to the public (again, except in matters of security). There are several classifications of information that are not available for either the press or the public, and the government separates them according to sensitivity: confidential, secret, and top secret. There are rumors among the conspiracy theory crowd that there are a number of levels above top secret, which is both reasonable and likely.

I asked my journalism experts how reporters would respond to attempts by authorities to control a situation such as a plague outbreak (with or without zombies).

Student says, "Authorities can, and sometimes do, ask for a delay off-the-record. Through court order, they conceivably can inhibit something that affects an ongoing case or puts the life of an agent/officer at-risk. Some news agencies run stories anyway depending on their assessment of the situation and if it is indeed life-threatening information. Policies vary newsroom-to-newsroom and editor-to-editor."

"If the government had the story," Viets says, "they wouldn't

3. Currently Great Britain has five classifications of D-Notice situations: DA-Notice 01: Military Operations, Plans & Capabilities; DA-Notice 02: Nuclear and Non-Nuclear Weapons and Equipment; DA-Notice 03: Ciphers and Secure Communications; DA-Notice 04: Sensitive Installations and Home Addresses; DA-Notice 05: United Kingdom Security & Intelligence Special Services. Britain maintains an official website for D-Notices: www.dnotice.org.uk/index.htm.

release it at all, they'd cover it up to prevent a panic. And by 'panic' I mean folks canceling everything, disrupting trade, impacting the stock market, damaging the flow of commerce. It isn't people running screaming through the streets that's the problem, it's the economy collapsing because of panic. Remember what happened during 9/11—everything got canceled, from air traffic (which you can understand) to church services and day-care (which is a bit extreme). Most likely the government, instead of trying to block the press, would just feed them some story they cooked up. They say it was a SARS scare, or something like that."

Small-town reporter Barr adds, "Well, of course they can say 'don't print that story' but in reality it is up to the editor and publisher whether or not a story will run. That is the beauty of the First Amendment. Now, it may forever damage the credibility of that newspaper in the eyes of said authorities, but if the story is important enough, a strong editor will take the heat and do what is right."

Viets adds, "I worked at the *Post Dispatch* during the release of the Pentagon Papers. The government tried to keep us from releasing them by taking us to court, citing 'National Security,' but it didn't work. On the other hand you can't yell fire in a crowded theater, so if the press is going to run a story they'd better make sure of their facts first."

The Zombie Effect

I asked my journalism experts to comment on how the press would handle a news tip that the dead were rising.

Barr remarks, "That's a tough one because of the disbelief factor intrinsic to the story itself. I'm not in Pittsburgh . . . so, zombies in Houghton, Michigan? Nearly everyone's first reaction would be to roll their eyes and go 'yeah, right.' However, a bored, but open-minded reporter would probably make a few inquiries, maybe interview the initial tipster and definitely try to get photos. If the tip panned out to be real, the whole community would be going nuts. I was taking a break from journalism when 9/11 happened and was working at a police/fire station in a town of about 13,000 in the Upper Peninsula of Michigan, which is

Art of the Dead – Sean Boley

Zombie Toons

"Zombies have captured and captivated audiences both young and old for years. As grotesquely disfigured and macabre as zombies are, people just can't help but be fascinated by the grossness of it all—those of us among the living tend to be weird that way."

about as far from New York and Washington as you can get culturally. You wouldn't believe the number of people who called and said something like 'There's an Arab walking down Ludington Street.' I replied, 'So?' and they said, 'Well, go arrest him. He's probably one of them terrorists.' It was just nuts. Fortunately, law enforcement kept their heads through all the nonsense."

Viets points out that the more fantastic news stories are often investigated just to break up boredom during slow stretches. "August is the ideal time to have weird things happen, 'cause nothing happens in August. That's when we'll go the extra mile to look into something oddball; that's when we'll drive out to the boonies to check out someone who called to say he saw a UFO—which always turned out to be swamp gas. I'd be heading out to the middle of nowhere with a cursing photographer hoping for something I could write about."

"If the reports were in any way reliable, or even potentially reliable the press would be all over it," Student assures.

Zach Martini, a freelance wire service reporter agrees, "If reporters heard the dead were rising they'd rush the story, grab it, squeeze every drop out it. Not just for glory—most reporters aren't really as cynical as we're sometimes portrayed. Jaded, maybe, but not completely heartless. We'd know that this was information that had to get out to the public. Especially if this was a national emergency. Lives would depend on the story getting out, and unless the Emergency Broadcast Network was kicked in—and when's the last time you ever heard of that? Not even during 9/11—it would fall to the press to keep the public informed."

In films like *Dawn the Living Dead* and its sequels, journalists are often depicted as unethical and disordered, providing outdated lists of shelters and safe zones just so they'd have something to report. I asked the reporters to talk about the efficiency of the modern reporter and how he or she would be able to stay on top of the story and as a result serve the public's need for reliable information.

Martini scoffs. "I saw those films and it pissed me off. Maybe you get a few total jackasses in the business, but there would be a mutiny if our news director was churning out false information like that. And we'd all be complicit in conspiracy and probably twenty other crimes. No, we'd send someone out to do a field report, and if a shelter became contaminated then *that* becomes the breaking news item. That would be what we'd need to tell the people right away."

Viets agrees. "The list of shelters would be news, no doubt; but more to the point the editors would *never* allow that kind of stuff to go out. Despite the bad PR the press often gets most of the people I've known in the 25 years I was a reporter were basically fair. You give out the wrong info knowingly and that will really come back to bite you."

"That's a tough one because modern newspapers aren't all that much different than they were fifty years ago," Barr says. "They are pretty much a very ethical bunch with a few bad apples. However, television coverage has changed dramatically thanks to the likes of Fox News and other media outlets that go for the shock factor. I don't know that is so much an ethics problem as the need to be the most outrageous in order to attract viewers. Humans love a good ol' fashioned bloodbath, and I mean that in all seriousness. It gives them something to talk about. Remember when someone posted the photos of the bodies following Princess Diana's crash? Millions of people said, 'How gross, how terrible, what an invasion of privacy.' Then, probably half of them looked at the photos. A good reporter will always try to balance the *ick* factor with common decency, but in a story that is sensational by its very nature, i.e., zombies, it would be very difficult not to come off sounding like the now-defunct *Weekly World News*. This is why having well spoken, honest officials on the record would be so important."

Student sees the matter as being multifaceted: "Deadlines and circumstance sometimes create a subset of ethics that are outside of what one might learn in J-school or follow as company policy. Basically, a reporter has to sometimes balance the information against what its implications are and what he/she can weed out through common sense. I have no doubt that some editors would want the reporter to actually have seen a zombie attack before reporting it as such, some would actually wait to pick up the story—especially in the days of the short-scoop (with the Web, as soon as you post info, it's everyone's story attributed to you, not just yours)—instead of running it first without conviction, confirmation, substantiation and attribution."

I asked the reporters about the newspaper headline from *Day of the Dead*, "The Dead Walk." Did that sound like a reasonable headline for a crisis of this kind? Viets assured me it was. "Absolutely. I worked for two editors who would go out of their way to run the corniest headline they could."

Student thought that it should have been tweaked: "Not if they are attacking people and eating their brains. You'd have something like DEAD ATTACK LIVING or 'ZOMBIE' MURDERS. Something more immediate and less vague but still sensational."

Viet points out that the wording of the headline depends a lot on the style of each paper. "If the *New York Times*, *The New York Daily Post*, and the *Daily News* all reported a zombie rising you'd have different styles. The *Times* would probably lead with something like EXPERTS BELIEVE THE DEAD MAY BE RETURNING TO LIFE. Something carefully worded; whereas the *Daily News* might actually run THE DEAD WALK, or maybe something even a little funny."

I asked my reporters if there was an ongoing conflict with the living dead, would reporters volunteer to become embedded with the military who are responding to the crisis? Just about all of them said yes, quickly and emphatically.

"Of course!" says Barr. "I can think of at least four or five reporters with whom I worked in my 10-year career who would have jumped at the opportunity to do something like that, myself included."

Student agreed wholeheartedly. "Sure. The profession, despite its relative shortcomings in salary and glamour, is filled with people who want to tell a (true) story that the world reads and remembers. This is an opportunity to write that story."

And Martini added, "Pardon the joke, but I'd *kill* for a story like that. You'd get out there on the front lines and you'd be reporting news that no one else has and you'd be making a difference, maybe even saving lives."

Viets sees it a little differently: "The young reporters looking to make a name for themselves would. The older guys would be happy to let them."

In related news . . . Just as the *Daily Show* with Jon Stewart is a fake news program that is nonetheless regarded as the best place to find the truth, the ZombieWorldNews (www.zombieworldnews.com) is the best place to find up-to-the-minute news stories about the living dead.

Created by Keith Harrop, ZombieWorldNews looks exactly like a straight-shooting Internet news site, with reporting from the field, stand ups by correspondents, and convincingly dry news articles about everything from zombie physiology to zombie disposal methods.

I asked Harrop about how ZombieWorldNews got started. "It actually started as one of those conversations me and my wife have after a bottle of wine. They always start with 'Hey, you know what would be a reeeaaalllly good idea?' Well, this was it. We try to approach it in the spirit of a real newscast. Which is difficult, because I am from the UK but have lived in the US for the last 20 years. So I have this mixed idea of what news media should be like. I have the droll, stoic delivery of the BBC and then the sensational, dramatic approach of CNN."

What's the ZombieWorldNews's approach: "There are too many Zombie movies that are just plain dumb. And the people who watch them deserve better. I committed from the beginning several things, they were—(A) not to dumb down the concept. (B) Not to satirize current events. (C) Not to sensationalize. (D) To pace the stories, even to the point where on some days mediocre events happened."

It seems like a lot of work for one guy. Harrop says, "I was just going to throw a couple of news items a month up on the site. But as it started to get popular I realized I had to really commit to this or it just would not work. As I started to write it, all sorts of issues and ideas started to come up. I had to recognize the human element. Ethics, politics, science and medicine. How do you dispose of a dead body? There must be rules, even in times like these. Is a Zombie clinically dead even? Where is its soul? Should it have some basic rights? How does human nature's natural tendency towards paranoia emerge in non-plague areas? What do we do with quarantine victims? Immigration?"

Harrop admits that he no longer does all of it himself. "About 50% is staff written at this point. The concept is to allow readers to write their own reports. If it fits the story direction as a whole then I print it. Other readers may write additional reports that take the story in an entirely different direction. You have to reel some people in at times though. They want to get straight to the third act. Submitting reports of thousands of Zombies holding America under siege. Well, where do you go from there? I think the slow burn is always best. Pace it. One well-written report of a missing hiker, or an outbreak on a cruise ship is equally engaging as any epic Zombie holocaust. That helps make ZombieWorldNews.com

Why Zombies?

- **"Our daily lives are filled with real monsters and real horrors. Monsters fly airplanes into buildings and abduct eleven-year-old girls from behind car washes and butcher their pregnant wives and strap their own children with bombs and send them to blow up other children. These are dark times that we live in, and people want an escape. People are scared of everyday life. Sometimes, it's good to curl up with a make believe monster, rather than the one outside your door. Make believe monsters offer us a release valve—an escape from the very real terrors that surround us. Who would you rather spend time with—a suicide bomber or a zombie?"—Brian Keene**
- **"Zombies tend to represent consumerism. Americans are the leaders of the world and the ultimate consumers in every way. For the future of the genre I'd like more exploration of the aftermath of consumerism—the post apocalypse and rebirth."—Sarah Langan, author of *The Missing*.**
- **"To quote a line from one of Romero's movies—'because we're them and they're us.' I think that's the key to it—we can become these nightmare creatures, and there's generally nothing we can do to stop it happening. We can put it off, but it's usually inevitable that the dead will catch up with you."—David Moody, author of the *Autumn* series of zombie novels.**

so unique. It's one huge, dynamic horror story told in real time with no specific author."

The Final Verdict: Extra, Extra, Read All About It

Disasters are news. Death is news. Pain and misery are news. Catastrophic loss is news. Wars are news. Epidemics are news. There's no doubt at all that if the apocalypse happened, you'd be watching it on TV or reading it in the morning paper.

11

To Die For

The Rise of Zombie Pop Culture

The Dead Elvi **by Chris Palmerini**

"Back in 1993, when the Chiller Theatre convention moved to a larger venue and a ballroom became available, promoter Kevin Clement asked his friend Chris Palmerini if he could help put together a band so Kevin could put on a costume ball. Thus was the birth of the Dead Elvi! Little did they think that twelve years later they'd still be performing, appear in several movie soundtracks, have a cut on a Rob Zombie CD, and appear on at least a dozen 'Something Weird' DVDs . . . and to be the last band to play a gig with the late, great Bobbie 'Boris' Pickett!"

—Reprinted with permission from www.deadelvi.com

Cecil B. DeMille is reported to have said, "Give me any two pages of the Bible and I'll give you a picture." We love taking the big (and small) events of our lives and making them into movies, songs, TV shows, documentaries, comics, and even T-shirts. We are a pop culture society.

How long after 9/11 did the first wave of movies hit the theaters? There are novels written about Hurricane Katrina. Whole TV episodes are built around recent headlines.

More than we love to write factually about the events of history—ancient or recent—we love to weave the top stories into the fabric of our pop culture. This is in no way a criticism—it's who we are, and to a degree it helps us understand the events that shape our lives. By using a media format, we can explore the nuances of an issue that might otherwise not be something folks could or would talk about. Look at the original *Star Trek* TV show: Despite the cool phasers and warp drives that appealed to our innate geekiness, there were also the weighty social issues in each episode, cleverly disguised as science fiction. During the incendiary 1960s, the show openly tackled racism with a crew that was racially mixed, the very first TV screen kiss between black and white races occured between Kirk and Uhuru,[1] an entire episode was used to mock the very nature of racism by depicting a struggle between aliens who were black on one side of their bodies and white on the other (the nature of their contention being the orientation—one was black on the left side, the other black on the right)[2]; and

1. Episode "Plato's Stepchildren" (airdate 11/22/68).
2. Episode "Let That Be Your Last Battlefield" (airdate 1/10/69).

the ongoing racism of human against Vulcan even among friends. Very touchy stuff back then.

But then theater has *always* taken issues of the day and made them into entertainment. Go ask Homer, Aeschylus, Euripides, and Epicharmus of Kos; or jump forward and see where William Shakespeare was getting his ideas. Same goes for just about anyone who wrote a play or a book, or wrote scripts for TV and film.

At this writing, we're all deeply embedded in the Iraq War. So far we've already had a number of movies set during this war, ranging from psychological studies, such as *Jarhead*, (2005) to pure exploitive entertainment, like *Transformers* (2007). We've had TV episodes and series by the dozen set in Iraq or touching on the lives of the men and women who have gone there to fight. Novels have been written about it; comics, too. Hollywood and the entertainment industries, political sides notwithstanding, recognize the war as a source of good storytelling. Or, more cynically put, they see it as a way to make money.

We've had feature films like *United 93* (2006) and *World Trade Center* (2006), and more of these are on the way. On a bigger picture scale, the global War on Terror is an endless source of entertainment. Middle Eastern terrorists and/or religious extremists have become the new standard movie villain.

All this offends a portion of our society, and these critics say that these are not fit subjects for entertainment, that it's too soon, that exploiting tragedy is in poor taste; and to a degree they're right. But they're not completely right because pop culture is not necessarily as shallow and ephemeral as all that. When Homer wrote the *Odyssey*, he certainly profited by it, but did that diminish its value? The book's been required reading for a couple of millennia and, let's face it, he played pretty fast and loose with the facts in order to tell a more compelling story. Was Dickens a cad for writing *A Tale of Two Cities*, when clearly so much human suffering was associated with the French Revolution? Was C. S. Forester merely pandering to his audience with his Horatio Hornblower Napoleonic war novels?

The answer will always be yes and no. A little bit of yes and a whole lot of no because art imitates life. It always has, since the first time a caveman painted a picture of a buffalo on the wall and tried to convince his in-laws that he'd actually seen something like that. Art—literature, dance, film, music—has grown up around the need to tell us stories, and many of those stories will be based in whole or in part on real events. It's how we explain our world to ourselves.

Just the Facts

Dead On!

Which brings us to zombies. If there was a zombie plague, there would be brand new zombie movies—even before the plague was resolved. I mean . . . we make movies about them *now* and there are no actual zombies. Do you want to sit there and tell me that if there were actual zombies we wouldn't be making films about them? Or books? Or comics? Of *course* we would. And we can justly say that Romero told us to. After all, *Night of the Living Dead* was a statement about the times as they were happening. So was *Dawn*, so was *Day*.

So often pop culture is either a mirror that we can hold up to view all the big pores, warts, pimples, and blackheads of our society; or it's a window into aspects of the world and points of view we can't otherwise see. Zombie films and books have frequently polished the glass on those mirrors and windows, or provided filters that block out distractions and allow us to see a specific thing with great clarity. It's a kind of Jonathan Swift effect. His *Gulliver's Travels* was no more about giants and little people than *A Modest Proposal* was about actually eating Irish babies. Along those same lines, *Night of the Living Dead* was not about monsters attacking humans, not on the level where the writer envisioned the story. Zombies were a by-product. For Romero, *Night* was, among other things, a way of shouting out about the state of our society, about the disconnect between human beings and their basic humanity, about the fracturing of openness and how human dignity takes a beating in the presence of uninformed bigotry. It was no accident that the hero of the piece, Ben, was played by a black actor. It was not an accident that the white majority hides behind locked doors.

What's so fascinating is that we probably already have a glimpse

The Zombie Presidents

Mount Rotmore **by Yale Redd Bender**

"Romero and his followers showed us that zombies and politics go hand in hand. Some people have taken that more to heart than others, and none more so than The Zombie Presidents. Founded by pop culture retailer Brett Dewey and Hollywood special effects artist Mark Tavares, the group promotes some very dry political humor (no one is spared) and also has a line of T-shirts and other merchandise. Dewey says, "The Zombie Presidents were conceived in the vein of the Zombie as social commentary. Seeing the current division in the country and frustration over the lack of inspiring leadership, the American voters cried out for leaders like the great ones of the past—and to everyone's surprise they answered! Why look for the next JFK or Ronald Reagan when you can have the original!"

of what the pop culture would look like if zombies were a reality. We have zombie movies by the hundreds; zombie novels, zombie comic books, zombie art, zombie music, zombie toys, zombie everything. In the summer of 2007, JCPenney launched a series of commercials in which zombified clothes attacked school children (granted it wasn't to munch on them but to amp up their post-grunge sense of style). Zombies are everywhere.

Johnny Gruesome

Johnny Gruesome by Zach McCain and Greg Lamberson

Zombies are usually the villains of the piece, but for subversive horror author Greg Lamberson the zombie is definitely the leading man. His creation, Johnny Gruesome, is the ghost of a murdered high school student who reanimates his own corpse in order to exact a bloody revenge. Johnny Gruesome has been turned into a comic book, a video short, and a head-banging CD. Zach McCain renders the comic with moody brilliance, and songwriter Giasone Italiano crafted the thrilling theme music.

I asked people in different aspects of the zombie pop culture to talk about what's hot in rot and what's cool for ghouls.

Expert Witness

Derrick Sampson, an actor and theater teacher from Chicago, was very frank about the role of race in the Romero films. "Romero was ballsy to cast a handsome black man—Duane Jones—as the lead in *Night of the Living Dead*. Especially in rural Pennsylvania. Most people are unaware that Pennsylvania has more KKK members than any other state in America. And *Night* was shot during the 1960s . . . not exactly the least turbulent time in American race relations. Duane played a strong, sensible, courageous man trying to do his best to protect the people in his charge—all of whom were white. Another director might have done that as a kind of stunt casting, but Romero is, if anything, fiercely outspoken when it comes to fairness. He may be cynical, but at the same time there is a thread of hope built into what he does."

Tony Todd, the actor who played the character of Ben in the 1990 remake of *Night* agrees. "I was always a big fan of the original *Night of the Living Dead*. It was so powerful, so iconic. And it had an African American leading man back in the 1960s, which you really didn't see that often. Not enough. Duane Jones did a terrific job as Ben. He had real power, real humanity. For Romero to have cast the movie that way showed insight and it showed backbone."

"Sadly," Sampson adds, "Romero was deeply mired in a dismal view of the world at the time and Ben is senselessly and tragically killed at the end of the movie. He's the strong one, the survivor who overcame predators and outlasted those too weak to follow his lead. He tried his best and deserved to live, but Romero isn't Disney, and he made another harsh social statement by having Ben gunned down at the end. Romero never said as much, but I remember talking with Duane about this about a year or so before his death,[3] and he admitted that he sometimes viewed that ending as a metaphor for the old racist view that 'you can't tell them apart,' switched

3. Duane Jones died of a heart attack in 1988 at age 52.

Zombie Crawls

***Zombie Walk* by Jill Hunt**

Philadelphia and Minneapolis may have helped zombie crawls to get started, but they are now worldwide. This picture of the Zombie Walk in Baltimore shows the living dead having a bloody good time.

from a comment about blacks or Chinese or any ethnic group to zombies. When the redneck hunters arrive in the morning they shoot everyone because in their eyes they all look like zombies."

The ending of *Night* changed in the remake. In the Tom Savini version, not only does Barbara escape but Ben actually becomes a zombie, succumbing to wounds received in the struggle to stay alive during that hellish night. As times had changed, the theme shifted from racism to sexism, and Barbara emerged as a feminist icon.

I asked Todd to comment on the different take on Ben in the remake. "When I heard that they were doing a remake of *Night of the Living Dead* I went straight over to the production offices and cornered Tom Savini and said: 'You have to test me for the part of Ben.' I think he was knocked out by my passion and determination. I *wanted* that role, and I *got* that role. Once we started shooting, though, I didn't want to do a retake on what Duane Jones did. That was his performance, this was mine and I wanted to give it a new sensibility. Ben was an interesting character to play. He's a reluctant hero. He didn't sign up for that crap. We get some hints about what happened to him before he gets to the farmhouse, we know that he feels like he failed his family during the crisis, and that's why he's so determined to keep everyone together and safe in the house. He didn't or couldn't save his immediate family so he doesn't want to fail his new 'family.' And, let's face it; somebody had to be a leader."

"Bad actors read lines," observes Sampson, "good actors become the character. Duane put a lot of depth and complexity into Ben. He made that character into a man, a human being. Ken Foree did the same with Peter in *Night*, Terry Alexander did with John in *Day*, and Tony Todd did in the underrated remake of *Day*. Strong black men and strong actors, each bringing qualities to the performance that rose above even the quality of the scripts. And each role, each character is a kind of statement of the times. Duane was the black man hated by the pale masses during the 1960s. In the late 1970s Ken Force plays a tough, competent SWAT officer—a sign of forward momentum showing that in just a decade blacks had gotten into the system, were part of it, were *crucial* to it, but were still black men with all of their individual and cultural integrity intact. Then we get to the dispirited 1990s and the character of John. He's strong and smart and valuable (he can fly the helicopter and none of the military grunts know how), but he's become disillusioned because becoming part of the system doesn't mean that the system has evolved or become better. Sometimes the grass on the other side of the fence has just as much crab grass as what's on your side. And yet Romero gives us more optimistic endings in both *Dawn* and *Day*, in which the races, white and black—seen in the microcosm of Peter and Francine in *Dawn* and John and Sarah[4] in *Day* escape together. Male and female, black

4. Francine was played by Gaylen Ross and Sarah by Lori Cardille.

and white, unified through shared adversity and hopefully with the appropriate cultural lessons learned. The actors all made these characters, these relationships, and these outcomes believable."

So what makes zombies so fascinating, and why do so many screenwriters and authors turn (and return) to this genre? I posed that question to a number of top writers in the field and got some illuminating responses:

As bestselling author Yvonne Navarro[5] sees it, "It's because to tell a truly frightening story, you need a truly frightening opponent, and zombies really fit that bill. Yeah, you can see them, so it's not like they're the big unknown. But it's that *known* that's the core of why zombies cause so much terror. First, in most of the stories, they're everywhere and they multiply faster than you can fight them. They'll pop out of bushes, closets, sewers, you name it, and there's no place to hide, day or night. Secondly, they are utterly relentless. Unless you can get a bullet or a machete to that sweet spot at the brain stem, they'll just keep coming. Finally, the Big Question as to why they make such a popular topic for horror stories: Who wants to be eaten alive?"

Bram Stoker Award-winner Weston Ochse says, "Nothing is

Tony Todd versus the Living Dead

I asked actor Tony Todd to speculate on how he would handle the events in *Night*. Would Tony become a zombie at the end of the flick?

"Hell no, Tony would have survived. Mainly 'cause Tony wouldn't have *stayed* there. You see with zombies it's all about keeping your calm. You can outrun them, outthink them, and that's what you do. Keep fighting, keep moving, and stay ahead of them. That's what I would do."

5. Yvonne Navarro is the author of *Hellboy* (Pocket Star, 2004), *Buffy the Vampire Slayer: Paleo* (Simon Spotlight, 2000) and, *Aliens: Music of the Spears* (Spectra, 1996).

more scary than encountering something that can't be reasoned with. Most of us believe we can talk ourselves our of any situation. Still others believe that they can fight their way out of any situation. Zombies represent something that can't be talked to and can't be fought. Cut off an arm? No biggie. I know the movies make it look easy, but the average Jack and Jill wouldn't know what to do regardless of the all cinematic and literary primers we've provided."

"The visual horror world needed a new archetype," says Rocky Wood, author of *Stephen King: Uncollected, Unpublished*.[6] "The

Zom Coms

Zombie comedies have become a genre unto themselves, anchored (though not started) by the cult classic *Shaun of the Dead* (written by Edgar Wright and Simon Pegg).

As frightening and intense as zombie films frequently are, there is also a tremendous amount of room for comedic expression. Romero pioneered this in *Dawn of the Dead*, which includes the satiric subplot of zombies compelled to return to a shopping mall because it was an "important place" in their lives. That film even had a bunch of bikers throwing custard pies in the faces of the ghouls.

Since then there have been a number of played-for-laughs zombie flicks, including Sam Raimi's *Evil Dead II* (1987) and *Army of Darkness* (1993); Dan O'Bannon's *Return of the Living Dead* (1985), Peter Jackson's *Braindead* (1992), Jonathan Wack's *Ed and His Dead Mother* (1993); Andrew Currie's *Fido* (2006), and others.

Haitian zombies were played for laughs, too, in films like *The Ghost Breakers* (starring Bob Hope. 1940), Gordon Douglas's *Zombies on Broadway* (with Bela Lugosi, 1945), Bob Balaban's *My Boyfriend's Back* (1993), and there are even comedic elements in Jean Yarbrough's classic *King of the Zombies* (1941).

6. Cemetery Dance Publications, 2005.

others having been worn close to the living (or dead) bone. While I like the socio-political angle behind the original upsurge my gut feeling is mindless cannibals with no socially redeeming features whatsoever were always likely to appeal to those who largely consume their horror in the movie theatre or through their video/DVD players."

"Romero-style zombies are a wonderful combination of fears: death, loved ones turning on us, disfigurement and disease, cannibalism, distorted artificial images of the human form (such as dolls and mannequins), and the notion that there is no afterlife (at least, not a heavenly paradise). As horror archetypes, they provide so much rich material for writers and film-makers," muses Tim Waggoner, author of *A Nightmare on Elm Street 3: Protégé* (Black Flame, 2005) and the Blade of the Flame series (Wizards of the Coast). "Zombie storytelling is marvelous because it allows for so much variety. There are so many good ones out there! So many favorite zombies: Bub from the original *Day of the Dead*, the Zombie Master and all his undead minions from Piers Anthony's *Xanth* books, all the zombies in *Shaun of the Dead*, the bizarre demon-possessed undead in the *Evil Dead* films, Big Daddy from Romero's *Land of the Dead*, the alien-slug infested zombies in *Night of the Creeps*, Simon Garth from Marvel Comics' *Tales of the Zombie*, the dead characters from *Corpse Bride*, the creepy tall zombie from Val Lewton's *I Walked with a Zombie*, Bud the Chud from *CHUD 2*, the zombies in Rich Hautala's novel *Moonwalker*, Brian Keene's undead in *The Rising* and *City of the Dead* . . . I could go on and on."

"The zombie model is incredibly flexible, which is great for writers," explains journalist Sam Anderson.[7] "Zombies don't have to adapt because they're already dead, so you can throw them in any situation and let the high jinks ensue. What, you need alien zombies? Alien zombies it is. How about zombie guppies? Those zombie guppies wouldn't even be relegated to staying in the water. Zombies offer possibilities that few other foils can. When you get the best writers working the most fertile soil—which this

7. Sam W. Anderson wrote "Swimming in the Sea of the Undead—A Look into the Soul of the Zombie Novel" for *Insidious Reflections* magazine.

Ramsey Campbell on Zombie Classics

Ramsey Campbell is one of the world's greatest masters of horror, the winner of more awards that we have pages here to list, and is also a reviewer. I asked him to comment on his favorite zombie movie.

"*I Walked with a Zombie* is director Hal Lewton's worst title and finest film (not to mention screenwriter Curt Siodmak's). It's the greatest zombie film too, though as far removed from the familiar genre as *Vampyr* is from vampire movies. The title was preordained by RKO and dismissed in the opening voice-over. While the basic concept of the film is *Jane Eyre* in the tropics, this becomes as elusive and ambiguous as the entire narrative. Far too delicate to be contained by even my definition of horror, *I Walked with a Zombie* shares an unemphatic sense of the supernatural with a very few other films (*Vampyr* and *Ugetsu Monogatari* among them). Its contradictions and subtleties resonate in the mind, leaving echoes of an experience almost impossible to define and aching for repetition. Even the final voice-over adds to the uncertainty, replacing the female voice with a disapproving male one that seeks to sum up the narrative more neatly than it achieves, instead directing the audience to look afresh. *Night of the Demon* is the Tourneur film I most love, but *I Walked with a Zombie* is arguably his masterpiece."

Ramsey Campbell's works include *The Grin of the Dark* (PS Publishing, 2007), *Secret Story* (Tor, 2007), and *The Overnight* (Tor, 2006).

---

genre certainly has—you're going to get some pretty special outcomes."

Canadian horror writer Steve Vernon, has a wickedly hopeful view of zombie popularity: "It's your ultimate mystery story, isn't it? What comes next? Everybody nowadays is worried about the coming apocalypse, and it's a great comfort to imagine we might all come back as part of a brainless headcheese-munching undead mob. Writers and storytellers have been messing with this theme from as far back as the days of Gilgamesh or Odysseus visiting the

Underworld. Everybody wonders what goes on beyond the grave. Once you bring someone back from the dead all bets are off. Removing extinction from the equation eliminates all sense of limitation."

Vernon also views zombies as an unlimited source of creative freedom, a view shared by many authors of the genre, who often bring in non-Romero elements to make the stories uniquely their own. "When I wrote *Long Horn, Big Shaggy*[8] I was searching for a melting pot mythos that could encompass any number of suppositions. I reached back into the roots of Native American mythology. These tales and legends often involved journey back and forth from the land of the dead. Then I poured a little Frankenstein science into the mix, spiced it off with a touch of dark Christianity, and let it steep and simmer for a while. In short, zombie potage."

"Zombies are monster icons," argues Stephen Jones, editor of *The Mammoth Book of Zombies* (Carroll & Graf Publishing, 1993), "and have been so now for more than seven decades. Vampires may still be the most successful, and Frankenstein and Dracula the most recognized, but zombies are now up there in popular culture with Mickey Mouse, Marilyn Monroe and Elvis! Show any small kid a picture of a grey-faced rotting corpse and the chances are that they will identify it as a zombie straight away! It can only be a matter of time before the walking dead are used to promote breakfast cereals and Happy Meals."

"I chose to write about zombies," says Scott A. Johnson, author of *Deadlands* (Harbor House Books, 2005), "because, to me, they're one of the most frightening of all the monsters. They are, in essence, our friends, relatives, and loved ones coming back to get us. In the span of a few moments, a person who was your wife or daughter could turn on you and try to eat your flesh. That concept gives me the creeps more than almost anything. When creating it I chose not to write strictly inside the Romero world. For the most part, I created my own mythology, though I definitely borrowed from the greats. From Lovecraft, I took the concept laid out in 'Herbert West: Re-animator' that we, playing God of course, might have created them. From Romero, I took the concept of the evolv-

8. KHP Publishing, 2004.

Stephen Jones on the Evolution of Zombie Popularity

"Although the cinema was slow to catch on to audiences' fascination with the resurrected dead—the 1932 independent film *White Zombie,* starring Bela Lugosi as the zombie master 'Murder' Legendre, was one of the first—there is no doubt that it was George Romero's equally cheap-looking *Night of the Living Dead* that influenced every zombie-themed project that followed it. But let's also not forget the part played by Italian filmmakers, such as Lucio Fulci, who did much to popularize Romero's film with unsanctioned sequels and rip-offs during the early 1970s!

"Since then, zombies have become firmly established in the pantheon of Monsters, albeit somewhat below the top-tier of recognizable Classic Creatures. This is perhaps because there has never been a single major zombie character along the same lines of Frankenstein, Dracula, The Wolf Man, The Mummy or The Creature from the Black Lagoon.

"That allows us to see the blank-faced zombies as metaphors for whatever we choose—from a statement on our uncontrollable consumer society (as in Romero's 1978 sequel *Dawn of the Dead*) to the disaffected dead of countless pointless wars (in everything from the obscure *Revolt of the Zombies* to Joe Dante's recent *Masters of Horror* episode, 'Homecoming').

"In literature, for the most part, zombies have been influenced by their more popular cinematic incarnations—from the anthologies of John Skipp and Craig Spector to David Wellington's enjoyable trilogy of 'Monster' novels, we are basically still in the world of Romero's flesh-eating ghouls."

Stephen Jones is a multiple award-winning editor and one of Britain's most acclaimed anthologists of horror and dark fantasy. He has had around 100 books published, including *The Mammoth Book of Monsters, The Essential Monster Movie Guide,* and *Clive Barker's A–Z of Horror.*

ing zombie. I drew from every zombie movie I'd ever seen, the visuals and the movements, and developed my own take from there."

And this from Rick Hautala: "My novel from a while back, *Moonwalker* (Zebra Books, 1989), was a zombie novel where I just had fun with the Romero version of zombies and put them in northern Maine. I also used the theme in my short story 'Perfect Witness,' which has a concept in it that I keep thinking I should develop into a novel some day. Zombies provide a social/political commentary on 20th Century life . . . I mean . . . in a way, aren't we all zombified to some extent or other? Whether it's TV, sex, politics, art, sports, or whatever, we're all kind of like the living dead when it comes to consuming."

Just the Facts

Zombies Go Global

Zombies in pop culture take many forms, and the love of zombies is expressed in many ways. Romero may be the big kahuna of zombie culture, but there have been others who have added their voice, shared their vision, and rebuilt the zombie world to fit their

Zombie Self-Empowerment

"Conflict between zombies and humans allow for the audience to see themselves in the role of the protagonists. We're not all secret agents or Chosen One vampire-slayers, though we may aspire to be as competent. Ultimately though, we all suffer in comparison to *Buffy, Blade,* or *Hellblazer*. Zombie films are all about ordinary folks, and generally from many different walks of life. The teen slasher films were all about random cuties getting killed off; there's no contest, it's just a spectacle. But a mix of people trying to work together, or undermine one another, and survive an (un)natural disaster, that's compelling for everyone and not just the pimply nerds who get off on either power fantasies (*Blade*) or revenge fantasies (*Friday the 13th*)."—Nick Mamatas, author of *Move Underground* (Prime Books, 2006).

image of how things might go. Let me say straight up, though, that very few zombie storytellers have thought things out as thoroughly as Romero or kept as firm a hand on the tiller as they sailed their projects through the dark waters of undead cinema and fiction.

Certainly the name that comes first to mind is Dario Argento. Though not a zombie director per se, Argento helped bankroll Romero's *Dawn of the Dead* and oversaw the recut of the film for European release. Argento's support of Romero and his efforts to push his cut of *Dawn*, called *Zombi*, kicked off a worldwide zombie mania. Without him the living dead films might have stalled at *Night*. That's a scary thought.

Argento was one of a number of Italian directors involved in the *giallo* genre of filmmaking, which overlapped the genres of horror, mystery, fantasy, and eroticism. Giallo film got started in the middle 1960s and by the 1970s this genre was dominated by Argento, Mario Bava (*Blood and Black Lace*, 1964; *Black Sunday*, 1960; and *Black Sabbath*, 1963); Umberto Lenzi (*Eyeball*, 1974); and Lucio Fulci. This genre was well known for excessive gore, nudity, and violence (often against women) and often dealt with psychological disintegration, madness, and emotional extremes. In a very real way they paved the way for thc worldwide slew of slasher films of the late 1970s and 1980s, and also informed the disturbing amount of antifemale violence found in many Italian zombie films of the 1980s and 1990s.

Of these directors, it's Lucio Fulci who has developed a worldwide following that, in some circles, rivals that of Romero. His *Zombie 2* (1979) was an extraordinarily gory film that was marketed as a sequel to *Zombie/Dawn of the Dead*, which it was not (it was already in production at the same time as *Dawn*). It was smart marketing, however, and it catapulted Fulci into the forefront of zombie film auteurs.

Fulci did not spend a lot of time trying to establish a credible reason for the dead returning to life. There are some vague references to a curse on a tropical island, so we can presume he links zombies to the supernatural, but we never really find out. What we get instead of a grounding in science is gore. Lots and lots and lots of gore. For example, there's one scene where a woman's eye is penetrated by a jagged piece of wood—and this scene is played out slowly and with excruciating attention to detail.[9] Very nasty and not really necessary, though one can make the case that the scene did accomplish what Fulci wanted in that it is one of two scenes in that film that are still being talked about thirty years later. The other scene—which I rather like—involves an underwater battle between a zombie and a shark. There's no comparable scene anywhere else in the whole zombie cinema library.

The explicit gore in Fulei's film earned it an X rating, and it was banned in many countries, forcing the producers to submit heavily cut prints in order to get it into theaters. It wasn't until 2005 that the complete and unadulterated Fulci version became available on DVD.

The next film in the Fulci series, *Zombie 3* (1988), gave directing credit to Fulci even though he only helmed part of the film, having had to back out due to illness. Bruno Mattei completed the film and went on to direct a number of low-budget zombie movies.

This film bears no thematic connection to *Zombi 2* or indeed to Argento's *Zombi* beyond the fact that they all include flesh-eating ghouls. In this one, a scientific reason (sort of) is floated: a bioweapon of some kind is stolen from a military base on a remote tropical island in the Philippines. The weapon is discharged accidentally and those exposed become your standard shambling zombies. Nothing much interesting happens, but a lot of people die and the bioweapon theme is never brought up again.

Released in 1988 was another name-only sequel, *Zombie 4: After Death*, directed by Claudio Fragasso, which veers even farther from the Romero model and gives us flesh-eating demons instead of living-dead ghouls.

Fulci returned to active zombie direction with 1982's *City of the Living Dead* (also known as *Gates of Hell*), and again we see zombies linked to the supernatural rather than the scientific. In this story, a priest hangs himself and the act somehow unlocks the gates of hell, which in turn allows the dead to rise. True to form, Fulci finds something truly outrageous to imbed the film into the moviegoer's psyche in that he has one character murdered by having a power drill used on his skull. Very graphic. That scene

9. The "eyeball gag" became a signature scene for Fulci, and in many of his later films he found new and inventive ways to slice, dice, impale, and remove the eyes of various characters.

was cut from a lot of the international prints and wasn't included in the official cut until the 2001 video release.

Fulci returned to further explore the metaphysical connections of life and death with 1983's *The Beyond*. Like *City of the Living Dead*, this was intended to be a film about the events surrounding one of the seven gates of hell, but the distributors didn't want that kind of film and put pressure on Fulci to make it a zombie movie. He did, and though the film has a strong following, it makes little to no sense. Fans don't seem to care because *The Beyond* frequently makes it onto lists of best horror films (including the 100 Scariest Movie Moments list presented by Bravo).[10]

Once the Italians had the genre in gear, the zombie movie craze shot into orbit. Soon every country seemed to be spawning its own line of zombie flicks, though most notably the British, Germans, Chinese, and Japanese.

21st-Century Zombie Madness

The twenty-first century launched a new age of zombie films, powered by advances in makeup effects and computer-generated imag-

The Zombie Cheerleader

TV, cable, and the Internet abound with horror-themed shows hosted by a variety of ghouls, vamps, mad scientists, and, in one case, a cheerleader turned zombie. The Zombie Cheerleader (a.k.a Nicole M. Brooks) is the hostess of her own online show, *The Zombie Cheerleader's School of Horror*, and can be seen in the first two seasons of *Monster Madhouse*. Her mission in *un*-life is to "educate the zombie masses so they may learn how to survive the impending fleshy onslaught." Fleshies are humans, and in her view they're the bad guys.

10. And, yes, despite its lack of scientific zombie grounding, I dig this flick, too.

Eat My Brains (EMB)

One of the coolest zombie websites is www.eatmybrains.com, run by Mike "Rawshark" Hewitt, Jim Smith, and Russell "Zomblee" Lee. It's raw, raunchy, and riotous, and features some of the best commentary, reviews, and zombie news anywhere; and they have a pedigree that sets them apart from most fans.

EMB: We met as zombie extras on the set of *Shaun of the Dead*. There were a lot of weirdos around, but some really nice zombies, too. It was only a matter of time before the three of us hooked up in our free time to watch as many horror flicks as we could before getting the last train home. The eatmybrains thing happened because everyone seemed to know their stuff, but the great thing was that we all had a passion for different areas. At the time, Jim was into a lot of Japanese horror, Rawshark loved Deodato's cannibals, and Zomblee dug anything Fulci or Carpenter. Eatmybrains was a logical consequence of watching and talking horror—the site was built just so that we could share this with like-minded horror fans who we hoped would like what we had to say.

ZCSU: What makes a good zombie movie?

EMB: This depends on whether you're looking for one of those zombie flicks that delve into social commentary and the human condition faced with the insurmountable challenge of an undead

ing (CGI), big budgets, and a fan base that crossed over from the vast world of computer gaming. The 2002 flick *Resident Evil* starring Milla Jovovich as zombie ass-kicker Alice,[11] is rather loosely based on the 1996 Sony PlayStation[12] game of the same name (known as *Baiohazado* in Japan where it was developed).

This franchise tells the story of a multinational conglomerate

11. The character of Alice was created for the movies and doesn't appear in the games.

12. Created by Shinji Mikami and developed by Capcom.

apocalypse, or whether you want to see a balls-out, gore-soaked, severed-head gut-muncher. For the former stick to Romero's works (*Dawn of the Dead* is probably the first on everyone's list), but for the latter you have options. You can go for the blood soaked Italian movies that came out in a rush straight after *Zombie Flesh Eaters* (aka *Zombi 2*, 1979); or you can catch one of the gore-drenched American comedy horror zombie movies from the mid-'80s instead (*Return of the Living Dead* and *Re-Animator* spring to mind). Alternatively there's a couple of top offerings from Asia if you fancy something different, with *Junk* (1999), *Versus* (2000), and *Wild Zero* (2000) being strong contenders for your time. I doubt if you'll be disappointed with any of those.

ZCSU: What makes a bad zombie flick?

EMB: What makes a bad zombie movie is even simpler; when there aren't even any zombies in it. Troma's god awful *Zombie Island Massacre* (1984) is one such culprit (they weren't zombies after all!) but *Zombie Aftermath* takes the biscuit as Steve Barkett and Sid Haig defend themselves from an undead horde of two that aren't really undead, they're more like radioactive mutants. Also stay away from the later *Zombie Flesh Eaters* movies after *Zombie Flesh Eaters 2* (aka *Zombi 3*, 1988) they either feature former porn stars or don't have any zombies in them, neither of which is good enough.)

called The Umbrella Corporation that, among other things, messes around with bioweapons technology. Naturally these things always get out of hand, first in the corporation's underground research complex, The Hive, and then above ground as an infection spreads to the closest large urban center, Raccoon City. Soon the dead are everywhere, along with all sorts of mutant critters.

Unlike most first-person shooter games, *Resident Evil* was actually very well written and pretty frightening. Terrific high-end graphics caught the right kind of Romeroesque mood, and the sales skyrocketed past 30 million units.

Eric S. Brown on Writing the Zombie Novel

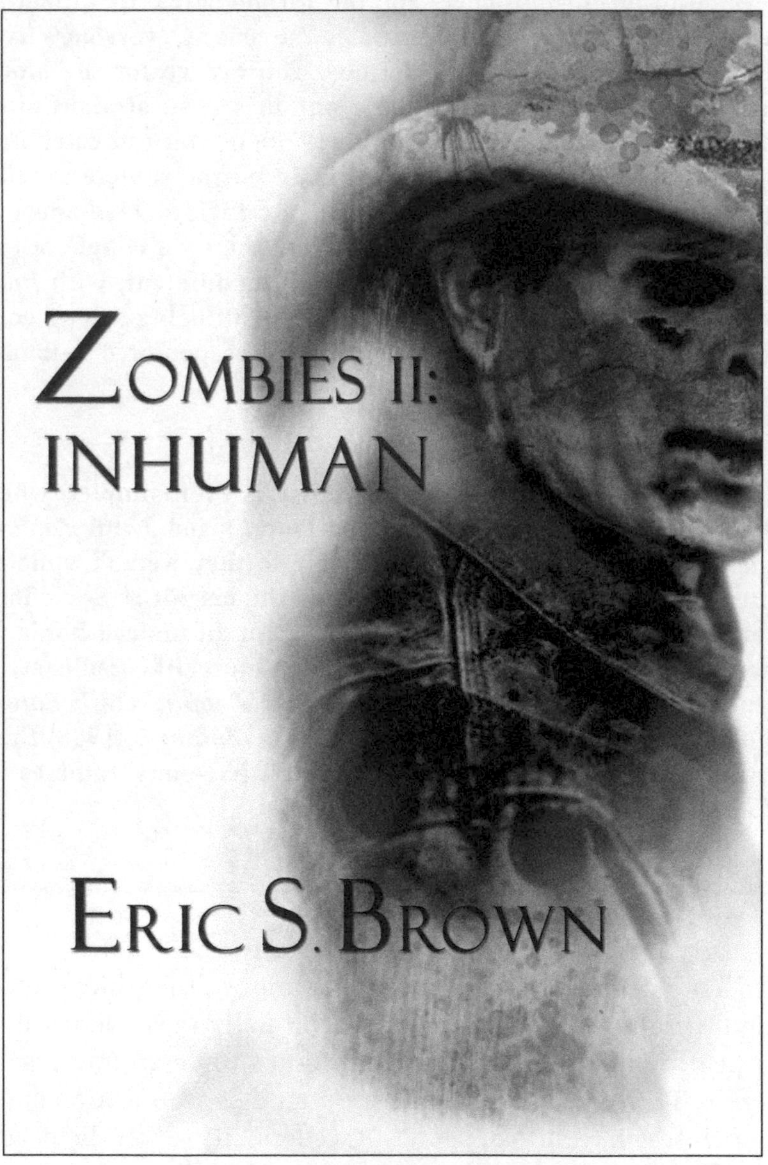

***Zombies II* by Eric S. Brown**
Cover Art by Donna Burgess

Eric S. Brown is the author of over 300 short stories and the recent novel, *Zombie II: Inhuman* (Naked Snake Books, 2007). I asked him to comment on the process of crafting zombie stories:

"I started out writing Romero type zombies but in the wake of *28 Days Later* and *The Rising* I began to break away from that type of zombie. I like the idea of the dead being intelligent enough to truly become the Earth's dominant species and create their own civilization. In my novella, *The Queen* (Naked Snake Books, 2006), the dead have set up breeding camps to raise their own humans as food and have rediscovered the ability to not use but also manufacture in a limited capacity technologies we take for granted.

"Marvel comics recently did a mini-series called Marvel Zombies which imagines the zombie virus as something that hops from world to world infecting the resident meta-humans and using them as the means to transfer the virus and keep it alive. In my latest book, *Zombies II: Inhuman,* I blend superheroes with zombies in a totally different way. With the human race facing extinction, it just makes sense that God, nature, or evolution would step in and try to come up with a way for the race to survive. So in my book, you have telepaths, speedsters, and many other types of super powered people who have developed powers in order to survive."

The first film in the series was the most effective, with a good cast fleshed out by Michelle Rodriquez at her snarling best, Eric Mabius looking stalwart, a sly and villainous James Purefoy, and a compelling Colin Salmon (underused and killed off too quickly). The movie moves like an *Aliens*-style bug hunt that turns into a zombie chase flick. Some of the action scenes, particularly in the earliest scenes when the zombies are first introduced, are genuinely creepy and had the film not tried to do so much of the video game plot (as in introducing slimy CGI monsters called "lickers"), it might have become a real classic of zombie cinema.

The story line that links all the films together and amplifies the zombie plot deals with the T-virus, a treatment created to cure a degenerative cell-destroying disease by reactivating the dead cells. That might be fine for those suffering from the disease for which it was intended, a plotline explored in the second film, but when introduced to uninfected humans, it first kills them and then reanimates them as the living dead. One wonders why a treatment used to treat tissue death would cause death before turning the dead into walking (and decaying) corpses. Why the virus works so antithetically is never adequately explored; instead they use those storytelling minutes to have the characters—good and bad, living and dead—kill lots and lots of people.

The virus story line ties the series to the zombie movie genre even though the films tend to use zombies as a setup before veering in the third act into fights with mutant monsters. And there are some zombie inconsistencies, such as the speed of the zombies. Mostly they are the kind of growling, shambling zombies we've come to know and love from the Romero films, and it's established that humans are faster and (it would seem from the fight scenes) a little stronger. However these zombies seem to speed up whenever the plot requires it, as shown with them sprinting up a flight of stairs after a potential victim early in *Resident Evil: Apocalypse* (2004). Of course, once the hero arrives to try and save the helpless female victim, the ghouls slow down again so he can kick the asses of a whole bunch of them. If you're just tuning in for the fun of it, the speed changes don't seem to matter, but if you're trying to suspend disbelief so you can make some degree of sense out of the story, these errors jump out. As a result some zombie flick purists dismiss the films. However, whether they fit in as true zombie films or not, they did contribute significantly to the momentum of the genre in the twenty-first century. Without it *Shaun of the Dead* (2004) might never have been made and probably would never have found the huge audience it did; and the same could be said of the remakes of *Dawn of the Dead* and *Day of the Dead*. This, too, has been the subject of extensive debate.

Jamie Russell, author of *Book of the Dead: The Complete History of Zombie Cinema* and an outspoken critic on the zombie genre, sees a link between the zombie pop culture and the larger world culture. "I think the recent resurgence in zombie movies definitely has something to do with the way in which we've

The Worst Zombie Films of All Time, Part 3

- ***Nudist Colony of the Dead* (1991): How could you possibly bore an audience with zombies and nudity? One answer: put all the nude actors into body stockings! Sheesh.**
- ***One Dark Night* (1982): Meg Tilly, a haunted house, Carrie-like telekinetic powers, and floating zombies. Just as silly as it sounds and not as much fun as it should have been.**
- ***The People Who Own the Dark* (1976): A mishmash inspired by *The Omega Man* that has a bunch of blind people laying siege to a house in which sighted people are holed up. Clearly nobody thought that through.**
- ***Shadow: Dead Riot* (2005): Love Tony Todd, hate the movie. Plot's not even worth talking about.**
- ***Nights of the Day of the Dawn of the Son of the Bride of the Return of the Terror* (1991): Looks like it was shot on a dare. And lost.**

become a more secular society. Once upon a time people went to church, they believed in heaven and hell, the soul and an afterlife. These days, especially in the West, we're less certain about such things and I think zombie movies are an expression of that. The zombie as a monster, as a reanimated corpse poses all kinds of questions about God, the afterlife and the soul. Are the living just zombies with brains, or are zombies the living without souls?"

The rise of the new zombie auteurs, Zack Snyder, Edgar Wright, Danny Boyle, and others raises the question as to whether the living dead torch has officially been passed.

"Romero will always be king," insists horror film critic Jim Dolan. "No matter how big someone else's films get, Romero's vision is the *official* vision of zombie cinema. Without him there wouldn't even be a genre."

Russell agrees. "For me, Romero is the Don of the Dead. It's his vision of social apocalypse that I think is the crux of what makes the zombie genre so frightening, really. That claustrophobic, there's-nowhere-to-run feeling that his films instill in the audience is one of the things I find most terrifying about zombies. It's a stark nihilism—a secular End of Days that suggests there isn't a God or an afterlife . . . We're all just hunks of meat."

Zombie Comics

Zombie comics have been hot for the last few years. I asked a few folks in that industry to comment on the upsurge of these illustrated zombie stories.

"Since the 1940's, some of the best American monster stories have appeared in comic books," says Trevor Strunk, comics expert and freelance writer. "Frankenstein was done first and best by Dick Briefer for Prize Publications in 1946; Marv Wolfman and Gene Colan defined the comic book vampire in their 1970's series *Tomb of Dracula;* and *Werewolf by Night,* by Gerry Conway and Mike Ploog translated the werewolf myth into the universe of the flawed Marvel Comics superhero. The zombie, however, one of the most popular monsters, has had a very limited presence in comic books."

Why so?

"The incidental nature of zombies in comics could be attributed to a couple causes," Strunk explains. "First, the Golden Age of horror comics of the 1940's and 50's came long before George Romero popularized zombies with his *Night of the Living Dead* films. Secondly, the Comics Code, a watchdog organization that limited violence, gore, and profanity, could not have looked kindly

New Monster Paradigm

"Stephen King calls zombies a new monster paradigm. Do I agree? Hey, if Stephen King said the sun rose in the west, I'd agree. He's Stephen King and I think, by now, he's earned the right to be right about everything."—Max Brooks, author of *World War Z*

on the concept of a reanimated corpse, especially one that devours still-living flesh. There were a few zombie-related series during Marvel Comics' 1970's horror revival—*Tales of the Zombie*, for instance, was published in magazine format and focused solely on the zombie—but the zombie comic has only recently recovered from its footnote status."

So, who is driving the new zombie comic genre?

Strunk doesn't hesitate: "Robert Kirkman and Tony Moore's *Walking Dead*, published by Image Comics, is a serious, large-scale zombie series, and Kirkman and Sean Phillip's *Marvel Zombies*, a tongue-in-cheek look at superheroes as zombies, has made the living dead more popular than ever in comic books. With high popular interest and more lax censorship standards, the comic book zombie's future has never been brighter."

I contacted Robert Kirkman and Bob Fingerman to see what they had to say about creating zombie comics. First thing I asked them was: Why zombies?

"Because, generally, they're a universal problem," says Fingerman. "They're the roach of the monster world; if you've seen one, you know there are thousands more where it came from. Also, they're scary because they can't be reasoned with. They're worse than children. But seriously, their lack of reasoning and their pure need-driven motivation are what make them frightening. That and the fact that they'll tear you limb from limb and devour all your soft tissue. Individually they're just gross and unsettling, but they always come in mobs and mobs are by nature terrifying."

Kirkman agrees. "Why not zombies? They're a mighty easy way to get things good and screwed up in a fictional world, and that leaves for some pretty interesting character development."

I asked what kind of feedback they've gotten about their books.

Fingerman says, "What I got was uniformly positive."

Kirkman, who slaughters all of Marvel's favorite superheroes (some get zombified, some get eaten), agrees. "Overwhelmingly positive response to be honest. And the formula was pretty damn easy: It was pretty easy. Zombie bites superhero, Superhero turns into zombie, bites more superheroes. Wash, Rinse, Repeat."

Kirkman says that the readers often form strong emotional connections to the characters in zombie comics. "Every now and then

Essential Zombie Comics — Trevor Strunk

- ***Essential Tales of the Zombie,*** **various authors. This new black-and-white collection from Marvel continues their tradition of cheap reprints under their Essentials line, but this time with zombies. This is a perfect collection if you want to understand the very beginnings of the comic book zombie as we know it.**
- ***The Walking Dead, Book One,*** **Robert Kirkman, writer; Tony Moore, Charlie Adlard, and Cliff Rathburn, artists. This hardcover collection includes the first twelve issues of Image Comics' premiere zombie series. Kirkman's writing is reminiscent of a Romero film, and the art, whether by Moore, Adlard, or Rathburn, is atmospheric and chilling. This is a great example of the modern zombie story in a sequentially progressive form.**
- ***Recess Pieces,*** **Bob Fingerman, writer and artist.** ***Recess Pieces*** **(Dark Horse) is an interpretation of the zombie myth from a much more independent, and a much more offbeat position. Set in an elementary school overrun with zombies, Fingerman's art complements the unsettling nature of the narrative. This is recommended for people who love zombies, but want their comic book reading done in one session.**
- ***Marvel Zombies,*** **Robert Kirkman, writer; Sean Phillips, artist.** ***Marvel Zombies*** **focuses on Marvel superheroes who also happen to be zombies. If that description has failed to sell the book for you, this might not be the zombie comic for you, but if you like your comics in the superheroic vein, then you'll certainly appreciate this tongue-in-cheek, violent meditation on zombies.**

someone will get upset about something I did to a character in *The Walking Dead*—but that really just means I'm doing my job. If they care about the fake people in the book—what I'm doing works."

And he summed it up for both of them by saying, "We're lucky enough to be working in very zombie-friendly times."

Art of the Dead – Collin Burton

Twilight Years of the Dead

"George Romero's *Night of the Living Dead* was showing on a late-night, local TV show called *Shock Theater* when I was nine years old. I remember not being able to watch past the point where they find the corpse on the stairs. A few years later I watched the whole thing and I've been drawn to zombies more than any other monster type ever since."

Zombie Music

Horror is a very popular theme in music—and has been for a long time. C'mon—you remember singing "Monster Mash" and "Purple People Eater," don't you?

Over the last thirty years a few subgenres of zombie-themed music have emerged from the music world, all sorts of styles like rock, pop, R&B, horror punk, death metal, dub, electro, indus, techno indus, blues, funk, industrial, gothic, and even hip hop. There's even an emerging fusion style called zombie country. The undisputed king of all zombie music is the master himself, Rob Zombie, who always incorporated living-dead themes into his music. But before Rob there was Black Sabbath, Alice Cooper, Harry and the Undertakers, Goblin, and scores of others.

I asked a few people who are really *into* zombie music for their opinions on why this subgenre is so strong and getting stronger all the time.

I asked author David F. Kramer,[13] a long-time devotee of horror music, to explain why zombie music is so popular. He said, "I'm quick to fall back on the words of Anton S. LaVey[14]—the Devil has always written the best tunes. Whether or not one believes in the diabolic nature of the devil's chord (tritone), the fact is—it's representative of dissonance—and that's really what the darkness is all about. So—"evil"music has really never gone out of style—at least not for the last few hundred years or so—and I hope it never will!"

So, what then makes for a great zombie song? Kramer says, "The best songs about zombies encompass all of the things for which zombies are known and loved—messily tearing through their graves to the surface to feast on the entrails and brains of slow witted (and moving) hapless human prey. Whether one is a fan of Goblin—the jazzy ensemble that's scored more than a few gut-chomping films since the 1970's; old school 1920's Southern Bluesmens' tales of the restless dead; or if you're just a death-grind-crust

13. David F. Kramer is coauthor, with Jonathan Maberry, of *The Cryptopedia: A Dictionary of the Weird, Strange and Downright Bizarre* (Citadel Press, 2007), winner of the Bram Stoker award for nonfiction.

14. Anton Szandor LaVey (April 11, 1930–October 29, 1997) was the founder and High Priest of the Church of Satan as well as author of *The Satanic Bible.*

Art of the Dead – Kevin Bias

Zombie Blues

"I think it's somewhat trendy to like zombies these days. I'm not sure why. There's *Night of the Living Dead* shirts at every Hot Topic store, and I just recently watched a TV commercial where laundry chased people like zombies. Maybe mankind is subconsciously aware of the imminent zombie apocalypse!"

fanatic—the message remains pretty much the same. And that message is BRAINS! Why split hairs when you could be splitting intestines?"

So who listens to this music? "Well," says Kramer, "I would

think that there's been 'horror music' since folks started banging on logs and telling stories to entertain other people. One need only look for biblical inspiration to know that bad news sells papers—and ultimately, record albums as well. Since the advent of the 20th century—feel free to point to the blues, rockabilly, rock and roll, heavy metal, punk, gangsta rap or the scapegoat of your choice for infernal inspiration." He adds, with a wicked grin, "At this point I would say that fans of zombies, horror and death metal are about as intertwined culturally as they will ever be. They all end up meeting when the entrails go stale."

Zombie Toys

Zombies are everywhere . . . your kids may even cuddle up with one at night. Well, that is if your kids are kind of strange. Zombie toys are the new big thing and leading the pack is the wonderfully imaginative Teddy Scares. I met with Joe DiDomenico, creator of Teddy Scares, to ask him how these adorable zombie dolls came into being.

"Teddy Scares are a group of unloved teddy bears that were discarded by their owners and now they have returned from the 'dead.' They reside in a trash dump and wish for the days to be loved again. The bears were a combination of my love of toys and horror and mixed them into an adorable package. Teddy Scares was something that I would want as a fan of horror and I thought others would like it as well."

Currently the product consists of 12″ bears (Series 1 and 2), 6″ bears (Morgue Minis), Graphic Novels (by Ape Entertainment), women's fashion tees (Headline) and Calendars (Universe Publishing). We hope to extend out to many more product lines in 2008!"

But . . . why zombies?

"I believe people can relate to zombies because they are us except they lack a conscience. I see it almost as though there is a level of 'realism' about the undead that isn't there with say vampires or werewolves."

David F. Kramer's Top Ten Zombie Songs of All Time

1. **"Night of the Living Dead"—The Misfits—from the EP *Night of the Living Dead* (1979)**
2. **"Revenge of the Zombie"—Six Feet Under—from the album *Warpath* (1997)**
3. **"Doomed by the Living Dead"—Mercyful[15] Fate—from the EP *Nuns Have No Fun* (1984)**
4. **"Now I'm Feeling Zombified"—Alien Sex Fiend—from the album *Curse* (1990).**
5. **"Black Juju"—Alice Cooper—from the album *Love It to Death* (1971)**
6. **"Pit of Zombies"—Cannibal Corpse—from the album *Gore Obsessed* (2002)**
7. **"Zombie Ritual"—Death—from the album *Scream Bloody Gore* (1987)**
8. **"Haunting the Chapel"—Slayer—from the EP *Haunting the Chapel* (1984)**
9. **"Death Metal"—Possessed—from the album *Seven Churches* (1985)**
10. **"Surfin' Dead"—The Cramps—from *The Return of the Living Dead* Soundtrack (1985)**

Big Old Web o' Zombies

Do a Google search on zombies. You will get more than thirty million hits. That's a lot of online references to our shambling friends. Granted not all of them refer to the zombies as we're defining them here, but even shaving off the references to Haitian culture, P-zombies, and colloquial uses of the word you're still

15. Please note that the spelling of Mercyful Fate with a *y* and not an *i* is correct.

Teddy Scares

Teddy Scares, created by Joe DiDomenico and Phil Nannay . . . these should rock your kids to sleep at night.

left with millions of sites, including tens of thousands of MySpace pages.[16]

Some of these sites (like the Zombie WorldNews mentioned elsewhere in this book) are devoted to establishing a higher stan-

16. Speaking of which, visit www.myspace.com/zombiecsu and www.zombiecsu.com.

dard of information and to providing the most reliable and accurate zombie data on all aspects of the genre.

One such site is *Revenant* Magazine (www.revenantmagazine.com), run by editor-in-chief Geoff Brough. I asked Brough to tell us about his ezine. "*Revenant* Magazine was established as the premiere online zombie magazine. There are some great horror publications out there that we really admire but we wanted to pay tribute to our favorite 'monster' by giving them the spotlight. We established our presence in an online format by covering all aspects of the zombie sub-genre, from books, film, comics, events, fiction, collectibles, etc. If it's about the walking dead, we're covering it. We hope to endeavor into a print format very soon."

Though *Revenant* covers all aspects of zombie pop culture, there is a definite sense of homage to Romero. I asked Brough to comment on that: "George Romero has lived in some pretty turbulent times. He's seen a lot of change in the world from the treatment of people in our country, wars, the civil rights movement, and assassinations, corrupt political figures . . . a lot of really crazy events. He's one of the first to utilize the undead as a reflection of our societal behavior. His social commentary on racism and the treatment of African Americans in *Night of the Living Dead* was eye-opening and shocking. The anti-consumerism stance in *Dawn* is widely talked about and blatantly obvious. His films bring a scope of realism in a rather unconventional way but it works so incredibly well. It's filmmakers like George Romero that not only keep the zombie film 'alive' but keep us on our toes about circumstances and events that shape our existence."

Another site chockfull of good zombie info is Dead-Central.com, which contains some of the best interviews with Romero cast members (from all his films) on the web; it's informative and has plenty of video, images, and fan forums.

Other popular undead sites include blogs: http://zombie-a-gogo.blogspot.com, http://zombiebloggers.blogspot.com, http://hungryzombie.blogspot.com; game sites: Undead Games (www.undeadgames.com), Kill the Zombies (www.killthezombies.com), Urban Dead (www.urbandead.com); general zombie pop culture sites: Eat My Brains (www.eatmybrains.com), Zombie Rama (www.zombierama.com), I Love Zombies (www.zombiejuice.com/

zombies.htm), All Things Zombie (www.allthingszombie.com); toys: My Pet Zombies (www.mypetzombies.com); zombie apocalypse preparedness sites: Zombie Squad (www.zombiehunters.org), Zombie Defense (www.zombiedefense.org), The Federal Vampire & Zombie Agency (www.fvza.org), Zombies Outside (www.zombiesoutside.com), Dead-Central (www.dead-central.com); how-to sites for turning yourself into a zombie: (www.zombiemaker.com); zombie pumpkin carving sites: (www.zombiepumpkins.com); zombie warning devices: (www.loris.net/zombie).

Zombie Games

Resident Evil is the king of zombie games, but it's in no way the only game in town. Zombie games, ranging from first-person shooters to RPGs (role-playing games) are vastly popular worldwide.

I asked Michael Tresca, author of *Blood & Brains: The Zombie Hunter's Guide*, a supplement for the d20[17] modern role-playing game, to comment on why zombie games are so incredibly popular. "Zombies are hilarious. They're dead, they lurch, they moan—it's hard to take them too seriously. Even in the undead hierarchy they're pretty ridiculous, well below ghosts and vampires. What other sub-genre of horror can be so disturbing and amusing at the same time?"

He talked about creating his zombie guide for gamers: "Beyond my love for Evil Dead, I decided that if I was going to write a book about zombies, I'd better become better versed in the zombie genre. My Netflix account got a lot of use. I bought as many books on zombies as I could find and read a lot on the Internet. And thus I discovered all kinds of zombies I didn't know about. Templar zombies, Nazi zombies, astro zombies, alien zombies, video zombies . . . there are endless varieties of zombies that scientists are creating even as we speak! Then it was just a matter of putting it all down in PDF format. The artist, John Longenbaugh, perfectly captured the style I was looking for. I added in my short story, 'Robots vs. Zombies,' about two geeks who defend a hardware store against cryogenic zombies. Chris Davis provided the green

17. The d20 system, released in 2000 by Wizards of the Coast, is a set of game mechanics for RPGs, based on the third edition of *Dungeons & Dragons*.

Blood and Brains cover art by Jeremy Simmons

"What other sub-genre of horror can be so disturbing and amusing at the same time?"—Michael Tresca, author of _Blood and Brains: The Zombie Hunter's Guide_

and red template and brickwork design that established just the right gritty feel."

David Jack Bell, author of *The Condemned*, thinks that the current upsurge in zombie popularity owes a lot to zombie video games. "I think video games are the biggest contributor to the modern resurgence of zombies in popular culture. Before that, the home video cassette market was a major contributor, because zombie movies were relatively cheap to make. In the era previous to home video and game consoles, zombie stories were an underground culture phenomena. In the old days, which I will call the 1980's; you had to look hard to find any sort of zombie literature. The only place it could be found was in comic shops and independent book stores that would carry the small press zines that were friendly to zombies and horror in general. One of the major breakthroughs into mainstream culture at this time was Skipp and Spector's *Book of the Dead* anthologies. But before those anthologies, only the die-hard fans would take time to search for this type of material. But now, zombie movies and games can be found virtually anywhere, and the ease of availability has attracted more people to the zombie genre in all its forms."

There are mass market big-ticket zombie games, and small underground games; there are licensed games and bootlegs, there are high-tech and low-tech games. There are a lot of games. Apparently a lot of folks want to shoot zombies.

Wither Now, Zombie?

I asked a bunch of zombie pop-culture folks what they'd like to see next in zombie storytelling, which avenues they think should be pursued. Here's a sampler of their replies:

"I'd like a great storyline about dysfunctional zombie families and their issues, how they cope with the day-to-day stress of being zombies." Cathy Buburuz, editor of *Champagne Shivers*

"In the dystopian novel *Noir* by K. W. Jeter, anyone who dies in debt is reanimated as a Zombie, forced to keep working until they have paid off their debts. I like the idea of forced redemption—the possibilities are endless." Amy Grech, author of *Cold Comfort* (Naked Snake Press) and over one hundred short stories

Art of the Dead – Shawn Conn

Zombies Worldwide

"I'd like to see zombies being able to somewhat inherit certain special abilities from the unfortunate humans they feast upon. Maybe not exactly become superheroes per se, but like say for instance a bodybuilder gets taken down by a zombie and gets devoured . . . that particular zombie then gains the upper advantage of gaining that bodybuilder's extra strength that lasts until the zombie is killed."

> **"More Big Picture, more global. We've got plenty of 'micro-horror', individual or group stories. I want to see how an entire country survives."**
>
> **—Max Brooks**

"I'm always up for the survival aspect. I don't really buy the end of the world thing—I think people are too smart to be completely exterminated by the dead. Bottom line: they're *dead*. They rot, they melt (ewwww), and eventually they can't even shamble after you."—Yvonne Navarro

"I grew up with the traditional voodoo zombie in the horror comics and movies I loved, so in my mind zombies are magical creatures. There are too many problems to overcome when telling stories about science-based zombies—how do they move with rotting muscles, where do they get the energy to move if they can't eat and digest food? They're closed systems, and they should cease functioning in a short time, a few days at the most. You don't have those sorts of problems with magical zombies. Plus, magic comes from the shadowy realm of the unknown, where science belongs to the world of cold hard facts. Magic—the dark kind found in supernatural horror—has a greater potential to be scary in fiction." —Tim Waggoner

"An intelligent explanation that gives rise to the dead. Give me science!"—Steve Alten

"Well, I'm not a huge fan of the socially aware zombie but it will be interesting to see how far that goes before the zombie-ism is lost. If zombies can exist on Earth surely they can exist in space/alien cultures? It may also be time to return the socio-political commentary Romero did so well."—Rocky Wood

"I wouldn't nudge it at all—because I'm doing what I would want everyone to do and I'd rather not have the competition. I just hate it when the stories end, so I'd want more long-term explorations of the world and the characters. I think there's a wealth of story potential in following a group of characters five, ten or twenty years into the end of the world . . . that's why I'm doing it with The Walking Dead."—Robert Kirkman

"Sexuality during the apocalypse is seldom if ever touched upon, and I'm just the guy to touch it."—Bob Fingerman

The Final Verdict: Zombies Forever

"It certainly would be fun to see how our bickering leaders and the politically correct media would handle a zombie crisis," muses screenwriter Andy Bark. "I recall the oil and petrol blockades in England a few years ago when a group, angry at fuel prices, blocked the tankers from leaving the depots. Things soon got quite surreal and I really got the feeling that it wouldn't take much for society to go over the edge. Who knows what would happen if the dead started returning? Against an ever growing army of contagious flesh eaters, unless the army got a grip on the situation fast, we'd be doomed. Anarchy would erupt on the streets and fuel and food stocks would vanish in a matter of hours. People would barricade themselves away, financial institutes would collapse making money worthless; in fact Romero probably got it right in *Dawn of the Dead*. Yep we'd be toast."

Closing Arguments

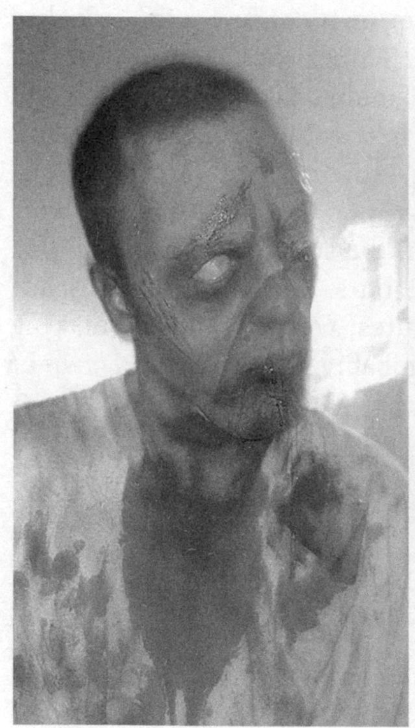

The Walking Dead by Nelson Robles

"Slow zombies would be contained I would think, of course it would be like any plague and continue to pop up in sporadic cases. Fast zombies would be the end of the world."

Here are some points to consider based on what we've learned from our experts.

The most logical scenario for a zombie uprising would be a plague. Not radiation, not demonic possession. Plagues start from a source and then spread outward, and this kind of thing would not—indeed *could* not—spread quietly.

In a post-9/11 world we are more prepared and we are *looking* for trouble to rear its head. Homeland, FEMA (the post-Katrina version), the various intelligence communities, the Centers for Disease Control, the World Health Organization, NATO . . . there are a lot of organizations ready and able to counter the spread of a new plague. Yes, there would be losses; but an apocalypse isn't likely.

Zombies are not going to overwhelm the cops. One-on-one they're no match; and it would take a fair number of them to overwhelm a police officer who can call for backup, can drive away, is trained to fall back in the presence of overwhelming threat, and has a variety of tools (OC spray, baton, shotgun with beanbag rounds, a Taser, and a sidearm).

If there was a zombie in the neighborhood, the cops would find it. Coordinated searches using helicopters, radios, K-9 dogs, and lots of backup would just overwhelm the zombie.

Zombies are also not going to overwhelm the military. They're not armed enemy combatants, and they're not secretive insurgents. They're brainless, organic-eating machines who don't have the sense to duck when someone shoots at them.

The idea that zombies would disregard gunfire flies in the face of physics. Whether a gunshot does fatal damage to the motor cortex or not, the impact of the shot is going to knock the unsteady zombie down or back, which allows for a second and possibly a third shot. With so many officers training with "failure drills"—two to the body and one to the head—the body shots will slow the attacker so that the third shot will flip the switch. The rise in the use of personal body armor has made everyone a bit better at head shots these days.

A zombie brought to a hospital is going to be restrained and a mouth guard will prevent biting. As its symptoms are assessed and the threat level recognized, any victim of the zombie will likewise be quarantined; and again we have protocols that will contain the spread of the infection.

The collection of forensic evidence, though generally used for legal issues, will aid scientists and doctors in the exploration of this new disease. Information sharing is more common these days, especially when dealing with medical crises; and computers and the Internet put vast resources at the disposal of forensics experts, medical professionals, and the police.

Even if no cure was discovered—which is dishearteningly likely if the disease turned out to be prion based—the infected would be quarantined and sterilization procedures would be put in place. Most likely all infected would be transported to ultrasterile and highly contained testing facilities for further study.

Any research from the medical research facility that inadvertently caused the plague would be subpoenaed or seized outright. Perhaps these materials might lead to solutions. If the threat were taken seriously enough, huge amounts of research monies would be granted to institutions investigating the plague. In time answers would be found.

From all the experts with whom I spoke during the research for this book—more than two hundred of them—not one of them believed that a plague of this kind would result in the end of humanity. Most doubted it would ever become a pandemic, largely

Eau de Zombie

When training dogs to sniff out cadavers, a special chemical is used to simulate the stink of decomposing flesh. It's an artificial version of cadaverine. Since zombies don't appear to attack one another—presumably they are not attracted to dead and rotting flesh—it seems like it would be a good idea to locate a supply of this chemical and use it as a zombie repellant by spraying it on clothes, etc. Not a pleasant thought, smelling like the dead, but it sure beats being on the menu.

because of the sensational nature of the plague. Society does not crumble that easily, and sometimes we do prove that we've learned from past mishandling of disasters. It might we be that we are better prepared at this moment to face a zombie uprising than we have ever been. It's probably the only useful side effect of global terrorism and global warming. We've seen the worst storms of our species' history in events like the World Trade Center attacks, Hurricane Katrina, the Christmas day tsunami and other tragedies. As wake-up calls go . . . those seem to have been pretty effective.

Will a disease like this ever happen?

Probably not. Well . . . maybe not. But anything's possible.

I just like to rest in the thought that if the dead rose up . . . then so would we.

APPENDIX A

Zombie Apocalypse Survival Scorecard

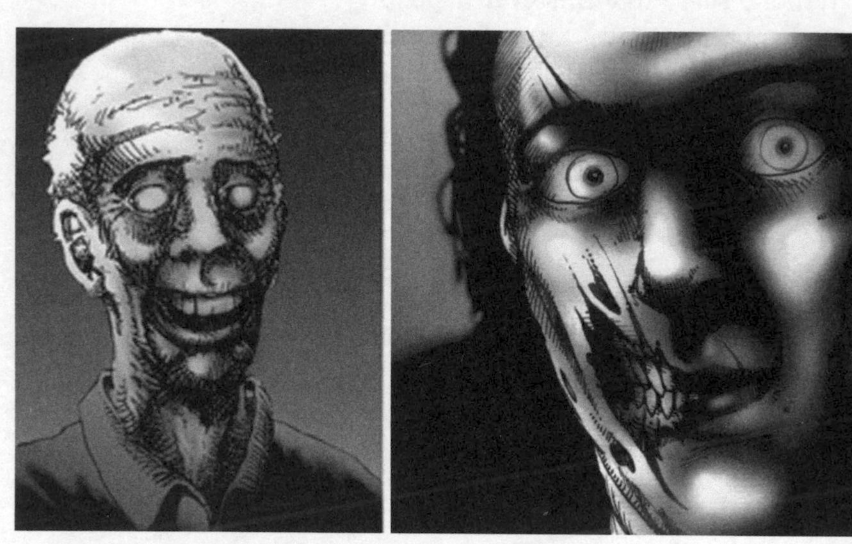

Faces of Death by Graham Pratt

"People are screwups and their leaders are worse. Water and poor engineering destroyed New Orleans. You think FEMA could handle zombies? *Please!*"

—Bob Fingerman, author of *Recess Pieces* and *Zombie World: Winter Dregs and Other Stories* (both from Dark Horse Books)

Now that we've explored the forensics of the zombie problem; followed it through the investigations of medical science; tracked the spread of the plague with world-class epidemiologists, and taken it to the streets with cops, SWAT, and the military . . . how do our chances stack up if the dead rose?

The answers depend on how the dead rise and what kind of zombies we'd be facing. Here's a summary of the major zombie subtypes along with some projections of how the twenty-first-century human race would do in a battle with the living dead.

Slow Zombies Rising as a Result of a Plague

This is the most common variation on the standard Romero model, and it's a far more plausible and practicable one. These zombies are the slow shufflers. They have very little brain function; they have poor balance; they fear fire; it takes a headshot to bring them down.

- Potential for Global Pandemic: Very high, but it would follow well-established epidemic spread patterns beginning with a patient zero and then increasing exponentially. Each vector would have the potential for unlimited contamination of human victims; each victim would become a disease vector upon reviving from human death.
- Limits to Disease Spread: Depending on where the infection begins, the spread of disease may be easily containable. In *Resident Evil*, for example, the disease would have been contained within the Vault had not human greed and a short-sighted desire to weaponize the disease overridden common sense and the sensible precautions built into all disease study and bioweapons research. If the disease begins spreading in a small town, there is the possibility of quarantine and purification (read: nuking the crap out of the town).
- Likelihood of Successful Human Opposition: Humans are smarter, faster, capable of using technology, and possess the ability to share information and form cooperative resistance. (Though in the movies they fail miserably at all of this so the movie zombie can ultimately win. Although this was a brilliant if cynical view put forward by Romero in *Dawn* and *Day*, the apocalypse-due-to-petty-humans theme has been way overused.) Considering the efficiency of military and local law enforcement, and the sophistication of their weapons and tactics, there is a solid chance that we would stay

ahead of the undead tsunami and eventually win. Based on the information from my experts, I give humanity a survival likelihood of 85 percent to 95 percent.

- Likelihood That We're All Toast: A lot of things would have to go wrong, more than just pettiness and infighting, for us to screw the pooch so badly that we'd all become dinner for the dead.

Slow Zombies Rising as a Result of Toxic Contamination

A number of films, with both slow and fast zombies, play the toxic spill card, as shown in films like *The Living Dead at Manchester Morgue, The Grapes of Death*, and *Toxic Zombie*.

- Potential for Global Pandemic: The severity of the outbreak depends on the number of people initially contaminated. If something gets into the water or major food source of a large population, then the outbreak could spin out of control.
- Limits to Disease Spread: Very little except that beyond the initial contamination of one or more patient zeroes the disease would spread by one-to-one bite attacks.
- Likelihood of Successful Human Opposition: Even if an entire city is infected, there would be slowdown points, such as bridges, tunnels, rivers, mountains, etc. Each of these could be used as a combat zone for hard-fire elimination of

---

Max Brooks on Zombie Realism

"Have you ever gone to a movie with your friends and one of them, that particular tight-assed nerd bag who won't shut up about how 'that would never happen' or 'this isn't realistic and here's why'? Well, I am that nerd bag."

—Max Brooks, author of *World War Z*

---

the infected. If more than a 5 percent population of a large city becomes simultaneously contaminated, then the military would need to use nuclear (or nuclear equivalent) weapons in order to sterilize large geographic sections. Continental survival following an infection of more than 5 percent of the population would be fifty-fifty. Oceans would stop the global spread. If, however, the toxic contamination affects a very small group (such as the staff at a toxic dump site or the population of a small and/or moderately isolated town), then our chances of survival jump to 95 percent or better. In either cases, there will likely be a high percentage of noninfected fatalities during the sterilization process.

- Likelihood That We're All Toast: See above.

Slow Zombies Rising as a Result of Unexplained Radiation

This results in all the recently deceased coming back to life. This is the classic Romero *Night of the Living Dead* scenario. These zombies are the slow shufflers. They have very little brain function; they have poor balance; they fear fire; it takes a head shot to bring them done.

- Potential for Global Pandemic: Absolute.
- Limits to Disease Spread: None.
- Likelihood of Successful Human Opposition: Zero, except in isolated pockets.
- Likelihood That We're All Toast: Virtually 100 percent. For storytellers interested in spinning a truly apocalyptic zombie story, the classic *Night* scenario is the way to go. But it's so completely unwinnable as to almost inspire a "who cares?" response. In the later Romero films, he subtly backed off from this stance. It may still have been part of his mythology, but he didn't belabor the point, or even raise it again as it negates the point of all resistance. Everyone dies, therefore, everyone will become a zombie . . . whether now or in forty years, so what's the point of fighting for survival? It would be

the same as taking a week's worth of food and locking yourself in a radiation-proof room during a worldwide nuclear war: sure, you'd survive for a week, but so what? The futility of this was eloquently explored in Richard Matheson's *I Am Legend*; but even here the author relents from total fatalism by providing a new "humanity" to inherit the earth once the original tenants have all been evicted. When writing the script for *Night*, Romero was undoubtedly not thinking of launching either a franchise or a genre, and from a creative standpoint the "all recent dead rise" mythology painted him into a corner. In the following films he concentrated more on the spread-through-bite theme, which allows for a great deal of creative freedom and flexibility.

Fast Zombies Rising Because of a Plague

This is the premise of the remake of *Dawn of the Dead*. Something starts the plague and it spreads very, very fast. Victims who die as a result of bites reanimate within seconds.

- Potential for Global Pandemic: Less likely than shown in the movie unless a lot of folks with bites suddenly hop onto airplanes to visit foreign countries. Once the disease becomes known in one country, the governments of neighboring countries would immediately start pointing missiles and very likely pressing buttons. If things got out of hand, it would be a race to see whether the plague or radioactive fallout would claim the most lives.
- Limits to Disease Spread: Most likely it would become an overwhelming disaster within the confines of connected continents. North and South America would fall within days or weeks if the infection starts there. Same with Australia. Since Europe and Asia are connected by shared borders, any plague that starts there would consume that land mass.
- Likelihood of Successful Human Opposition: Slim to none. The disease spreads too fast to allow reaction, study, preparation, and response. It's the same nihilistic view as the radi-

ation raising all the dead, and from the storytelling point of view, there is one story to tell. At best you can try for episodic survivor tales, but that's it.

- Likelihood That We're All Toast: There are two views on this. If you stick to the mythology as shown in the *Dawn* remake, then yeah, we're toast; but since the disease in that film doesn't operate the way any disease is likely to act, then we probably have a shot. No matter how virulent and aggressive a disease is, there has to be time for it to spread through the bloodstream. The thought that an infected person reanimates after hours or days is plausible; and the fact that they reanimate quickly makes some degree of sense, especially in justifying why they are fast and more coordinated: They are not in rigor yet and they've suffered significantly less damage to the brain. Fewer brain cells have died and, therefore, more of their motor cortex is working even if cognition is diminished. But the thought that a person who is bitten to death *immediately* reanimates and is a completely infectious vector is less likely. If they die from a bite to the throat (as does Ana's husband in *Dawn*) and bleeds out from a torn artery, there won't have been time for the disease to have taken hold throughout the entire body. The mouth won't yet contain a sufficient (if any) amount of the pathogen to make them an instant carrier for the disease. So, the whole scenario where the disease spreads out of control and *everyone* immediately becomes a murderous zombie doesn't hold up to close scrutiny. Makes a helluva movie, though.

Fast, Thinking Zombies Rising Because of a Government Experiment Gone Wrong

This is the *Return of the Living Dead* model, and it has other tweaks on the model. The infected die over a period of a few hours and then reanimate as fully cognizant zombies. They can think, talk, strategize, and work cooperatively. They also have a desire to eat only human brains, and their own bodies are remarkably difficult to kill. Even severed limbs are active, as if every cell in the

***Lab Rats* by Ryan Allen**

"Who knows what today's government-funded mad scientists are cooking up?"

body has become a separate being. How this works with an arm detached from the central nervous system, not to mention the supportive and cooperative structures of the rest of the shoulder's tendons and bones, is a bit hard to explain (which is why even as a kid I always thought that films like *The Crawling Hand* were just plain silly).

- Potential for Global Pandemic: If we accept the mythology in its entirety, then the spread of the disease begins as a standard one-to-one oubreak with pandemic potential; but when we add to this a deliberate and hostile intelligence, then it becomes a battle on the level of ethnic genocide.
- Limits to Disease Spread: Whomever has the best weapons will win; but with an enemy that can never be completely destroyed (even ash from incineration is a contaminate), there is no foreseen limit to the spread of the disease.

- Likelihood of Successful Human Opposition: Unless it starts on an island or in some place that can be contained without using incineration (and that depends on how fast we can erect a fifty-foot-high concrete wall around an entire town), then our chances of stopping it would be very small.
- Likelihood That We're All Toast: Isolated communities capable of fortification may survive until the zombies acquire weapons. And even that fifty-foot-high concrete wall will yield to a tank or fifty determined thinking zombies with jackhammers.

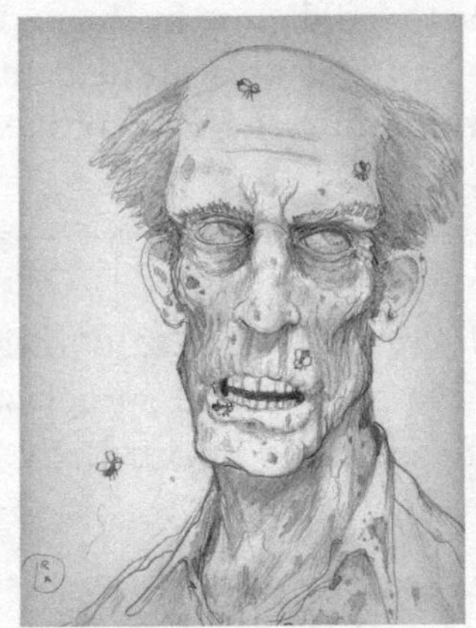

***Zombie Rage* by Ryan Allen**

"If it happens too fast it may be too late."

Fast Human Zombies Rising Because of a Virus

This was the model used in Romero's *The Crazies* and *28 Days Later*: A government experiment gone wrong in *Crazies* and a rage virus accidentally released in *28*. The infected humans, especially in recent films, are incapable of controlled or rational thought and are, for all intents and purposes, fast zombies—even if they are technically alive.

Nuclear Meltdown

One thing that might settle the hash of both zombies and surviving humans is the reality of worldwide nuclear meltdown. In an apocalyptic situation, with no active infrastructure or an absence of human staff at nuclear power plants, the cooling towers would very quickly cease to operate; they require constant human supervision. With no one at the controls, the water used to cool the rods would evaporate and the superheated gasses would result in meltdowns of every one of the approximately four hundred nuclear power plants worldwide—more than a hundred of which are in the United States. Each meltdown would release massive amounts of radioactive vapor. We'd not only be toast, but that toast would glow in the dark. One very small consolation is that radiation causes tissue damage and cellular decay, so the zombies would bite the radioactive dust, too.

- Potential for Global Pandemic: Like *Dawn*, the premise requires that we accept that infection spreads instantly and completely through the entire body within seconds of contamination.
- Limits to Disease Spread: While this premise is frightening, it's unlikely. More likely the process would take hours during which the infected would experience a decrease in rational behavior and an increase in hostility. Triage and quarantine would come later once order is restored.
- Likelihood of Successful Human Opposition: Since the disease would have to have a lag time of a few hours, this would likely spin out of control for a while and then it would smash into the kinds of disaster-response protocols that *all* governments have in place. Losses would be high, and among them would be many uninfected who would be killed because the initial military responses would have to take a big-picture view of containment.
- Likelihood That We're All Toast: If things were handled with the lack of military efficiency shown in the movies, then the

whole world would go down in less than a year, except for isolated islands and fortified pockets. But I doubt that any military would crumble as easily as the occupying U.S. military does in *28 Weeks Later*. Some of my military experts (see Chapters 5 and 9) tell me they groaned louder than a hungry zombie when they saw the way military tactics were portrayed. Although they all liked the movie from a fan point of view, they all agreed that no one would ever have made it out of England (as they did in the film, using a stolen military helicopter). Captain Dick Taylor, US Army (retired) put it this way: "Knowing the potential for a global disaster, anything . . . and I mean *anything* flying out of that country, especially after a known outbreak, and not heading directly to a secure quarantine spot, would be shot out of the sky before they cleared the outbound coastline. There is not the slightest doubt about it."

Deliberately Reanimated Dead

Authors and filmmakers have been kicking this concept around for a long time, and there are some zombie experts who consider *Frankenstein* by Mary Shelley, published in 1918, to be the very first entry in this subgenre. There's some weight to the argument since it does involve the dead being brought back to life and, once revived, demonstrates decidedly hostile tendencies. In H. P. Lovecraft's 1922 short story "Herbert West—Reanimator"[1] a scientist's attempts to create a reagent that will restore life to the dead backfires resulting in reanimated but mindless and aggressive corpses who bear a striking resemblance to the flesh-eating ghouls of Romero's *Night of the Living Dead*. Director Stuart Gordon filmed this as *Re-Animator* in 1985 based on a script he cowrote with Dennis Paoli and William Norris, and in this landmark film the zombie element was played up, both for laughs and for real shocks. These creatures are typically very strong, uncontrollably violent, but they can be destroyed.

1. First published in serial form in *Home Brew* from February through July 1922.

- Potential for Global Pandemic: Only moderate.
- Limits to Disease Spread: The dead are reanimated during a scientific process (electrochemistry in *Frankenstein*; injections of a reagent in *Re-Animator*; etc.), which means that any spread would be very slow unless a more efficient process was developed.
- Likelihood of Successful Human Opposition: Once the threat is known, then any armed response would likely end things pretty quickly.
- Likelihood That We're All Toast: *Slim to none.*

Demon Zombies

Movies like Sam Raimi's *Evil Dead* series and books like Brian Keene's *The Rising* and *City of the Dead* use demonic forces as the reason the dead rise. The demons of *Evil Dead* possess dead (and sometimes living) bodies and turn them into raging, bloodthirsty killing machines that can only be stopped by cutting them into harmless pieces. In the Keene novels, the demons inhabit all dead things, including insects and animals. Destroying the body of one does little since the demonic force can just switch to another host.

- Potential for Global Pandemic: Absolute.
- Limits to Disease Spread: None.
- Likelihood of Successful Human Opposition: Not a chance.
- Likelihood That We're All Toast: Prepare to meet thy maker.

Revenge Zombies

These are stories of the dead returning to life in order to redress some wrong or to resolve some unfinished business. The waterlogged zombies of *Creepshow* have come back for revenge; as is the sort-of-a-cyborg zombie in *Deadly Friend*. In the *Blind Dead* series, a bunch of slaughtered Knights Templar return from the

Art of the Dead – Joseph Adams

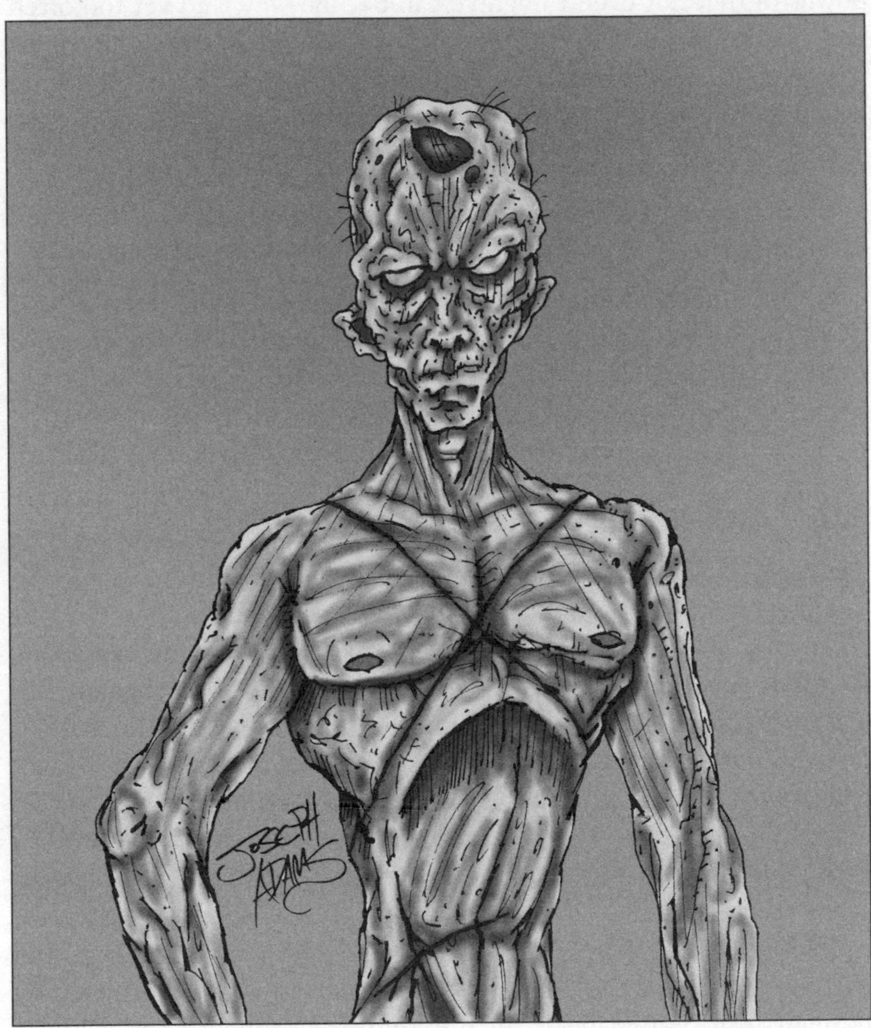

"The gruesome thought of a diseased, cannibalistic horde of the walking dead scares the crap out of people. Even the sight of it drawn out on paper frightens them."

grave to exact revenge on descendants of the villagers in whose town the knights were murdered. In many of these stories, the logic is warped in that there is supposed to be a need for justice so powerful that not even the grave can bar the way, and yet too often the murder spree of the zombies continues on long after the right is wrong, or more often, a large number of uninvolved civilians are killed just to satisfy the body-count fix of the audience.

- Potential for Global Pandemic: Small, if any.
- Limits to Disease Spread: These cases tend to be localized incidents.
- Likelihood of Successful Human Opposition: There's a long and valued history of villagers with torches. Seems to work pretty well.
- Likelihood That We're All Toast: None.

Alien Zombies

This is a storytelling form that allows all known rules of science to be quietly chucked out the window by taking the stance that "It all makes sense if it comes from outer space." In some cases this is just lazy storytelling, as in dreck like the 1969 el cheapo film *Astro-Zombies* (with John Carradine) and Fred Olin Ray's 1980 piece o' junk *Alien Dead*, and the all-time worst film ever, *Plan 9 from Outer Space*; while on the other hand it's been used to great effect (by better writers) for storylines like the Marvel Zombies series of comic books written by Robert Kirkman (in which an alien plague begins infecting all of the Marvel superheroes, including Spider-Man, Captain America, the Fantastic Four, and the Avengers); and the 2006 movie *Slither*, written and directed by James Gunn, which dealt with a zombie outbreak caused by an alien organism that crash-lands on earth in a meteor.

- Potential for Global Pandemic: This varies depending on the type of infection. In Marvel Zombies the plague spreads as fast as it does in the films *Dawn of the Dead* and *28 Days Later*, and the problem is exacerbated by having super-powered zombies. That's a no-win scenario; but in *Slither* and films of its genre the problem spreads with relative slowness.

- Limits to Disease Spread: Potentially none in all cases unless deliberately stopped.
- Likelihood of Successful Human Opposition: For *Marvel Zombies* it's zero; for the others we stand a fair chance.
- Likelihood That We're All Toast: For most of the genre, we have a shot at staying alive; but if a zombified Incredible Hulk shows up at your door, just pack it in.

The Final Verdict: Us and Them

To get the total zombie experience, sit back with the 1960s band *The Zombies* on the CD player (I recommend their self-titled debut album from 1965, which has "She Not There" and "Tell Her No"), leaf through a stack of zombie comics (my personal favorite is an even split between Fingerman's *Recess Pieces* and Kirkman's *The Walking Dead*), cue up the five-disc changer on the DVD player to play the complete Romero collection, and start sipping an icy cold Jamaican zombie (light and dark rum, apricot brandy, with lime, orange, pineapple, and passion fruit juices and garnished with an orange slice and a cherry).

And try to tune out the dreadful moans coming through the gaps in the boards you've crookedly nailed over all the windows. Just make sure your gun is loaded before you are.

Don't worry about calling the police . . . they're probably already on the case. Just sit back, listen to some tunes, watch some flicks, browse a book, and sip your drink. And wait. The cops are coming. Those shots you hear are the SWAT teams retaking the street.

Kick back and relax. It'll all be over soon enough.

One way or the other.

APPENDIX B

Artist Index

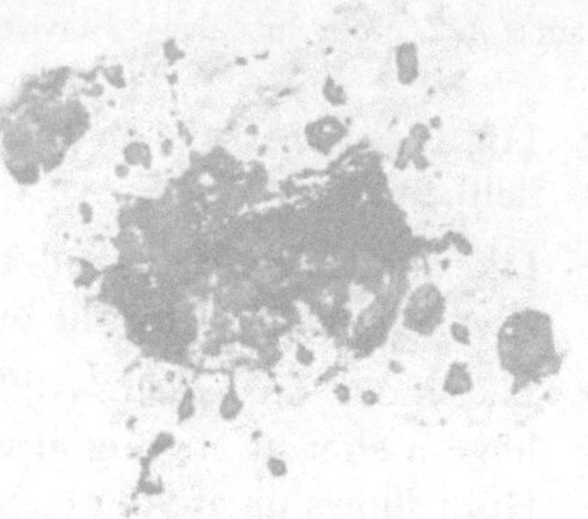

Joseph "Jody" Adams a.k.a Von Monstersteiner, comes from Nicholasville, Kentucky, He is a member of the Honorable Order of Kentucky Colonels, a disability rights activist, and former mayoral candidate. Joseph is an accomplished cartoonist, horror illustrator, and known to be an artist in the modern-day lowbrow art movement. His artwork can be seen in publications such as *The Hacker's Source*, *Black Hills Folk Press*, and *Unspeakable Press*. One of his most notable artistic endeavors has been as the production illustrator for the Solomon Mortamur film, *It Came from Trafalgar*. Contact him at adams4hire@yahoo.com. Joseph's official website: www.freewebs.com/jody_adams/index.htm; Joseph's MySpace page: www.myspace.com/smoke_if_ya_got_em.

Ryan Allen lives in Iowa with his wife Ronda and their pup, Mortimer. Ryan is an eclectic and creative soul who draws, paints, and sculpts. His creativity also spills over into writing. His creative endeavors are usually weird, horrific, sometimes funny, and almost always gory. Ryan traces his creative and artistic development back to being contaminated as a kid by the genres of science fiction, fantasy, and horror in all their various media. These, along with a heavy dose of comic books and the art of James Holloway, Ryan knew he wanted to be an artist. Contact him at infernalengines@aol.com.

Matthew "Six" Bahr has always tried to be as creative as possible, and you can see this in his artwork at his website, www.robo6.net. He's a huge zombie fan and has always loved drawing the flesh-hungry ghouls. During the day, he's the art director for Native Sons, www.nativesons.com, and is also the executive creative officer/part owner of a surf clothing company called Embryo Surf Co., www.embryosurfco.com.

But at night, his favorite project is the zombie comic book he's illustrating called *After the Rising*. A mini-series set in the time period just after the world is lost to the zombie hordes. Expect to see it in early 2009. Six lives in Myrtle Beach, South Carolina, and has two beautiful daughters that have probably seen more zombie movies than your average horror movie fan.

Jason Beam's illustrative storytelling style that melds the macabre with surrealistic sensuality has established his work among gothic and horror enthusiasts, writers, musicians, and feature film and entertainment industry clientele. He is the owner and creative director of WeeGee Creative in Phoenix, Arizona, and spends his free time cruising for zombies in his hot rod hearse. His work can be seen at www.weegeecreative.com and on the cover of *The Cryptopedia: A Dictionary of the Weird, Strange & Downright Bizarre* by Jonathan Maberry and David F. Kramer (Citadel Press, 2007).

Alan F. Beck has been a science fiction, fantasy, and surrealistic artist and illustrator for over thirty years doing work for many major corporations. His art has been published in magazines and on book covers and has been exhibited in shows and science fiction/fantasy conventions all across the United States. His visions and concepts are produced using acrylics, watercolors, pastels, 3-D modeling, and image manipulation programs. Contact him at alanfbeck@earthlink.net. Website: www.alanfbeck.com.

Geff Bertrand's published works include a self-published limited edition 150-page art book and illustrations for a few stories in *Black Ink Horror* Magazine, *Raw Meat—Bedtime Stories for the Sick & Deranged* plus a few other small publications and CD covers. You can see more of his art at dr-twistid.deviantart.com. Contact him at bringeruvdeth@hotmail.com.

Kevin Bias, from Easthampton, Massachusetts, has been drawing ever since he was able to hold a pencil. He cites his comic art influences as Jack Kirby, John Byrne, and Bernie Wrightson, preferring the campy art of the 1970s and 1980s. He creates art for local bands out of Western Massachusetts for the web and for CDs and T-shirts; and does the occasional freelance job. You can find him at www.myspace.com/kevthedevil, and performing onstage around New England with his band, Pallet. Contact him at Kevlen72@charter.net.

Sean Boley is better known for his offbeat and twisted humor in his cartoons, but is certainly no stranger to illustrating. His work has been featured in various publications over the years, and he has done other things as well, including designing logos and tattoos. While on that quest for the elusive holy grail of an art career, he lives in Washington, Virginia, where he "draws" (pardon the pun!) inspiration from anything imaginable, warning people that nothing and no one is safe from his paper and pen. Contact him at kr2nist@yahoo.com.

Kevin James Breaux is a professional graphic designer with over ten years experience with design tools such as Photoshop. He graduated from Tyler School of Art in 2000 with a B.F.A. and since worked designing major motion picture merchandise for the X-Men movie franchise. Review his online portfolio of digital art and photography at www.browebdesigns.com. Kevin is a fantasy writer, and actively seeking agents for his first series. He is also writing several horror short stories and one dramatic graphic novel. His author website can be found at www.kevinbreaux.com; contact him at kbreaux23@yahoo.com.

Peter Brown is a dark arts pen and ink illustrator who has done commissioned work for several book and magazine publications. His childhood love of comic book art, horror stories, and monster movies kick-started his imagination and artistic drive. He also creates photo manipulations for realistic fantasy-horror pieces. He is currently illustrating for *Black Ink Horror* Magazine and enjoys working on special projects/collaborations with other DA artists. View his website at rayznhell.tripod.com or contact him to work on your next project at rayznhell@lycos.com.

Donna Burgess is the owner and editor of Naked Snake Press. She is a poet, author, and an artist whose credits include the covers of several Eric S. Brown collections and novellas.

Collin Burton is an advertising graphic designer by day, freelance illustrator by night, who lives in Colorado Springs, Colorado. He uses mixed media and Photoshop to create his dark and fascinating images. Contact him at collin@fizzleandpop.com. To see more of his work, visit sketch.smugmug.com/Portfolio.

Shawn Conn grew up a farm boy in upstate New York, where he lived with very supportive parents and three equally creative younger brothers. His interest in art began almost at the same time he discovered "the monster movie." Growing up in the age of Hammer films, Godzilla, and the drive-in monster fests, he would begin to create his own worlds of fantasy and horror on paper and canvas. He went on to study art at the Rochester Institute of Technology, as well as served in the Army. Shawn is currently accepting limited commissions and has an apparel line devoted to zombies distributed by Punk and Pissed, called Armageddon 2012. Contact him at shantyshawn@yahoo.com.

Scott Cramton is a freelance photographer specializing in scary photos. He's also the director of The Haunt, one of the most acclaimed haunted houses in the country and a place Scott has found plenty of subjects. When not shooting, he is writing for websites such as www.herealms.com and www.the-haunt.com. Scott has written three plays that were produced by Grand Valley State University. Recently one of those plays was picked up for a successful run by the Detroit's Players Club. Contact him at thehauntman@gmail.com for more information about his work.

Tootie Detrick, at an early age, knew art would become her main focus. Studying graphic design and fine art after high school at Bowling Green State University, she is working as a full-time graphic designer, freelance artist, and web page designer. She is also an experienced architectural illustrator. Tootie has attended many art shows throughout her career and began selling her art on the Internet in 2007. To request graphic design, artist, or illustrator services, visit www.tootiedetrick.com.

Frank Dietz's love for monsters and fantasy has led to his career in the film industry as a writer, producer, director, actor, and Walt Disney feature animation artist. His work can be seen in *Hercules*, *Mulan*, *Tarzan*, *Fantasia 2000*, and others. He continues to work as a screenwriter and is the author and illustrator of the popular *Sketchy Things* sketchbook series. In 2007 he was awarded the first Rondo Hatton Classic Horror Award for artist of the year. See more about Frank's work at www.sketchythings.com.

Kelly Everaert was born in southern Ontario, Canada, where he grew up on a steady supply of monster movies and comic books. After surviving his childhood, he went on to college where he graduated with a diploma in fine arts. After a road trip across Canada in 1995 with his now wife, Michelle, they settled in Vancouver, British Columbia. Kelly now tries to make a living as a freelance artist working for a variety of clients producing book illustrations, storyboards, and concept drawings for the film industry, comic books, and paintings. If you would like to see more of his work check out Keltic Studios online at members.shaw.ca/kelticstudios/Keltic_Studios.htm.

Shannon Freshwater is an artist and illustrator who grew up in Las Vegas where zombies sit in front of slot machines twenty-four hours a day. Shannon enjoys painting bodily decay because it exorcizes her own fears of death and sickness. She attended Art Center College of Design for illustration, and currently lives and works in Los Angeles. Website: www.shannonfreshwater.com. Contact her at airandwater27 @hotmail.com.

Lisa Russo Gressen holds a B.F.A in painting from Arcadia University and a Desktop Publishing certification from Moore College of Art and Design. She worked for Chilton Publishing and TVSM/The Cable Guide, has published several poems, and completed her first supernatural thriller, *Kindred*. Her new musical, *Dreamweavers*, had a well-received reading on Broadway. She is president and CEO of Good Show Productions, Inc. Lisa also teaches art appreciation to over 500 elementary students each year through Art Goes To School. Lisa can be contacted at dreamweaverlisa@comcast.net.

Steve Hester is a self-employed house painter, artist, and musician, living in Fountain Inn, South Carolina. His fascination with the intricacies of life are realized in his surreal artwork . . . much of which he is unable to interpret himself. As a result, Steve is always intrigued by what those who appreciate his art are able to *see* in it.

Brandon Hildreth is a self-taught artist whose work reflects a wide variety of styles, always changing when it comes to texture and depth, often dwelling in the realm of science fiction and horror-like genres. His work can be viewed online at www.lunarisart.com.

Jill Hunt in an artist and amateur photographer living in northern Virginia with her husband and three cats. She is studying zombie movies, comics, and books in preparation for the zombie apocalypse.

Jonathan Maberry is the Bram Stoker Award-winning author of *Ghost Road Blues*, as well as *Dead Man's Song*, *Vampire Universe*, *The*

Cryptopedia, and *Bad Moon Rising*. He is an artist, amateur photographer, and writing teacher. His website is www.jonathanmaberry.com.

George Martzoukos was born on March 23, 1982, in Athens, Greece. His work has appeared in *The New Masters of Fantasy*, volumes 2 and 3, and Jonathan Maberry's *Vampire Universe.* He is currently collaborating with Visionary Comics Studio on various projects and has also designed many CD artworks in Greece, contributed art in projects such as: ". . . Erth Chronicles" and *The Fleshrot* Magazine. Recently he has illustrated art inspired from Steven Savile's *The Heart of Thera* and exhibited his original art at Fanfare Sports & Entertainment, Website: Inc. www.myspace.com/martzoukos. Contact him at martzoukosarts@yahoo.gr.

Lori Ann McAdam's art is either tattoo art or paintings—but all of it features some representation of death. She has a perpetually growing obsession with zombies and zombie films. The graphic undertones are reflected in the way she paints or draws. Her best advice: "Always remember, the zombies *are* coming." Contact her at makeouterwart @yahoo.com; www.myspace.com/makeoutcrew.

Rob McCallum is a graduate of Glasgow School of Art where he started drawing comics while still a student. He's worked for Dark Horse, DC Comics, 2000ad in the United Kingdom, and Marvel Comics (where he worked for Stan Lee on his unpublished Excelsior line). Having made his own short films, Rob moved into film storyboards and concept art, working with directors such as George Romero, Richard Donner, Barry Levinson, Danny Boyle, and John Singleton on the films *Land of the Dead, Resident Evil Apocalypse, 16 Blocks, Four Brothers, Hairspray*, and many others. Rob can be contacted through his website: www.mecallumart.com.

Zach McCain is an internationally published artist whose work ranges from designing book covers, illustrations for books and magazines, to artwork for trading cards and games. He has illustrated the works of such authors as Paul Finch, Steve Vernon, Charles M. Grant, William F. Nolan, and many more. His clients include Cemetery Dance Publications, Gray Friar Press, Hero Games, and Z-Man Games. Artwork and current projects can be viewed at his official website: www.zachmccain.com.

Mark McLaughlin is an artist and widely published writer. His books of short stories include *Pickman's Motel, Slime After Slime*, and *Motivational Shrieker* (he also did the cover art for the last two). He is the coauthor, with Rain Graves and David Niall Wilson, of the Bram Stoker Award-winning poetry collection, *The Gossamer Eye*. Also, he has written a novel, *Monster Behind the Wheel*, with collaborator Michael McCarty. Visit him online at www.myspace.com/monsterbook.

Ken Meyer, Jr. is an illustrator by trade and has been working at it for close to twenty years, working in comics, games (paper and online), educational media, and more. He is back in school pursuing his M.F.A. He puts together the Tori Amos RAINN benefit calendar each year (www.rainn.org), plays tennis, drinks Dr Pepper, plays with his daughters, and idolizes Stephen Colbert. Okay, maybe that's too strong . . . but he likes him a whole lot. See his work at www.kenmeyerjr.com/port.

Peter Mihaichuk is an art director, photographer, artist, and family man who found his calling in dark art at an early age, when he was brought before a child psychologist to discuss a disturbing piece that consisted of an all-consuming tornado wreaking havoc with human and animal captives. For over ten years, he has worked as a concept artist, illustrator, and art director. Peter's work has been featured in such magazines and publications as *EXPOSÉ 5*, *ImagineFX*, *Apex*, *Doorways*, *Post Mortem*, *Cthulhu Sex*, and *Dark Discoveries*, among others. Peter created www.aimfortheheadshot.com in 2007, giving people access to a unique portrait service. Peter's work can be seen at www.mihaichuk.com and www.aimfortheheadshot.com.

Brian Orlowski was born at the lousy end of the 1960s. He grew up happy but was always obsessed with the darker aspect of life. His true fear came when he saw *Night of the Living Dead*. Zombies became his dread of choice, permeating his writing and artwork. In college, Brian majored in fine arts and creative writing. He later graduated from the Joe Kubert School of Cartooning & Graphic Arts. He currently has a novel under consideration and a comic strip vying for syndication. He can be seen every month in several magazines: *Ideas, Goals and Dreams*; *Doorways*; *Girls & Corpses*, and others. Website: www.drawnofthedead.com. Contact him at brianjorlowski@gmail.com.

Christopher Palmerini, professional musician and artist, has been entertaining audiences for the past three decades and has performed in every major club in the tristate area. He is an in-demand studio musician who has opened for national acts and backed up many famous performers such as Ray Manzarek, Pete Best, Mick Taylor, Denny Laine, Jane Weidlin, Buckethead, Tiffany, and Billy Mumy. He's written and cowritten music for half a dozen horror movies with his band The Dead Elvi. He also appears on Rob Zombie's *Halloween Hootenanny* CD. You can see clips of him performing at www.deadelvi.com and www.thehoundsmusic.com.

Robert Papp has illustrated everything from *King Kong* to the *American Girl of the Year*, to *P is for Princess*. His picture books such as *The Scarlet Stockings Spy* and *M Is for Meow* do not have zombies in them, but they have won awards nationwide. Robert lives with his artist wife, Lisa, and their orange cat in historic Bucks County, Pennsylvania. You can see more of his art at www.robertpapp.com and feel free to contact him if you'd like yourself "zombified."

Jacob Parmentier was raised by two loving parents in Middletown, Connecticut, and at a very young age Jacob became interested in horror movies. Quite often he would create drawings of the movies he had loved so much. Nowadays Jacob still resides in Connecticut, except now with his lovely girlfriend. You can usually find Jacob's artwork in the pages of *Black Ink Horror* Magazine and other independent publications that show a strong interest in the horror genre. He can be contacted through his websites, beardomcweirdo.tripod.com, www.myspace.com/beardomcweirdo, and www.beardomcweirdo.deviantart.com; or by e-mail at *beardomcweirdo@hotmail.com*.

Graham Pratt is a freelance artist specializing in T-shirt and album cover design and has recently been doodling for an up-and-coming band from Manchester, England—The Freezing Fog. He tends to favor blood and guts instead of paint, as this usually gives more depth to the piece being created. He also uses technology to further enhance and mutate the raw materials into splatter-filled chunks of visual wonderment. Website: www.myspace.com/zombie_mastermind. Contact him at zombie@shoppingmall.freeserve.co.uk.

Redd Hott Artwork is comprised of two artists, Redd and Lisa. Both are award-winning artists who specialize in Kustom Kulture. Their love for all things morbid and vintage is reflected in their art. From capturing the resurrection of a timeworn vehicle that was left to rot and the undead pin-up girl who drives it, to an undead cruise at a local cemetery diner, Redd and Lisa inject a uniquely fun style into their art. Artwork and information on these two artists can be found at www.reddhottartwork.com. Contact them at: ReddHottArtwork @comcast.net.

Nelson Robles is a writer, illustrator, thinker, father, husband, and one of the undead. Visit him on MySpace at www.Myspace.com/ undeadartist.

Elizabeth Lopez Romero studies audiovisual arts in Mexico at the University of Guadalajara, where she also resides. After school she intends to become an active part of the new Mexican cinema scene, with a goal of working in the related fields of make-up effects and special effects. Contact her at child_ofthe_night@hotmail.com.

Seth Rose is a digital artist from Canada whose work encompasses a dark surrealistic style deeply inspired by music, horror movies, fetishism and eroticism, comics, and society itself. His work has been seen round the world via the Internet and other sources. Seth has worked with such bands as Front Line Assembly, Shaolin Temple of Boom, and Doomsday Refreshment Committee as well as many more. His work can be seen at syntheticlamb.deviantart.com as well as on MySpace at www.myspace.com/syntheticlamb.

Rob Sacchetto was born and raised in Sudbury, Ontario, Canada, where he still resides to this day. He has spent some twenty years dedicated to the visual arts and has worked in a variety of mediums, including commissioned work, illustrated film, comic book illustration, and concept design. With many creative projects on the go, Rob is always at his art table. He is currently working on two separate comic books, which he will be self-publishing. His most recent project, www.zombieportraits.com, however, is by far his favorite. For more information or to contact him directly, visit the website, or call 705-675-3528.

Doug Schooner resides in Boulder, Colorado, working on music, literature, and art and says that his first paintings can be most enjoyed in very specific lighting environments. He attended Notre Dame College in Manchester, New Hampshire, as a commercial art major. He plays guitar, has recorded music, done interviews for local television shows, performed festivals, opened for national acts, published poetry, performed computer animation voiceovers, and is working on a novel. In 2005, Doug's Rock N Roll Art Gallery began. Experience DR RAGS at www.myspace.com/drrags. Contact him at denverdrgn@gmail.com.

Jeremy Simmons has been working in RPG design and cartography for over six years, and a professional designer for twice that. Since working in this industry is more of a labor of love than anything else, working for RPG Objects on projects like *Blood and Brains* is a perfect example of how much fun one can have doing so. Jeremy is dedicated to creating the best work he can on every piece, he is easy to work with, and very professional. And in this case, he is glad to have the chance to prepare for the zombie apocalypse.

Harold Vincent was born in Granite City, Illinois, and discovered early in his life that he was fascinated by the world of horror movies. The youngest of five children, he relied on his imagination to keep him company. Combining his love for monsters and fantasy art, Harold incorporates raw emotion and creativity to bring to life a new strain of characters. He is now working on a personal sci-fi/horror project, which he hopes will be published soon. Harold lives in Huber Heights, Ohio, with his wife Shelby and their three children. Visit him at www.myspace.com/faith_and_rage. Contact him at necropolis126@yahoo.com.

Chad Michael Ward, director, photographer, and artist, has spent the last decade entertaining audiences with his dark, and oft times erotic, horror art. His work has been featured in dozens of publications around the world including *NME*, *Skin Two*, *Aphrodesia*, *Spectrum*, *Gothic Beauty*, *Tattoo Savage*, *Carpe Noctem*, *Club International*, *Gallery*, *Pit*, *Dark Realms*, and *The Third Alternative* and is frequently commissioned by musicians such as Marilyn Manson, The Cruxshadows, Fear Factory, Collide, The Blank Theory, Soilwork, Pissing Razors, Naglfar, and Darkane. His work can be found at www.digitalapocalypse.com.

John C. Worsley was born in 1978 in Sacramento, California, but has spent the last twenty-two years in comically idyllic Portland, Oregon. Since 2003 John has been self-employed as a minimum-time programmer/over-time illustrator, self-publishing comics such as the science fiction neomythological *Painkillers*, and the contemporary horror comic *Dead Valentines*. He has also contributed illustrations to games such as Iron Realms' *Achaea*, Pinnacle's *Deadlands: Reloaded*, and Wizkids' *Pirates of the Spanish Main*. Staying generally active in the miniature comics mecca that is the Portland comics scene, he is also the maintainer of Shannon Wheeler's Too Much Coffee Man website and the Stumptown Comics Fest. Website: www.openvein.com. Contact him at jcworsley@gmail.com.

APPENDIX C

Answers to Gregg Winkler's Zombie Quiz

PART 1

1. A Crimson Head
2. David J. Schow's "Jerry's Kids Meet Wormboy"
3. Draugr
4. An orb above the earth's South Pole made up of worms
5. *The Rising* by Brian Keene

PART 2

1. "Re: Your Brains"
2. Tom Savini—he played a zombie named Blades (or Machete Zombie) in both *Dawn of the Dead* and *Land of the Dead*.
3. "Trojan, Ramses, Magnum, Sheik!"
4. *Stacy*
5. Captain America

PART 3

1. The conflicts in Northern Ireland known as "The Troubles."
2. *King of the Zombies*
3. *Braindead*
4. C.
5. C.

Art of the Dead – Lori Ann McAdam

Zombie Geisha

"*Night of the Living Dead* is definitely the foundation of zombie pop culture. My grandmother even remembers being scared out of her wits, how could you not love that thought?"

About the Author

Jonathan Maberry is a *New York Times* bestselling author, five-time Bram Stoker Award-winner, and comic book writer. His vampire apocalypse book series V-Wars was a Netflix original series. He writes in multiple genres including suspense, thriller, horror, science fiction, fantasy, and action; for adults, teens, and middle grade. He is the editor many anthologies, including *The X-Files*, *Aliens: Bug Hunt*, *Don't Turn Out the Lights*, *Nights of the Living Dead*, and others. His comics include *Black Panther: DoomWar*, *Captain America*, *Pandemica*, *Highway to Hell*, *The Punisher*, and *Bad Blood*. He is a board member of the Horror Writers Association and the president of the International Association of Media Tie-in Writers. Visit him online at www.jonathanmaberry.com.